The SNES Encyclopedia
EVERY GAME RELEASED FOR THE
SUPER
Nintendo
ENTERTAINMENT SYSTEM

CHRIS SCULLION

WHITE OWL

AN IMPRINT OF PEN & SWORD BOOKS LTD.
YORKSHIRE - PHILADELPHIA

First published in Great Britain in 2020 and reprinted in 2023 by
White Owl
An imprint of
Pen & Sword Books Ltd
Yorkshire - Philadelphia

ISBN 978 1 52673 783 0

Typeset in 11/13 pts Adobe Devanagari by Aura Technology and Software Services, India.

Printed and bound in the UK by CPI Group (UK) Ltd, Croydon, CR0 4YY.

Pen & Sword Books Limited incorporates the imprints of After the Battle, Atlas, Archaeology, Aviation, Discovery, Family History, Fiction, History, Maritime, Military, Military Classics, Politics, Select, Transport, True Crime, Air World, Frontline Publishing, Leo Cooper, Remember When, Seaforth Publishing, The Praetorian Press, Wharncliffe Local History, Wharncliffe Transport, Wharncliffe True Crime and White Owl.

For a complete list of Pen & Sword titles please contact

PEN & SWORD BOOKS LIMITED
47 Church Street, Barnsley, South Yorkshire, S70 2AS, England
E-mail: enquiries@pen-and-sword.co.uk
Website: www.pen-and-sword.co.uk
or
PEN AND SWORD BOOKS
1950 Lawrence Rd, Havertown, PA 19083, USA
E-mail: uspen-and-sword@casematepublishers.com
Website: www.penandswordbooks.com

To Mum and Dad: thank you for recognising and encouraging my love of gaming by following up my NES with a SNES, rather than worrying you were doing more harm than good.

To my wee brother Kevin: cheers for the countless late-night and early morning International Superstar Soccer sessions. The reason the SNES was one of my favourite systems was because it was the one I played most with you.

To my incredible wife Louise: not only did you not complain when I said I was writing a second book, you were an absolute star when I was going out of my mind trying to get it finished in time. I love you more than words can say, which is a bit worrying considering this is a book and words are sort of its thing.

And finally, to my beautiful wee girl Serena: the countless wonderful experiences your daddy had playing these games over the past three decades are all nothing compared to a single smile from you. I will love you forever.

FOREWORD

When I heard Nintendo was replacing the NES I was really excited about it. Don't get me wrong, the first system was a great machine. As a developer, though, I was always hit with 'sprite per line' issues when creating end-of-level bosses in side-scrolling games. I was also getting a little bit bored of the small colour palette available and the rather dull sound channels.

Eventually, two Japanese machines appeared in the office at Rare, each with Super Mario World packed in. My first impression was that it really was a 'Super' Nintendo. It did everything the NES did, but far better. Bigger sprites, higher resolution, more colours, amazing sound, fully rotating backgrounds with a special Mode 7 which could also be used to create fantastic perspective '3D' effects, and the fantastic transparency feature.

However, this was a problem for me as I was already very much in love with my Mega Drive. So much so, in fact that I didn't really want to believe that the SNES was going to be as 'Super' as it was, because that would mean I'd be buying one immediately: and where would that leave poor old Sonic & Co? But, after drawing comparisons with Ghouls 'n Ghosts on both systems, I decided I had to go and get one. So, sure enough, my Mega Drive was turned off for the last time and I ordered a SNES through Rare along with a few games to kick off with.

When I began working on my first few projects on the system, it was clear to see that it was an awesome piece of kit. Gone were the days of trying to box up 8 x 8 pixel, 3-colour sprites together to make something that resembled a Battletoad, and in came a huge range of colours to choose from, with a palette of 15 for each sprite. Gone was the slightly feeble channel 2 'hum' that struggled to create any form of bass, and in came orchestral sounding anthems filled with samples and fantastic FX created by my buddy David Wise. At last: the games were going to look and sound like I'd imagined them to! I'd go as far to say that we were spoiled by the machine's capability, and I don't think

I had ever had quite so much fun experimenting with graphics on any other machine as I did on the SNES. But just when I thought things couldn't get any better I was given the chance to create something really special, that actually did look 'Super': I got the chance to recreate Donkey Kong.

The Super Nintendo handled the colours of Donkey Kong Country's rendered models beautifully, making really gorgeous, solid-looking sprites. People were baffled as to how things looked so good, and often we were asked if we had performed any special hardware modifications under the hood of the cartridge. But it was just the SNES doing what it was supposed to do extremely well. We were also able to add environmental effects like snowflakes and water, all thanks to that transparency (none of that 'dithered' pixel stuff). These effects weren't only a visual feast at the time; they added a new dynamic to the gameplay side of things too. All in all, the game looked Super, it sounded Super, and it played really well on that Super controller too.

If the truth be told, I was very sad to have to go back to basics when I moved onto the Nintendo 64, because things really took a step backwards when it came to graphics production. Of course, once we'd mastered the art of making things look great in 3D it was all ok, but there was something really special about the SNES that I missed: even the way it looked. Sniff. I loved the way it looked. So much better than its little brother… and I'm not even going to compare it to the N64. That thing was just plain ugly.

Thanks, Nintendo, for getting every single thing right with the Super Nintendo and making the 16-bit era so great! I'll be playing on my SNES Mini long after they wheel me away to the old people's home. And I can't wait.

Kevin Bayliss
Rare Ltd: 1987 – 2005
Playtonic Games: 2015 – Present

INTRODUCTION

The arrival of the SNES affected me in a different way to that of its predecessor. When a four-year-old me first discovered the NES, it was unlike anything I'd ever seen before. I'd gone from the occasional dabbling with my dad's Atari 2600 and ZX Spectrum, to staring mouth agape at the groundbreaking wonder of Super Mario Bros. Nintendo had entered my life and my tiny wee mind was blown.

The SNES arrived in the UK a few days after my ninth birthday. In the previous five years I'd gone from

a wide-eyed sprog, gazing in amazement at a wondrous new contraption, to a complete gaming die-hard. The NES had become the most important thing in my young life: I adored every new game release, devoured countless magazines to glean every word of knowledge I could, got up early in the morning to watch the *Super Mario Bros Super Show* and *Captain N*, and was generally the biggest Nintendo fan imaginable.

I was a fan of video games first and foremost, and so for much of that five-year period the Sega Master

System also found a home next to my NES. In the Christmas of 1991, the 16-bit era entered my household when I got my Sega Mega Drive, complete with Altered Beast and Sonic the Hedgehog. So when I finally got my hands on the SNES in the summer of 1992, it's perhaps understandable that its impact on me – a grizzled nine-year-old gaming veteran who'd seen it all – was different from what had come before.

And yet, what an impact it had. F-Zero's lightning fast speed and pseudo-3D Mode 7 graphics absolutely blew me away. Super Soccer was unlike any football game I had ever played (bearing in mind this was before FIFA existed). Mario was always my first love, though, and so the highlight was undoubtedly the enormous Super Mario World and its introduction of Yoshi.

In the years that followed, the SNES would be responsible for countless iconic moments that have stuck with me throughout the rest of my life. Many of these moments are well-trodden territory in games writing because they affected so many of us: fighting Ridley at the start of Super Metroid, entering the polygonal era in Star Fox (or Starwing, as we in Europe knew it), and simply seeing Donkey Kong Country for the first time and wondering how in the hell that system was capable of such incredible '3D' sprites.

However, as was the case with the NES Encyclopedia – which, at the risk of a cheap plug, is still available from all good booksellers – this book is about more than those pivotal, industry-defining moments that were enjoyed by the masses. Yes, it of course gives due respect to the Earthbounds, the Killer Instincts, the Street Fighter II Turbos and the… um, Pilotwingses. But it also ensures that every SNES game you played growing up also gets the nod it deserves. Did you rent Cutthroat Island from Blockbuster Video and stay up all night trying to beat it? Was working your way up the rankings in Riddick Bowe

Boxing one of your greatest accomplishments when you were younger? Were you the 'fortunate' recipient of a copy of Bronkie the Bronchiasaurus from a well-meaning grandparent trying to help you learn more about your asthma? These games never get mentioned among the nostalgic retrospectives in today's gaming websites, but that doesn't mean they were any less important to your childhood. Those were your memories, and with any luck this book will jog some of them.

This book was harder to write than the *NES Encyclopedia*: not because of the content, but because of my personal circumstances. When I wrote the NES book I was a happily married man, but by the time I started writing the SNES book I had become both a happily married man and a hopelessly devoted father. My daughter Serena is the greatest thing to have ever happened to me, but I'll be damned if writing a book this size wasn't infinitely trickier given that her needs had to be juggled into the mix too (and always took priority).

With that in mind, I'm probably even prouder of this book than I am of its predecessor, and I really hope you get a kick out of it: especially from the notable increase in bad jokes, which were partly added to keep me sane throughout the process. If you enjoy the book, please do let me know on Twitter @scully1888 because that would mean the world to me.

Thank you so much for reading the *SNES Encyclopedia*: I hope it gives you a detailed and entertaining look at Nintendo's iconic 16-bit system. There are always two sides to every story, though, and it's important to remember that there were two participants in the 16-bit war of the '90s. With any luck, then, I'll see you again next year, when we'll look closer at the system that started this war. Or, rather, was part of its genesis.

Chris Scullion

THE HISTORY OF THE SNES

By 1990, Nintendo was on top of the world. Just a decade earlier the Kyoto company had been struggling with its own identity: hanafuda playing cards were no longer enough to sustain the business alone, and while its foray into the toy market saw some notable successes, in the grand scheme of things it was still a small koi in a pond containing the likes of Bandai and Tomy. None of that mattered now, however. After some dabbling in early arcade games saw mild to moderate returns, it was the launch of Donkey Kong in 1981 that turned around Nintendo's fortunes and gave crystal clarity to its new mission: this was now a video game company.

Not content with merely competing in the arcade space, Nintendo made clear its intention to also take over the home, when in 1983 it launched the Famicom in Japan. A couple of years later, with a westernised rebranding and a new name – the Nintendo Entertainment System – the company took another

giant step by making its presence felt in homes outside of its native Japan. The subsequent years were nothing short of glorious for Nintendo and its customers, with the NES playing host to a steady stream of classics that, unbeknownst at the time, would go on to form franchises spanning decades. Super Mario Bros, The Legend of Zelda, Metroid, Mega Man, Castlevania, Final Fantasy, Dragon Quest, Kid Icarus, Cheetahmen: they all started on NES and all continue to enjoy huge fanbases to this day. Okay, maybe not Cheetahmen.

Resting on your laurels can lead to a thorn in your bum, though, and while Nintendo was content to continue releasing NES games for the foreseeable future, the market was changing around it. In 1987, NEC Home Electronics released the PC Engine, which then came to North America in 1989 as the TurboGrafx-16. Although it still used an 8-bit CPU, its 16-bit GPU gave it a notable graphical edge over Nintendo's 8-bit system. Then, in 1988, an even bigger threat arrived in the shape of the Sega Mega Drive, a true 16-bit powerhouse that also came to America in 1989 (under the name Genesis). The result of all this was that even though Nintendo was indeed still the market leader, by the end of the '80s the NES found itself now competing with two new systems that were far more powerful. As sales of NES consoles and games started their inevitable decline, Nintendo grudgingly got to work on a successor that would allow it to attend the 16-bit party (albeit fashionably late).

The result was the Super Famicom, which launched in Japan on 21 November 1990. It boasted a 16-bit CPU for faster processing than the original Famicom, and a graphics unit that could display up to 256 colours from a palette of 32,768 (compared to the NES's support for 25 colours from a palette of 54). It offered programmers eight different video modes – including

the much-hyped Mode 7, which we'll get to – giving a great deal of flexibility to game creators. Its dedicated Sony-produced audio chip could make stereo sound and offered eight channels of audio along with a sampling system: this meant developers could add their own 'instrument' noises and compose with those rather than working with standard blips and bloops.

Just two games were available for the Super Famicom at launch in Japan, but they were two massively important titles that would be good indicators of what was to come. The first was Super Mario World, the fourth game in the Super Mario Bros series and the most effective opening shot Nintendo could have hoped for as it parachuted into the 16-bit war. Mario was easily the most popular video game character by this point, and there was no head-start long enough to help NEC and Sega compete with the fact that Nintendo had Mario, while they only had Bonk and Alex Kidd (not that there was anything massively wrong with them, mind you). The other Japanese launch game was F-Zero: while at the time it was a brand new IP and an unknown name, it could be argued that it would become the more influential of the two games when it came to the console's future library. F-Zero was the first game to show off the aforementioned Mode 7 effect: an impressive video mode that let developers create a large sprite and perform zoom, rotate and perspective effects on it to give the illusion that it was moving in 3D, all at an extremely smooth 60 frames per second. In F-Zero, Nintendo made the sprite look like a track and overlaid car sprites over it: the impression given was that players were racing on a 3D track when in reality the car wasn't moving at all: the player was instead controlling the floor sliding underneath them. Mode 7 was such a striking effect that countless developers used it in their games, even shoehorning it in when it wasn't really

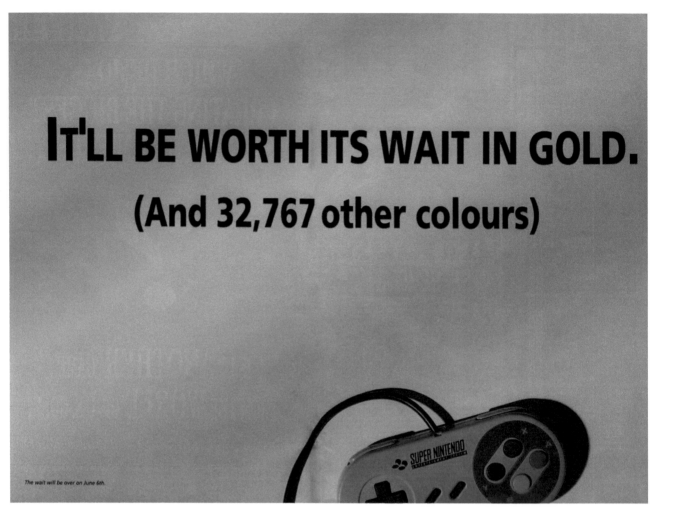

IT'LL BE WORTH ITS WAIT IN GOLD.

(And 32,767 other colours)

The wait will be over on June 6th.

Streetfighter II.

Sega owners... dream on.

STREET FIGHTER II

If you want to play Streetfighter II, it's got to be Super Nintendo.

SUPER NINTENDO
ENTERTAINMENT SYSTEM™

Will you ever reach the end?

necessary: as you read through this book, keep an eye out for how many side-scrolling platformers threw in a couple of Mode 7 levels for no real reason.

The Super Famicom launched in North America on 23 August 1991 with a suitable name change: the Super Nintendo Entertainment System, or SNES for short. It then came to Europe over the summer of 1992, with the UK and Ireland getting it first on 6 June. Nintendo had levelled up, and fans were delighted. The ride wasn't as easy for Nintendo this time around, however. NEC eventually waved the white flag and discontinued the TurboGrafx a couple of years after the SNES launched, but Sega's Mega Drive / Genesis was a force to be reckoned with. The Japanese gaming giant had enough time to prepare for the SNES's arrival, and launched Sonic the Hedgehog in June 1991, two months before the SNES landed in America and a full year before most of Europe got it. Sonic gave Sega an attitude that helped it appeal to older kids: the 10-year-old NES fans who were now 15 and 16 and looking for excuses to rebel. The result was arguably the most competitive console war of any generation, with playgrounds across the world divided into red and blue teams, each with their own valid reasons as to why their console was better than their friends'. The SNES still managed to outsell the Genesis in North America by a considerable margin, but this wasn't the case across the board: in the UK, for example, the Mega Drive was the clear winner.

Regardless of what side you fall on, there can be no denying that the SNES remains one of the most important video game consoles in the history of the medium. So many of the games in this book are fondly regarded as classics today, and the system launched so many more new franchises – F-Zero, Pilotwings, Super Mario Kart, Donkey Kong Country, Star Fox, Mega Man X, Super 3D Noah's Ark – and inspired so many others that it's hard to think what state the industry would have been in had it never existed, and had so many of these great games never had the chance to influence future developers. Okay, maybe not Super 3D Noah's Ark. As for Sega's console? Well, that's for another book.

THE GAMES

The SNES could have offered all the Mode 7 trickery and other gizmos it wanted, but it would all have been a waste of time if it didn't have entertaining games. Thankfully, the SNES enjoyed some of the greatest games ever released, all of which you're about to see in this book. One of the reasons the SNES enjoyed such an impressive library was Nintendo's ability to retain many of its most trusted third-party publishers. Although it's obvious that the likes of Mario, Zelda and Metroid were instrumental in the success of the NES, it would still have struggled had it not also been home to a steady stream of quality titles from companies like Konami, Capcom, Square, Enix, Tecmo and Koei. When the SNES launched, the third-party publishers stuck around, ensuring Nintendo's new console wouldn't be short of quality games any time soon.

One thing that did change, however, was Nintendo's level of control over the games on its system. The NES was infamous for the number of hoops publishers had to jump through in order to get their games on Nintendo's console: Nintendo had to approve every game's content, developers could only release five games per year, only Nintendo was allowed to make the cartridges, and any games released first on the NES weren't allowed to launch on another system for two years. The library's overall quality may have thrived because of these rules, but Nintendo's relationship with developers suffered.

Realising that the popularity of the Mega Drive / Genesis may cause some publishers to say 'fine, we'll just take our games to Sega', Nintendo relaxed these rules when it came to the SNES. The only one it continued to stick by was its insistence on approving the content of each game: it was still a family-friendly company and didn't want to give that up. This famously came to bite the company in the backside when Sega's version of Mortal Kombat outsold the SNES one by nearly three to one because Nintendo had the blood removed.

One of the more interesting and ultimately fruitful ideas Nintendo came up with for the SNES was to ensure its cartridges – or Game Paks, as it called them – offered developers the option to add extra coprocessor chips to them. This made sure that even as the SNES hardware became older and more out of date, the cartridges themselves could include extra processing power to help keep its games looking modern. This was best demonstrated with the Super FX chip, which could perform complex functions (like the drawing of polygons, texture mapping and enhanced sprite scaling) that would otherwise be impossible on the actual SNES hardware.

This book contains 779 games released for the Super Nintendo Entertainment system in North America, Europe and Australia during the console's original run. Multi-game re-releases – like the Super Mario All-Stars + Super Mario World cartridge and the Speed Racer / Mountain Bike Rally cart that came with the Exertainment exercise bike – haven't been included, just to avoid boring repetition. I also haven't included any of the new batch of independently released SNES games that have started to become popular: while these are perfectly valid games in their own right I want this book to be a definitive collection and not a work-in-progress, and as such I'm only focusing on games released during the console's main run.

A large number of SNES games (far more than on the NES) had different names in North America and Europe. Given that this book will be available in both regions, I've listed each game by the title it had in the region it first launched in (where possible). For example, Wings 2: Aces High launched in North America before it came to Europe as Blazing Skies, while football game Striker was released in the UK before America got it as World Soccer 94: Road to Glory. If you can't find a game in the book, please check the index at the back, because chances are it was called something different in another country and all known alternative titles are included in the index.

3 NINJAS KICK BACK

Year	1994
Publisher	Sony Imagesoft
Developer	Malibu Interactive

BASED ON THE sequel to the mediocre movie *3 Ninjas* (known in the UK as *3 Ninja Kids*), the SNES version of 3 Ninjas Kick Back is an action platformer in which bash-happy brothers Rocky, Colt and Tum-Tum have to find a magical dagger for their ageing master (played in the movie by Victor Wong). After choosing which lad you want to control – each is armed with their own unique ninja weapon – you fight your way through five stages filled with all manner of enemies, from rival ninjas and bats to sumo wrestlers and an evil syringe-wielding nurse. Which, you've got to admit, doesn't tend to pop up in video games too often. It also includes a two-player co-op option, which was unusual for the time. ∎

FACT

The game was also released for the Mega Drive and Mega CD. The latter version features video clips of Victor Wong giving you sass.

THE 7TH SAGA

Year	1993
Publisher	Enix
Developer	Produce

A TURN-BASED RPG with more frequent combat than most other games of its type. It has you choosing one of seven distinct characters before being tasked with finding the seven powerful runes needed to defeat an evil entity called Gorsia. The characters are notable for their diversity: as well as standard RPG fare like a knight, a cleric, a dwarf and an elf, you can also choose to play as a demon, a spiked alien made of fire, or the bizarre LUX TIZER: a robot created 5,000 years ago by an ancient civilization. Without wishing to spoil too much, the plot chucks in all manner of time travel and resurrection nonsense, in an attempt to make sure things remain interesting throughout. ∎

FACT

Enix and Produce! later developed another RPG called Mystic Ark. It was going to be sold as The 7th Saga II in the west but never made it out of Japan.

90 MINUTES EUROPEAN PRIME GOAL

Year	1995
Publisher	Ocean Software
Developer	Namco

DESPITE INDEED FEATURING European football as described in the title, Namco's 90 Minutes European Prime Goal is actually a westernised port of the third game in its J-League Soccer: Prime Goal series in Japan. Whereas those Super Famicom games naturally feature teams from Japanese club football, here you get your pick from 14 European nations, including Scotland, England and Northern Ireland (um, sorry Wales). The game itself is standard arcade style fare, with typically stereotypical fake player names: Scotland contains such mildly offensive players as R. Sporran, J. Kaber and B. Connolly. One unique addition is the You're a Hero mode, in which you're placed in various scenarios and have to turn things around to win the game in suitably dramatic fashion. ∎

FACT

All three J-League Soccer Prime Goal games were released in Japan for the Super Famicom. The menu backgrounds featured the J-League mascot, but for the European rebrand they were replaced with garish Ocean Software logos.

AAAHH!!! REAL MONSTERS

Year	1995
Publisher	Viacom New Media
Developer	Realtime Associates

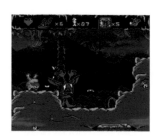

NICKELODEON'S QUIRKY ANIMATED series followed a trio of young monsters trying to graduate from monster school to become fully qualified scarers. The inevitable platform game spin-off lets players switch between the three heroes – Ickis, Krumm and Oblina – and use each of their strengths to get past various obstacles. Ickis can fly over gaps, Krumm can use his detached eyeballs to search the area for hidden rooms and collectibles, and Oblina can stand on top of the other two and use her height to reach otherwise inaccessible platforms. Despite the inventive subject matter, the Real Monsters game is a fairly unremarkable platformer that was critically received at the time with less of an 'AAAHH!!!' and more of a 'meh'. ∎

FACT

The late Christine Cavanaugh, who voiced Oblina in the *Real Monsters* cartoon, also voiced Bunnie Rabbot in the *Sonic the Hedgehog* cartoon series in 1993. She was better known, though, as the voice of Chuckie from *Rugrats*, Dexter from *Dexter's Laboratory* and Babe the Pig.

ABC MONDAY NIGHT FOOTBALL

Year	1993
Publisher	Data East
Developer	Data East

 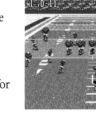

OF ALL THE American football games released on the SNES, ABC Monday Night Football is… well, it's one of them. A fairly unremarkable example of the genre, it opts for unlicensed teams that at least do have fitting names, if not very exciting ones: the Buffalo Wings, the Philadelphia Bells, the San Francisco Bridges and the like. One official licence Data East did secure for the game, though, was obviously that of the ABC *Monday Night Football* show, complete with the classic theme tune the show was famous for, and even a digitised version of sportscaster Frank Gifford looking all serious at you on the main menu. He doesn't do much else though, other than giving the scores from other matches during the game's career mode. ◼

FACT

Monday Night Football red on ABC from 1970 until 005, when it was moved to ter network ESPN. This made one of the longest-running prime time shows on network TV.

ACME ANIMATION FACTORY

Year	1994
Publisher	Sunsoft
Developer	Probe

THIS SURPRISINGLY COMPLEX Looney Tunes themed animation studio was designed with the SNES Mouse in mind, though you could also use a standard SNES controller (as long as you didn't mind drawing circles that looked more like squares). Users can create their own animations one frame at a time, making use of a variety of tools from copying and pasting, to mixing colours and using stamps to add a variety of Looney Tunes characters including Bugs Bunny, Porky Pig and Yosemite Sam. There's a standard drawing mode for those who just want to create still artwork, a Music Hall where players can create their own musical compositions, and a 'Game Arcade' consisting of a single memory match style mini-game. ◼

FACT

The game's manual teaches you how to set your SNES up to a VCR, in case you want to record any of your animations onto a VHS tape.

ACTRAISER

Year	1991
Publisher	Enix
Developer	Quintet

FOR HUNDREDS OF years an evil being called Tanzra has ruled the world, splitting it into six parts and giving control of each to one of his guardians. The peace-loving 'Master', who's been hiding in their Sky Palace, finally decides it's time to fight back. ActRaiser is split into two distinct gameplay types: Simulation mode and Action mode. In the former, you have to develop the land and 'purify' it, in turn growing the population and levelling The Master up in the process. The latter, meanwhile, is more traditional action platformer fare, in which The Master possesses a statue which then wanders through each land, clearing it of Tanzra's monsters. An interesting game that deserves the cult following it's gathered over the years. ◼

FACT

The rather deep ending eveals that all the shrines in the game are now empty because e world's people are no longer uffering. 'Should we yearn for a time when people will no longer need to ask for our help?' it asks.

ACTRAISER 2

Year	1993
Publisher	Enix
Developer	Quintet

THE SEQUEL TO ActRaiser completely ditches the simulation mode, instead offering a straight action platformer free of major gimmicks (other than the fact that you have a large pair of wings you can use to glide during jumps). This time the game's seven stages are named after the seven deadly sins, as The Master sets out to destroy Tanzra's mightiest demons (referred to as the Chosen 13 in the manual). This is a more difficult game than its predecessor – it can feel quite cheap at times – though you can also acquire seven types of magic attack, ranging from the ability to breathe fire on enemies to the wonderfully named 'Raging Bomb'. ◼

FACT

Both Actraiser games were changed in the west to avoid Nintendo's tendency to object to religious iconography in any games appearing on its consoles. In the Japanese versions, The Master and Tanzra are instead God and Satan.

THE ADDAMS FAMILY

Year	1992
Publisher	Ocean Software
Developer	Ocean Software

THERE AREN'T MANY licensed properties that can boast a trio of SNES releases, but The Addams Family can. This first title is based on the 1991 movie starring Raul Julia and Anjelica Huston, and has Gomez exploring the Addams mansion and its surrounding grounds as he tries to rescue all his family members (who've been imprisoned by evil lawyer Tully Alford). For the most part the standard Super Mario-decreed 'jumping on enemy heads to kill them' rule is in effect, but you can also equip Gomez with a fencing sword to him help attack from the side, or find golf balls that he can throw at foes from a distance. If that isn't frivolous enough there's also a little Fez with a propeller that lets him fly around for a limited time. ∎

FACT

The bottom-left corner of the main 'Hall of Stairs' area contains a hidden door that leads to a whole heap of 1-ups and other power-ups.

THE ADDAMS FAMILY: PUGSLEY'S SCAVENGER HUNT

Year	1993
Publisher	Ocean Software
Developer	Ocean Software

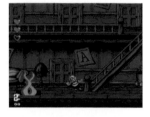

BASED THIS TIME on the animated TV series broadcast between 1992 and 1993, Pugsley's Scavenger Hunt plays similarly to its predecessor, though this time there's obviously a new protagonist and more cartoonish sprites. The plot is far less sinister too: rather than having an evil solicitor locking up all the Addams family members, this time you're simply having a bit of fun. Wednesday Addams has set up a scavenger hunt for her brother Pugsley, so you have to explore the Addams mansion in search of all six hidden items. The dark comedy of *The Addams Family* also helps justify the various enemies and traps you encounter along the way: they were deliberately put there by Wednesday to make things more dangerous (and therefore fun) for Pugsley. ∎

FACT

Whereas other versions have a password system, the SNES version doesn't. Given that it's a tricky game, this is considered a big loss.

ADDAMS FAMILY VALUES

Year	1995
Publisher	Ocean Software
Developer	Ocean Software

FOR ITS THIRD Addams Family game on the SNES, Ocean decided to go in a different direction and instead opted for a top-down action RPG in the style of the early Zelda games. The source of inspiration this time is the second live-action movie in which Gomez and Morticia have a third child called Pubert. In the game, Pubert has been kidnapped by evil nanny Debbie Jellinski who wants control over the Addams estate as ransom. The family track her down to a deserted mansion on the outskirts of town and set about trying to find Pubert. While all the family members can be found dotted around you play as Uncle Fester in this one (much like in NES game Fester's Quest), exploring the mansion grounds and eventually the mansion itself. ∎

FACT

Perhaps aware that this can be a difficult adventure, the manual lists all 43 items in the game and explains exactly which puzzles they solve (so if you get stuck, you have no excuse).

THE ADVENTURES OF BATMAN & ROBIN

Year	1994
Publisher	Konami
Developer	Konami

ARKHAM ASYLUM, THE least secure asylum in modern times, has seen its umpteenth breakout and once again all of Gotham's criminals are on the loose. It's up to Batman and Robin to put a stop to The Joker, The Riddler, Poison Ivy, The Penguin, Catwoman, Two-Face and Scarecrow so they can be locked up again (at least until they escape half an hour later). Well, I say 'It's up to Batman and Robin' but in reality this is very much a Batman-only action platformer (despite the game's name), with Robin relegated to cutscene roles. Still, good old Batters can equip himself with all manner of gadgets, from his trademark Batarang and Grappling Gun to less Bat-standard items like a pair of X-Ray goggles and a 'spray gun' that makes enemies temporarily fall down. ∎

FACT

Robin barely features because the game is based on *Batman: The Animated Series* and was we into development when it emerge the second season would be called *The Adventures of Batman & Robin*.

THE ADVENTURES OF DR FRANKEN

Year	1993
Publisher	DTMC
Developer	MotiveTime

FRANKY IS A '90s style 'cool' version of Frankenstein's monster: he's hip, he's funny and he's very much a dude with a 'tude. He's also got a girlfriend called Bitsy, and the pair want to take a holiday to New York, but there's just one problem: she doesn't have a passport. Since she's also a monster made up of spare body parts, the decision is made to cut her into small pieces and mail her to their destination. However, a mix-up sends Bitsy's bits to 20 different locations all around the world so it's up to Franky to travel the globe and put his missus back together again. Each level in this platformer has its own unique enemies, so travelling to the UK puts you up against punk rockers and kids on space hoppers (that well-known British stereotype). ■

FACT

Prototype versions of Dr Franken were made for the NES and Game Gear, but although they were nearly finished they were never released.

THE ADVENTURES OF MIGHTY MAX

Year	1995
Publisher	Ocean Software
Developer	Ocean Software

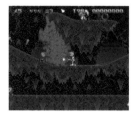

MIGHTY MAX WAS the 'boy' equivalent of the Polly Pocket playsets from the early '90s which featured tiny little figures (less than an inch in height) in little environments that could be closed over like compact mirrors. As well as the Mighty Max toys there was also a short-lived animated series: this game was based on that. Playing as either Max or one of his friends Felix or Bea – who are just as powerful, so he can't be that mighty – you have to collect the scattered pieces of a bunch of massive weapons to stop the evil SkullMaster from using them to dominate the world. A ridiculously high jumping mechanic prevents the Mighty Max game from being anything other than an exercise in frustration. ■

FACT

In the *Mighty Max* cartoon Max was voiced by Rob Paulsen, better known for voicing two Teenage Mutant Ninja Turtles: Raphael in the '80s series, and Donatello in the 2002 series.

THE ADVENTURES OF ROCKY AND BULLWINKLE AND FRIENDS

Year	1993
Publisher	THQ
Developer	Imagineering

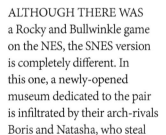

ALTHOUGH THERE WAS a Rocky and Bullwinkle game on the NES, the SNES version is completely different. In this one, a newly-opened museum dedicated to the pair is infiltrated by their arch-rivals Boris and Natasha, who steal three of its most valuable artefacts. It's up to the duo to travel across a mountain, cave, mine, mechanical whale, ghost ship and castle to catch up to the villains and get the items back. Lengthy jumping sections with tiny platforms can make this one a little tricky, and collision detection is more than a little ropey, but it's got enough charm to make it worth a look. It also has mini-games based on spin-off characters Dudley Do-Right and Peabody & Sherman. ■

FACT

The intro sequence is interrupted when Rocky asks why the game has the same plot as the Game Boy version. The narrator reassures him the game itself is completely different.

THE ADVENTURES OF TINTIN: PRISONERS OF THE SUN

Year	1996
Publisher	Infogrames
Developer	Infogrames

THE SECOND OF two Tintin games released on the SNES (the first being Tintin in Tibet), this one follows the Tintin story of the same name – as well as its predecessor, *The Seven Crystal Balls* – as the ginger reporter tries to track down and rescue the kidnapped Professor Calculus while also trying to figure out why a group of explorers have all fallen into a coma. Whereas the book takes place mainly in Peru, the game is instead set all over the world with stages as diverse as a museum, a ship, a jungle and… um, a newspaper. That last one's a puzzle stage where you have to arrange scraps of torn paper to form an image. A visually impressive game for its era, and one relatively easy to find despite the fact it was only released in Europe near the end of the SNES's life. ■

FACT

Prisoners of the Sun was also ported to the Game Boy Color. Despite the obvious drop in graphical detail, it's actually remarkably faithful to the SNES game.

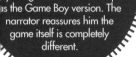

ADVENTURES OF YOGI BEAR

Year	1994
Publisher	Cybersoft
Developer	Empire Software

ALSO KNOWN AS Yogi Bear's Cartoon Capers in Europe (though both versions just say 'Yogi Bear' on the title screen), this serviceable platformer stars everyone's fourth favourite cartoon bear as he tries to save his home, Jellystone Park, from being turned into a chemical dumping zone by industrial developers. It's not quite clear whether the series of unrelated enemies you're up against – including killer snowmen and cute hopping bunnies who can still somehow hurt you – are in cahoots with the chemical dumpers, or whether the fact they want to kill you too is just a tragic coincidence. Either way, while its stages are fairly nondescript woodland-based environments for the most part, one highlight involves surfing on the back of a beaver to cross water. ■

FACT

The closing credits end with the message 'thank you for playing' followed by 'have fun', which seems a tad belated by that point.

AERO FIGHTERS

Year	1994
Publisher	Video System
Developer	Video System

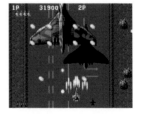

DESPITE BEING A port of a relatively popular arcade shoot 'em up, Aero Fighters is considered one of the rarest SNES games, purely because it was released in such small numbers. It's a shame, because it's a decent little shooter that does a good job of taking the vertically-oriented arcade version and squashing everything down into a standard TV aspect ratio. Playing as one of four 'aero fighters', you have to destroy 'unknown alien forces' by blasting your way through seven stages, culminating in a final boss fight against a giant rocket. An unnecessarily long cheat code lets you play as Rabio, the hero of another Video System arcade shooter, Rabbit Punch. The game claims to be developed by Mc O'River: this was just the temporary name for Video System's US arm. ■

FACT

Designer Shun Nakamura wasn't happy that Video System was planning to make Neo Geo games, because he preferred vertical screen layouts. As a protest, he and some colleagues left to form a new studio, Psikyo.

AERO THE ACRO-BAT

Year	1993
Publisher	Sunsoft
Developer	Iguana Entertainment

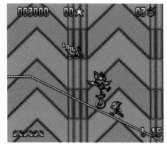

A DISGRUNTLED FORMER clown named Edgar Ektor decides to get revenge by sabotaging the World of Amusement Circus and Funpark. Unfortunately, he didn't reckon with Aero the Acro-Bat, a death-defying stuntman (well, stuntbat) who works for the circus and decides to save the day. Armed with a diagonal drill jump move (similar to that of Cat Mario in Super Mario 3D World) and the obligatory sassy attitude, Aero has to make used of cannons, unicycles, trapezes and trampolines on his way to the Museum of Horrors for a final showdown with Edgar and his sidekick, Zero the Acrobat (who was later renamed Zero the Kamikaze Squirrel and eventually got his own game, found elsewhere in this book). ■

FACT

TV company Saban Entertainment was going to create an animated series based on Aero the Acro-Bat, but the plans fell through when Saban instead found success with *Mighty Morphin' Power Rangers*.

AERO THE ACRO-BAT 2

Year	1994
Publisher	Sunsoft
Developer	Iguana Entertainment

THE 16-BIT GENERATION was very much the era of animal mascots with attitude (thank/blame the success of Sonic the Hedgehog for that). Very few of them stuck around long enough to get a sequel, though, so fair play to Aero for earning this encore performance. Set immediately after the events of the first game, Aero finds a magician's box in Edgar's museum that teleports him to a mysterious world where he meets a beautiful Eastern European bat called Batasha (groan). Little does he know, though, that Zero saved Edgar and the pair are getting ready to launch the sinister-sounding 'Plan B'. Gameplay is more of the same, though the levels are longer and you can now drill directly downwards (rather than being limited to diagonal attacks). ■

FACT

Just in case it wasn't quite clear just how 'radical' Aero is, there's a stage called Boardin' Zone where you get to snowboard down some 'gnarly' hills and such.

AEROBIZ

Year	1993
Publisher	Koei
Developer	Koei

KOEI MAY BE better known for its historical simulation games (especially those based on ancient China), but it's been known to dabble in other areas too. Aerobiz is a shining example of this: putting you in the expensive shoes of an airline CEO, you have to expand your business and outdo your three rival airlines. There are two time periods to choose from: the 1963–1995 scenario has each airline competing to be the first to cross the Pacific Ocean without refuelling, while the other scenario opens with the advent of supersonic travel in 1983 and continues well into the future (2015). Whichever of these you choose, the eventual aim is the same: connect all 22 of the game's cities through your air routes. ■

FACT

World events shape the game's difficulty: set your line in Moscow and it's hard to buy anything other than Russian planes until the Cold War ends.

AEROBIZ SUPERSONIC

Year	1994
Publisher	Koei
Developer	Koei

DESPITE AEROBIZ'S AIM to join together world cities, Koei decided that didn't extend to game publishing and so it chose not to release its sequel in Europe. It's a shame, because it's a superior game in practically every sense: there are now 89 cities available, as well as over 50 airplane types (including supersonic ones, obviously) and four new scenarios: 1955–75, 1970–90, 1985–2005 and the futuristic 2000–2020. Although (like its predecessor) it uses real-world events to affect your game, the latter scenario obviously had to predict future events. Most (like Russia, Belarus, Ukraine and Switzerland joining the EU) didn't happen. Of course, little did Koei know that the events of 11 September 2001 would change the aerospace industry forever, making the 2000–2020 scenario a charmingly innocent 'what if' situation. ■

FACT

The Aerobiz games are known as Air Management I and II in Japan. A third game, Air Management '96, was released in Japan for the PlayStation and Saturn.

AIR CAVALRY

Year	1995
Publisher	Cybersoft
Developer	Synergistic Software

EA'S DESERT STRIKE (found elsewhere in this book) may be the first game most people think about when it comes to helicopter combat, but it was far from the only example. Cybersoft's Air Cavalry puts you in control of four different models – the AH-64A Apache, AH-94A Valkyrie, OH-6D Defender and UH-60A Black Hawk – as you take on various missions in the Middle East, Central America and Indonesia. Whereas Desert Strike had an isometric viewpoint, Air Cavalry puts the camera right behind your chopper and uses Mode 7 for a 3D effect. Despite its impressive visuals, it was heavily criticised for its high level of difficulty: enemy units are remarkably accurate and have a habit of shooting you down extremely quickly. ■

FACT

The briefing screen features a rendition of Wagner's *Flight of the Valkyries*. In the movie *Apocalypse Now*, US soldiers in helicopters play *Flight of the Valkyries* through loudspeakers to intimidate the Vietnamese.

AL UNSER JR'S ROAD TO THE TOP

Year	1994
Publisher	Mindscape
Developer	Radical Entertainment

TWO-TIME INDY 500 winner Al Unser Jr seemingly wasn't content with lending his name to a single game (Data East's NES title Al Unser Jr's Turbo Racing), so here's a second effort from a different publisher and developer. Road to the Top has players working their way up the motorsport ladder as they take on four different disciplines on their way to the titular top, where they meet Mr Unser Jr for a final race. Starting off with go-kart racing, players will take on snowmobiles and IROC (International Race of Champions) cars before finally getting to race in Indy cars. All four disciplines use the same Mario Kart style Mode 7 viewpoint and generally handle similarly with the only major difference being speed. ■

FACT

Al pops up to give you advice before each race. One of his most illuminating tips is that 'snowmobiles are a totally different beast than the go-kart'.

ALADDIN

Year	1993
Publisher	Capcom
Developer	Capcom

ALADDIN IS A rare example of a 16-bit movie tie-in that's completely different on each system. The Mega Drive / Genesis version was developed by Virgin Interactive and published by Sega, because Sega had acquired the licence to make an Aladdin video game. However, Capcom still held a longer-running exclusivity licence to make Disney games for Nintendo consoles, and so the SNES version of Aladdin is an entirely different game developed by Capcom and designed by Shinji Mikami (later known for directing and producing the Resident Evil games). Starting off in the marketplace, Aladdin's journey takes him through the Cave of Wonders, a giant pyramid and even the Genie's lamp itself before he arrives at Jafar's palace for a final showdown. There's also a bonus stage based on the magic carpet section from the film, in which Aladdin and Jasmine enjoy an evening fly set to *A Whole New World*. The differences between the SNES and Mega Drive versions make for a fascinating study in how two studios handle the same source material in both different and similar

FACT

In a 2014 interview, Mikami revealed that given the choice between each version he'd rather play the Mega Drive one. '[It] had a sword, actually,' he explained. 'I wanted a sword.'

ways: both games have you collecting apples and throwing them at enemies for long-range attacks, but while the Mega Drive version also features sword-based combat, Capcom instead opts for the tried-and-tested platforming trope of jumping on enemies' heads to defeat them. Aladdin can also find a large white sheet that he can use to glide across the sky: this can make for some almost parkour-style moments where he's leaping off heads, climbing ledges and flipping over poles. ■

ALIEN 3

Year	1992
Publisher	Acclaim
Developer	Probe

ANOTHER MOVIE TIE-IN that's completely different on the SNES. Whereas other versions of Alien 3 have you running through numerous levels as you try to find a certain number of hostages before time runs out, the SNES version is a slower-paced, free-roaming affair

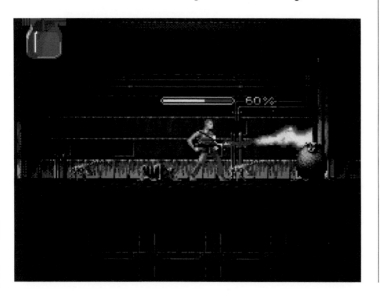

that feels more like a mission-based Metroid adventure (which is fitting, given that Metroid was inspired by Alien). As in the controversial movie of the same name, Ripley has found herself on the prison colony Fiorina 161, and she's brought an alien with her. However, as with the other games, that's where the similarities end: whereas the movie's central premise is based on the fact that Ripley and her new prisoner chums are stuck on a planet without weapons facing a single Alien, here you're armed to the teeth as you fight endless hordes of them. This time, though, instead of simply running and gunning your way from left to right, you take on a series of missions located at the various computer terminals located around the prison. These have you doing anything from fusing doors shut before an egg hive hatches and breaks loose, to repairing pipes to keep the cooling system from breaking down, to powering up generators. There are multiple routes to each objective and you have free movement around each stage, meaning you have to use the terminal's map to try to determine the easiest and safest routes to take. Its surprising depth makes the SNES version of Alien 3 one of the best movie tie-ins of the 16-bit era. ■

FACT

The game ends like the movie does (spoilers), with Ripley jumping into a pool of lava to stop Weyland-Yutani getting the Alien inside her. This is done with a Mode 7 effect looking down into the pool as Ripley falls into it.

ALIEN VS PREDATOR

Year	1993
Publisher	Activision
Developer	Jorudan

 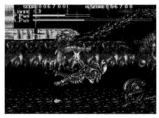

AN ARCADE-STYLE BEAT 'em up, not to be confused with the actual AvP arcade game released by Capcom a year later. Set in the year 2493 on the planet Vega 4, workers digging a subway tunnel in New Shanghai find some dormant Alien eggs, which hatch and attack everyone. A distress signal is picked up by a Predator, who – sick of hunting humans and looking for a challenge – decides to help out. Combat is a little clunky and the constant stream of Aliens, each with a needlessly long power bar, make this a fairly repetitive affair, and although the ending teases that there may be a sequel set on another planet, lacklustre reviews made sure Jorudan wouldn't be at the helm regardless. ■

FACT

The credits in the Japanese version of the game correctly lists the names of everyone involved in the making of the game, but the western version replaces 'K. Nakabayahi' with 'Dr Banana' for unknown reasons.

AMERICAN GLADIATORS

Year	1993
Publisher	GameTec
Developer	Imagitec Design

WHEREAS THE NES version of American Gladiators took some liberties with the hit TV show's format, the SNES game is a far more authentic product: partly because all of the events play like they do on the show but also because only a few people in the world will truly conquer it. Playing through Imagitec's 16-bit interpretations of Assault, Human Cannonball, Atlasphere, Joust, Powerball, The Wall and the Eliminator is an exercise in patience as each event tries to outdo the others to offer the worst controls on the SNES. Players can play one-on-one shows (with either male or female contestants), or put together a 16-player tournament if they fancy cutting 15 friends out of their life and want a quick way to ditch them all at once. ■

FACT

There were a total of 33 American Gladiators over the course of the show's five seasons, from long-term favourites like Nitro and Zap to the likes of Bronco and Jade, who each only appeared on a single episode to replace an injured Gladiator.

AN AMERICAN TAIL: FIEVEL GOES WEST

Year	1994
Publisher	Hudson Soft
Developer	Shimada Kikaku

THE JEWISH-UKRAINIAN MOUSEKEWITZ family emigrated to America in 1885, but realised life there wasn't all it was cracked up to be. Five years later, the evil Cat R. Waul tells them a better life can be found out west, so the family sets off. Separated from them, young Fievel learns that Cat R. Waul actually wants to turn them into mouseburgers, so it's up to him to reunite with his folks and put a stop to the scheme. This Hudson-published platformer arms Fievel with a pop gun so he can take out his enemies. He can also collect special types of ammo that can be used for certain tasks: for example, collecting the water ammo and firing at flaming platforms puts them out and lets you jump on them without taking damage. ■

FACT

There was another Fievel Goes West game released for DOS PCs. Rather than a platformer, it's instead a point-and-click adventure.

ANDRE AGASSI TENNIS

Year	1994
Publisher	TecMagik
Developer	Radiance Software

THIS BASIC TENNIS game features exhibition matches or a tournament mode where you play against each of the game's eight characters, culminating in a match against eight-time Grand Slam champion Andre Agassi himself. The other seven tennis players featured are completely fictional, and range from speedy Bob Chin to the accurate Cassie Nova (who 'puts 'em where she wants 'em', according to the manual). As well as standard matches – you can only play the best of one or three sets – you can also play 'skins' matches, in which every hit in a rally adds $100 to the bank, and whoever wins the point gets to keep the whole lot. It's an interesting feature in a game that, unlike the man himself, is otherwise rather unremarkable. ■

FACT

The manual is also full of advice from Agassi, including 'it's all attitude, go for it!' and 'the forehand is my weapon: expose my forehand to hit regular winners'. There's probably a euphemism in there if you try hard to find it.

ANOTHER WORLD

Year	1992
Publisher	Interplay
Developer	Delphine Software

WHILE WORKING ON his particle accelerator in his lab, ginger genius Lester Knight Chaykin suddenly finds himself in a sticky situation when a bolt of lightning hits the building and creates a tear in space and time, transporting Lester to a barren alien planet. Can Lester escape the hostile aliens trying to kill him and return back home? Spoilers: yes and no, respectively. Another World (known as Out of This World in North America) is a visually unique adventure game designed by French developer Éric Chahi, who was responsible for everything except the music. Unlike most other side-scrollers of the time, Another World has no HUD showing your score, health, lives or the like: it's designed to be a cinematic adventure rather than a standard action game. This extends to the impressive cutscenes, which were far and away ahead of anything else like it, partly because of Chahi's use of vector art and rotoscoping to give the game a polygonal look, long before that became the norm. Playing the game itself is more of an exercise in trial and error, however: each new scene introduces not only new hostile beings – from the underwater plant monster on the very first screen to the evil shadow wolf – but new control mechanics too, meaning players often get to see Lester's various grim death scenes before figuring out what they're supposed to do each time. Think of it as more of a cinematic puzzle game, then, than an actual platformer. ■

FACT

Near the end of the game you run past a pool area where some female aliens can be seen bathing in the foreground. The SNES version is slightly censored here: the aliens' bum cracks have been removed.

ANIMANIACS

Year	1994
Publisher	Konami
Developer	Konami

RATHER THAN GO down the standard 2D platformer route, Konami's take on Warner Bros' popular animated series is instead a pseudo-3D affair with Yakko, Wakko and Dot able to travel not just left and right, but also up and down as they go in search of their script's 24 missing pages. As well as a jump and dash attack, the trio can pick up and throw items and even stack on top of each other for a higher jump. This only works when you have a full team, though: when a character is caught by a guard or 'dies' they're out of the game permanently. Collecting coins triggers a slot machine at the bottom of the screen which can give various bonuses or resurrect fallen heroes. ■

FACT

The Mega Drive version is a more traditional 2D platformer and was far better received by critics, who felt the SNES game was too difficult and awkward to play.

ARCADE'S GREATEST HITS: THE ATARI COLLECTION 1

Year	1997
Publisher	Midway Games
Developer	Digital Eclipse

CALIFORNIA-BASED DEVELOPER DIGITAL Eclipse has a reputation for delivering high-quality ports of retro games. It's been doing this for over 25 years now, and one of its earliest products was this SNES compilation featuring home renditions of six of Atari's most popular arcade games: Asteroids, Battlezone, Centipede, Missile Command, Super Breakout and Tempest. Considering the 8-bit generation was infamous for a steady stream of half-hearted and generally inept ports of arcade titles, the level of accuracy here is extremely impressive: everything looks, feels and sounds just like it should, proving that Digital Eclipse had the whole arcade-to-home thing nailed pretty much straight away. Each game also gets a full array of options and two-player modes, meaning at the time they were considered the definitive home versions of each classic game. ■

FACT

The compilation was also released on the PlayStation and Saturn: these versions also included a video documentary called *The Golden Age of Atari.*

ARCANA

Year	1992
Publisher	HAL Laboratory
Developer	HAL Laboratory

CARD-BASED RPGS ARE generally better suited to real-life board games than video games, which is probably why Arcana flirts with the idea but ultimately doesn't commit to it. Playing as Rooks, the son of the last Card Master

in the land of Elemen, you have to head off on an adventure to stop the awakening of the evil empress Rimsala. Although Rooks and the other members of his party are represented by cards, Arcana is instead a more traditional first-person dungeon crawler where you explore a series of dungeons and take out the enemies you encounter. Although its card-based theme was interesting, it was notorious for its high difficulty level, partly due to its small inventory size, its limited save points, and bosses appearing out of nowhere. ▪

FACT

An early plan for the game let players find and equip various rings to get new abilities. The idea was scrapped but the unused code for 17 different rings remains on the cartridge.

ARKANOID: DOH IT AGAIN

Year	1997
Publisher	Nintendo
Developer	Taito

WHEN A NEW potentially habitable planet is discovered by a sensor ship, Commander Therle jumps into his Vaus ship and heads out to investigate. Before he gets there, the evil floating head DOH (the final boss from the first Arkanoid game) appears and starts putting blocks in his way. Therle has to destroy all the blocks and then kill DOH so he can reach the planet and see if a new colony can be set up there. All of which is clearly a ridiculously elaborate story for what's just another bat-and-ball game where you have to clear the blocks on all 99 levels. There's also a level editor mode, where players can create their own stages (and yes, I'm sure making rude pictures out of the blocks has been done before). ▪

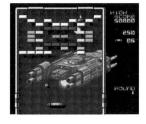

FACT

When you beat level 99, Therle decides the planet is habitable and says: 'We will never repeat the mistakes of the past. Humanity and environment will co-exist together.'

ARDY LIGHTFOOT

Year	1994
Publisher	Titus Software
Developer	ASCII Entertainment

THE EVIL KING Visconti is seeking the shattered pieces of a scared rainbow, because whoever finds them all will have their dreams come true. He sends his henchmen out to get the pieces, but they aren't alone. Also looking for the pieces is Ardy, a feline adventurer who, accompanied by his little blue chum Pec, quite fancies having his wishes granted too. Cue a fairly tricky platformer in which the player is armed with a variety of moves, from a pogo tail jump to the ability to throw Pec at enemies and obstacles. Along the way he meets various chums, most notably Indiana Jones knock-off Don Jacoby, who turns up every now and then to help out. An inventive and enjoyable game, if a difficult one. ▪

FACT

A stage set inside a giant worm shows boss character Catry lying unconscious. In the Japanese version you instead see her skeleton, dissolved by stomach acid. Could be worse: a beta version shows a semi-decomposed corpse instead.

ART OF FIGHTING

Year	1993
Publisher	Takara
Developer	Monolith Corporation

ALTHOUGH FATAL FURY and The King of Fighters are the series that tend to spring to mind when it comes to SNK, the Neo Geo creator also created a prequel trilogy called Art of Fighting, the first game of which made it to the SNES. Despite taking obvious influences from Street Fighter II it also offers its own unique features, most notably a single-player story mode in which you can choose between two characters (Ryo and Robert) as they fight their way through the notorious South Town district trying to save Ryo's sister Yuri. It also introduces 'desperation attacks' – high-power moves that can only be performed when your energy meter is dangerously low and flashing – and a 'spirit gauge' which weakens your special moves the more you use them. ▪

FACT

Spoilers: while the Story mode in other versions of Art of Fighting stops short of revealing the identity of final boss Mr Karate, the SNES version goes on to show that he's Ryo and Yuri's father.

A.S.P. AIR STRIKE PATROL

Year	1994
Publisher	SETA (US), System 3 (EU)
Developer	Opus

THE GULF WAR influenced a number of air combat games in the early '90s, but not all were bold enough to explicitly state it. That's why A.S.P. (known as Desert Fighter in Europe) isn't about Iraq invading Kuwait, but Zaraq invading Sweit. Completely different, you see. As an air force commander, it's your job to fly into the warzone and carry out various missions, usually involving blowing loads of things up.

The game is played with an isometric viewpoint and you're given the option to fly in either an A-10 Thunderbolt II or an F-15 Strike Eagle. After each mission you're graded on your performance in a number of areas: this affects the ending text you get when you complete the game's eighth and final mission. ■

FACT

Lose too many lives and the ending will tell you that families turned up at the victory parade with yellow ribbons for fear their loved ones didn't return. You're then told to 'go back to war college'.

ASTERIX

Year	1993
Publisher	Infogrames
Developer	Infogrames

THE POPULAR FRENCH comic *Asterix* has been around for over 60 years and is much loved worldwide: though maybe not so much in the US, which may explain why this SNES platformer didn't make it there. It's certainly America's loss because it's a decent little game, if a difficult one: you play as the titular Gaul who has to travel all the way from home to Rome to find his big pal Obelix, who's been captured. Along the way you'll encounter your fair share of Romans to beat up, accompanied by the same delightful 'PAF!' bubble from the comics. You can also pick up Getafix's magic potion – which gives a variety of powers from invincibility to temporary flight – or a bone, which makes Obelix's pet Dogmatix appear and bite the nearest enemy. ■

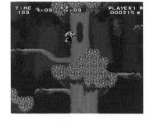

FACT

Asterix and the Chieftain's Daughter, released in 2019, was the 38th book in the Asterix series. It was translated to over 20 languages at launch with 5 million copies printed (only slightly more than this book).

ASTERIX & OBELIX

Year	1996
Publisher	Infogrames
Developer	Infogrames

ASTERIX'S FRIEND OBELIX is loved just as much (if not more) than the main man himself, so the fact he wasn't playable in the first SNES game disappointed some fans. This was rectified with Asterix & Obelix, a second platformer in which players can now choose to play as either hero. This time the pair decide to travel the world and bring back a souvenir from every country, then send them to Caesar to show him they can go wherever they like. These include a rugby ball from Britannia, Olympic laurels from Grecia and a gold pyramid from Egyptia. Although it's clearly based on its predecessor's game engine, Asterix & Obelix improves the animation substantially to the extent that it's arguably one of the better looking SNES games. ■

FACT

Obelix fell into the magic potion when he was a child so he's permanently blessed with super strength. Despite this, a couple of hits will still kill him here.

AXELAY

Year	1992
Publisher	Konami
Developer	Konami

THE ARMADA OF Annihilation is invading, working its way through the various planets in the Illis solar system. All that remains between the invaders and total destruction is the *Axelay*, a small stratafighter armed to the teeth. This Konami shoot 'em up includes both side-scrolling and vertically scrolling stages, the latter using a strange visual effect to make the background 'roll' underneath you (contrary to popular belief, this isn't a Mode 7 trick). Rather than collecting power-ups, you're instead given new weapons after each stage and have to choose which three of them to take with you into the next level. If you take a hit you'll lose one of these weapons, meaning you have to resort to a weaker gun until you eventually die and get your arms restored. ■

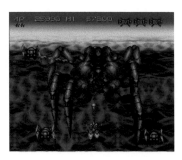

FACT

If you beat the game three times in a row you'll get a message saying: 'See you again at Axelay 2.' A sequel was never released.

BALLZ 3D

Year	1994
Publisher	Accolade
Developer	PF Magic

WITH POLYGONAL FIGHTING games like Virtua Fighter starting to make their presence known, California-based developer PF Magic decided to swap squares for spheres with Ballz, a game in which all of its fighters are made entirely of balls. Characters range from ballet dancer Devine to a rhino named Crusher, to Yoko: a small monkey that specialises in farting at its opponents. There are also five unplayable bosses, including an ostrich, T-Rex and kangaroo. In case you can't tell, it isn't the most serious game, to the extent that Nintendo asked PF Magic to change the intro sequence: it says 'to be the champion, you gotta have Ballz' in the Mega Drive version, but was changed to 'you gotta play Ballz' for the SNES. ■

FACT

Although Ballz 3D wasn't massive success, PF Magic kept its art style for its PC virtual pet games Petz, Dogz, Catz, Oddballz and Babyz.

BARBIE: SUPER MODEL

Year	1993
Publisher	Hi-Tech Expressions
Developer	Software Creations

BARBIE HAS BEEN asked to participate in the National Super Model Competition (despite being 12 inches tall), but before she gets to the big event in New York she has to enter tryouts in Hollywood, Hawaii and Colorado first. The game consists of three elements: side-scrolling sections (where you have to avoid obstacles in a car, rollerskates or skis), memory mini-games (where you have to study Barbie's appearance then match her hair, clothes and accessories) and catwalk stages. Each show has a sequence of button presses you need to pull off on the catwalk: you can practice it beforehand but then need to pull it off without button prompts. Score at least 5,000 points in total and you'll go down as a legendary supermodel. ■

FACT

A second Barbie game entitled Barbie: Vacation Adventure was seemingly completed, but despite getting reviewed in *Nintendo Power* and *GamePro* magazines it was never released.

BARKLEY: SHUT UP AND JAM!

Year	1994
Publisher	Accolade
Developer	Accolade

A CLEAR ATTEMPT to capitalise on the success of the NBA Jam games, Barkley: Shut Up and Jam! takes the same two-on-two formula as Midway's arcade title but moves it to the streets instead. Players can choose their pair from a roster of 16 characters: these consist of NBA superstar Charles Barkley and 15 other fictional ballers, from the dreadlocked T-Bone to the mean-looking D-Train, to Jimi Hendrix lookalike Funky D and a few others who don't have initials in their names. One area where it does better than NBA Jam is in courts, however: rather than its single stage there are eight to choose from here, with settings ranging from a beach to the rooftops to what the manual politely describes as 'the ghetto'. ■

FACT

In 2008 an indie RPG called Barkley: Shut Up and Jam Gaiden was created. It's set in 2041, where basketball has been outlawed after a powerful Barkley dunk killed a number of onlookers.

BASS MASTERS CLASSIC

Year	1995
Publisher	Malibu Games
Developer	Malibu Games

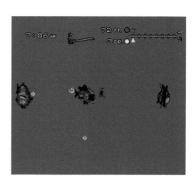

THE SNES GOT its fair share of fishing games, with particular focus paid to bass fishing, for some reason. As the name suggests, Bass Masters Classic is indeed all about the bass, and contains the official Bass Anglers Sportsman Society (B.A.S.S.) licence. There are six different anglers to choose from, ranging from Hooker B. Sharp (who 'uses chemically sharpened hooks') to Zoe Shelby (who is delightfully described as 'the most attractive angler on the pro circuit, to bass at least'). The aim is to take on a series of four tournaments, finishing in the top five in each to progress to the next. You can visit a shop in between rounds to stock up on different lures, reels, rods, lines, fish finders and boat engines. ■

FACT

The largest ever bass caught during a Bassmaster Classic (the SuperBowl of bass fishing) was 11 pounds 10 ounces, caught by Preston Clark in 2006.

BASS MASTERS CLASSIC: PRO EDITION

Year | 1996
Publisher | Malibu Games
Developer | Malibu Games

CLEARLY SOMEONE AT Malibu Games decided that Bass Masters Classic wasn't a comprehensive enough bass fishing experience, and so gamers were blessed with the Pro Edition. As you may expect, this isn't a complete sequel to the original but rather a tweaked version that addresses some of its issues. Most notable is the inclusion of 'amateur' and 'pro' difficulty levels, the former adding some new aids to help players catch fish easier. While amateur mode lets you play as a new helping of fictional anglers (from 'young sprout' Nick Casey to 'spunky oldster' Earl Green), pro mode now features six real-life bass fishing experts, from Tom Mann Jr to all-time pro bass fishing money winner Kevin VanDam (who's netted over $6 million in prize money over the years). ∎

FACT

If you decide you fancy trying the real thing, the manual includes a voucher to become a B.A.S.S. member for $14 instead of the usual $20.

BASSIN'S BLACK BASS

Year | 1994
Publisher | Hot-B
Developer | Starfish

NOT SO FAST, Bass Masters Classic. Japanese studio Hot-B – which had been responsible for NES fishing games The Blue Marlin and The Black Bass – decided to cast its lure into the SNES pond with its own bass fishing offering. Much like Malibu's titles it too has its own sponsorship (this time with *Bassin'* magazine) and its own pro angler tie-in (two-time Bassmaster Classic winner Hank Parker). The general idea remains the same: there are three lakes and a river to choose from, and the aim is to catch the biggest fish you can. In this game, however, you're also given the option to recruit an assistant who'll head out into the water with you and give you useful advice on where to look for fish. ∎

FACT

Bassin' magazine was established in 1981 and is absolutely adamant that it remains 'America's number 1 "how to" bass fishing magazine for the weekend angler.' Who am I to argue?

BATMAN FOREVER

Year | 1995
Publisher | Acclaim
Developer | Probe

THE THIRD BATMAN movie wasn't quite as critically acclaimed as the first two, but gamers were at least given an authentic home console experience because Acclaim's tie-in game was just as disappointing. Despite being an action platformer, Batman Forever actually uses a heavily modified version of the Mortal Kombat fight system, as evidenced by the presence of uppercuts, sweeps, roundhouse kicks and quick punches (as well as the use of real actors digitised into the game). Players can choose to play as Batman or Robin but whoever you select the result is the same: awkward controls, repetitive fighting and gadgets that are so cumbersome you start to wonder how Batman made it to a third film without getting his head kicked in. ∎

FACT

It's rare for a SNES game to feature visible loading screens, but every time you enter a new room in Batman Forever you're met with a black screen and the words 'hold on'.

BATMAN RETURNS

Year | 1993
Publisher | Konami
Developer | Konami

A COUPLE OF years before Batman Forever was stinking up SNES systems worldwide, Konami delivered a much better effort to coincide with the second movie, *Batman Returns*. It's a beat 'em up in the style of Final Fight and sees Batman punching and kicking his way through Gotham in an attempt to put a stop to the Penguin, via Catwoman. Some of its stages are side-scrollers and there's also a Batmobile level, but the game's most unique feature is its grappling system, where walking into an opponent grabs them by the throat and lifts them into the air: from here you can slam them into background scenery like windows and fences, or quickly grab a second enemy and bash both their heads together. ∎

FACT

Beat the game in Mania mode, the hardest difficulty level, and you'll be rewarded with a photo of Batman looking suitably moody with the message: 'You are the true Dark Knight.'

BATTLE BLAZE

Year	1994
Publisher	American Sammy
Developer	Aicom

BATTLE BLAZE WAS originally released in arcades in 1992, and felt fairly basic back then. By the time it made it to the SNES in 1994, where it was compared to the likes of Super Street Fighter II, it seemed positively prehistoric. You play as a single character, the Conan-like Kerrell, as he tries to win a 'Tournament of Champions' and defeat the evil demon Autarch to avenge his father's death. Your quest consists of just five fights in total, including battles against similarly generic opponents – a beast-man, a knight, a female warrior and an orc – and you're armed with a single attack button. There's a separate mode called The Battle where you can play as anyone, but only in single matches. ■

FACT

case two players wanted to play as Kerrell in The Battle mode, Aicom added a Battle-only character: his twin brother Lang, who is identical in every way.

BATTLE CARS

Year	1993
Publisher	Malibu Interactive
Developer	Namco

IN THE POST-APOCALYPTIC twenty-second century, the world's surviving population demands a new sport that accurately represents the general disillusionment they're feeling. Step forward Battle Cars, a series of races in cars armed with powerful weapons, set in the likes of Newtroit, Nuevo Vegas, Katmando and… um, Dakar. Because not every city was renamed, it seems. It's basically Mad Max, then: in fact, it's Mad Max meets F-Zero, as Battle Cars owes a lot of its visual style to Nintendo's futuristic racer, right down to the Mode 7 tracks and the way they turn to a horizontal shot as you cross the finish line. As in many other racers of the time, winning races earns you money that can be spent on upgrades to your car and weaponry. ■

FACT

Malibu Interactive was a spin-off of '80s publisher Malibu Comics, which was bought out by Marvel. It was rebranded in 2012 and is now a digital agency.

BATTLE CLASH

Year	1992
Publisher	Nintendo
Developer	Intelligent Systems

A HANDFUL OF SNES games were created for the Super Scope, Nintendo's bazooka-shaped light gun (see Super Scope 6 for more information). Battle Clash is one of the more interesting efforts, as rather than a typical shooting gallery it's actually a series of nine one-on-one boss fights in which you pilot a giant mech called an ST (Standing Tank) and have to take down another ST. As well as attacking your opponent by shooting their weak point, you have to shoot their own bullets to prevent them damaging you. While your main form of attack is a rapid fire shot, you can also charge up a large energy shot that does more damage and can block certain stronger attacks that your normal bullets can't stop. ■

FACT

Battle Clash's soundtrack was composed by Yuka Tsujiyoko. She's better known for composing the first seven Fire Emblem games, including its main theme still used today.

BATTLE GRAND PRIX

Year	1993
Publisher	Hudson Soft
Developer	KID

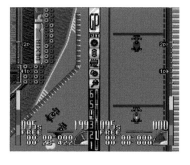

THIS TOP-DOWN FORMULA One game comes courtesy of Tokyo-based studio KID, which had previously worked on NES titles like Low G Man, Isolated Warrior and the G.I. Joe games. Despite its F1 theme it doesn't have any official licences to speak of, meaning you'll be signing up to race for teams with meaningless names like Team Bend, Team Milla and Keng Team. The tracks are also completely unrelated to real-life F1, with circuits in Cairo, Toronto and Bombay among others. There are single and two-player modes yet, oddly, you still get a split-screen display if you choose the former. While your car is shown on the left side, the right shows the car closest to you. This can be a difficult game due to its high speed and zoomed-in view. ■

FACT

There's nothing like the personal touch: among the game's end credits are a Special Thanks to 'Mr and Mrs Ichikawa and their child.'

BATTLETOADS & DOUBLE DRAGON: THE ULTIMATE TEAM

Year	1993
Publisher	Tradewest
Developer	Rare

THIS ODD CROSSOVER with Technos' Double Dragon series had launched on the NES six months prior, but SNES fans weren't to be denied their share of the action. Battletoads Zitz, Rash and Pimple have to team up with Billy and Jimmy Lee to take down the evil duo of the Dark Queen and Shadow Boss, and the best way to go about that is to beat their countless henchmen senseless. Despite both games sharing the title, this plays a lot more like Battletoads than Double Dragon, from the elaborate special attacks that transform your hands and feet into oversized weapons, to the presence of a speeder bike level, which should cause anyone who played the similar stage in the original Battletoads to break out into a cold sweat. ■

FACT

Shadow Boss wasn't a known Double Dragon enemy. The name seems to be based on the NES Double Dragon, where it's revealed that Jimmy Lee is secretly a criminal leader called Shadow Boss (even though he's a playable hero here).

BATTLETOADS IN BATTLEMANIACS

Year	1993
Publisher	Tradewest
Developer	Rare

IT'S THAT CLASSIC story: a Tibetan video game company has created a portal-based console called the Psicone T.R.I.P.S. 21 that literally puts you in the game. When the game's enemies enter the real world, kidnap Zitz and pull him into the game, it's up to Rash and Pimple to enter the game and save the day before the Dark Queen can use the portals to bring the game world into the real world and rule the Gamescape Kingdom. Or something. Despite launching before Battletoads & Double Dragon, Battlemaniacs is technically a more impressive game (perhaps because it didn't require a NES port too). Character sprites are large and chunky, and the combat feels a little more solid, if a tad tricky at times. ■

FACT

Oddly, the characters are assigned to controller ports: player 1 is always Pimple and player 2 is always Rash. If you want to play as Rash in a single-player game, plug your controller into the second port.

BAZOOKA BLITZKRIEG

Year	1992
Publisher	Bandai
Developer	Tose

THE EVIL CORPORATION Sylon's robots have begun to attack your home city ('cause unknown', the game helpfully adds), so your task is to grab your trusty bazooka and reduce them to scrap metal. This 'bazooka' acts suspiciously like a machine gun, mind you: by holding the main fire button on your Super Scope light gun you can spray a steady stream of bullets across the screen, while the secondary fire button fires more bazooka-like missiles for extra damage (naturally, these are limited). The game itself is a relatively generic shooting gallery in which you slowly slide along five stages on your way to Sylon's base to destroy its mainframe (which appears to be a floating Mode 7 Terminator head, because reasons). ■

FACT

The game ends with you destroying Sylon's headquarters, at which point it's revealed that your character is a man in a ninja suit for absolutely no given reason whatsoever.

BEAUTY AND THE BEAST

Year	1994
Publisher	Hudson Soft
Developer	Probe

'TALE AS OLD as time, song as old as rhyme.' Presumably Hudson Soft felt the *Beauty and the Beast* theme was also missing the lyric 'game as hard as nails' because that's what we have here. It generally follows the plot of the movie: playing as the Beast you have to defeat the evil Gaston, rescue Belle and break your spell so you can return to human form and live happily ever after. However, unlike in the film, it would appear that every insect, creature and object in the Beast's castle (not to mention every book in his library) is trying to kill him, which makes you wonder why he still lives there. This makes the game notoriously difficult, especially given its target audience of younger gamers. ■

FACT

The most infamous stage has you catching a seemingl endless supply of snowballs being thrown at you by Belle. Drop three and you die (presumably of shame).

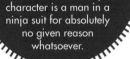

BEAVIS AND BUTT-HEAD

Year	1994
Publisher	Viacom New Media
Developer	Realtime Associates

NOTHING SCREAMS MID-90s popular culture like MTV's dysfunctional teenagers Beavis and Butt-head, so a SNES game was a no-brainer (literally). The pair want to see their favourite band GWAR in concert but they don't have any money, so

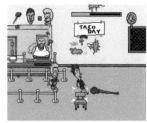

they hope that by taking photos of themselves doing cool stuff they'll be let into the show for free. It's a side-scrolling 'platformer' (though there aren't many platforms) in which the pair are both visible on-screen. You can switch between them with the Select button, or play co-op with another player, as you wander through each stage thwacking anything that comes close. A bonus stage lets you try 'couch fishing' as you use rods to grab food that's dropping outside your window to regain health. ■

FACT

You can control the show's iconic laughing intro on the title screen. Pressing any direction on the D-Pad makes Beavis 'heh heh', while pressing A, B, X or Y will make Butt-head 'huh huh'.

BÉBÉ'S KIDS

Year	1994
Publisher	Motown Software
Developer	Radical Entertainment

EASILY ONE OF the most obscure licensed games, Bébé's Kids is based on a stand-up routine by comedian Robin Harris that was later made into an animated movie: sadly though, the film was critically shrugged at and made a mere $8.4 million box office. Despite this, someone at Motown Software clearly decided it was ripe for a SNES rendition and so we have this beat 'em up in which you play as LaShawn or Kahlil (Bébé's titular sprogs) and have to cause general chaos at a theme park. It was received even worse than the movie: combat is poor, enemies take an absolute age to defeat and an impossibly strict time limit means if you don't speedrun it you'll probably run out of time. ■

FACT

Kahlil was voiced in the movie by Marques Houston, who was in the R&B group IMx and would later star as Roger in Nickelodeon show *Sister Sister*.

BEETHOVEN: THE ULTIMATE CANINE CAPER

Year	1993
Publisher	Hi Tech Expressions
Developer	Riedel Software Productions

DESPITE THE NAME, this is actually based on the second movie in the Beethoven series, *Beethoven's 2nd*. Indeed, that's what the title screen says, and that's the name the game goes by in Europe. Playing as the titular St Bernard, you have to explore four locations – the suburbs, the park, the kennels and the wilderness – in search of your four missing puppies. Each area is split into two stages: the first is standard platforming fare as you try to reach the end, whereas the second has you trying to escort your newly rescued puppy back to its mum, Missy. In these latter sections you have to decide when to carry the dog in your mouth (making you unable to perform some actions) and when to let it fend for itself briefly. ■

FACT

At the time of writing there have been no fewer than eight Beethoven films and a TV series. The most recent was 2014's *Beethoven's Treasure Trail*.

BEST OF THE BEST: CHAMPIONSHIP KARATE

Year	1993
Publisher	Electro Brain
Developer	Loriciel

FRENCH DEVELOPER LORICIEL'S take on kick boxing enjoyed something of a cult following due to its more 'realistic' take on martial arts. There are 55 different types of attack available to you, but you can only assign 13 of these to your fighter: they're then executed using combinations of D-Pad directions and the B button. No other face buttons are used, presumably because the game was originally developed in Europe for home computers (which often used single-button joysticks). The key to success, then, is building a moveset that best suits your style then learning the timing and distance needed to execute each move in order to defeat your opponent. Button-mashing will get you nowhere in this deliberately slow and methodical game. ■

FACT

The manual opens with a spiritual quote from Tae Kwon Do legend Suh Chong Kang, but then later explains that 'the name of the game is pound or be pounded'. So that's nice.

BIG SKY TROOPER

Year	1995	
Publisher	JVC	
Developer	LucasArts	

THIS LESSER KNOWN LucasArts game is an interesting mix of Asteroids clone and top-down exploration game. The evil Sultan of Slime and his Space Slugs have invaded the galaxy, so it's up to you – a new recruit on the space ship *Dire Wolf* – to complete a series of missions to help end their attack. From your central base on the ship you choose which planet to visit next: when you reach it you then have to take out surrounding Slug ships in an Asteroid style mini-game. After this you have to descend to the surface and take out enemies in a top-down adventure section (similar to LucasArts' Zombies Ate My Neighbours) in order to safely deploy a transport relay that lets you move to the next planet. ■

FACT
The game opens with the LucasArts logo being destroyed, after the Sultan of Slime accuses it of being nothing more than bones and advertising.

BIKER MICE FROM MARS

Year	1994	
Publisher	Konami	
Developer	Konami	

A RACING SPIN-OFF based on the umpteenth 'cool anthropomorphic animal' cartoon series that tried to take the throne from the Teenage Mutant Ninja Turtles, the Biker Mice game is actually pretty entertaining. Players can choose between the three titular rodents (Throttle, Modo and Vinnie) and three of their TV show villains (Limburger, Greasepit and Karbunkle) and take part in a five-season racing career spanning a total of 30 unique tracks. Every lap you complete grants you a power-up, ranging from a clock that stops every other racer in their tracks, to a massive earthquake that reduces everyone to a crawl. After each race your prize money can be spent on upgrading your bike, or stocking up on missiles you can fire at your opponents. ■

FACT
The EU version of the game contains product placement for Snickers, including a Snickers power-up that makes you invincible, speeds you up and makes fireworks appear.

BILL LAIMBEER'S COMBAT BASKETBALL

Year	1991	
Publisher	Hudson Soft	
Developer	Hewson Consultants	

BRITISH DEVELOPER HEWSON Consultants was responsible for this odd futuristic basketball game seemingly inspired by the similarly UK-developed Speedball 2. It stars Detroit Pistons player Bill Laimbeer, who was notorious for being a dirty player. It apparently paid off for him, though: by the year 2031, where this game is set, Laimbeer – now 74 years old – is the commissioner of a no-rules combat-based basketball league with team names including Danger Dudes, Ruffians and Direct Action. The game is played with a top-down viewpoint and has a similar scoring system to basketball, but charging into players is allowed and icons on the court let you activate weapons like homing missiles and spinning saw blades. Despite his age, you can still buy Laimbeer for your squad: naturally, he's the game's best player. ■

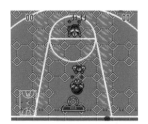

FACT
Basketball superstar Dennis Rodman, who played with Laimbeer at the Pistons, wrote in his autobiography that he 'was more than a thug, but that's what he'll be remembered for.'

BILL WALSH COLLEGE FOOTBALL

Year	1993	
Publisher	Electronic Arts	
Developer	EA / Visual Concepts	

WITH THE JOHN Madden Football series building momentum year by year, EA decided to make a spin-off game focusing on college football. The game doesn't have the official NCAA licence, so the teams are named after the cities each school is based in, rather than the school name itself (for example, BYU Cougars are instead known as Provo). Similarly, there are no real player names in the game, but they can still be identified by their numbers. There are 48 teams in total: 24 current teams (the best ranked teams from the previous season) and the 24 all-time greatest college teams since 1978, such as Notre Dame 1988 and Florida 1984. Walsh appears before each match to give his opinion on each team's stats. ■

FACT
A second Bill Walsh game was released the next year, followed by the Walsh-free College Football USA 96. Both sequels were only released on the Genesis (Mega Drive).

BIOMETAL

Year | 1993
Publisher | Activision
Developer | Athena

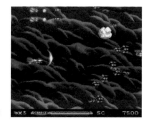

AN EVIL RACE of mechanised animal aliens called the BioMetals will take over the Milky Way in a matter of hours, unless the starship *Halbard* and its two-person crew Kid Ray and Anita can stop them. If the names Ray and Anita are familiar to you, that may be down to your obvious love of early '90s Dutch techno music, because they're named after the duo better known as 2 Unlimited. In fact, the entire soundtrack for BioMetal consists of SNES versions of songs from 2 Unlimited's debut album, including breakout hit *Get Ready For This*. The game itself is a speedy side-scrolling shoot 'em up where you're armed with the G.A.M. (Gel Analog Mutant), four blue blobs that can act as a shield and also fly out to attack enemies. ■

FACT

2 Unlimited is best known [fo]r its single *No Limit*, which [fea]tured on their second album. [Sa]dly, BioMetal only launched shortly after that album, so *No Limit* is nowhere to be heard.

BLACKTHORNE

Year | 1995
Publisher | Interplay
Developer | Blizzard

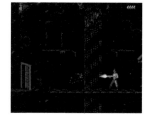

KNOWN AS BLACKHAWK in Europe, Blackthorne is an adventure platformer with realistic rotoscoped animation, similar to the likes of Prince of Persia and Flashback. You play as Kyle Vlaros, otherwise known as Blackthorne, as he returns to his home planet to save his people, destroy the evil Sarlac and take the throne (he was the heir, you see, but his dad sent him to Earth to save him from Sarlac's invasion). Kyle is armed with a shotgun, which he can either shoot forwards or blindly shoot behind him in an impractical but admittedly cool-looking manner. There's a lot more dialogue here too than in many platform games of its time, making it one of the most plot-heavy SNES games that isn't an RPG. ■

FACT

The cover for the SNES version of Blackthorne was designed by Jim Lee, the legendary comic book artist who drew the 1991 *X-Men #1* and is now the COO of DC Comics.

BLAZEON: THE BIO-CYBORG CHALLENGE

Year | 1992
Publisher | Atlus
Developer | A1

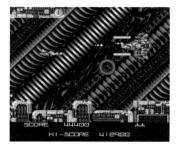

AT FIRST GLANCE BlaZeon seems hugely disappointing: it's an extremely slow side-scrolling shoot 'em up where you're armed with a measly gun, a weird rocket gun that doesn't do much more damage and no ability to collect any power-ups whatsoever. That's because the Garland TFF-01 – the ship you're controlling – isn't designed to be your main vehicle. When you hit some of the larger normal enemies in the game with your rocket gun, they'll freeze and turn blue. If you fly into them you'll then possess them, meaning you have access to their unique weapons. The result, then, is a game where you don't simply collect little power-up orbs: the power-ups are actually the enemies you're fighting against. It's still slow, mind you. ■

FACT

[B]laZeon was originally [a]n arcade game which [sp]orted a nifty two-player [c]o-op mode. That mode was ditched for the SNES version.

THE BLUES BROTHERS

Year | 1993
Publisher | Titus Software
Developer | Titus Software

DESPITE SHARING THE same title as the Blues Brothers game on the NES, this SNES adventure is actually the sequel, released on Game Boy and PC as The Blues Brothers: Jukebox Adventure. Jake and Elwood have been sucked into a magical jukebox for some reason, so it's up to them to make their way through 24 stages filled with evil bear traps and giant killer robot snails (it's safe to say there's been a little artistic licence used here). There are two main level environments: a moody underground one and a psychedelic overground one. Although you can play the game in single-player mode, it's designed to be played cooperatively with two players: Jake and Elwood can jump on each other's heads to help navigate trickier jumping sections. ■

FACT

John Belushi was paid $500,000 for his role as Jake in *The Blues Brothers* movie, but Dan Ackroyd was only paid $250,000 to play Elwood.

B.O.B.

Year	1993
Publisher	Electronic Arts
Developer	Gray Matter

NOT TO BE confused with the American rapper (who was only five years old when this was released), B.O.B. is an entertaining action platformer set in outer space. The titular B.O.B. is a teenage robot who takes his robo-dad's car out to go on a robo-date, but ends up robo-crashing it and landing on an asteroid (which is distinctly non-robo). Rather than the usual 'repair your ship' mission plots like this usually line up, B.O.B. has instead to make his way through each stage, blasting hostile enemies, in search of other cars he can use to help him reach his date. Which seems a little selfish, but I suppose robots aren't known for strong feelings of guilt. ◼

FACT

Just to prove how shallow B.O.B. is, the game ends with him reaching his date (a large blue robot), getting annoyed with her and ditching her for a slim red one. What a charmer.

BONKERS

Year	1994
Publisher	Capcom
Developer	Sun L

THE DISNEY ANIMATED series that was absolutely nobody's favourite actually spawned a surprisingly entertaining Capcom platformer. Bonkers the police cat's (far more competent) partner Lucky is in hospital, so when Hollywood's three most valuable treasures – the Genie's lamp from *Aladdin*, the Little Mermaid's voice and the Sorcerer's Hat from *Fantasia* – are stolen, he has to get them back on his own. While he can jump on some enemies' heads to hurt them, Bonkers' main attacks are a dash move (which damages anything he speeds into) and a limited supply of bombs. With its six stages taking place in the likes of Wackytown Studios, downtown Hollywood and Toon World, the game's littered with cameos, including one from Mickey Mouse and Donald Duck. ◼

FACT

The Continue screen takes place in a comedy club where a stick of dynamite is telling bad jokes. If you choose 'laugh' you'll continue, if you choose 'ignore' he blows up and it's Game Over.

BOOGERMAN: A PICK AND FLICK ADVENTURE

Year	1995
Publisher	Interplay
Developer	Interplay

BOOGERMAN IS A massive, gloopy, green example of an era when gross-out products were popular. Millionaire Snotty Ragsdale works at mad scientist Professor Stinkbaum's lab, located near a landfill called Takey Dump (ugh). When Snotty accidentally creates a portal into another world, a large arm comes out and steals Stinkbaum's new invention. Snotty changes into his alter-ego, Boogerman, and enters the portal to get it back. As you'd expect, Boogerman is armed (well, nosed) with a bunch of grim attacks, from flicking big green globs of snot at his enemies to charging up enormous belches and farts to clear the screen. If it's subtlety you're looking for, it's safe to say you probably aren't going to find it with this one. ◼

FACT

A Kickstarter attempt to bring back Boogerman only raised $40,000 of its $375,000 goal, so if you were hoping for an HD sequel it snot going to happen (sorry).

BOXING LEGENDS OF THE RING

Year	1993
Publisher	Electro Brain
Developer	Sculptured Software

THE RING IN this instance isn't just a boxing ring but the long-running boxing magazine first published in 1922. The game's roster, then, consists of eight legendary middleweight boxers from the history of the sport: Sugar Ray Robinson, Sugar Ray Leonard, Jake LaMotta, Marvin Hagler, Roberto Duran, Thomas Hearns, James Toney and Rocky Graziano. You can either take part in one-off exhibition fights, put together a 'Battle of the Legends' (which just puts all eight in a tournament bracket) or play the Career mode, where you create an original boxer and send the poor sap into the ring to take on all eight legends one at a time. Fights take place in the Las Vegas Hilton (the Japanese version has a generic arena with Electro Brain advertising instead). ◼

FACT

Mexico got a rebranded version of this game called Chavez II, starring Julio César Chávez and other generic boxers. If you're curious about Chavez I, look up Riddick Bowe Boxing.

BRAIN LORD

Year	1994
Publisher	Enix
Developer	Produce

WHEN REMEER'S DAD, the last of the dragon warriors, heads out to find and kill a dragon, he never comes back. Years later, Remeer (who can be renamed to whatever you like) heads out to find him, accompanied by four chums. While Enix is best known for its turn-based RPGs like Dragon Quest, Brain Lord is instead more of an action RPG like The Legend of Zelda: you're initially armed with a sword (though you get plenty more weapons later) and can swipe freely at enemies. Although there are only five dungeons and two towns (one of which is called Toronto, oddly), it's still a reasonably lengthy adventure. You can also find and equip 'jades', little creatures that give you special powers like lighting up dark rooms, spitting fireballs and healing. ■

FACT

The manual offered an official Brain Lord strategy guide for $9.99. The guide was an impressive black-and-white book full of information and Enix's official artwork.

THE BRAINIES

Year	1994
Publisher	Titus Software
Developer	Titus Software

THE BRAINIES ARE a bunch of coloured blobs whose sole purpose in life is seemingly to find and reach the exits that correspond to their colour. You don't control the Brainies directly: you instead move a cursor around, selecting Brainies and telling them which direction to go. When a Brainy starts walking, it won't stop until it hits a wall – think of it as your typical video game puzzle where a character's on ice and you have to use the scenery to slide them over to the other side, Pokémon used to do it all the time – meaning you have to think ahead and figure out how to beat the stage before the often harsh time limit runs out. There are 101 levels in total. ■

FACT

The Brainies was originally released on home computers in Europe in 1991, often under the name Tiny Skweeks.

BRAM STOKER'S DRACULA

Year	1993
Publisher	Sony Imagesoft
Developer	Psygnosis

FRANCIS FORD COPPOLA'S superb gothic horror was a massive success when it hit cinemas in late 1992, but the subsequent video games – which were different on most platforms – by and large failed to reach the same level of critical success. The SNES version puts you in the boots of Jonathan Harker (Keanu Reeves) as he explores Dracula's castle, Hillingham Estate and Carfax Abbey in search of Count Dracula. Although it's an action platformer, combat can be a little on the frustrating side: especially given that Harker's main form of attack – swinging a sword – barely extends in front of him, meaning you have to be right next to an enemy to do any damage, obviously opening you up to attack. ■

FACT

Dracula was only the second game co-developed by Traveller's Tales (who worked alongside Psygnosis). The studio would go on to become known for its licensed Lego games.

BRANDISH

Year	1995
Publisher	Koei
Developer	Koei

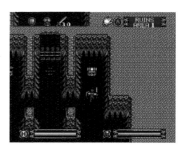

FIVE YEARS AFTER he was falsely accused of murdering the sorceress Alexis's master, swordsman Varik finds himself face-to-face with her. The ensuing skirmish leads to them both collapsing through the ground into the lost ruins of Vittoria, a land that once stood there 1,000 years ago. Playing as Varik, you have to make your way out of the ruins' 40 stages, while still bearing in mind that Alexis is on your trail too. Originally designed for Japanese computers, Brandish is a top-down dungeon crawler with mouse-style controls that are initially confusing (as is the odd way it reloads a rotated map when you turn, rather than just turning the camera). At one point you get the chance to save Alexis, changing the game's ending. ■

FACT

Brandish was popular enough to spawn three sequels. Brandish 2: The Planet Buster, Brandish 3: Spirit of Balcan and Brandish VT were only released in Japan.

BRAWL BROTHERS

Year | 1993
Publisher | Jaleco
Developer | Jaleco

THE SEQUEL TO Rival Turf! (found elsewhere in this book), Brawl Brothers takes the heroes from the first game, renames them Hack and Slash, and throws in three other playable characters including a ninja, a judo master and a female wrestler. It's a beat 'em up heavily inspired by Final Fight, but whereas its predecessor was criticised for its stiff animations and boring gameplay this is a more solid game overall. It isn't without its inventive quirks either, although some are more successful than others: while the optional 'Angry Mode' (which sees you going briefly invincible and powerful when you're stuck in an annoying attack loop) is welcome, the maze-like sewer level was received less warmly, with many a young gamer stuck there for hours. ■

FACT

Press B, A, X, Y repeatedly on the Jaleco screen to unlock the Japanese version of the game, Rushing Beat Ran, which changes character names, makes the sewer section less annoying and reinstates a censored groin kick move.

BREAKTHRU!

Year | 1994
Publisher | Spectrum Holobyte
Developer | Artech

IN A SOMEWHAT cheeky move, Spectrum Holobyte insisted on putting Tetris creator Alexey Pajitnov's face on both the box cover and title screen of Breakthru! in order to give the impression he created it. In reality, he had nothing to do with it whatsoever beyond endorsement: it was actually created by a chap called Steve Fry for Japanese developer Zoo Corporation. Being blunt, it's clear that it isn't the work of Mr Tetris: it's a fairly spiritless puzzler in which you're presented with a wall of coloured squares and have to clear it by selecting the squares that are touching similarly-coloured ones. As you complete stages you'll travel to various countries (Berlin, London, Moscow and the like), which give you different images when you clear the wall. ■

FACT

BreakThru! was also released on the Game Boy where it was significantly less intuitive to play given the lack of a colour display.

BREATH OF FIRE

Year | 1994
Publisher | Square
Developer | Capcom

CAPCOM MAY NOT immediately be associated with RPGs but that's not to say it didn't dabble: it was responsible for the Breath of Fire series, which found a small but dedicated following over the years. Originally planning to only release it only in Japan, Capcom struck up a publishing deal with Square, who set about translating it into English and publishing it in North America.

The game tells the story of Ryu (not that one), a member of the Light Dragon Clan. The clan is down to a handful of remaining members thanks to an attack by their rivals, the cleverly-named Dark Dragon Clan. When the Dark Dragon Clan kidnap Ryu's sister Sara, he sets off to try and rescue her, during which time he also discovers his ability to turn into a dragon. Which is useful. Transformation is one of the key themes of the game in general. As Ryu proceeds on his quest he encounters and adds seven other characters to his party, all of whom have some sort of transforming ability. Gobi can turn into

FACT

Supporting character Karn (known as Danc in Japan) had his appearance changed for the west because he appears to be in a form of blackface in the Japanese version.

a huge fish, Mogu can turn into a mole and dig holes, and Bleu is a sorceress whose lower body is a snake's tail.

With character designs by Keiji Inafune (best known for working on Mega Man) and a soundtrack by Capcom's iconic Alph Lyla team – also responsible for the likes of Street Fighter II, Final Fight and Strider – Breath of Fire may not break any new ground in terms of RPG mechanics, but is a polished and critically well regarded title nonetheless. ■

BREATH OF FIRE II

Year | 1995
Publisher | Capcom
Developer | Capcom

SET 500 YEARS after the previous game, Breath of Fire II once again has you playing as a young chap called Ryu (not that one, or the other one). When he returns home one day to discover that his family is missing and nobody in his village recognises him, Ryu and his pal Bow leave town, beginning an adventure that once again leads to recruiting a bunch of animal-transforming party members and the inevitable discovery that Ryu is descended from the Light Dragon Clan and can also turn into a dragon. Although praised for its detailed plot, Breath of Fire II was also criticised for being notably longer than its predecessor and failing to introduce more than a handful of major new gameplay innovations. ■

FACT

There have been a total of five Breath of Fire games, as well as a Japan-only free-to-play online game called Breath of Fire 6, which was widely hated and shut down a year after launch.

BRETT HULL HOCKEY

Year | 1994
Publisher | Accolade
Developer | Radical Entertainment

THIS ICE HOCKEY game is endorsed by legendary right-wing (not like that) St Louis Blues player Brett Hull, but more importantly also includes the NHLPA licence, meaning all the players have real names. What it doesn't have, however, is the NHL licence, which means those real-life players are playing for generic teams named only after their cities (meaning the New York Islanders are now Long Island, for example). The game itself is a smooth and entertaining rendition of the sport, accompanied by commentary from legendary announcer Al Michaels. This commentary is an impressive feat for a SNES cartridge, though it does get quite old hearing him say 'crosses the blue line' every single time a player does just that. Which, in ice hockey, is a lot. ■

FACT

There were versions of Brett Hull Hockey in development for the Mega Drive / Genesis, Atari Jaguar and Jaguar CD but all three were scrapped, meaning it was only released on the SNES.

BRETT HULL HOCKEY '95

Year | 1995
Publisher | Accolade
Developer | Radical Entertainment

THIS FOLLOW-UP CAME a year after the original Brett Hull Hockey and is very much more of an annual upgrade than a complete sequel. Other than updated rosters and some minor control tweaks – you now switch players with B instead of X, for example – this plays more or less like its predecessor with very few changes on the rink (some improved visuals aside). Al Michaels once again returns to provide play-by-play commentary and it's just as remarkable a technical achievement as it was the year before, though his obsession with blue line crossing remains alive and well, causing one to think that there wasn't too much tweaking going on behind-the-scenes (since someone surely had to have brought up how annoying it was). ■

FACT

Brett Hull continued playing until 2005 and became the fourth highest scorer in NHL history with 741 career goals. His jersey number 16 was retired by the St Louis Blues.

BRONKIE THE BRONCHIASAURUS

Year | 1995
Publisher | Raya Systems
Developer | WaveQuest

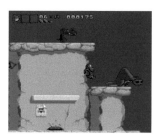

ONE OF A series of four games released by Raya Systems (later renamed Click Health) to help educate children about various medical conditions, Bronkie the Bronchiasaurus is a platformer starring a dinosaur with asthma. After meteors strike the town of San Saurian, the resulting dust clouds cause many of its population (including young Bronkie) to develop asthma. You have to help find the missing parts needed to build a wind machine that'll blow the dust away and clear the air. Along the way you'll encounter a bunch of asthma-unfriendly hazards, including cigarette smoke, animals and tar, and every now and then you'll be given a trivia question about asthma that will give you bonus points if you get it right. ■

FACT

Clinical trials of Bronkie in the mid '90s suggested that urgent care and emergency visits for asthmatic children were (allegedly) reduced by 40 per cent for those who played the game.

BRUNSWICK WORLD: TOURNAMENT OF CHAMPIONS

Year | 1997
Publisher | THQ
Developer | Tiertex

THERE'S REALLY ONLY so much you can do with a bowling game, but Brunswick World tries its best to do it all. After creating your own bowler, you can compete in one of six tournaments (ranging from the Combat Zone classic to the titular Tournament of Champions), or take part in a league. There are different lane types, each with different oil patterns that affect the way the ball spins. And, just to make things extra spicy, there are 12 real-life pro bowlers in the game, from all-time record holder Walter Ray Williams Jr to the moustachioed Johnny Petraglia, who the game reliably informs you is known as 'Rags' to his fellow pros. It's still a bowling game when all is said and done, but fair play. ■

FACT

The best bowler bio in the game belongs to 'the soft-spoken Mike Aulby'. 'If an athlete can quietly become a legend in his sport,' it claims, 'then Mike Aulby is that athlete.'

BRUTAL: PAWS OF FURY

Year | 1994
Publisher | GameTek
Developer | Eurocom

THIS AMBITIOUS FIGHTING game has a cast of anthropomorphic animals as its combatants. Whether playing as Kung-Fu Bunny (the Ryu of this line-up), Tai Cheetah, Ivan the Bear, Foxy Roxy – a vixen in hot pants, but don't worry, it's okay because she's also 'a UN executive' – or any of the other four playable fighters, the goal is the same: win the Brutal Island Tournament and defeat the boss, Dali Llama (ugh). The main game differs from most other Street Fighter clones in that you start with a basic array of punches and kicks and learn new special moves as you progress. While this makes things more interesting, critics complained that it also made the game's earlier stages a bit bland. ■

FACT

An updated version of the game called Brutal Unleashed: Above the Claw was released o Sega 32X and PC. It included two new characters, a mole called Chung Poe and a cat called Psycho Kitty.

BUBSY IN CLAWS ENCOUNTERS OF THE FURRED KIND

Year | 1993
Publisher | Accolade
Developer | Accolade

FEWER MASCOTS CAME closer to reaching the heights of Mario and Sonic did than Bubsy the Bobcat. In the months leading up to his debut, Accolade swamped the gaming press with hype, building Bubsy up to be the next big thing. He was going to be the best animated, most charismatic character in gaming to date. In reality, when the game eventually launched in May 1993, the general consensus was that it was good… but not great.

Aliens called Woolies have invaded the planet and want to plunder it of all its yarn. Bubsy, being a cat and all, is rather fond of yarn and as such doesn't have a good 'feline' about this (I'm so sorry), so decides to head out and put a stop to the Woolies' invasion. As well as the token ability to jump on enemies' heads to kill

FACT

Some levels were originally going to include catnip, which would drive Bubsy mad and affect the controls. Because it looked suspiciously green and leafy, Accolade changed it to banana skins to keep Nintendo happy.

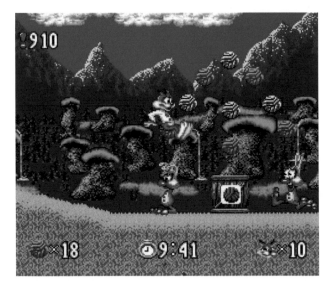

them, Bubsy also has a glide move he can execute to soar through the sky while travelling slowly downwards. While this is a useful move, it's often used for the wrong reasons: the game's camera is zoomed in too close and doesn't give the player enough of a heads-up on what's coming next, so the glide is usually used for protection during the many blind jumps players need to pull off.

Its awkward camera aside, Bubsy does at least fulfil the promise of having a lot of character: there are numerous death animations, and Bubsy has a whole host of one-liners too (though whether that's a good thing depends on your tolerance of terrible jokes). ■

BUBSY II

Year	1994
Publisher	Accolade
Developer	Accolade

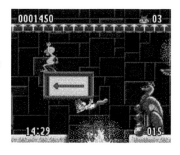

ACCOLADE WAS SO certain Bubsy would be a smash hit that it got to work on the sequel before the first game had even launched. Bubsy II is set in the Amazatorium, a virtual reality theme park where visitors can travel to a bunch of historical places and eras. It soon becomes clear that it isn't virtual reality but actual reality: the evil Oinker P. Spamm is using the Amazatorium to capture time itself and steal ancient artefacts. Cue Bubsy as he tries to put a stop to these nefarious shenanigans. Bubsy is similar to its predecessor in most regards, although now instead of a linear level structure you get to choose which world to visit next. Bubsy can now take three hits too, meaning fewer frustrating deaths. ▪

FACT

The working title for the game was Bubsy 2: Still No Pants, an obvious reference to the fact that Bubsy wears a t-shirt but nothing on his lower half.

BUGS BUNNY RABBIT RAMPAGE

Year	1994
Publisher	Sunsoft
Developer	Viacom New Media

ALTHOUGH EACH STAGE in this game is based on a different Looney Tunes animated short, the general idea is based on the 1955 cartoon *Rabbit Rampage*, in which a bad-tempered animator makes life miserable for Bugs by drawing and erasing things on the screen. In the original cartoon the animator is revealed to be Elmer Fudd but this time it's someone else (see the Fact), meaning Elmer gets to be one of the game's numerous villains, along with the likes of Yosemite Sam, Taz and Wile E. Coyote. You're able to collect a number of ACME devices to help you take out your enemies, ranging from a bulls-eye you can place on the ground (making an anvil drop on anyone who walks over it) to the classic crowd-pleaser, the cream pie. ▪

FACT

Admit it, you're curious to know who the mischievous animator is. It's none other than Daffy Duck, who you fight in the game's 10th and final stage.

BULLS VS BLAZERS AND THE NBA PLAYOFFS

Year	1992
Publisher	Electronic Arts
Developer	Electronic Arts

THE FOURTH GAME in EA's NBA Playoffs series of basketball games (but the first to get a SNES release), Bulls vs Blazers refers to the teams that made it to the NBA Finals the previous year. Given its NBA licence, EA's hoop 'em up offers truly authentic presentation with all the correct team names, logos and players. Thirty-four of the biggest superstars even have their own 'marquee shots' similar to those of their real-life counterparts: Michael Jordan has his famous 'kiss the rim' dunk, for example, while Magic Johnson does a fake no-look pass into a layup. The only thing missing is… well, nearly half the teams. Although there were 27 NBA teams that season, you can only choose from the 16 that made it to the NBA Playoffs in the 1991–92 season. ▪

FACT

The previous games in the series were Lakers vs Celtics, Bulls vs Lakers and Team USA Basketball: the latter was based on the Barcelona 1992 Olympic team.

BUST-A-MOVE

Year	1995
Publisher	Taito
Developer	Taito

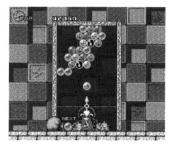

THIS SPIN-OFF OF Bubble Bobble ended up getting more sequels than its source of inspiration did. It's little wonder, to be fair: even with this first effort (a port of an arcade title released a year earlier) Taito had already pretty much nailed the bubble-shooting mechanic that makes it so well-loved. The aim is to use your harpoon gun to fire coloured bubbles at the large bundle of bubbles above you. Match three or more touching bubbles and they'll pop, potentially causing a collapse of any others they were joined to. Clear all the bubbles containing enemies and you'll move onto the next of the game's 100 levels. It was known as Puzzle Bobble in both Europe and its native Japan. ▪

FACT

There's a hidden message inside the game code that says in Japanese: 'It's bad to copy games, kids. Copying games is for old, bad men.'

CACOMA KNIGHT IN BIZYLAND

Year	1993
Publisher	SETA
Developer	Affect

PRINCESS OPHELIA OF Bizyland has been kidnapped by the evil Queen Wagamama of Lasyland, so it's up to two young kids called Jack and Jean, and a robot called RB93, to save the day with their magic chalk.

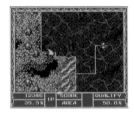

This is all just an elaborate container for what is in reality a fairly simple imitation of the popular action puzzler Qix. As in that game, the aim here is to draw unbroken lines – using your aforementioned chalk – across a large square stage, splitting it into smaller sections. Every time you fully complete a division, the smaller side is filled in. Once you fill in a target percentage of the stage, it's onto the next one. With only 21 levels though, it can be beaten in 15 minutes. ■

FACT

Cacoma Knight is unusual in that it comes with a full set of test modes, letting you check your TV's colour range and make sure every controller button is working.

CAL RIPKEN JR BASEBALL

Year	1992
Publisher	Mindscape
Developer	Mindscape

GIVEN THAT THERE were nearly 20 baseball games released for the SNES over the course of its life, it would take something fairly special to be considered one of the best of the bunch.

Cal Ripken Jr Baseball takes the bold decision to do nothing of the sort, instead offering the bare minimum. There are a total of 16 teams to choose from, none of which have real names, logos or player rosters. As you'd imagine, then, the only licensed element in the game is Cal Ripken Jr, the 'Iron Man' of baseball (who once played 2,632 games in a row). With only exhibition and league modes to choose from, this is easily among the most feature-light baseball games on the system. ■

FACT

Hold L & R and press the Start button on the Team Select screen to unlock the All-Cals, a team composed entirely of Cal Ripkens. Because why not.

CALIFORNIA GAMES 2

Year	1992
Publisher	DTMC
Developer	Silicon Sorcery

THE SUCCESS OF Epyx Games' 8-bit sports compilation California Games led to this sequel, which featured a further five events based on things you can theoretically do in the Golden State. The disciplines

on offer here are hang gliding, jet ski, snowboarding, bodyboarding and skateboarding, each of which has a completely different control style. Although California Games II was generally believed to be inferior to the first game, notable mention does have to go to the jet ski event, which made use of Mode 7 on the SNES to create a large pseudo-3D course made of buoys. This doesn't excuse the chap in the top corner constantly shouting things like 'bogus', 'dweeb' and 'ay caramba' at you, of course. ■

FACT

Oddly, the SNES box art for California Games II is a recreation of the 1990 PC version's box art, with the models used in that replaced with new models striking the same pose.

CANNON FODDER

Year	1994
Publisher	Virgin Interactive
Developer	Sensible Software

BRITISH DEVELOPER SENSIBLE Software's anti-war game gathered its fair share of controversy for a number of reasons, ranging from its use of a poppy on the title screen, to the graveyard of fallen soldiers that grew as you lost lives, to the game's title itself. Look past the drama and there's an entertaining action game there that's part real-time strategy, part point-and-click adventure (the game supports the SNES Mouse). Your team of soldiers are promoted each time you complete a stage, but if one dies they're gone forever, represented by a gravestone and replaced by one of the many young hopefuls joining an ever-growing queue of wannabe soldiers lining up across the map screen. An extremely dark game, then, but a welcome one. ■

FACT

If you think the SNES version is controversial, at least the intro music doesn't have the Amiga version's lyrics, which croon that 'war has never been so much fun'.

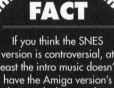

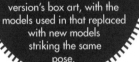

CANNONDALE CUP

Year	1994
Publisher	ASC / Life Fitness Entertainment
Developer	Radical Entertainment

A MOUNTAIN BIKING game more notable for what it was compatible with rather than its actual contents, Cannondale Cup nevertheless makes decent use of Mode 7 in its eight courses and gives you eight fictional riders to choose from, ranging from fairly normal characters (Marc Gullickson, Alison Sydor) to more bizarre ones (the green-faced Mountain Demon or the white-masked 'Mystery'). Around the same time it launched, it was also released as Mountain Bike Rally and made compatible with the Life Fitness Exertainment System, a full-sized exercise bike with a built-in SNES and television display. Naturally, the faster you pedal the bike, the faster you ride in the game. Don't have an Exertainment bike? Then you'll be constantly tapping the B button to pedal instead: not quite as intuitive, but much cheaper. ■

FACT

Two games were compatible with the Exertainment bike: [thi]s and Speed Racer. The bike was bundled with a 2-in-1 cart, which can sell online these days for up to $5,000.

CAPCOM'S MVP FOOTBALL

Year	1992
Publisher	Capcom
Developer	Equilibrium

CAPCOM'S TAKE ON American football includes the NFL licence, meaning all the team names are correct. As well as the expected Exhibition mode, you can also take part in a playoffs bracket or attempt the unique MVP mode. Here you're put in situations from past NFL games and asked to meet a certain criteria to succeed. For example, the first challenge has you controlling the Chicago Bears against the New York Jets: there are three minutes to go, you're 45 yards from the goal line and you're four points down, which means you probably need to go for a game-winning touchdown. If you aren't much of a player you can also choose to coach the team instead, as the game plays out for you. ■

FACT

The game's music was composed by Ed Bogas, who also composed the soundtracks to a whole host of *Peanuts* and *Garfield* cartoons in the '80s.

CAPCOM'S SOCCER SHOOTOUT

Year	1994
Publisher	Capcom
Developer	A-Max

DESPITE THE NAME suggesting otherwise, Soccer Shootout isn't 'Capcom's'. It's actually a Japanese game called J. League Excite Stage: developed by A-Max and published in Japan by Epoch, it was translated and licensed to Capcom so it could get some of the football game market in the west. As well as your typical exhibition and league modes – there are 12 teams so you can have a 22-game or 44-game league – there are also slightly less common features. These include an All-Star mode, where you play an exhibition match with the best (fake) players in the game, and a seven-a-side indoor mode where the ball bounces off walls instead of going out for throw-ins or goal kicks. ■

FACT

There were five more J. [Le]ague Excite Stage games [rel]eased in Japan: two more for the Super Famicom, two on Game Boy Color and one on PlayStation.

CAPTAIN AMERICA AND THE AVENGERS

Year	1993
Publisher	Mindscape
Developer	Realtime Associates

WHEREAS THE NES version of Captain America and the Avengers was a platformer, the SNES title is instead a port of the popular four-player Data East arcade game. Rather than handling the port directly as it did with the Mega Drive version, Data East handed the reins over to Mindscape and developer Realtime Associates, resulting in a version many believed was inferior to that on Sega's console. Playing as either Captain America, Iron Man, Hawkeye or Vision, you have to take on the army of supervillains assembled by the evil Red Skull in order to stop him taking over the world. While most of the game is standard beat 'em up fare, there are also shoot 'em up sections where your hero takes to the sky to fight airborne enemies. ■

FACT

Data East followed Captain America up with a 1995 fighting game called Avengers in Galactic Storm. It was only released in arcades and didn't get a home port.

CAPTAIN COMMANDO

Year	1995
Publisher	Capcom
Developer	Capcom

IN THE YEAR 2026, Metro City – the same city that featured in Capcom's beloved Final Fight – is under attack by a gang of intergalactic ne'er-do-wells called the Super Criminals, led by the evil Scumocide. It's up to the Commando Team, led by the heroic Captain Commando, to save the day. Originally an arcade beat 'em up, Captain Commando retains all four playable heroes: the Captain himself, a dagger-wielding mummy called Mack the Knife, a ninja named Ginzu and the bizarre Baby Head, a tiny genius baby inside an adult-sized mech. Although the arcade version included a simultaneous four-player mode, this SNES port only supports up to two players: still welcome, given that the same couldn't be said for Final Fight (as seen elsewhere in this book). ■

FACT

Captain Commando made his debut long before this game: he regularly appeared in the instruction manuals for Capcom's NES games, congratulating players on buying them.

CAPTAIN NOVOLIN

Year	1992
Publisher	Raya Systems
Developer	Sculptured Software

WHILE BRONKIE THE Bronchiasaurus helped educate players about the dangers of asthma, Captain Novolin instead tackles the topic of diabetes. A group of aliens have landed on Mount Wayupthar and have been instructed by their leader, Blubberman, to take over the Earth. Disguised as sugary foods, they've kidnapped the mayor of Pineville, who happens to be diabetic and only has enough supplies for 48 hours. Cue Captain Novolin, the world's greatest diabetic superhero, who has to make his way through eight stages dodging those sugary swines, while also collecting food along the way. Eat too many sugary foods – or not enough – and your blood sugar levels will hit an extreme high or low, killing you. A harsh but fair lesson, I suppose. ■

FACT

Captain Novolin may be a diabetic superhero, but spare a thought for diabetic villain Marcu, a centaur who fought Deadpool i a 2014 comic and had his hoove chopped off after confessing he was worried he'd lose them to diabetes.

CARRIER ACES

Year	1995
Publisher	Cybersoft
Developer	Synergistic Software

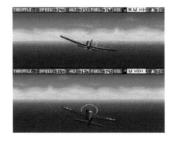

SET DURING THE Second World War, this air combat game lets you fight on either the US or Japanese side. From your aircraft carrier, you can choose which types of plane will head out. There are four types to choose from on each side: the Japanese options are a Nakajima B5N Kate torpedo bomber, an Aichi D3A1 Val dive bomber, a Mitsubishi A6M2 Zero or a Mitsubishi A6M5 Zero. US pilots get to choose between an SBD Dauntless dive bomber, a TBF Avenger torpedo bomber, an F4F-3 Wildcat or F6F-5 Hellcat. Planes with rear guns have an obvious offensive advantage but they're slower at turning, whereas planes that can only fire forwards are more agile in the air. Missions include one-on-one dogfighting, dive bombing on ships, torpedo runs and landing on your carrier. ■

FACT

The second mission claims that the Japanese destroyer the *Yamato* is well ahead of the rest of its fleet. In reality, the *Yamato* was an extremely heavy battleship that could travel at 27 knots: much slower than a destroyer.

CASPER

Year	1996
Publisher	Natsume
Developer	Imagineering

THE *CASPER* MOVIE starred Christina Ricci as Kat, a young girl who realises that the mansion her parapsychologist dad is investigating is being haunted by the (friendly) ghost of a young boy. The SNES tie-in has you controlling Casper as he helps Kat make her way through the house. If he roams too far from Kat she'll be abducted by the evil Carrigan Crittenden or her assistant Dibs, so he has to stick close and use his ability to transform into various objects to protect her. For example, turning into a pillow helps her fall long distances and land on him. If you're worried about the young girl dying, don't be: the ghost of her mum swoops in to take her away if you 'lose a life'. ■

FACT

Japan got an entirely different Casper game for the Super Famicom. It's an isometric adventure developed by Natsume in which you play as Kat instead.

CASTLEVANIA: DRACULA X

Year	1995
Publisher	Konami
Developer	Konami

IN 1993, KONAMI released Castlevania: Rondo of Blood on the PC Engine CD in Japan. It was widely considered to be one of the greatest games in the series, so a couple of years later the game was remade for the SNES as Dracula X (or Castlevania: Vampire's Kiss as it's known in Europe). Playing as Richter Belmont – a direct descendant of the original game's hero Simon – you have to make your way through Dracula's castle, rescuing a number of young women along the way to finding your kidnapped girlfriend Annette. Though its direct sequel Symphony of the Night would become more famous, Dracula X is believed by many to be the last great old-school (i.e. linear) Castlevania adventure. ◼

FACT

Richter Belmont appeared as a playable character in Super Smash Bros Ultimate on Switch. His default costume is based on the outfit he wears in Dracula X.

CHAMPIONS WORLD CLASS SOCCER

Year	1994
Publisher	Acclaim
Developer	Park Place Productions

A RELATIVELY BARE-BONES and unremarkable football game that offers two options: an exhibition match or a tournament mode. There are 32 teams to choose from, with some unusual choices not necessarily known as footballing powerhouses (such as the United Arab Emirates). Various European versions of the game featured stars from their respective countries on the packaging. The UK version, for example, featured Manchester United star Ryan Giggs on the box: Acclaim was clearly keen to celebrate this as his name is larger than the game's logo. The German version also included an unfortunate typo: if your game goes to a penalty shootout the game doesn't say 'schiessen' (which is German for 'shootout'), but instead says 'scheissen' ('shit'). ◼

FACT

As a Scot, I feel obliged to point out the game's biggest scandal: the Scotland flag is wrong (a light blue cross on a white background, instead of a white one on dark blue).

CHAMPIONSHIP POOL

Year	1993
Publisher	Mindscape
Developer	Bitmasters

THERE AREN'T MANY video games that are officially endorsed by the Billiard Congress of America… though given that most games aren't about pool that probably makes sense. Regardless, Championship Pool offers numerous variations on ball-smacking, from 8-ball and 9-ball to rotation pool and cut-throat pool. As well as a freestyle mode – where you can just pot balls freely – and a challenge mode where you try to get a high score, there's also a tournament mode where you take on a series of opponents in an attempt to qualify for and then win the Billiard Congress of America world championship. Of note is the 3D view mode, where you can see the table from an angled perspective: it's fairly useless, but certainly looks nice. ◼

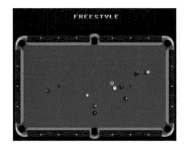

FACT

Championship Pool was also released on the NES, and is remarkably similar to its 16-bit brother in terms of gameplay modes and general presentation.

THE CHAOS ENGINE

Year	1993
Publisher	Spectrum Holobyte
Developer	The Bitmap Brothers

KNOWN AS SOLDIERS of Fortune in North America, The Chaos Engine was originally developed by East London studio The Bitmap Brothers for the Commodore Amiga home computer before it was ported to the SNES (among other systems). It's a steampunk action game that tells the story of a time traveller from the future who travels to the 1800s and accidentally lets his technology get in the hands of an inventor, who uses it to create a sentient contraption called the Chaos Engine that spawns monsters everywhere. Time to start shooting loads of stuff. It's a co-op game with six characters – Brigand, Mercenary, Gentleman, Navvie, Thug and Scientist – and you can either play with a friend or with an AI partner (no solo missions here). ◼

FACT

An Amiga-only sequel (cleverly called The Chaos Engine 2) ditched the standard action in favour of head-to-head deathmatches where two players had to fight against each other to clear a level first.

THE CHESSMASTER

Year	1991
Publisher	Mindscape
Developer	Mindscape

THE CHESSMASTER SERIES has been released on nearly 20 systems over the years, and while the SNES version wasn't the first console port – it launched on NES and Game Boy the year before – it's still a relatively early one. Like its peers at the time, it offers 16 difficulty levels ranging from absolute newcomer to 'infinite' (where it'll think about its next move indefinitely until you prompt it). It's notable for its 'teaching mode', which helps players learn the rules of chess by showing which spaces a piece is able to land on. You can also choose a 'get advice from Chessmaster' option, which shows you which move the Chessmaster thinks you should make next. Which is nice of him, considering you're playing against him. ∎

FACT

Although the SNES version launched a year after the Game Boy one it doesn't have the Game Boy version's most impressive feature: sampled speech saying things like 'capture' and 'checkmate'.

CHESTER CHEETAH: TOO COOL TO FOOL

Year	1992
Publisher	Kaneko
Developer	Kaneko

THIS 2D PLATFORMER stars Chester Cheetah, the hip, laid-back cat who happens to be the official mascot for Frito-Lay's Cheetos snacks (although, oddly, there are no Cheetos to be found anywhere here). Chester's stuck in Four Corners Zoo, so players have guide him through each stage as he searches for a bunch of motorcycle parts that he can use to escape (because apparently he's a mechanic too). While visually impressive, the game's pace is as relaxed as its star, meaning movement may be a little slow for some players. It's best known for its terrible manual, which was seemingly written in Japan and attempts to create some cool rhymes but ends up with stuff like 'as is CHESTER CHEETAH way, this is a one person play'. ∎

FACT

Cheetos have been released in some strange flavours overseas, most notably in Japan, where they've been available in strawberry, Pepsi and Mountain Dew flavour.

CHESTER CHEETAH: WILD WILD QUEST

Year	1994
Publisher	Kaneko
Developer	Kaneko

AFTER ESCAPING FROM the zoo, Chester Cheetah's adversary Mean Eugene scuppers his plans by tearing his map into 10 pieces and scattering them across America. It's up to Chester to collect the pieces while avoiding capture by Eugene. Each of the 10 locations – some of which now include driving stages instead of standard platforming – is a (terrible) play on words of a real-life US city: Omaha, Nebraska becomes Omahog and takes place on a farm; Little Rock, Arkansas becomes Little Shock and has electrical shocks scattered throughout the stage, and so on. Whereas the first game was criticised for being too slow, the sequel is perhaps a little too fast with overly twitchy movements. Sadly, there was no Goldilocks-style third game for Kaneko to get the pacing just right. ∎

FACT

It would appear the punster who named the levels ran out of steam at some point as Great Falls, Montana and Clearwater, Florida are instead Not-So-Great Falls and Un-Clearwater respectively.

CHOPLIFTER III

Year	1994
Publisher	Extreme Entertainment Group
Developer	Beam Software

LIKE ITS PREDECESSORS, Choplifter III is a side-scrolling action game where you pilot a helicopter through a series of warzones in an attempt to rescue hostages. In between gunning down enemies, you have to safely land at various points, wait for nearby hostages to climb aboard, then take off and return them to your home base where they can safely leave. The twist is that your chopper can only hold so many hostages, meaning you'll have to make repeat journeys in order to rescue them all. The game has 16 stages in total, with four different environments: jungle, desert, sea and city (the latter being the most difficult because you also have to contend with numerous large buildings getting in your way). ∎

FACT

Choplifter III is also available on the Game Boy and Game Gear, but neither is a port of the SNES game; they're both based on the Game Boy-only Choplifter II.

CHRONO TRIGGER

Year	1995
Publisher	Square
Developer	Square

ALTHOUGH THE FINAL Fantasy games will generally be foremost in most people's minds when thinking of Square RPGs, there are those who consider Chrono Trigger the company's high point due to its time-travelling plot, which offered an impressive degree of depth for the time. The game's main protagonist is Chrono, a young chap who lives in 1000 AD and generally spends his days hanging out with his inventor friend Lucca. At the Millennial Fair in their hometown, Lucca's dad shows off a new teleporter: when a girl called Marle offers to test it out, her mysterious pendant reacts with it and creates a portal that sends her 400 years into the past (to be fair, I've been to worse events). Chrono and Lucca decide to create their own portal to try and rescue Marle, and so begins an enormous adventure that takes in a bunch of time zones (65,000,000 BC, 12,000 BC, 600 AD, 1000 AD, 1999 AD and 2300 AD) and introduces a host of characters. Some of these – like the anthropomorphic amphibian Frog, the memory-wiped android Robo and the prehistoric tribeswoman Ayla – can be recruited to join your team, each bringing their own unique qualities to the table.

The game makes use of Active Time Battle 2.0, an updated version of the turn-based combat system created for Final Fantasy IV in which each character has

FACT

Composer Yasunori Mitsuda worked so hard creating Chrono Trigger's 54 tracks that he frequently passed out and was eventually hospitalised with stomach ulcers. Final Fantasy composer Nobuo Uematsu stepped in to finish the soundtrack for him.

a timer gauge: when the gauge runs out, they can attack. It differs from most other RPGs, however, in the way you engage in battles. Rather than hitting a 'random' encounter and switching the action to a separate battle screen, all of your enemies are visible as you explore and battles take place on the same exploration screen, allowing you to seamlessly jump in and out of fights without having to tolerate transition animations, skip through results screens and the like.

Chrono Trigger's development staff was considered something of a who's who of creative minds at the time. The game was designed by Hironobu Sakaguchi, the man who created Final Fantasy and with it essentially saved Square from going out of business. The artwork was created by Akira Toriyama, the manga legend who created Dragon Ball. Meanwhile, the plot was drafted by Yuji Horii – the creator of Dragon Quest – and refined by Masato Kato, who would go on to work on the likes of Final Fantasy VII and Xenogears. With a team like that involved, it's perhaps little wonder that Chrono Trigger quickly became one of Square's most loved games.

At least, it was in Japan and North America. Much like many other JRPGs at the time, Chrono Trigger never saw a release in Europe (presumably because of the translation work that would have been required). As a result, while the game regularly found itself at the top of Japanese and American 'best SNES games' lists, Europeans wouldn't be given the chance to play it – emulation aside – until nearly a decade and a half later, when an enhanced port was released on the Nintendo DS in 2009 (Europe also got the original SNES version on the Wii Virtual Console in 2011). ■

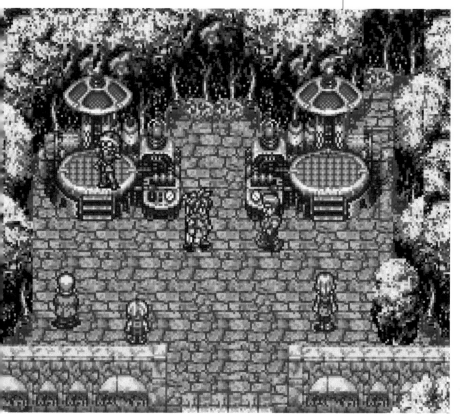

CHUCK ROCK

Year	1992
Publisher	Sony Imagesoft
Developer	Core Design

CHUCK ROCK IS a prehistoric caveman with a problem: his glamorous wife Ophelia Rock – awkwardly described in the game's manual as 'a swell little cavemaker' – has been kidnapped by the nasty Gary Gritter (a pun that definitely hasn't aged well) so off he goes on a rescue mission. Chuck is armed with a number of attacks, from the ability to hit enemies with his belly to more standard fare like jumping kicks. His main trick, though, is being able to lift large boulders and lob them at his enemies, hence his name. This serves other purposes too: any rocks he picks up can be used as shields against falling debris, and laid down as platforms to reach higher areas. ■

FACT

A sequel called Chuck Rock II: Son of Chuck was released on other systems and starred Chuck's club-wielding baby.

CIVILIZATION

Year	1995
Publisher	Koei
Developer	Microprose

ORIGINALLY CREATED AND developed by Sid Meier for MS-DOS PCs in 1991, Civilization is considered the first major example of what's since become known as the 4X genre of strategy games ('explore, expand, exploit and exterminate'). Players choose a starting civilization from a list of 14 – ranging from the Romans and Babylonians to the Aztecs and Mongols – and, starting off as a smaller settler unit in the year 4000 BC, have to build and expand in order to progress through the centuries and millennia with the ultimate aim being to reach the future and colonise space. The SNES version is a relatively faithful port of the PC game, though there are a few changes: the Zulu civilization has been replaced with the Japanese, for example. ■

FACT

A bug in some versions of Civilization affects the peace-loving Mahatma Gandhi, eventually turning him into an extremely aggressive leader desperate to use nuclear weapons.

CLAYFIGHTER

Year	1993
Publisher	Interplay
Developer	Visual Concepts

A COMEDY FIGHTING game that parodies Street Fighter II, with the added twist that all the characters are made of clay: more specifically, they're all circus performers who've been infected with a goo that's turned them into clay-like beings. There are eight fighters in total, ranging from a clown called Bonker and a hulking wrestler known as Tiny to an Elvis impersonator named Blue Suede Goo and an evil snowman who goes by the name Bad Mr Frosty (which is probably where the 'circus performers' plot falls apart a bit). While it wasn't quite as accomplished as the Street Fighter games, its sense of humour gathered a cult following, to the extent that US magazine EGM declared it the best Street Fighter imitator of 1993 (of which there were many). ■

FACT

The game's official canon declares that Tiny won the ClayFighter tournament, and went on to turn the circus into a huge wrestling gym.

CLAYFIGHTER: TOURNAMENT EDITION

Year	1994
Publisher	Interplay
Developer	Visual Concepts

THIS UPDATED VERSION of ClayFighter was only available for rental at Blockbuster Video stores in North America (although some gamers bought ex-rental copies once they'd run their course). It's essentially the original ClayFighter with the addition of a new tournament mode for up to 16 players. Visual Concepts also took the opportunity to fix some of the game's bugs and a few of its cheaper exploits. The most important of these is the Blob's buzzsaw move, which slices opponents clean in half: in the original release if this was blocked it would continue to bounce off your opponent six or seven times, chipping enough of their health away to actually do more damage than if the attack had landed. In the Tournament Edition the move only hits once when blocked. ■

FACT

Keep an eye out for the fox that runs past a the beginning of each round. It's one of the playable animals in Claymates.

CLAYFIGHTER 2: JUDGMENT CLAY

Year	1995
Publisher	Interplay
Developer	Interplay

CLAYFIGHTER'S SEQUEL DIALLED back the humour a little and made the sprites smaller in an attempt to make it a more legitimate, accomplished fighting game. Only three characters from the first game – Bad Mr Frosty, Tiny and the Blob – return, and are joined by five new fighters: living banana Nanaman, the squid-like Octohead, foul-mouthed giant baby Googoo, boxing kangaroo Kangoo and the game's lead character, a Schwarzenegger-esque rabbit named Hoppy. Each character also has an evil 'twin' character that can be unlocked: although they look the same – they're the same sprites with a different colour palette – they're actually more than mere clones: their moves are entirely different, their fighting stance is different and they have completely unique win animations and endings. ■

FACT

A third game called ClayFighter 63⅓ was released on the Nintendo 64... but that's for another book (hopefully).

CLAYMATES

Year	1993
Publisher	Interplay
Developer	Visual Concepts

INTERPLAY AND VISUAL Concepts were all in on the whole clay thing, so much so that ClayFighter wasn't the only clay-based game it had in the works. Claymates is a platformer about a young lad called Clayton whose dad has figured out how to turn clay into living animals. Clayton's dad is then turned into a ball of clay by a witch doctor, who kidnaps his dad for good measure (well, when you name your kid Clayton you have it coming). Finding different coloured blobs of clay will turn you into one of five animals: Muckster the cat, Oozy the mouse, Goopy the fish, Globmeister the gopher and Doh-Doh the bird. Each has their own special abilities: you can fit into tight squeezes with Oozy, for example. ■

FACT

According to programmer Brian Greenstone, Claymates was actually created before ClayFighter, but since fighting games were so popular at the time Interplay released that first.

CLIFFHANGER

Year	1993
Publisher	Sony Imagesoft
Developer	Malibu Interactive

THERE WERE NUMEROUS games based on Sylvester Stallone's hit 1993 mountain-climbing action movie. While NES owners were 'treated' to a fairly bog-standard side-scrolling platformer, those with a SNES were instead 'treated' to a fairly bog-standard side-scrolling beat 'em up. Playing as Stallone's character Gabe Walker, you have to work your way up a snowy mountain, fighting a bunch of generic grunts as you try to reach the evil megalomaniac Eric Qualen and give him a swift kick in the cold bits. Unlike most beat 'em ups, you're armed with a block button in Cliffhanger: this goes some way to making your enemies' attacks a little less frustrating (only some way, though). As in the movie, you also have to make some death-defying leaps over large chasms to progress. ■

FACT

Cliffhanger was nominated for three Oscars: Best Sound, Sound Effects Editing and Visual Effects. It made the mistake of releasing in 1993, though, because *Jurassic Park* claimed all three instead.

CLUE

Year	1992
Publisher	Parker Brothers
Developer	Sculptured Software

A VIDEO GAME version of the popular board game *Clue* (or *Cluedo*, as it's known in its native UK). Some poor chap by the name of Mr Boddy has been murdered in a massive mansion in the English countryside, so players have to explore the mansion's various rooms and suggest possible theories in order to deduce – through the process of elimination – the identity of the killer, the room where the murder took place and the weapon that was used to send Mr Boddy to the big country house in the sky (there are 324 different possible solutions). While this SNES interpretation plays like the board game for the most part, it does add a little flourish by showing cutscenes of each of the suggestions and accusations made. ■

FACT

In 2016, Hasbro released a new version of *Cluedo* that ditched the ditzy servant Mrs White and replaced her with Dr Orchid, a plant scientist.

COLLEGE FOOTBALL USA '97: THE ROAD TO NEW ORLEANS

Year | 1996
Publisher | Electronic Arts
Developer | Black Pearl Software

FOLLOWING THE RELEASE of Bill Walsh College Football in 1993, EA decided not to release its two sequels – Bill Walsh College Football '95 and College Football USA '96 – on the SNES. After this EA decided to open its arms to Nintendo fans again, though many believed they should've stayed shut. On paper this is a solid offering: all 111 NCAA Division I-A teams are included, complete with official uniforms (no player names, however), and players can take part in either a 12-week season or a tournament. However, something went terribly wrong somewhere when porting the game to the SNES, and while the Sega Genesis version feels like a fairly straightforward Madden spin-off the SNES port suffers from a shockingly low frame rate that renders the game nearly unplayable. ∎

FACT

The SNES version was one of the worst scoring games in the 22-year history of US magazine *GamePro*, scoring 1.5 (out of 5) for Graphics and 0.5 for Sound, Control and Fun Factor.

COLLEGE SLAM

Year | 1996
Publisher | Acclaim
Developer | Iguana Entertainment

FOLLOWING THE SUCCESS of NBA Jam and its Tournament Edition upgrade, Acclaim decided to see if the formula would be just as successful with college basketball. The result was College Slam, which featured 44 of the most popular NCAA Division I teams with some odd exceptions: Notre Dame are nowhere to be seen, for example. Like other NCAA licensed games, there are no real players in the game – as 'amateurs', NCAA players are forbidden to make money from the use of their likenesses – but an Edit Team option lets you input player names manually. As well as single head-to-head matches you can also start a tournament from the semi finals or the last 16, or start Season Matchup mode where you start at the bottom of a ladder and work your way up. ∎

FACT

The decision not to feature every NCAA team led to some awkward moments: Mississippi State University isn't in the game, but managed to reach the Final Four that year.

THE COMBATRIBES

Year | 1993
Publisher | American Technos
Developer | Technos Japan

A BEAT 'EM up set in New York in the near future. Well, you're playing as cyborgs, so probably not that near. Berserker, Bullova and Blitz are a trio of streetfighting machine-men who have come to the Big Apple in search of a criminal organisation called Ground Zero. Along the way, they have to fight a series of gangs in small self-contained stages much smaller than those in typical side-scrolling beat 'em ups. As well as the expected array of fighting moves available to you, you can also grab a fallen opponent by the ankles and spin them round (much like WWE superstar Cesaro), hitting other enemies with them. The game's penultimate boss is called Swastika in Japan, but this was renamed to M. Blaster for fairly obvious reasons. ∎

FACT

Because the intro opens with the heroes standing in front of the World Trade Center and referring to Ground Zero, the Wii Virtual Console re-release in 2009 renamed the enemy group to Guilty Zero.

CONGO'S CAPER

Year | 1993
Publisher | Data East
Developer | Data East

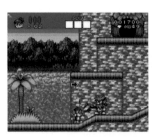

CONGO AND HIS 'chimp-chick' (the manual's words, not mine) were hanging out in a tree one day when a magic ruby fell out of the sky, turning them both human. Suddenly, a demon appeared and kidnapped Congo's lady chum: no prizes for guessing what happens next. Congo's Caper is an underrated platformer consisting of 35 levels which includes a hit system similar to that of Capcom's Ghouls 'n Ghosts: you begin the game in human form, and if Congo takes a hit he'll turn back into a monkey. A second hit will kill him outright, though you can find more magic rubies to become human again. Hitting some enemies with your club will curl them into a ball that you can then roll or hit towards others. ∎

FACT

In Japan the game's called Tatakae Genshijin 2. The original Tatakae Genshijin was Joe & Mac, meaning Congo's Caper is essentially Joe & Mac 2 with a new hero.

CONTRA III: THE ALIEN WARS

Year	1992
Publisher	Konami
Developer	Konami

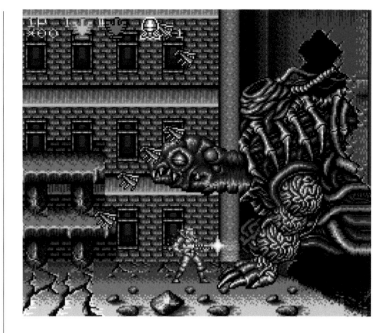

ALTHOUGH THE ORIGINAL Contra wasn't the first ever run 'n' gun game, there can be no denying that it created many new fans of the genre by being one of its finest examples. The same can be said for Contra III (known as Super Probotector in Europe): once again it doesn't actually do anything truly inventive from a mechanics standpoint, but it handles everything – the look, the feel, the sound, the challenge – so superbly that the sum of its parts feels revolutionary. Set on the oddly specific date of 14 February 2636, you play as Jimbo and Sully, the descendants of the original game's Bill and Lance, as you attempt to put a stop once again to the evil Red Falcon army (an alien force consisting of extraterrestrial enemies and brainwashed humans). In order to do this you have to fight your way through six stages: four of these are traversed via the obligatory method of running and/or gunning, whereas the other two are top-down stages that make use of the SNES's Mode 7 effects to rotate and scale the environment underneath you.

While a few of the weapons from the previous Contra games make their return here, Contra III also introduces some new firearms to the mix. These include the controversial Homing Gun (which fires small, weak missiles that home in on enemies, making it hard to aim at specific foes when there are a bunch on-screen), the Crush Gun (which has a short range but

explodes on impact) and the Fire Gun (which is essentially a flamethrower). There's also a new 'Helio Bomb' weapon that acts like a smart bomb: trigger it and it kills everything on the screen (except bosses, who instead receive heavy damage).

While the original Contra focused more on gritty combat, Contra III director Nobuya Nakazato decided that this SNES sequel should contain more ridiculous moments that were so over-the-top they were almost funny. This was achieved in numerous ways, be those subtle (hold L and R and your character will face the screen and hold both guns up in the air in an unashamedly '90s action movie stance), or notable: one stage has you clinging to and jumping between giant missiles as they zoom through the air. It also extends to the boss fights, which are some of the most memorable on the SNES. Many players will fondly remember the first time they entered a room with a large metal door in the background, and felt their jaw dropping as Big Fuzz – an enormous screen-filling robot skeleton – pulled it open and started attacking.

The original Contra was renamed Probotector in Europe and, sure enough, Contra III got the same treatment, becoming Super Probotector: Alien Rebels. As in the NES original, the human protagonists were also replaced with robot ones: say goodbye to Jimbo and Sully, say greetings (or whatever you say to a robot) to RD-008 and RC-011. Despite this notable aesthetic change, each version remains fantastic to this day. ■

FACT

The original Contra was also originally set in the future but the US release changed the plot to the present day. In Japan, then, Contra III only takes place a couple of years after the original and the heroes are still Bill and Lance.

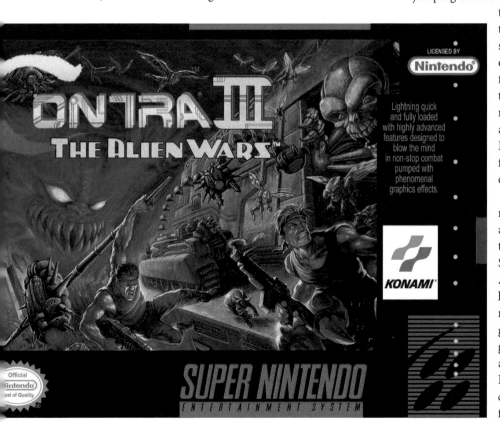

COOL SPOT

Year	1993
Publisher	Virgin Interactive
Developer	Virgin Interactive

WHEN IT COMES to licensed tie-ins, Cool Spot is perhaps one of the more initially subtle examples considering that its hero is the small red dot that appears on the logo for drinks brand 7up. Turns out that all you need to do with a dot is put a pair of sunglasses on it and you have a character: a cool one at that. Spot has to rescue his friends Spot, Spot, Spot, Spot, Spot and Spot (seriously), who've been trapped in cages by the evil Wild Wicked Wily Will who has been trying to prove for years that Spots exist. Each stage has a caged Spot to find, but you can't free them right away. You have to build your 'cool' percentage by collecting smaller dots that are, well, dotted around the stage: when you hit a certain amount the cage will be unlocked and you'll be able to bust the lock open with your

FACT

If you beat the game on Hard while collecting every letter and without continuing you're shown a special screen. Players who took a photo of the screen and sent it to Virgin Games would receive a mystery prize, which was a PVC figure of Spot.

'Cool Shot' (a projectile that's basically a blast of 7up bubbles). While for the most part the 7up branding is minimal – the 1-up collectible says 7up instead but that's about it – the bonus stage is the exception. Here you're placed inside a giant 7up bottle and have to bounce off the bubbles to reach the top and collect one of six letters that eventually spell out UNCOLA (the 7up Company had been referring to its drink as 'the uncola' in various advertising campaigns since the late 1960s). ∎

COOL WORLD

Year	1992
Publisher	Ocean Software
Developer	Painting By Numbers

WHEREAS OTHER VIDEO game adaptations of Paramount's part live-action, part animated box office flop had you playing as Brad Pitt's character, the SNES version is the only one that puts you in the cartoon shoes of Jack Deebs, played in the movie by Gabriel Byrne. The aim is to get to the top of the Ocean Hotel in Las Vegas and get the 'Golden Spike of power' before animated bombshell Holli Would (played in the movie by Kim Basinger) reaches it and potentially destroys both the real and cartoon worlds. It's essentially a point-and-click adventure game where the pointing and clicking are replaced with clunky action platforming controls and an annoying tendency to find yourself being chased by the toon police, before being arrested and warned or fined by the detective (Pitt). ∎

FACT

Paramount sat a 75-foot cut-out of Holli Would on the 'D' of the Hollywood sign in Los Angeles to promote the film. It only stayed up for a week but that was long enough to enrage local residents who filed a lawsuit.

CUTTHROAT ISLAND

Year	1996
Publisher	Acclaim
Developer	Software Creations

IF *COOL WORLD* was a box office disappointment, *Cutthroat Island* was an absolute disaster, contributing to the closure of struggling studio Carolco and making pirate movies toxic for nearly a decade (until *Pirates of the Caribbean* came alone). This SNES tie-in lets you choose between Morgan Adams (Geena Davis) or William Shaw (Matthew Modine) as they buckle all manner of swash in an attempt to reach the uncharted Cutthroat Island and find the treasure there. Players can choose between two fighting styles – swordplay and brawling – which determine whether your character focuses more on fencing or fisticuffs. While most of the game consists of scrapping with enemies, two of its 10 stages break things up a little by having you race through an area in a minecart or on horseback. ∎

FACT

The movie's budget was nearly $100m but it only made $10m at US cinemas earning the Guinness World Record for biggest box-office bomb of all time.

CYBER SPIN

Year	1992
Publisher	Takara
Developer	Takara

YOU ARE CHUCK Davis, a 17-year-old boy racer who dreams of being world famous. Oh, and it's also the future (well, it's 2015) and you're racing in a Cyber Car, a state-of-the-art vehicle that can reach crazy speeds of

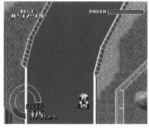

up to 384 km/h. Can you race your way around a 10-track season unscathed and find yourself top of the leaderboard once all the cyber-dust has cyber-settled?

Cyber Spin is a top-down racer that splits its races into two parts: you have to complete a lap within a certain time in order to qualify for the main race against seven CPU opponents. The game is speedy as it is but a turbo boost lets you go even faster, at the expense of your energy bar (which can be topped up in the pits). ■

FACT

The Japanese version of Cyber Spin is based on the anime *Future GPX Cyber Formula*, and contains completely different characters and vehicles.

CYBERNATOR

Year	1993
Publisher	Konami
Developer	NCS

CYBERNATOR IS THE second game in NCS's Assault Suits series (in Japan it's called Assault Suits Valken). It's a run 'n' gun game where instead of running you're stomping around in an enormous mech that's four or five storeys

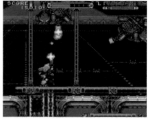

tall. This obviously has an effect on your movement, making Cybernator feel a little more sluggish than other games in its genre. The payoff, however, is a hefty arsenal of weaponry, a pleasantly flexible aiming mechanic and the ability to upgrade your various firearms. It's been censored a bit, though that's perhaps understandable: the Japanese version features a scene where you confront the enemy president, who then takes out a gun and shoots himself in the head. It's no big shock that this scene was removed for the west. ■

FACT

The first Assault Suit game was Assault Suit Leynos for the Sega Mega Drive. Like Cybernator, it too was given a western release, under the name Target Earth.

DAFFY DUCK: THE MARVIN MISSIONS

Year	1993
Publisher	Sunsoft
Developer	ICOM Simulations

THIS SNES PLATFORMER is based on *Duck Dodgers in the 24½th Century*, a seven-minute long cartoon released by Warner Bros in 1953 as part of its Merrie Melodies series.

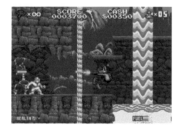

Marvin the Martian is trying to take over the Earth, so it's up to Duck Dodgers (i.e. Daffy Duck in a cape) to head to Mars and stop him. There are five different types of gun for Daffy to use: these can be found dotted around each of the game's 19 levels, though you can also buy them at the shops you occasionally encounter. Combat is a little off in this one: there's a hefty recoil effect every time Daffy shoots (which bounces you up enough to hit bullets even if you're ducking them) and most enemies don't visibly react to shots. ■

FACT

A proper *Duck Dodgers* cartoon ran on Cartoon Network for 39 episodes in 2003. The theme tune was performed by Tom Jones and The Flaming Lips.

DARIUS TWIN

Year	1991
Publisher	Taito
Developer	Taito

DARIUS TWIN IS the third in Taito's Darius series of shoot 'em ups, and the first to be created specifically for a home console (the previous two were arcade releases). Set centuries after the events

of the previous games, Darius Twin has players jumping in their Silver Hawk ship and trying to take down the galactic tyrant Belser, who's returned once again to generally smash loads of stuff up. The 'Twin' in the title refers to the presence of simultaneous two-player mode, something that's relatively uncommon among SNES shoot 'em ups. The game also offers a choice of different paths to travel through the game: while you'll take on seven stages on your way to the end credits, there are actually 12 in total, making multiple playthroughs essential. ■

FACT

The first two Darius games were designed with multiple arcade monitors in mind: the original could be played over three screens whereas Darius II could be played over two or three.

DAVID CRANE'S AMAZING TENNIS

Year	1992
Publisher	Absolute Entertainment
Developer	David Crane

WHEN A GAME'S title namechecks its designer, you know it's going to at least offer something interesting. Such is the case with David Crane's Amazing Tennis, designed by the man behind the likes of Pitfall!, A Boy and His Blob and the original Ghostbusters game. The selling point here is the unique viewpoint, which sits the camera far lower than you would usually expect in a tennis game: rather than looking down on the action from above, you're essentially standing at one end of the court at ground level. While some praised this for its originality and claimed it gave players a greater feeling of immersion, others complained that it made it difficult to play on the far end of the court, since you can't really judge depth there. ■

FACT

David Crane was one of five men who founded Activision. The initial aim was to publish Atari 2600 games that would give the developers more credit and make their names known to gamers.

THE DEATH AND RETURN OF SUPERMAN

Year	1994
Publisher	Sunsoft
Developer	Blizzard Entertainment

THE DEATH OF Superman was one of DC's most controversial comic events, for a number of reasons (not least because he didn't actually die). Such was its impact that a video game based on it was released a year or so later. It's a beat 'em up that puts you in charge of five different 'Supermen' over the course of the game: the original Superman, Superboy, the metallic-suited Steel, the morally dubious Cyborg Superman and the Last Son of Krypton, also known as the Eradicator. Character diversity aside it's a fairly standard game, though it does have one satisfying move: if you grab your opponent and hold Up on the D-Pad while throwing them you'll slam them into the background scenery, potentially damaging it. ■

FACT

The *Death of Superman* comic arc was created because Superman comic sales had been declining and the writing team wanted to teach readers not to take him for granted.

DAZE BEFORE CHRISTMAS

Year	1994
Publisher	Sunsoft
Developer	Funcom

THERE HAVE BEEN surprisingly few Christmas-themed games over the years, which is what makes the existence of Daze Before Christmas all the more welcome (though it only made it to Europe and Australia). The evil Louse the Mouse has stolen the children's presents and cursed them, turning them into enemies. Playing as Santa himself, you have to use your magic dust to return them to their original gift-like state, then give Louse and his cronies a kick in the chestnuts for good measure. Perhaps the oddest feature is the ability to turn into the 'Anti-Claus': by collecting a cup of tea Santa will turn blue and swap his magic dust for the tried-and-tested method of swinging his sack of toys at enemies. One for the naughty list, surely. ■

FACT

Hidden in the game's program code is a quote by Shirley Temple: 'I stopped believing in Santa Claus when I was six. Mother took me to see him in a department store and he asked for my autograph.'

DEMOLITION MAN

Year	1995
Publisher	Acclaim
Developer	Virgin Interactive

DID YOU KNOW that in the mid '90s gung-ho cop Sylvester Stallone and psychopathic criminal Wesley Snipes were both frozen in a cryogenic prison, only to awaken in 2036 and discover that crime is a thing of the past? Only joking, it was a film: ha ha! Should've seen your face. Acclaim's tie-in loosely follows the plot of the movie and has John Spartan (Stallone) trying to hunt down Simon Phoenix (Snipes) while gunning down his armed cronies along the way. The majority of the game is a side-scrolling action platformer – an extremely fast one, at that – but on a couple of occasions it switches to a top-down shooter and tasks you with rescuing hostages. Just to stress again, this didn't happen in real life. ■

FACT

A different Demolition Man game was developed for the 3DO console, featuring a mix of light fun, fighting, FPS and racing stages. Stallone and Snipes shot exclusive FMV scenes for it.

DEMON'S CREST

Year	1994
Publisher	Capcom
Developer	Capcom

WHILE PLENTY OF love has been (rightly) showered on Capcom's Ghosts 'n Goblins and Ghouls 'n Ghosts, it's also worth acknowledging its spin-off trilogy starring enemy demon Firebrand. Following Gargoyle's Quest on the Game Boy and its NES prequel Gargoyle's Quest II, Demon's Crest concludes the saga with Firebrand trying to find and gather six elemental crests (each of which give him new powers) in the hope of making the all-powerful Crest of Infinity appear and earning unlimited power. An action platformer with a fun hovering mechanic – a simple double-tap of the jump button 'locks' you at your current height until you press it again to drop – Demon's Crest also has Metroidvania elements: some areas can't be reached without certain crest powers, meaning some backtracking is essential. ■

FACT

Demon's Crest had a built-in anti-piracy measure to stop it being sold on bootleg carts. If the game detected that it wasn't legit, all the enemies became invincible.

DENNIS THE MENACE

Year	1993
Publisher	Ocean Software
Developer	Ocean Software

UK READERS, TEMPER your expectations: this isn't the same Dennis the Menace who's been gracing *The Beano* comic for nearly 70 years. Instead, it's the US comic strip – simply known as *Dennis* in the UK – that features a little blonde-haired scamp and was subsequently turned into an animated series and a 1993 live-action movie. It's the film that forms the basis for this game: after crook Switchblade Sam breaks into Dennis's neighbour Mr Wilson's house and steals his coin collection, it's up to Dennis to find each of the coins and return them. The problem is that Mr Wilson thinks Dennis is a pest who was responsible for the mess, meaning you have to avoid a large Walter Matthau roaming around while carrying out your task. ■

FACT

The first issue of *The Beano* to feature the UK Dennis the Menace went on sale on 12 March 1951, whereas the US Dennis the Menace made his debut in American newspapers on... 12 March 1951.

DESERT STRIKE: RETURN TO THE GULF

Year	1992
Publisher	Electronic Arts
Developer	Visual Concepts

THERE WERE A number of military games inspired by the Gulf War in the early '90s but none were quite so well-received as Desert Strike. The evil General Mubaba – who's known as General Kilbaba in other versions of the game and definitely isn't supposed to be Saddam Hussein, honest – has seized and become dictator of an unnamed Gulf state, so the US Army sends in a sole helicopter to carry out a series of low-key missions to try and bring him down.

These missions generally fall into one of two categories: destroying stuff (be that radar dishes, airstrips, chemical weapons plants, Scud launchers, what have you) and rescuing allies with your chopper's useful winch and ladder. What makes Desert Strike so compelling is its deliberate limitations designed to make the game more realistic: weapons, fuel and armour are strictly limited and you have to find more throughout your mission or you won't have enough to beat it.

FACT

Some may be frustrated that the Gulf state in Desert Strike is never named, but it could be worse: according to Posehn, the game was originally going to be called Beirut Breakout.

DANGER ZONE!

Meanwhile, the helicopter moves with momentum, meaning mastering it is a skill in itself. Rather than showing the action from a first-person cockpit view or side-on like so many other war games of the time, designer Mike Posehn opted for an isometric viewpoint instead and developed an interesting 'elliptical' rotation system for the camera. This meant that any time you turned, the camera would swoop around so that the back of your helicopter was always near the edge of the screen, letting you see further ahead regardless of what direction you were facing. ■

D-FORCE

Year	1991
Publisher	Asmik Ace Entertainment
Developer	Asmik Ace Entertainment

A 'POWERFUL OIL-RICH dictator in the Middle East has waged war on the world' (sounds familiar) so off you pop in D-Force, a 'super-modified nuclear Apache helicopter' to take him down. The game's split

into two styles: levels 1, 3 and 5 are 'shooting' stages and play like a normal vertical shoot 'em up, whereas levels 2, 4 and 6 are 'exploration' stages that play similarly but have enemies at two different heights. You have to use the L and R buttons to switch between high and low altitudes in order to hit both types of enemy. An option on the title screen lets you play only the shooting and exploration modes should you wish, but you can only access the final seventh stage by playing them all. Oh, and there are dinosaurs in it, because reasons. ■

> **FACT**
>
> The manual provides ample encouragement: 'If the ol' apple pie and baseball are to remain as symbols of our country, you'd better get on the ball.'

DIG & SPIKE VOLLEYBALL

Year	1993
Publisher	Hudson Soft
Developer	Tose

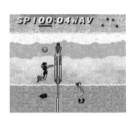

WHEN IT COMES to volleyball games, which should you go for: professional indoor volleyball, or casual beach volleyball? Dig & Spike shrugs its shoulders and asks 'why not both?'. For starters, you can take part in two-on-two women's beach volleyball, with both exhibition games and a tournament mode on offer. Then, for the main course, there's full six-on-six indoor men's volleyball, with eight countries to choose from: Cuba, USA, Italy, Netherlands, Brazil, Japan, Algeria and everyone's favourite nation, the Commonwealth of Independent States (which would later become Russia). If these seem like odd choices, to volleyball fans they make perfect sense: these are eight of the twelve teams that played in the volleyball tournament at the 1992 Olympic Games in Barcelona. ■

> **FACT**
>
> In case you're wondering, the gold medal for men's volleyball at the '92 Olympics went to Brazil, who beat the Netherlands in the final. Algeria finished 12th, which means Spain (who finished 8th) should have been in Dig & Spike instead.

DINOCITY

Year	1992
Publisher	Irem
Developer	Irem

MOVIE TIE-INS RARELY get more obscure than this one, which is based on a made-for-TV film called *Adventures in Dinosaur City*. Young chums Timmy and Jamie want to watch a video tape of their favourite TV dinosaur show but the television they're using is rubbish, so they decide to sneak into Timmy's dad's laboratory to use his massive telly there. Turns out it isn't a normal TV: it creates a portal and sucks the pair into the show, trapping them in its prehistoric world. Although there's a device that can send them home, one of its fuses has been stolen by Mr Big, the leader of a gang called the Rockeys. It's up to Timmy and Jamie to get it back, but they'll be doing it as a quartet. You see, they've befriended a pair of anthropomorphic dinosaurs called Rex (who's a T-Rex) and Tops (a Protoceratops), who offer to help them on their adventure. When you start the game you can choose between Timmy and Rex or Jamie and Tops, each pair

> **FACT**
>
> A cavewoman enemy called Cindy had a large bust and an angry face in the Japanese version of the game. This was changed for western releases, but it feels a bit like you're attacking someone friendly.

offering a different type of combat: Rex can punch and swing his tail whereas Tops throws projectiles at enemies instead. Regardless of which you choose, the other notable mechanic is the ability to get off your dino at any point by pressing the R button. While this can make you vulnerable, it's necessary for solving some platforming puzzles later in the game. Both film and game have been mostly forgotten these days, but while I can't speak for the former, the latter is underrated. ■

DINO DINI'S SOCCER

Year	1994
Publisher	Virgin Interactive
Developer	Eurocom

DINO DINI WAS a game designer best known for creating the much-loved computer football games Kick Off and Kick Off 2. Dino Dini's Soccer – known as Goal on computers – was considered the spiritual successor to Kick Off 2, but the SNES port had nothing to do with Dini and he distanced himself from it. It's a shame, because it's still a good football game but feels different to Dini's trademark style: most notably, the ball sticks to players' feet like glue whereas the Kick off games were notorious for making players learn how to control the ball. There are nearly 100 national teams to choose from, ranging from the usual big hitters to the likes of Zaire, Sierra Leone and Liberia. ■

FACT

Dino Dini made a return in 2016 with Dino Dini's Kick Off Revival on PS4. It was savaged by critics and Metacritic declared it one of the 10 worst games of 2016.

DIRT RACER

Year	1995
Publisher	Elite Systems
Developer	MotiveTime

THE ORIGINAL SUPER FX chip (see Star Fox) was used in just five games, and oddly two of them included Dirt in the title. Dirt Racer is the lesser-known of the two, since it was only released in Europe: it's a rally game consisting of head-to-head racers against single CPU opponents. You can take part in either a knockout cup or a league format, the latter featuring divisions you move up and down depending on how many races you win. At first, this will likely not be very many: the cars handle like a canoe in a storm and are extremely sensitive to control, with the slightest movement on the D-Pad swinging you round and potentially spinning you out. Getting round a corner feels like an accomplishment in this one. ■

FACT

MotiveTime and Elite were working on a second Super FX racer called Powerslide which offered more intuitive handling. It was planned for the SNES and 3DO but was cancelled.

DIRT TRAX FX

Year	1995
Publisher	Acclaim
Developer	Sculptured Software

ACCLAIM'S SINGLE SUPER FX game is this technically impressive motocross game in which you choose between eight different characters and take part in a series of races. While the game makes use of the Super FX to offer polygonal tracks with various dips, bumps and walls, the racer models are just sprites: while this initially seems like a cop-out the reality is that this frees up some power and gives Dirt Trax FX a significantly higher frame rate than any of the other games that used the original Super FX chip. It isn't without its issues, though:

FACT

The Super FX chip has 'MARIO' printed on it. It stands for Mathematical, Argonaut, Rotation and Input/Output.

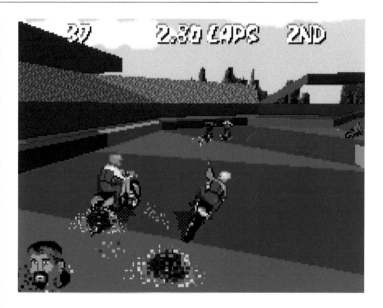

each racer has a theme tune that plays while they're in first place, which means any races where the lead is constantly changing become a mess of sound. ■

DONKEY KONG COUNTRY

Year	1994
Publisher	Nintendo
Developer	Rare

BY THE END of 1994 the SNES was beginning to see some serious competition. Sega's Mega Drive already had a CD-ROM add-on and another piece of kit was imminent that would offer 32-bit visuals. Meanwhile, in Japan, the Sega Saturn and Sony PlayStation were about to launch, declaring in no uncertain terms that the era of CD-based polygonal gaming was very much arriving. Eager to show that the SNES was still capable of packing a punch, Nintendo turned to UK-based developer Rare, who had recently bought a pair of Hollywood-quality £80,000 Silicon Graphics workstations and had impressed Nintendo with a boxing game prototype using the new tech. The boxing game never happened but Rare asked to make a game based on Donkey Kong, a character who had been mostly dormant since Nintendo's early arcade days and had certainly never been portrayed as a hero before. The result was Donkey Kong Country, one of the most visually stunning platformers seen at the time and a game that still holds up well today.

The game's plot is your typical rescue mission, but there's no damsel in distress this time. Instead, Donkey Kong is trying to retrieve his enormous stash of bananas, which has been stolen by King K. Rool and his Kremling henchmen. Joining him on his quest is his young pal Diddy Kong, who DK is currently training to be a hero. Each has their own unique abilities: Donkey is more powerful and can slap the ground to find secrets, whereas Diddy is faster and can jump higher. There

are also five animal chums – Rambi the rhino, Enguarde the swordfish, Expresso the ostrich, Winky the frog and Squawks the parrot – who can be found trapped in crates and can be ridden when rescued.

Although it's a fantastic game to play, its most notable aspect is easily its presentation. The music was primarily the work of David Wise, Rare's in-house composer, and is considered by many to be his greatest work (listen to the Aquatic Ambience track for convincing proof). Most immediately striking, however, is the game's graphics. The secret was those expensive Silicon Graphics computers, which at the time were renowned for creating the CGI dinosaurs in Jurassic Park. The SNES clearly couldn't handle anything like that level of power, so Rare's clever trick was to render everything – Donkey Kong, Diddy, the enemies and all the background environments – as individual CG models, then capture still images of them and turn them into normal sprites that the SNES could easily deal with (similar to the way Mortal Kombat used photos of actors as sprites). The result was a game that acted like any other 2D platformer, but had an incredibly futuristic 3D CGI look and felt like it should be running on far more powerful hardware instead.

The Sega 32X hit America on the same day as Donkey Kong Country. Nintendo sent all its Nintendo Power magazine subscribers a promotional VHS showing off the game, and declaring that you won't find it 'on 32X adapters'. Donkey Kong Country ended up becoming the third best-selling SNES game with 9 million copies sold worldwide. The 32X bombed. ■

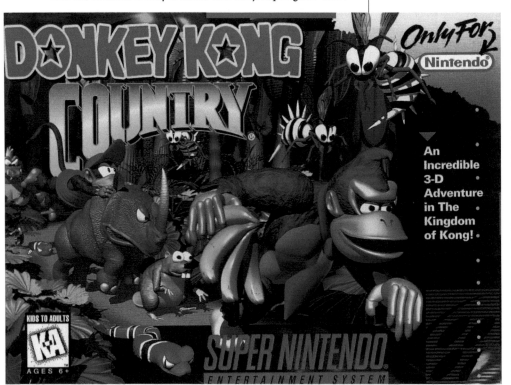

DONKEY KONG COUNTRY 2: DIDDY'S KONG QUEST

Year	1995
Publisher	Nintendo
Developer	Rare

IT'S A GOOD job Diddy Kong was getting all that hero training, because this time Donkey Kong himself has been kidnapped by K. Rool (who now fancies himself as a pirate and is going by Kaptain rather than King). His ransom? The banana stash he failed to successfully steal in the first game: he really can't let that lie, it seems. Clearly unwilling to pay, Diddy heads out to rescue his big buddy, though he doesn't go solo: this time he's accompanied by his girlfriend Dixie Kong, who can jump even higher than Diddy and can spin her hair around to float in the air. Unlike in the first game, each hero can now grab their partner and launch them at enemies as if they were a barrel. Animal buddies return too, but this time you transform into them instead of riding them. Furthermore, Expresso and Winky

have been replaced by Squitter the spider and a rattlesnake with the inspired name Rattly. Other than these changes the majority of the gameplay is similar to that of the original game, with Rare very much employing an 'if it ain't broke' strategy and instead opting to focus on making the sequel more difficult. As a result, the game's main difference over the original (other than the new protagonist pairing) is its general tone: whereas the first Donkey Kong Country was set primarily in jungle environments, Diddy's Kong Quest (conquest, geddit) has more of a pirate theme. ◼

DONKEY KONG COUNTRY 3: DIXIE KONG'S DOUBLE TROUBLE

Year	1996
Publisher	Nintendo
Developer	Rare

still use her pigtails like a helicopter to hover in the air, while Kiddy plays the Donkey Kong role this time, using his strength to defeat certain enemies Dixie can't beat. Animal buddies return once again with Ellie the elephant among the new recruits, and there's a new ongoing side-quest involving a group of bears called the Brothers Bear. Each needs a certain item to help them out with a problem: if you can find that item and trade it with them you'll get a 'banana bird'. Get all these and you'll free the Banana Bird Queen, who helps you defeat K. Rool. Um, I mean Baron K. Roolenstein. Definitely not the same person. ◼

DECIDING TO TAKE a break after the events of the second game, Donkey Kong and Diddy Kong go on vacation to the Northern Kremisphere, where they're both kidnapped by the suspiciously named Baron K. Roolenstein. That leaves Dixie to take on the role of lead protagonist this time and go on a rescue mission: which is good of her, when you consider her boyfriend didn't invite her to join him on holiday. This means the role of sidekick needs filling once again, so step forward Kiddy Kong, Dixie's younger cousin, who's essentially a large baby and is somehow allowed to accompany Dixie on her dangerous quest (we get it, Kongs, you have no interest in security whatsoever). As before, the Kongs each have their own unique abilities: Dixie can

DOOM

Year	1995
Publisher	Williams Entertainment / Ocean
Developer	Sculptured Software

🇺🇸✓ 🇪🇺✓

DOOM HAS SEEN more ports over the years than a cruise ship captain, but most have been on systems expected to be able to handle it. A SNES version of Doom was considered impossible until the Super FX 2 chip – an enhanced upgrade of the Super FX that doubled the clock speed from 10.5 MHz to 21 MHz – made it a reality. As with all other versions of the game, you play as a space marine who has to destroy a seemingly endless horde of monsters who've arrived from Hell, in order to prevent them reaching and taking over the Earth. Despite its lower resolution, the SNES rendition of Doom is an otherwise impressive effort, containing nearly all the levels from the PC original and even including some monsters – like the Cyberdemon and Spiderdemon – that aren't present in the more powerful Sega 32X, Jaguar and 3DO versions.

FACT

The SNES port of Doom was programmed by Randy Linden, who went on to develop Bleem!, a commercial PlayStation emulator for PCs that was eventually crippled by Sony lawsuits.

That said, the console's limitations do mean that some elements of the game play differently on the SNES than other systems. Most notably, enemies can only be seen facing you: they have no sprites for looking away. This means it's impossible to sneak up on them and kill them without them spotting you, and also means the occasional instance of enemies turning on each other (after one shoots the other by mistake) can't happen either. Despite these concessions and the SNES's relative lack of power overall, this still manages to be a perfectly playable version of an important, genre-defining game. ■

DOOM TROOPERS

Year	1995
Publisher	Playmates
Developer	Adrenalin Interactive

🇺🇸✓ 🇪🇺✗

DOOM TROOPERS IS a run 'n' gun platform shooter based on Mutant Chronicles, a pen-and-paper RPG created by Swedish company Target Games that spawned a card game spin-off named Doom Trooper. You choose between two titular troopers – Mitch Hunter and Max Steiner – as they travel from planet to planet killing any Dark Legion mutants that get in their way in order to protect the galaxy from them. It's a surprisingly gory game, with enemies exploding in a shower of blood and heads popping off all over the place, though given that you're dealing with mutants that doesn't always mean the end: it's not uncommon for headless baddies to continue blindly running around and shooting at you even after you've relieved them of their noggin. ■

FACT

A crowdfunding campaign to turn the Doom Trooper card game into a digital version was successfully funded in September 2017.

DOOMSDAY WARRIOR

Year	1993
Publisher	Renovation Products
Developer	Laser Soft

🇺🇸✓ 🇪🇺✗

WHILE FIGHTING GAMES became 10 a penny in the wake of Street Fighter II's success, Doomsday Warrior deserves at least some credit for trying to bring something new to the table (even if it doesn't quite manage it). It has specific block and jump buttons, rather than assigning them to the D-Pad. It has some truly unique characters, such as Nuform, a 'living liquid' character who looks a bit like the T-1000 in *Terminator 2*. Most notable though is its interesting levelling up system: your health in each fight is split into four smaller gauges, and after a win any full gauges can be spent on powering up certain aspects of you character. This means your fighter's eventual strength depends on how convincingly you beat your CPU opponents. ■

FACT

Laser Soft was a branch of Japanese game publisher Telenet Japan. Other branches include RiOT and Wolfteam: the latter developed Tales of Phantasia for the Super Famicom and eventually became Namco Tales Studio.

DOUBLE DRAGON V: THE SHADOW FALLS

Year	1994
Publisher	Tradewest
Developer	Leland Interactive Media

ALTHOUGH PRACTICALLY EVERY gamer thinks of the Double Dragon series as beat 'em ups, Double Dragon V is a rare exception. Instead, it's a one-on-fighting game in the style of Street Fighter II. Players choose their fighter from a roster of 10 – mainstay heroes Billy and Jimmy Lee, and eight enemy characters – and fight their way through either an arcade-style Tournament mode or one-off Versus battles. There's also Quest, which is a story mode where you can only choose between the Lee brothers as they attempt to fight their way to the Shadow Master to stop him releasing a plague on the city. Most of the enemy characters come from an ill-fated *Double Dragon* cartoon series which launched around the same time as this game. ◾

FACT

The entire manual is a full-colour comic book in which Billy and Jimmy explain the game's controls and options to each other in a painfully drawn-out way (so to speak).

DRAGON: THE BRUCE LEE STORY

Year	1995
Publisher	Acclaim Entertainment
Developer	Virgin Interactive

DRAGON WAS A critically acclaimed 1993 movie telling the life story of the legendary martial artist and movie star Bruce Lee. Virgin's video game adaptation follows the movie's plot to some extent – it misses out the entire subplot about his relationship with his wife Linda – with still images telling the story in between each fight (because in case it wasn't already clear, it's obviously a fighting game). The most notable element of Dragon is its support for fights with up to three characters, meaning on occasion you'll be taking on two enemies at once. You can turn the tables, however, by playing two-player co-op, where one of you plays as Bruce Lee and the other plays as… um, Bruce Lee but with red trousers. ◾

FACT

In the *Dragon* movie, Bruce Lee's daughter Shannon has a cameo as a singer at a party. At this party, Bruce's wife Linda tells him that she's pregnant: with Shannon.

DRAGON BALL Z: SUPER BUTODEN

Year	1993
Publisher	Bandai
Developer	Tose

ALTHOUGH *DRAGON BALL* now has a huge following in the west, that wasn't the case at first. While France was the first country to get a localised dub back in the late '80s, it didn't actually air in the US until 1995 and didn't hit UK television until 2000. As a result, after Super Butoden launched on the Super Famicom in Japan, France was the only country to get a localised SNES release. Super Butoden is the first ever one-on-one fighting game based on *Dragon Ball*, and contains a Story mode (in French, obviously) that covers the Piccolo Jr Saga and goes up to the Cell Games Saga. If plot isn't for you, there's also a standard versus mode where you can choose from the 13 playable fighters. ◾

FACT

The Super Famicom version of Super Butoden was re-released on the Nintendo Switch, but only as a free bonus for anyone who pre-ordered Dragon Ball FighterZ.

DRAGON BALL Z: LA LÉGENDE SAIEN

Year	1994
Publisher	Bandai
Developer	Tose

SUPER BUTODEN SOLD around 1.4 million copies in Japan alone, so Super Butoden 2 was a no-brainer. French gamers were once again treated to their own localised version, this time renamed La Légende Saien. Once again it has a story mode, this time starting with the Cell Games Saga and taking in three of the *Dragon Ball Z* movies, but as a unique twist the story can change depending on whether you win or lose a fight, meaning your performance can turn things decidedly non-canon. As with its predecessor, combat takes place over enormous stages set on both ground level and in the sky: if you stray too far from your opponent the screen will split and a little radar will show your positions relative to each other. ◾

FACT

The Japanese version was included as a pre-order bonus for anyone who bought Dragon Ball Z: Extreme Butoden on the 3DS. Noticing a theme here?

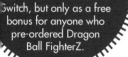

DRAGON BALL Z: ULTIME MENACE

Year	1995
Publisher	Bandai
Developer	Tose

SUPER BUTODEN 3 came to Japan the year after its predecessor and, once again, it was translated for the French market and given a new name. Ultime Menace is set during the show's Majin Buu Saga, but there's no story mode this time: instead, you simply get a standard arcade-style tournament mode where you choose from one of 10 characters – Majin Buu, Majin Vegeta, Supreme Kai, Dabura, Android 18 and Super Saiyan versions of Goku, Goten, Trunks, Gohan and Future Trunks – and fight your way through the rest. It plays very similarly to its predecessor, with one major difference: the time needed to charge your Ki only takes a short while, compared to several seconds in La Légende Saien. ∎

> **FACT**
> Super Saiyan Future Trunks is a hidden character. To unlock him, press Up, X, Down, B, L, Y, R, A during the game's opening sequence.

DRAGON BALL Z: HYPER DIMENSION

Year	1997
Publisher	Bandai
Developer	Tose

THE FOURTH AND final Super Butoden game brought back the Story mode when it launched for the Super Famicom in Japan, this time taking place from the Frieza Saga through to the Kid Buu Saga. However, when the inevitable French port was released, this Story mode was missing, leaving players with the standard Tournament and Single Battle modes seen in the previous game. It does at least play a little differently this time: while the standard idea of the large play area and the ability to take to the skies remain intact, energy bars are replaced with a number up to 999, which you can replenish during fights. When your energy drops below 80 you can trigger 'desperation' moves, which do massive amounts of damage. ∎

> **FACT**
> Although the Story mode isn't present in the French SNES version of the game, all its music tracks can still be found in the Sound Test in the Options menu, which suggests it was simply ripped out unceremoniously.

DRAGON VIEW

Year	1994
Publisher	Kemco
Developer	Kemco

A SEQUEL OF sorts to Drakkhen (see the opposite page), Dragon View ditches the whole party-of-four idea and resorts for a far more conventional 'save the girl' storyline. The lady in question this time is Katarina – the fiancée of the game's hero Alex – who's been kidnapped by evil wizard Argos. Alex (who's a descendant of one of the heroes from Drakkhen) has to head out and rescue her while also finding out exactly what Argos wanted with her in the first place. And if you think it involves dragons, you're on the right path. Speaking of right paths, Dragon View borrows the first-person exploration that made Drakkhen so impressive, but replaces its turn-based battles with a beat 'em up style system. This makes it an ideal starter RPG for those more used to action games. ∎

> **FACT**
> Dragon View was ported to Steam (under the name Dragonview) and is essentially a SNES emulator running the game, so there's no need to go looking for a pricey cartridge.

DRAGON'S LAIR

Year	1993
Publisher	Data East
Developer	MotiveTime

THE ORIGINAL ARCADE version of Dragon's Lair was a breakthrough for gaming visuals. Running off laserdiscs, it was a full-motion video adventure that offered limited gameplay but impressed arcade-goers regardless. Naturally, Nintendo systems couldn't handle this, so when it came to Nintendo versions a different solution had to be sought. The platformer released for the NES was a disaster (see the *NES Encyclopedia*), but developer MotiveTime had another crack with this SNES game. It was a great improvement – as well as obviously looking significantly better it controlled better too – but suffered from poor hit detection and a number of cheap deaths. As a result, even though it outdid its 8-bit sibling in every way it was still panned by critics. ∎

> **FACT**
> Although it was considered impossible, an authentic recreation of Dragon's Lair was actually released on the humble Game Boy Color in 2000, and did a commendable job of recreating its cutscenes.

DRAKKHEN

Year	1991
Publisher	Kemco-Seika
Developer	Infogrames

ORIGINALLY DEVELOPED BY French studio Infogrames and released on home computers in 1989, Drakkhen came to the SNES very early in its life and initially suggested that Nintendo's system could be a feasible home for ports of PC RPGs. This co-production with Japanese studio Kemco-Seika included numerous differences compared to its computer counterpart (including far less emphasis on its text-based adventure log) but kept many of the game's most important elements, most notably its impressive first-person overworld exploration mechanic. It was also far more difficult, mainly because it didn't come with the book of short stories that accompanied the computer versions and which gave numerous tidbits of advice on how to defeat the various enemies you encounter. The story is also far less comprehensible, given its translation to Japanese and back again. ■

FACT

The computer version of the game features a 'Love Monster' that appears as the silhouette of a woman saying 'I love you' in a series of odd voices. The SNES version removes the voices with generic enemy grunts.

DREAM TV

Year	1994
Publisher	Triffix
Developer	Triffix

CHARLIE AND JIMMY are national video game champions, so there's nothing they won't play. One day a mysterious game called Dream TV turns up in the mail, but when they try to play it they end up getting sucked into a world overseen by the mysterious and evil Critic. You have to make your way through its four worlds (Egyptian, Medieval, Futuristic and Prehistoric) collecting nine puzzle pieces in each. The twist is that Dream TV is designed for co-op play, with the screen splitting if the two heroes wander too far away from each other. While playing with two players is obviously preferred you can still play on your own, using the R button to switch between characters: this does make boss fights much harder, though. ■

FACT

Triffix was a small Montreal-based publisher that only published three games: Dream TV, Castelian on the NES and Game Boy, and Space Football: One on One for the SNES.

THE DUEL: TEST DRIVE II

Year	1992
Publisher	Accolade
Developer	Distinctive Software

THE TEST DRIVE series has always focused on racing exotic cars through public roads while avoiding the police, and the second game is a prime example of this. The 'Duel' moniker is key here, because whereas the first Test Drive only allowed you to race against the clock, here you can also choose to race against a single CPU opponent. There are three cars to pick from – the Porsche 959, Ferrari F40 and Lamborghini Diablo – and four courses to race through, each based in the US (the last course, for example, shows the Space Needle in Seattle in the background at one point). Its in-car view was relatively uncommon at the time, but enjoy it while it lasts: it's very easy to be pulled over by the cops for speeding. ■

FACT

A total of 20 Test Drive games and spin-offs have been released, ranging from the Test Drive Off-Road titles to the open-world Test Drive Unlimited games on Xbox 360 and PS3.

DUNGEON MASTER

Year	1993
Publisher	JVC
Developer	FTL Games

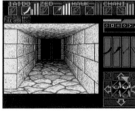

DUNGEON MASTER WAS originally released on the Atari ST in 1987 and was ported to a number of other home computers over the years until finally coming to the SNES a full six years after launch. It's credited for being the first dungeon crawling RPG that featured real-time combat rather than turn-based battling. Playing as Theros, the apprentice of the Grey Lord Librasulus, you have to resurrect four dead champions (from a selection of 24) and explore a labyrinthine dungeon in search of the firestaff, which will let Librasulus take human form and defeat the evil Lord Chaos. If you're the rebellious type who doesn't take kindly to commands, you can find the firestaff and just leave the dungeon, but Librasulus will turn up and kill you himself. ■

FACT

If you were hoping for a more detailed version of the game's plot here, good luck: the manual takes a whopping 17 pages of full text to explain it.

EARTHBOUND

Year	1995
Publisher	Nintendo
Developer	Ape / HAL Laboratory

 ✓ ✗

MOST 8-BIT AND 16-bit RPGs – indeed, most modern RPGs too – have a fantasy setting. Dragons, magic, dungeons, that sort of thing. By offering players an RPG adventure in a normal, modern day environment, Earthbound (and its Japan-only predecessor Mother) did something special: it focused on the ordinary and in turn created something extraordinary. The game tells the story of Ness (who later found fame in the Smash Bros games), a young lad with psychic powers whose town is shook one night by the impact of a meteorite crashing into a nearby hill. It soon becomes apparent that it's the work of Gigyas, an evil alien force who's engulfed the world in hatred and turned its humans and animals evil. It's up to Ness and three other characters he meets along the way – telepathic 13-year-old Paula, tech-head Jeff and martial artist Poo – to defeat Gigyas and bring kindness and empathy back to the world.

The game's real-world setting continually provided the player with ways to relate to Ness's adventure. Rather than fighting orcs, demons and goblins, the game's turn-based battles had Ness and chums facing off against angry bears, cranky old women, enraged fire hydrants and, in the game's words, 'new age retro hippies'. Rather than earning gold, defeating enemies earns you cash that's deposited remotely into an ATM account by your dad and has to be manually withdrawn. And as one of the first Nintendo games localised specifically with

FACT

Earthbound is known as Mother 2 in Japan. Shigesato Itoi named the game after the John Lennon song of the same name, which made him cry the first time he heard it.

Americanised jokes (with references to the likes of Spinal Tap and Bugs Bunny) rather than a straight translation from its native Japanese, Earthbound simply felt more contemporary and approachable than most other stony-faced RPGs.

The game's eccentricity extended to the way it was sold and promoted in North America. Conscious that the RPG genre had still to properly be accepted *en masse* by western audiences, Nintendo included a full 135-page *Player's Guide* with each American copy of Earthbound: not only did this help players get to grips with the game's mechanics, it actually took them through the entire game, right up to the final battle with Gigyas. Oh, and it included a set of scratch-and-sniff stickers too, just in case it didn't seem quirky enough already.

Written, directed and co-produced by Japanese copywriter Shigesato Itoi and his development team Ape Inc, Earthbound's lengthy development meant it was continually threatened with cancellation until HAL Laboratory's Satoru Iwata came on board to co-produce and take on lead programming duties. It's a good job, too: had Iwata not been asked to get involved, the world may have been unwittingly deprived of one of the most well-loved RPGs of all time. That's not to say parts of the world weren't anyway, of course: the game was never released in Europe, meaning the first time gamers in that region were able to (legally) buy and play the game was on the Wii U's Virtual Console service in July 2013, a full 18 years after launch. For many, it was worth the wait. ∎

EARTHWORM JIM

Year	1994
Publisher	Playmates
Developer	Shiny Entertainment

IN THE EARLY '90s, Dave Perry was hot property. The Northern Irish programmer had been working for Virgin Games and was partly responsible for three extremely successful licensed platformers: the McDonalds-themed Global Gladiators, Cool Spot and Aladdin. When Playmates Toys – rolling in money from its Teenage Mutant Ninja Turtles action figures – decided it wanted to get into video game publishing, it teamed up with Perry and funded a brand new independent studio for him: Shiny Entertainment. Perry gathered some other Virgin Games colleagues (including animation director Mike Dietz and lead artist Steve Crow, two men crucial to the previous games' incredible visuals) and teamed up with animator Doug TenNapel to create Earthworm Jim, an entirely original platformer designed to spawn an action figure line and animated series.

Jim was a harmless, unassuming earthworm minding his own business until a hi-tech, indestructible space suit fell out of the sky and landed on him, giving him human-like properties. Now Jim's being pursued by a bunch of nasty types looking to steal his suit: we're talking the likes of the similarly humanified Psy-Crow, the self-explanatory Professor Monkey-for-a-Head and the main villain, known as Queen Pulsating, Bloated, Festering, Sweaty, Pus-filled, Malformed Slug-for-a-Butt (now you know why this game got a whole page). Can Jim stop his suit falling into the wrong hands and rescue the kidnapped Princess What's-Her-Name in the process? I mean, that's more or less up to you.

FACT

Remember the dig at Earthworm Jim in Donkey Kong Country 2 (see the Fact on that page)? That was actually a response to the Mega CD version of Earthworm Jim, which featured a cheat code that replaced Jim's face with that of Donkey Kong, complete with dumb expression and an arrow through his head.

In case it wasn't already clear, Earthworm Jim's main characteristic is its ridiculous sense of humour, with absurd moments occurring on a regular basis. One boss fight has you taking on an evil goldfish named Bob, who's beaten by simply walking into his bowl and smashing it on the ground, leaving him flopping around. Another stage has you indulging in a bungee jump fight against a giant snot monster. Perhaps silliest of all, though, is the cow launch: near the start of the game you have to drop a refrigerator onto a see-saw to launch a cow into space. When the game ends and you finally rescue Princess What's-Her-Name, the celebrations are cut somewhat short when the cow re-enters the stratosphere and lands directly on her, crushing her.

The Playmates action figure line was cancelled after one series, meaning the planned second wave, including key enemies like the Queen and the memorable Professor Monkey-for-a-Head (and his simian sidekick Monkey Professor-for-a-Head) was never released. The animated series, meanwhile, lasted 23 episodes before it too was axed, despite being genuinely funny with Dan Castellaneta (aka Homer Simpson) voicing Jim. Those relative disappointments should never take away from the success of the game, however: maybe Earthworm Jim was simply never supposed to be a toy line, or a cartoon, or a comic strip. When he's in game form, trying to avoid giant hamsters and launching cows into space, that's when fans know and love him best. ■

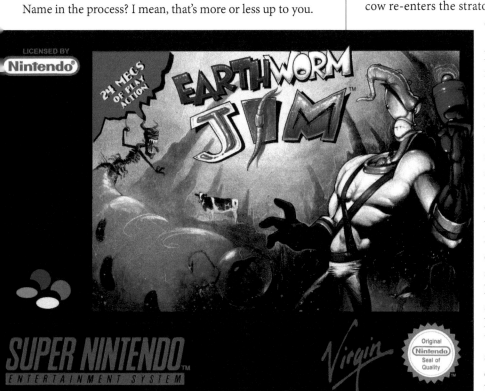

EARTHWORM JIM 2

Year	1995
Publisher	Playmates
Developer	Shiny Entertainment

THE TOYS AND cartoon may not have been a smash hit but the Earthworm Jim game was much-loved by many and so the inevitable sequel followed a year later. Spurred on by the knowledge that the first game's abstract sense of humour had gone down well, Shiny included even more ridiculous scenarios and moments in Earthworm Jim 2. One minute players are riding a stairlift while avoiding falling grannies, the next they're trying to help prevent cows being abducted by UFOs by carrying them safely to a barn while avoiding the electric chairs conveniently lying around. While not every idea is a hit – an isometric shoot 'em up section is rather slow and dull – these are easily outnumbered by the more hilarious moments. There aren't too many games that feature head inflations, luchador lawyers and a rescue mission where you have to save puppies being flung out of a building by trying to make

> **FACT**
>
> The music in the Cave Salamander stage is Beethoven's Moonlight Sonata. This piece is no stranger to video games, having also appeared in the likes of Dr Franken, Phantasy Star Online 2 and most notably as part of a puzzle in Resident Evil.

them land on a giant marshmallow. Easily the strangest moment, however, is the level entitled Jim's Now a Blind Cave Salamander, in which you swim around the intestinal tract of a massive monster while collecting mealworms: the more you get, the more questions you get asked in the Earthworm Jim gameshow at the end of the stage. There are more than 70 of these questions chosen randomly, and they're all suitable silly. Sample question: 'Can Psy-Crow beat Jim at arm wrestling?' Answer: 'Jim has no arms.' ■

EEK! THE CAT

Year	1994
Publisher	Ocean
Developer	CTA Developments

BASED ON THE Fox Kids cartoon that ran from 1992–97, Eek! The Cat is a modified version of Sleepwalker, a home computer game released by Ocean in 1993.

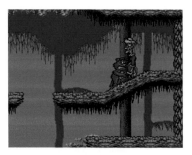

Sleepwalker had you playing as a dog that had to guide a sleepwalking boy past a series of dangerous obstacles. Eek! The Cat is exactly the same, although this time the dog is now the titular cat and the boy has been replaced with various characters from the show, each in either a dizzy state or wearing a costume that conveniently covers their sight. The final stage has you guiding a walking present to an orphanage: manage this and Eek opens the present to find a note from Santa saying he's getting a party. Which is nice, but presumably means the orphans get nothing. ■

> **FACT**
>
> Sleepwalker was released to make money for Comic Relief in the UK, and featured soundbites from comedians Lenny Henry and Harry Enfield.

EMMITT SMITH FOOTBALL

Year	1995
Publisher	JVC
Developer	Bitmasters

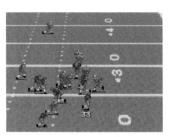

WHEN IT COMES to getting a big name athlete for your American football game, Emmitt Smith is up there with the best of them. A three-time Super Bowl champion who still holds the NFL record for most rushing yards in his career (18,355), Smith was a perfect face for JVC's pigskin sim. Unfortunately, it seems that Mr Smith's presence is the most notable thing about what's otherwise a pretty bare-bones package. The game has no official NFL or NFLPA licence (meaning no real team or player names), and there's no season or tournament mode to speak of, meaning you're limited to just exhibition matches. A clever play-editing mode lets you save up to 64 custom plays and use them during matches, but that's about all the depth on offer here. ■

> **FACT**
>
> Emmitt Smith is only one of two non-kicking players to score more than 1,000 points in his career. The other is Jerry Rice, best known for his time at the San Francisco 49ers alongside Joe Montana.

EQUINOX

Year	1994
Publisher	Sony Imagesoft
Developer	Software Creations

THIS IS THE sequel to NES title Solstice: The Quest for the Staff of Demnos, and uses a similar isometric viewpoint to that game, albeit with far more impressive graphics. The hero of the original game, Shadax, has been kidnapped by his apprentice Sonia (that's gratitude for you) and imprisoned in her ice palace. Playing as Shadax's son Glendaal, you have to clear the world's seven kingdoms of the hordes of monsters that have shown up, then head to the ice palace in Death Island and get your old man back. The majority of the game consists of exploring the eight dungeons, collecting the 12 shiny blue tokens hidden in each and using these to summon the boss. ■

FACT

Why Equinox and not Solstice II? Well, the titles are linked. It's to do with the Earth's orbit around the sun. In astrology, a solstice is when the sun is at its greatest distance from the Earth's equator, and an equinox is when it's at its closest.

ESPN BASEBALL TONIGHT

Year	1994
Publisher	Sony Imagesoft
Developer	Park Place Productions

A DEAL BETWEEN Sony and ESPN resulted in a bunch of officially licensed ESPN sports games in 1994. Only Baseball Tonight (the first to be released) made it to Europe. It's got the official MLB licence – meaning all the official team names and logos are present – but doesn't have the MLBPA licence, which means players are represented only by their numbers, not their names. It's got a unique visual style: practically the entire game is played as if it were shot with a single camera behind home plate. While this gives the game an interesting feel, the tight perspective does make it quite difficult to catch anything that's hit to the outfield. ESPN host Chris Berman appears before each game to give his analysis, and commentator Dan Patrick calls the plays. ■

FACT

Adverts for pizza chain Little Caesars can be seen in the game as part of a promotional tie-in. Little Caesars restaurants sold the game at launch and offered a mail-in deal for a VHS tape called ESPN Best of Sports.

ESPN NATIONAL HOCKEY NIGHT

Year	1994
Publisher	Sony Imagesoft
Developer	Sony Imagesoft

SONY'S DEAL WITH ESPN extended to a video game based on its popular ice hockey show. As with Baseball Tonight, the game features the full NHL licence – so the Toronto Maple Leafs, Detroit Red Wings, the newly formed Anaheim Ducks and every other team had their official name and uniform – but not the NHLPA licence, meaning once again players could be identified by number only. It also follows Baseball Tonight's lead by including the actual host from the show: in this case, Bill Clement turns up to break down the teams' stats. While the game defaults to a horizontal TV-style camera, you can choose to switch to a vertical viewpoint to make it look more like EA's hockey games: a fairly unique option for its time. ■

FACT

National Hockey Night started on NBC in 1992 and ran until the infamous 'NHL lockout', which meant there was no 2004–05 season. When hockey returned the following season, the Outdoor Life Network (now NBCSN) got the rights instead.

ESPN SPEED WORLD

Year	1994
Publisher	Sony Imagesoft
Developer	Sony Imagesoft

BASEBALL? TICK. ICE hockey? Tick. But what about NASCAR? Step forward Speed World, based on the ESPN show that ran from 1979 to 2006. While the show covered all manner of motorsports including CART, F1 and NHRA drag racing, the focus here is on stock-car racing. Although it doesn't have the official NASCAR licence, its 15-race season mode is based on the NASCAR circuits of that time. Some of the tracks have been renamed too for licensing reasons, meaning the likes of Daytona, Talladega and Sears Point are now Florida, Alabama and Oregon respectively. Hosting duties this time go to Dr Jerry Punch, who appears before each race in a well-animated screen that almost looks like actual video if you squint a bit. ■

FACT

ESPN Speed World has four different control configurations to choose from, though the third and fourth are bizarre: presumably designed for left-handed gamers, they involve holding the SNES controller upside down.

ESPN SUNDAY NIGHT NFL

Year	1994
Publisher	Sony Imagesoft
Developer	Absolute Entertainment

YOU CAN'T HAVE a baseball game and an ice hockey game without American football getting in on the action too, and sure enough this one's based on ESPN's *Sunday Night Football* show (which started in 1987 and ended on New Year's Day in 2006, when ESPN decided it wanted the rights to *Monday Night Football* instead). If you've already read about the other ESPN sports games you should probably know the drill by now: you've got the full NFL licence here to ensure that all teams and logos are present, but once again the lack of an NFLPA licence means we're looking at numbers instead of names. Not satisfied with simply appearing in ESPN Baseball Tonight, Chris Berman turns up for pre-game analysis here too. ■

FACT

If you're wondering why there wasn't an ESPN basketball game, there actually was. ESPN NBA Hangtime '95 was also handled by Sony Imagesoft but was only released on the Sega CD. That'll need to wait for the Mega Drive Encyclopedia.

E.V.O. SEARCH FOR EDEN

Year	1993
Publisher	Enix
Developer	Almanac

SOME GAMES HAVE a plot that spans a lengthy period of time, but E.V.O. probably has them all beat, given that it takes place over the course of a billion years. Initially starting off as a fish in the year 500,000,000 BC, the aim is to swim around, fighting other fish and eating their meat. This gives you experience points that can then be spent on evolving different body parts like your jaws, fins and so on. As you progress through each stage you'll eventually travel through various ages and evolve into other creatures: an early land-walker in 300,000,000 BC, a reptile during the age of dinosaurs, a mammal during the ice age, and eventually a human. ■

FACT

E.V.O. is based on a Japan-only game called 4.6 Billion Year Story: The Theory of Evolution, which was released on the NEC PC-9801 home computer in 1990 and has many of the same principles.

EXTRA INNINGS

Year	1992
Publisher	Sony Imagesoft
Developer	Sting Entertainment

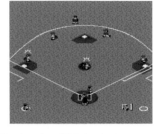

THIS EARLY SNES baseball game is an English translation of Tokyo-based studio Sting's Super Famicom title Hakunetsu Pro Yakyuu Ganba League. It features 12 fictional teams (with names like the Surfers, Condors, Valiants and um… Bunkers), split into six-team American and National leagues. As well as exhibition games and an all-star mode – where each league's best players join forces – there's also a Pennant Race mode, where you choose your team and five opponent teams, and play them a set number of times to see who can become the champion. If playing as the Rains or Metallics doesn't sound like your cup of tea, there are two Edit Teams which can be fully customised, letting you edit the names of all eight players and set their stats from a pool of points. ■

FACT

If you've got runners on first and third base, you can get an easy run by making each runner keep trying to steal and run back. The CPU always tries to put a runner out, so each time they throw to the guy on first you can move the guy on third closer to home.

EYE OF THE BEHOLDER

Year	1994
Publisher	Capcom
Developer	Capcom

EYE OF THE Beholder is a dungeon-crawling RPG set in the *Advanced Dungeons & Dragons* universe. Like the seminal Dungeon Crawler before it, the game is played with a first-person perspective and has you travelling through a dungeon beneath the city of Waterdeep in order to find out the source of the evil lurking there. You initially start with four heroes, who you can customise by entering their name and choosing their gender, appearance, race (human, elf, half-elf, dwarf, gnome or halfling), class (fighter, cleric, thief or a combination of two) and alignment (lawful, neutral or chaotic, and good, neutral or evil). Along the way you can come across other NPCs who you can recruit to join your team, increasing your party size to a maximum of six. ■

FACT

There were two more Eye of the Beholder games: The Legend of Darkmoor and Assault on Myth Drannor. Neither was given a console port.

F-ZERO

Year	1991
Publisher	Nintendo
Developer	Nintendo

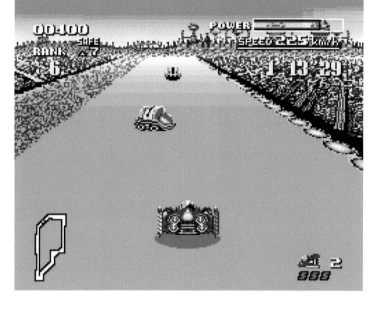

FEW LAUNCH GAMES have shown off a console's new features as well as F-Zero did. Releasing alongside the system in Japan, America and Europe, Nintendo's futuristic racer was the perfect showcase for the SNES's impressive new Mode 7 functionality. Mode 7 was a new graphical effect that allowed developers to take a background layer and scale and rotate it smoothly and quickly. With F-Zero, Nintendo demonstrated one of the most useful ways Mode 7 could be used: to create pseudo-3D tracks in racing games. By taking a large background sprite – which serves as the track – and using Mode 7 to quickly rotate and slide it under the sprite of the player's car, the game gives the impression that you're racing on a 3D road (when in reality your car is static and you're actually controlling the road).

As the sole racing game at launch, F-Zero was the first title to show off this effect and it was considered mind-blowing at the time. Not only was Mode 7 heralded as a way to produce jaw-dropping 3D visuals that hadn't been seen before, the fact it also did this so quickly and smoothly was even more exciting.

It helped that the game itself was brilliant too. It's set in the year 2560, a time where intergalactic trade and intercultural relationships are the norm. Bored of their wealth, the billionaires who made their fortunes trading with other planets decide to fund a galactic-scale racing league, similar to the F1 races held centuries earlier, only held on massive tracks 300 feet in the air with hovering magnetic cars that can travel at speeds up to 478 km/h. Players can choose between four different racers – bounty hunter Captain Falcon, medical practitioner Dr Stewart, alien soldier-turned-hitman Pico and gang leader Samurai Goroh – each of whom has their own unique vehicle with varying acceleration, top speed and weight stats. The latter is more important here than it is in other racing games because many of F-Zero's tracks come with large jumps, and failure to land back on the track will result in your car immediately exploding and your race ending.

The game consists of three separate Grand Prix events – Knight League, Queen League and King League – each consisting of five different tracks. Unlike most other racing games, here you're given a target position (15th, 10th, 7th etc) for each lap and have to make sure you're in at least that position by the time the lap ends, otherwise your race is immediately over.

F-Zero's combination of high-octane racing and visual spectacle made it a huge hit among Nintendo fans, leading to a number of sequels spanning the Nintendo 64, GameCube and Game Boy Advance. While fans continue to be serviced with various cameos in other games (such as Captain Falcon starring in the Super Smash Bros games and a pair of F-Zero courses being added to Mario Kart 8), at the time of writing it's been 16 years since the last proper F-Zero game, meaning the wait for a sequel continues. ∎

FACT

The manual includes an eight-page comic giving Captain Falcon's backstory, which includes Dr Stewart saying: 'I shall win to honour beautiful women everywhere.' Come on doc, it's the twenty-first... um, twenty-sixth century.

The Race of the 26th Century!

F1 POLE POSITION

Year	1993
Publisher	Ubisoft
Developer	Human Entertainment

THE FIRST IN a pair of Formula 1 games developed in Japan by Human Entertainment and published in the west by Ubisoft. It has the official Formula 1 licence, which means all the racers and cars are official, with one exception: although Ayrton Senna was racing for Williams at the time, Sega had the exclusive rights to feature his image in video games. As a result, he's replaced here by Michael Andretti instead. All 16 tracks used in the official 1992 Formula One season are included here, and there's a wide variety of tuning options you can tinker with before each race to ensure your car behaves exactly how you want it to. If that all seems a bit too much, there's also an 'auto' option which recommends a setup for you. ∎

FACT

The Japanese version of the game (known as Human Grand Prix) not only includes Senna, but also has advertising for the likes of Camel and Marlboro. These tobacco sponsorships were removed for the western version.

F1 POLE POSITION 2

Year	1994
Publisher	Ubisoft
Developer	Human Entertainment

SINCE F1 POLE Position focused on the 1992 F1 season, you'd expect its sequel to be based on the 1993 season. In fact… nah, you're right. Once again all the official tracks, racers and manufacturers are present and accounted for, though once again Ayrton Senna doesn't appear (this time replaced by not only Michael Andretti but Mika Hakkinen too). The new Edit mode also lets you swap drivers into different teams, and even slot in one of three other drivers: Nigel Mansell, Satoru Nakajima or a custom character you can create yourself. This Edit mode actually goes to surprising degrees of detail in some areas: you can actually select different engine contracts for each manufacturer, so if you ever wanted the Ferrari team to use a Yamaha engine instead, you're in luck. ∎

FACT

The F1 Pole Position games were based on the Human Grand Prix series in Japan. Two more games (cleverly titled Human Grand Prix III and IV) were also released on the Super Famicom but didn't make it to the west.

F1 ROC: RACE OF CHAMPIONS

Year	1992
Publisher	SETA / Ocean
Developer	SETA

SETA'S TAKE ON Formula One was released in Europe under its original Japanese title, Exhaust Heat. It's based on the 1991 F1 season, but only loosely: while it includes all 16 circuits from that season, the order in which you race them is completely different (it appears that they've been rearranged to make the tracks get progressively harder, as the likes of Monaco and Suzuka appear near the end of the season). Although the Formula One logo on the box may suggest a fully licensed game, in reality there are only eight racers and their names are fake: Ayrton Senna becomes A. Seta, Nigel Mansell becomes N. J. Myden and so on. Like many similar racing games, F1 ROC uses Mode 7 to rotate its tracks. ∎

FACT

Although you can head into the pits in the game, the only reason is to repair your car so you don't lose so much money at the end of the race. There's no refuelling because mid-race refuelling was banned in F1 from 1983 until 1994.

F1 ROC II: RACE OF CHAMPIONS

Year	1994
Publisher	SETA
Developer	SETA

THE SEQUEL TO F1 ROC is substantially improved and has one of the most detailed career modes in a 'serious' 16-bit racing game. Rather than simply focusing on Formula One cars and the 16 circuits in an F1 season, ROC II starts players off in 'Group C' prototype cars and gives them eight original tracks to race on with the aim being to earn enough money to pay your R&D team to upgrade your vehicle. Eventually you then move on to Formula 3000 racing (with a new set of tracks) before finally reaching Formula One. Since each class of car has its own unique tracks, this means that whereas the original game had 16 circuits there are 32 on offer here. ∎

FACT

There are two hidden mini-games in ROC II. On the copyright screen, use the second controller to enter X, X, X, X, Y, Y, Y, Y, X, X for a block-breaking game and Y, Y, Y, Y, X, X for a Space Invaders style game.

F1 WORLD CHAMPIONSHIP EDITION

Year	1995
Publisher	Acclaim
Developer	Domark

JUST IN CASE you hadn't gotten all the Formula One racing out of your system by the time the SNES was coming to the end of its life, up popped Acclaim and Domark with this Europe-only affair. Based on the 1994 F1 championship season, F1 World Championship Edition is actually a sequel of sorts to the 1993 Mega Drive, Master System and Amiga game simply called F1 (which instead used a first-person, in-car viewpoint). Whereas F1 only contained 12 circuits, the World Championship Edition features all 16 circuits from the 1994 season, and almost all of the official drivers. The main exception is once again Ayrton Senna but not for licensing reasons this time: Senna tragically crashed and died three races into the 1994 season. ■

FACT

Domark's F1 games were based on Vroom, a 1991 Amiga racing game developed by French studio Lankhor. Domark got involved and secured the official F1 licence.

FAMILY DOG

Year	1993
Publisher	Malibu Games
Developer	Imagineering

IN CASE YOU aren't familiar with it, *Family Dog* was a very short-lived animated series that had a great deal of hype behind it – it was produced by Steven Spielberg and Tim Burton – but ultimately didn't even last a full season (only 10 of the 13 commissioned episodes aired). The video game tie-in didn't fare much better in terms of popularity, but in its defence it isn't exactly the worst game you'll ever play. Playing as Jonah, the titular pet, you have to make your way through a handful of stages set in your family home, a large dog pound complex and eventually the forest (with the odd fetch mini-game thrown in along the way). It isn't the longest game ever: you can beat it in about 15 minutes. ■

FACT

Tim Burton's involvement included the character design of the dog, which may go some way to explaining why it looks incredibly similar to the dog in his later animated movie *Frankenweenie*.

FACEBALL 2000

Year	1992
Publisher	Bullet-Proof Software
Developer	Xanth Software

DESCRIBED BY THE manual as 'the greatest virtual reality sport of the future', Faceball 2000 is a polygonal deathmatch game where you roam around a series of mazes shooting at avatars shaped like smiley faces. Originally an Atari ST game named MIDI Maze, the development team at Xanth decided to port it to the Game Boy as Faceball 2000 (where it supported up to 16 players!) then brought it to the SNES the following year. There are two main modes, Arena and CyberZone. Arena is a two-player battle mode, whereas CyberZone is the main single-player mode. It consists of 41 stages, and the aim is to shoot a set number of constantly spawning enemies, at which point an exit panel will appear to teleport you to the next stage. ■

FACT

The official term for your avatar in the game is a Holographically Assisted Physical Pattern Yielded For Active Computerized Embarkation, or HAPPYFACE for short.

FAMILY FEUD

Year	1993
Publisher	GameTek
Developer	Imagineering

GAMETEK WAS A publisher known for specialising in video game versions of popular gameshows, and the SNES era was no different. This 16-bit take on *Family Feud* (known as *Family Fortunes* in the UK) is based on the era when Ray Combs was the host, and includes the quick-fire Bullseye round that was introduced in 1992. As in the real show, players have to guess the most popular answers for surveys taken by 100 people. It isn't exactly the easiest game these days, partly due to inaccuracies ('Name a country that's an island' – England, 'Name something associated with Scotland' – Scotland Yard) but mainly because it's outdated: the top answer for the slightly questionable 'name a blonde bombshell of today' is Loni Anderson, bizarrely. ■

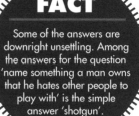

FACT

Some of the answers are downright unsettling. Among the answers for the question 'name something a man owns that he hates other people to play with' is the simple answer 'shotgun'.

FATAL FURY

Year	1993
Publisher	Takara
Developer	Nova

MUCH-LOVED JAPANESE STUDIO SNK is best known for its Neo Geo fighting games, and Fatal Fury was where it all began. It follows the story of Terry and Andy Bogard and their friend Joe Higashi as they enter a tournament called the King of Fighters in the hope of reaching and confronting Geese Howard, the crime boss who killed Terry and Andy's dad a decade earlier. Although the obvious conclusion to reach is that Fatal Fury is another Street Fighter II clone, in reality both the arcade version of SNK and Capcom's games were being developed at the same time. In fact, Fatal Fury was actually designed by Takashi Nishiyama, who created the original Street Fighter game before moving to SNK shortly afterwards. 'Fatal Fury was my Street Fighter II,' Nishiyama once said in an interview. The game was also notable for a few quirks that stood it apart from Street Fighter II, the most obvious of which being the ability to jump between the foreground and background, making it possible to dodge projectiles and perform attacks from one plane to the other. This SNES port, however, makes a number of changes, including ditching the two-plane system in favour of a standard linear fighting system. Also ditched are the Neo Geo version's two-on-one battles – cut because the SNES couldn't handle them – and its arm wrestling mini-game, though the latter is replaced with tyre-punching mini-game instead, if thwacking rubber is more your thing. And why wouldn't it be? ∎

> **FACT**
>
> Fatal Fury is known as Garou Densetsu: Shukumei no Tatakai in Japan, which translates to the far better Legend of the Hungry Wolf: The Battle of Destiny.

FATAL FURY 2

Year	1994
Publisher	Takara
Developer	Nova

THE SECOND FATAL Fury game improved on the original's foundations by adding more attack buttons: rather than a single punch and kick, players could now perform light and strong variations. Whereas the first game only had three characters to choose from (Terry, Andy and Joe), Fatal Fury 2 offers eight, including the debut of SNK's most popular female character Mai Shiranui. The SNES port is more of an authentic recreation than that of the original game: most notably, the ability to jump between two planes is present this time, meaning you can move the action from the foreground to the background. It's particularly entertaining in Jubei's stage, where you can hide behind large paper screens and burst through them into the foreground. ∎

> **FACT**
>
> Fatal Fury 2 was SNK's second '100-Mega-Shock' game, which meant the cartridge size clocked in at an enormous 100 Mb. The SNES version was on a 20Mb cart, which shows just how impressive the port is.

FATAL FURY SPECIAL

Year	1995
Publisher	Takara
Developer	Takara

FATAL FURY SPECIAL is to Fatal Fury 2 what Super Street Fighter II is to Street Fighter II. Rather than an outright sequel, it's an enhanced version of Fatal Fury 2 with a bunch of new features designed to make it the definitive Fatal Fury game (at the time, at least). Whereas the main version includes eight playable characters, that number doubles to 16 in Fatal Fury Special: the standard eight, the four previously unplayable boss fighters, three returning characters from the first Fatal Fury, and a guest appearance by Ryo Sakazaki, the main hero from Art of Fighting. A new combo system has been added too, allowing players to string together moves to do extra damage to their opponent. Easily the best Fatal Fury game on SNES. ∎

> **FACT**
>
> There were three anime movies about Fatal Fury. They were called Fatal Fury: Legend of the Hungry Wolf, Fatal Fury 2: The New Battle and Fatal Fury: The Motion Picture.

FIFA INTERNATIONAL SOCCER

Year	1994
Publisher	Electronic Arts
Developer	Extended Play Productions

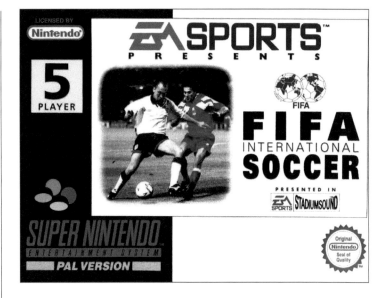

THE WORLD OF soccer games was very different in the early 1990s. Although a number of studios had tried their hand at making 'realistic' interpretations of football, almost all of them were reviewed negatively: the relative lack of power in the 8-bit and 16-bit days made it harder to create a nuanced passing, shooting and defending system, let alone an AI capable of behaving like a real football team. It was widely believed, then, that the best football games around were 'arcade' style efforts that threw realism to the wayside, ditching tactics and teamwork in favour of big looping shots, extreme slide tackles and laser-sharp passing. Sensible Soccer, Nintendo World Cup, SNK's Super Sidekicks and the like were heralded as the best football games, and anyone seeking something more realistic could… well, just watch the real thing on TV. Step forward Electronic Arts, with a game that would change this perception forever.

Originally released for the Sega Mega Drive / Genesis, FIFA International Soccer was an attempt to provide a game that played more like real football than anything that had come before it. Its unique isometric viewpoint added a welcome depth, making it easier for players to judge passes not only up and down the pitch, but to the wings too. Rather than sticking the ball to players' feet and allowing them to make pinpoint passes, players were able to knock the ball ahead of them, prod it out of opponents' legs while they dribbled past and generally create situations that felt less scripted and more organic. Arcade-like elements were still present, like long-range shots, but the fact the build-up was more realistic meant that such ridiculous goals felt like an accomplishment rather than the norm. And even though the 30 international teams on offer here all have fake player names, the fact that each player has their own internal stats means the likes of Joe Della-Savia, H. Van Smeiter and Janco Tianno became well-loved names among fans of the game (incidentally, Janco Tianno is named after Jan Tian, the game's designer, so it's little wonder the guy's got a hell of a right foot on him).

Given that these days FIFA is EA's biggest money-spinner by a country mile – the microtransactions in its Ultimate Team mode alone are said to generate over $800 million a year – it may be somewhat surprising to learn that the publisher originally had no interest in making a football game in the first place. Or maybe not, given that EA is based in the US. Only a promise from a UK-based senior exec that the game would sell at least 300,000 copies convinced the San Francisco-based bigwigs to start development, under the working title Team USA Soccer (it's a good job football's governing body agreed to a liccnsing deal). Ultimately, the promise turned out to be a conservative estimate: the original FIFA International Soccer went on to sell half a million copies. ∎

FACT

While designer Jan Tian was visiting his ill father in his native China, he thought of a solution to make the game's players position themselves properly. He had to implement it quickly but all flights back to EA were booked, so he got a plane ticket by bribing airport staff.

FIFA SOCCER 96

Year	1995
Publisher	Electronic Arts
Developer	Extended Play Productions

BY THE TIME the port of the first FIFA eventually made it to the SNES, EA was already gearing up to release a sequel called FIFA 95 for the Mega Drive / Genesis. Rather than knock out a SNES port of FIFA 95 mere months after the first game EA decided to hold fire, skip FIFA 95 on the SNES and bring both systems in line with each other for the next game, FIFA 96. While the isometric viewpoint remained and general gameplay felt similar, FIFA 96's biggest change was the addition of 11 club leagues from around the world. Players could take part in league and cup competitions for the American, Brazilian, English, French, German, Italian, Dutch, Scottish, Spanish, Swedish and… um, Malaysian leagues, each featuring real player names for the first time in FIFA. ∎

FACT

FIFA 96 was also the first game in the series to launch on the PlayStation and Saturn. While FIFA 96 remained similar on the SNES and Mega Drive, the CD-based versions featured brand new polygonal graphics using tech that EA had branded Virtual Stadium.

FIFA 97

Year	1996
Publisher	Electronic Arts
Developer	Electronic Arts

BY THE TIME FIFA 97 came around, EA's focus was very much trained on the next-gen, polygonal versions of the game on PlayStation, Saturn and PC. Still wishing to support the 16-bit systems, though, it committed to a version of FIFA 97 on SNES and Mega Drive (subtitled the Gold Edition on the title screen) that continued to use the previous year's engine but updated the player names to reflect the latest transfers. More exciting, though, is the fact that EA also decided to carry over the new mode that was making its debut in the next-gen versions too: the ability to play indoor football. The same 11 club leagues from the last game are still present (you're in luck, Malaysian league fans), but the indoor mode gives FIFA 97 a welcome freshness. ∎

FACT

John Motson, the commentator in the early CD-based FIFA games, recorded a hidden dance track for the PlayStation version of FIFA 97 which included him saying 'we've got some funky stuff in the house' and 'that is the phattest bottom end I've ever heard'.

FIFA: ROAD TO WORLD CUP 98

Year	1997
Publisher	Electronic Arts
Developer	Electronic Arts

BY THIS POINT nobody would have taken issue with EA drawing a line under SNES support and concentrating solely on the PlayStation generation, but it had one more 16-bit FIFA in its locker and it was a doozy. While indoor football was ditched for FIFA 98, a far more impressive mode named Road to the World Cup was added in its place. This is a lengthy tournament mode where you pick any country and try to qualify them for the upcoming 1998 FIFA World Cup. And when I say any country, I mean it: there are no fewer than 172 nations to choose from here, meaning those dreams of winning the World Cup as the Democratic Republic of the Congo can finally be realised. ∎

FACT

The well-known 'EA Sports, it's in the game' intro that opens most EA Sports titles used to be longer. Early magazine ads for EA Sports games used the full slogan: 'If it's in the game, it's in the game.'

FIGHTER'S HISTORY

Year	1994
Publisher	Data East
Developer	Data East

AS IS ALREADY obvious if you've been reading this book in order, the release of Street Fighter II inspired countless other developers to have their own go at making a one-on-one fighting game. While most of these games took at least some influence from Street Fighter II, Fighter's History was the only one that was 'influenced' so much that Capcom took its publisher Data East to court. In Capcom's defence, it's fairly blatant, from the flame-based logo to the Ryu-style martial artist (whose moves are similar right down to his double-kick when you press Forward and Strong Kick), to even the specific shade of blue that appears in the background in the 'smack talk' screen after each fight. It's a fun little fighter, mind you. ∎

FACT

Capcom lost the court case after a judge claimed that Fighter's History's alleged infringements were 'scenes a faire' which means they were things that almost had to be in a fighting game and would have been hard to avoid.

FINAL FANTASY II

Year	1991
Publisher	Square
Developer	Square

BEAR WITH ME, because this is a tiny bit confusing. The relative success of the original NES Final Fantasy in North America was enough to convince Square that it should probably keep translating the series for western audiences. The problem was, by the time it realised this, the NES was already coming to the end of its life and the SNES was on its way, meaning Square had a dilemma: did it take Final Fantasy II and III – released on the Famicom in Japan – and translate and port them to a nearly dead system, or did it skip ahead to Final Fantasy IV, in development for the 16-bit Super Famicom? Given that each Final Fantasy game is a standalone story, it opted to go for the latter, meaning the Final Fantasy II you see on this page is actually Final Fantasy IV as we know it today. Look, just go with it.

The game follows Cecil Harvey, a dark knight who captains a special air force called the Red Barons. After returning from a mission to attack a city and steal its water crystal, Cecil – feeling guilty about the innocent lives ruined – asks the king what his intentions are. Insulted by the implication that he's morally dodgy, the king strips Cecil of his rank and sends him off on a quest to hunt a summoned monster. When he realises the king's new mission was actually designed to trick Cecil into bombing another village, he forms an alliance of warriors to take the king down.

FACT

This was actually supposed to be the fifth Final Fantasy game. Square was working on a fourth Famicom title that was to be called Final Fantasy IV, but decided to abandon it when it was around 80 per cent complete.

Although much-loved for its story, Final Fantasy II/IV was more important for introducing Active Time Battle, a new battle system designed to make turn-based combat more interactive and less formulaic. Prior to Active Time Battle, most turn-based RPGs had you selecting all the moves for each character in your party at the same time, then watching the whole thing play out (with heroes' and enemies' speed stats determining the order in which they took their turn). Active Time Battle changes all this by assigning each character and enemy their own time gauge that gradually fills up (again, the speed stat determines how quickly this happens). When one of your characters gets a full gauge, you then get to choose their next move in real-time, while all the other gauges continue to rise. It's a more exciting way of taking part in battles, because the aim is to set each command quickly enough so you can pull it off before the enemy's own gauge fills up and it gets an attack in first.

Final Fantasy II/IV continues to be heralded for its story to this day, to the extent that it was even given its own sequel in 2008: something rare for the Final Fantasy series. Final Fantasy IV: The After Years was set 17 years later and focuses on Cecil's son as he and most of the original game's characters investigate the reappearance of a mysterious second moon. ∎

FINAL FANTASY III

Year	1994
Publisher	Square
Developer	Square

NOT FULLY CONTENT with messing up the Final Fantasy numbering system in the west, Square decided that Final Fantasy V wasn't going to get an English-language release either. After localisation began, it was soon decided that the game was too difficult and not accessible enough for western audiences, and so plans were scrapped. Instead, Final Fantasy VI was the next game to make it to North America, under the new title of Final Fantasy III. And you thought the *Rambo* films had confusing names.

Set in a steampunk planet known simply as the World of Balance – one with a southern hemisphere ruled by the evil Gestahl Empire and opposed by the rebellious Returners group – Final Fantasy III/VI offers one of the most complex plots in the series' history, and also offers 14 main playable characters, more than any other Final Fantasy before or since. These aren't just an arbitrary selection of

> **FACT**
>
> Although Square chose not to release Final Fantasy V in the west, it did at least try a couple of times first. At one point it toyed with the idea of releasing the game as Final Fantasy Extreme.

characters who all serve more or less the same purpose but just offer different abilities: each one has their own backstory which the game explores in impressive detail.

It could be argued that Final Fantasy III/VI is perhaps too overwhelming for many gamers, and that by creating an epic story that gives noteworthy time to each of its numerous protagonists Square made a game that offers so much information it's hard to take it all in. Those up for the challenge of sticking with its lengthy and detailed plot, however, will find one of the most story-rich games ever released, past or present. ■

FINAL FANTASY MYSTIC QUEST

Year	1992
Publisher	Square
Developer	Square

DESIGNED TO BE a sort of beginner's version of Final Fantasy, this spin-off does away with some of the series' more complicated elements, resulting in a more streamlined game that's an ideal starting point for those who may be keen to get into the RPG genre but are a bit intimidated by its depth. The plot is far less complex than in other Final Fantasy games too: playing as a young chap called Benjamin, you have to retrieve four stolen crystals to stop the world being destroyed.

Mystic Quest scraps a number of RPG staples in favour of more accessible alternatives: instead of having save points, you can save whenever you want. Instead of aimlessly exploring a massive world map, you instead travel between specific areas on the map represented by icons. Instead of random battles, all enemies are seen on-screen.

> **FACT**
>
> Square had already repurposed a bunch of Game Boy RPGs as Final Fantasy spin-offs: the first three games in the SaGa series were renamed Final Fantasy Legend I, II and III in the west. Mystic Quest was always designed to be a Final Fantasy game, though.

Instead of endless grinding, the world map has a series of 'Battlefields', which offer 10 separate battles and reward the player with loads of XP, gold or other important items. The main exploration is slightly more action-oriented too: although it's never quite Zelda, you can still use various skills that wouldn't be seen in a typical turn-based RPG's overworld, such as the ability to cut down trees, blow up doors with bombs and use a grappling hook. If you've always wanted to play a 16-bit RPG but have been worried about how hard they are to initially get into, this is the perfect gateway game to get you used to the genre's general pace and structure. ■

FINAL FIGHT

Year	1991
Publisher	Capcom
Developer	Capcom

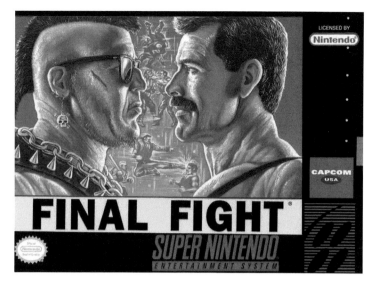

THERE WAS A time when Metro City was one of the most dangerous areas in America. The crime rates were off the charts, gang warfare was rife… it was basically Glasgow in the 1970s. That all changed when former pro wrestler Mike Haggar become the mayor and cleaned up Metro City, much to the delight of all. All, that is, except the Mad Gear gang, who have decided that they quite fancy the idea of continuing to terrorise the city, thanks very much. After failing to bribe Haggar to turn a blind eye to their shenanigans, the Mad Gear kidnap his daughter Jessica, which prompts the big man to head out into the streets, wrestling gear on, looking for a rumble (which is basically like modern day Glasgow).

Your arcade wasn't really an arcade in the early '90s if it didn't have a Final Fight machine: along with Double Dragon (and later Streets of Rage) it's one of the most important and much-loved examples of the beat 'em up genre. Taking such a popular coin-op game and porting it to the SNES was a no-brainer, but that's not to say it was an entirely smooth process: although the SNES was undoubtedly more powerful than any other console Capcom had worked on to date, it still had significantly less oomph than Capcom's CP System arcade hardware. As a result, a number of concessions had to be made in order to make the SNES port of Final Fight a reality.

Some of these changes were relatively minor, like the fact that the SNES version didn't show most of the transition animations between each stage. Beat the initial street stage, for example, and when you reach the subway stairs at the end your character won't go down them like they do in the arcade version. Many changes had more of an effect, however: while the arcade version occasionally had you fighting up to 10 enemies at once, the SNES couldn't handle anything like that number and instead you never really came up against more than a few at a time. This also led to the removal of co-op multiplayer, which was a much-loved feature of the arcade game: it's a strictly solo affair on the SNES. There's also an entire level missing here. The most controversial move, however, was the removal of one of the three playable characters. While the arcade version let you choose between Haggar, Cody (Jessica's boyfriend) and Guy (Cody's pal), the SNES version ditches Guy altogether, leaving the player with just two characters to choose from. This naturally upset the Guy fans: all six of them.

It's a testament to the core game's quality, though, that despite removing the multiplayer, a whole stage, a third of the roster and other various bits and pieces, what's left is still a hugely playable beat 'em up. The SNES version of Final Fight may have been far from an arcade perfect port, but it retained the essence of its source material and remained a popular game as a result. ■

FACT

The western SNES version of Final Fight was heavily censored. Female enemies Roxy and Poison were replaced with men, darker skinned enemies were given lighter skin and the beer and whisky health pick-ups were replaced with rootbeer and vitamins.

FINAL FIGHT 2

Year	1993
Publisher	Capcom
Developer	Capcom

THE MAD GEAR gang are back, and now they've gone global. This time they've kidnapped Guy's fiancée Rena (which must be confusing for SNES players who didn't get to play as Guy last time) and her dad. With Cody and Guy off on holiday, Haggar teams up with two new characters: Rena's ninjutsu-practising sister Maki and Haggar's sword-wielding friend Carlos. Since Final Fight 2 is unique to the SNES and not based on an arcade game, Capcom was able to build it around the SNES hardware and bring back some of the features it had to remove from its predecessor, like two-player co-op. This aside it plays much like the first Final Fight, except that its six stages are now based in different countries around the world instead of various Metro City districts. ∎

FACT

The game's first stage is set in Hong Kong. If you look closely at one point you can see Chun-Li from Street Fighter eating noodles at a restaurant in the background.

FINAL FIGHT 3

Year	1995
Publisher	Capcom
Developer	Capcom

A NEW GANG called the Skull Cross has started a massive riot in Metro City, so Haggar and Guy team up with new characters Lucia (a detective) and Dean (a mysterious street fighter) to head out into the streets to stop it. Unlike the second game, Final Fight 3 does actually make notable changes to the game. Players can now dash, and can also build a Super Street Fighter II Turbo style super gauge to pull off a special move. Some stages now have multiple routes, meaning you can access different areas for a change of scenery. There's also the interesting option to play a co-op game with a CPU partner, which is handy for those who want the two-player experience but don't have a chum nearby. ∎

FACT

Potentially left in by mistake, the European version of Final Fight 3 shows a full debug menu if you hold down Select during the Capcom logo. Options include a level select and being able to kill every enemy on-screen by pressing X.

FINAL FIGHT GUY

Year	1994
Publisher	Capcom
Developer	Capcom

THOSE GUY FANS were really upset about his removal from the SNES version of Final Fight, so Capcom threw them a bone with this tweaked alternative (which was initially only available to rent from Blockbuster Video but then got a limited release). As the title suggests, Guy is indeed a playable character this time around, snazzy orange suit and all. There's just one problem: it's still just a modified version of the original SNES port, which means all the technical issues of that initial release remain here. There's still no two-player mode and, just as importantly, it can still only support two playable characters. That means in order to keep Guy fans happy, Capcom had to remove Cody from this version instead. Swings and roundabouts. ∎

FACT

The intro text has been changed to explain Cody's absence: he'd been training with Guy in Japan to get ready to fight the Mad Gear gang, but Guy went home early.

THE FIREMEN

Year	1994
Publisher	Human Entertainment
Developer	Human Entertainment

OF ALL THE SNES games that were released in Europe but not North America, The Firemen is probably the most entertaining. Set in the year 2010, the game revolves around a fire that breaks out during a Christmas party at a chemical facility. Playing as fireman Pete Grey (and accompanied by a CPU partner named Daniel McClean), you have to make your way through the building's various floors, using your hose and water bombs to put out the fire. Along the way you rescue trapped workers to regain health, all while communicating regularly on your radio with Winona, your assistant at the fire station. Although The Firemen is a short game, it's an impressive one that tells a fun story and keeps players' interest until the credits roll. ∎

I'm getting a life reading on my detector.

FACT

The Firemen got a Japan-only sequel for the PlayStation called The Firemen 2: Pete & Danny. This time the pair have to put out a massive fire at a theme park on Christmas Eve.

FIREPOWER 2000

Year	1992
Publisher	Sunsoft
Developer	Sales Curve Interactive

 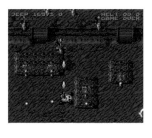

THIS IS KNOWN as Super SWIV in Europe, which is a more logical title given that it's a sequel to UK developer Sales Curve's SWIV (which itself was a sequel to Tecmo's Silkworm). It's a top-down shoot 'em up where the main gimmick is the choice to play as either a helicopter or a jeep. Naturally, each has their own strengths and weaknesses: the helicopter is faster and can happily fly over any ground obstacles, but it can only fire upwards. The jeep, meanwhile, can fire in all directions and can pass under flying enemies without taking damage, but you have to navigate it around debris on the ground. If you want the best of both worlds, there's a two-player co-op mode where you each take a different vehicle. ■

FACT

A fourth and final SWIV game called SWIV 3D was released on PC in 1996. It was polygonal and was set to be ported to the PlayStation after Interplay bought the rights, but the PS version never materialised.

FIRESTRIKER

Year	1994
Publisher	DTMC
Developer	Axes Art Amuse

THIS CURIOUS MIX of action RPG and bat-and-ball games like Arkanoid has you playing as Slader, a Firestriker who has the ability to control the Trialight, a ball of fire that can be thwacked at enemies. The aim is to progress through four kingdoms, whacking the Trialight against blocks and enemies along the way, as you try to kill the four boss monsters summoned by an evil archmage. This isn't a solo journey: as well as being able to recruit a few more Firestrikers later in the game, you're also accompanied by a nameless wizard who stays at the bottom of the screen. This wizard acts as a last resort: if you miss the Trialight you can move him left and right with the shoulder buttons to try and stop it. ■

FACT

Firestriker has a four-player mode that splits players into two teams. The aim is to hit the Trialight into your opponent's goal.

FIRST SAMURAI

Year	1993
Publisher	Kemco
Developer	Kemco

ORIGINALLY DEVELOPED IN 1991 for the Amiga and Atari ST home computers by London-based studio Vivid Image, First Samurai was ported to the SNES by Kemco. Players control the titular First Samurai as he hunts down the Demon King, seeking vengeance for the death of his sensei. Here's the twist: the Demon King has travelled to the future, so the First Samurai has to learn magic from a Wizard Mage to get there too. This is a fairly entertaining action platformer, which comes with a number of off-puttingly cheesy audio samples (such as the hero shouting 'OH NO, MY SWORD' every time you lose your blade). While the game lost a number of the stages from the computer version and was censored fairly heavily, it still retained much of what made the game a favourite among Amiga owners. ■

FACT

A sequel called Second Samurai launched on the Amiga and Mega Drive in 1994, and saw the player travelling not only to the future, but to prehistoric times too.

FLASHBACK

Year	1994
Publisher	US Gold
Developer	Delphine

KNOWN BY THE fuller title Flashback: The Quest for Identity in North America, this cinematic action platformer is often associated with Delphine's previous title Another World (aka Out of This World), even though the two are actually unrelated. Set in the year 2140, you play as a ginger chap called Conrad Hart who's lost his memory. After being pursued by a bunch of mutants and crash-landing his hoverbike in a jungle, he finds a holocube that projects a recording of himself telling him to head to New Washington. So begins a beautifully animated adventure, but one with a 'realistic' control scheme that takes some getting used to: running and jumping in particular are strictly tied to the character's momentum-based animation, similar to the first Prince of Persia. ■

FACT

Although Flashback isn't a sequel to Another World, there is a proper sequel to Flashback. Fade to Black launched on PC and PlayStation in 1995 and was a third-person action adventure game.

THE FLINTSTONES

Year	1995
Publisher	Ocean Software
Developer	Ocean Software

BASED ON THE live-action Universal Pictures film of the same name, The Flintstones has you playing as Fred (represented by a decent likeness of John Goodman) as he tries to rescue Pebbles and Bam-Bam from his company's evil vice-president, Cliff Vandercave (who just about looks like Kyle MacLachlan if you squint a bit). You actually rescue the kids fairly early on in the game, but Vandercave isn't done, and over the course of the game's cutscenes he goes on to kidnap Barney and Wilma too. The platforming is fairly straightforward, with more of an emphasis on combat than usual: as well as a club that Fred can use to bash enemies, you can also collect bowling balls and rocks to chuck at them. ■

FACT

A Sega Genesis version of the game was released exclusively on the Sega Channel download service in North America. It hasn't been seen again for 25 years.

THE FLINTSTONES: THE TREASURE OF SIERRA MADROCK

Year	1994
Publisher	Taito
Developer	Taito

THE GRAND POOBAH is retiring from the Royal Order of Water Buffaloes, and decides to hold a contest to pick a replacement: whoever can find the Treasure of Sierra Madrock first will be the new head honcho. Based on the animated series this time (as opposed to the movie), this offers an odd take on the platforming genre, in that the world map plays like a board game, where you roll a dice and then move Fred or Barney (you alternate between them) to whatever stage they land on. It's usually a platformer stage but you may also get a shop or a mini-game (such as a race against another Water Buffalo member). If Fred or Barney land on Wilma or Betty respectively, they'll be dragged back a few spaces. ■

FACT

The title is a play on *The Treasure of the Sierra Madre*, a 1927 novel turned 1948 Humphrey Bogart movie which was notable for the line 'We don't need no badges, I don't have to show you any stinkin' badges'.

FOOTBALL FURY

Year	1993
Publisher	American Sammy
Developer	American Sammy

PROMOTED IN MAGAZINE ads as 'a football game with a difference: it's easy to learn', Football Fury is an arcade-style American football game that looks interesting but is very limited in terms of modes and features. There's a single playoffs mode where you choose one of the teams on offer and make your way to the final, and a two-player exhibition mode: that's about it, really. With no NFL licence, all the team names are fake, though they're still based on the actual cities that had NFL teams at the time: say hello to the Cleveland Bees, New York Titans, Phoenix Condors and such. The main innovation is the passing system, where a power bar appears that lets you set exactly how far your quarterback throws the ball. ■

FACT

As with most things in life, the Japanese name for Football Fury is much better. Over there it's known as Ultimate Football: Try Formation!

FOREMAN FOR REAL

Year	1995
Publisher	Acclaim
Developer	Software Creations

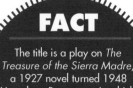

A SEQUEL OF sorts to Activision's George Foreman's KO Boxing. As the name implies, Foreman For Real attempts to create the most realistic boxing game to date by featuring digitised versions of each boxer, including George Foreman himself. The result is fairly impressive, though the boxers' arms are a little on the long side. Foreman is the only real boxer in the game: the other 19 available sluggers are all completely fictional (you'd hope so too, with terrible names like Savage Sammy Swift, Keith 'Hammerhead' Glascoe and Rob 'The Killer' Jones). As well as the ability to play as Big George in Exhibition and Tournament modes, there's also a Career mode where you choose one of the other no-names and fight your way through the rest to reach Foreman. ■

FACT

After retiring from boxing, Foreman lent his name to the George Foreman Grill. It's estimated that he's made at least $200 million from this endorsement, which is more than he ever earned boxing.

FRANK THOMAS BIG HURT BASEBALL

Year	1995
Publisher	Acclaim
Developer	Iguana Entertainment

IF YOU THINK the title's awkward, don't worry: it makes sense. The Big Hurt was the nickname given to Frank Thomas, a five-time MLB All-Star best known for his 15-year stint with the Chicago White Sox. Big Hurt Baseball sports the MLBPA licence but not the MLB one, meaning the player names are correct but the teams are simply city names (so just Toronto, Cleveland and so on). As well as the usual Exhibition, Season and Playoff modes, you can take part in a Home Run Derby and also a mode called Clutch Time, which gives you 16 different scenarios to try and win. Pitching is particularly detailed: you have a series of menus where you choose your pitch type, direction, height and speed before each throw. ∎

FACT

There was also a pinball machine called Frank Thomas' Big Hurt, produced in 1995 by Gottlieb. It can be found as a downloadable table in some versions of modern pinball game The Pinball Arcade.

FRANTIC FLEA

Year	1996
Publisher	GameTek
Developer	Häus Teknikka

THE INSIDEOS ARE a group of one-legged aliens who decide to travel to the planet Fleaworld and capture all the fleas living there as punishment for having not only two legs, but four arms as well. All the fleas, that is, except for Frantic, who now has to infiltrate the Insideos' mothership and rescue his fellow fleas. Oh, and he's activated a special device that makes him grow to the same height as the Insideos, which is useful for collecting his still-tiny pals. The aim is to collect enough fleas in each level to make an exit door open. The more you collect, the larger the trail of fleas behind you, and the more powerful your attacks become (because the fleas copy your movements). ∎

FACT

Despite the name, Häus Teknikka was actually based in the UK. Frantic Flea was its only video game before it moved onto CGI work: it created a range of idents for BBC 2 to celebrate the 10th anniversary of *Red Dwarf*.

FROGGER

Year	1998
Publisher	Majesco
Developer	Morning Star Multimedia

SOMETIMES THE GREATEST of battles can end with a whimper. Frogger was the last game released in North America for both the SNES and the Sega Genesis, bringing to an end the hard-fought 16-bit console war that lasted through most of the '90s. It's just a shame that this had to be both systems' swansong: it's an extremely lazy port of the arcade game that offers a straight recreation and not much more. In fact, rather than offering unique music and sound effects, Frogger just lifts the sound code from another publisher's SNES game, Ren & Stimpy: Buckaroo$. It's well-hidden but by using an Action Replay cheat cartridge you can access all the unused Ren & Stimpy music, which still remains on the cartridge. ∎

FACT

In 1998 Majesco did a deal with Hasbro to release a bunch of arcade titles on the SNES and Game Boy, of which Frogger was one. Hasbro released a completely different Frogger game on the PlayStation which, confusingly, has the same cover image as the SNES one.

FULL THROTTLE: ALL-AMERICAN RACING

Year	1994
Publisher	Cybersoft / GameTek
Developer	Gremlin Interactive

THIS MODE 7 racer would be relatively unremarkable were it not for the fact that it offers two very different types of vehicle to race on. For some of your races you take to the roads of America in a high-speed motorbike, whereas others have you zooming (well, moving at a fairly average speed) along rivers in a jet ski. Each of the game's tracks is based on a real-life American location, though there are generally used for background scenery rather than anything of note: the San Francisco track, for example, shows the Golden Gate Bridge in the distance but you never actually get anywhere near it. Oddly, Full Throttle only lets you choose between music and sound effects: it isn't possible to get both. ∎

FACT

The game was published in the US by Cybersoft, which was actually a subsidiary of GameTek focused on publishing those of its SNES games that weren't based on game shows.

FUN 'N GAMES

Year	1994
Publisher	Tradewest
Developer	Leland Interactive Media

THIS RELATIVELY RARE compilation game gives players four activities to choose from under the names Paint, Games, Music and Style. Paint is a basic art package, with various stamps and brush types (as well as the option to colour in some black-and-white images). Games consist of two basic mini-games: a Pac-Man clone starring a mouse and a first-person space combat game. Music is a simple music composer, where the player places notes on an octave and can choose between 15 different instruments. Finally, Style has you choosing clothes for a paper doll or mixing monsters' body parts. Although the game can be played with a standard SNES controller, it is clear that it was really designed with the SNES mouse in mind (particularly when it comes to freehand drawing). ■

FACT

Fun 'n Games was also released on the Sega Genesis, and included a third mini-game called Whack a Clown. You'll have to guess what it's about.

GEMFIRE

Year	1992
Publisher	Koei
Developer	Koei

KOEI IS GENERALLY best known for its strategy games based on real-life historic conflicts, but it has been known to dabble with pure fiction from time to time. Gemfire is a good example of this: it takes place in the fictional island of Ishmeria, where the daughter of a corrupt king has taken his magical crown Gemfire and scattered its six gems, which are all actually wizards (don't ask), across the land. Each gem/wizard now resides with one of six families: your aim is to choose one of these families and conquer the rest of Ishmeria, unifying it and putting an end to the king's reign of terror. The colourful plot aside, the rest of the game is pure Koei, with a number of different scenarios and typical turn-based strategy gameplay. ■

FACT

Gemfire is known as Super Royal Blood in Japan. It wa[s] popular enough to spawn [a] sequel called Royal Blood II, which was only released on PC.

GENGHIS KHAN II: CLAN OF THE GREY WOLF

Year	1993
Publisher	Koei
Developer	Koei

SPEAKING OF KOEI'S more historical-themed titles, Genghis Khan II is a sequel to the NES game Genghis Khan (as opposed to a game about his son, who I'm reliably informed wasn't called Genghis Khan II anyway). The game consists of four different scenarios: the first lets you play as either Temujin (who would become Genghis Khan) or one of three other rivals as you try to take over Mongolia. The other three are variations of a similar goal – take over the entire world, not just Mongolia – each set at a different time period. Here you aren't limited to Mongolian leaders: you can play as the likes of Philip II of France, Charles I of Sicily or Richard the Lionheart of England. ■

FACT

Although it's called Genghis Khan II, this is actually the third in the series. The first was the Japan-only Aoki Okami to Shiroki Mejika, which translates as Blue Wolves and White Does.

GEORGE FOREMAN'S KO BOXING

Year	1992
Publisher	Acclaim
Developer	Beam Software

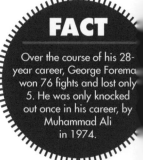

A FEW YEARS before Foreman For Real launched on the SNES, Acclaim released a slightly less real George Foreman game on the system (as well as for the NES and Mega Drive). Whereas For Real featured digitised boxers, KO Boxing goes for good old-fashioned sprite work, and shows the action from directly behind your boxer, rather than an over-the-shoulder viewpoint. This gives the game a look similar to that of Nintendo's Punch-Out!! series, though it doesn't play like it at all. Whereas Punch-Out!! is about finding an opponent's weakness and exploiting it, KO Boxing is more of a slugfest where each fighter simply tries to wear their opponent's energy down by flinging punches at each other non-stop. Not the most sophisticated boxing game, then. ■

FACT

Over the course of his 28-year career, George Forema[n] won 76 fights and lost only 5. He was only knocked out once in his career, by Muhammad Ali in 1974.

GHOUL PATROL

Year	1994
Publisher	JVC
Developer	LucasArts / Motion Pixel

THIS SNES-EXCLUSIVE SEQUEL to Zombies Ate My Neighbours offers similar monster-blasting action but this time the plot takes you to different time zones. Zeke and Julie, the heroes from the first game, visit a ghost exhibit at a library and accidentally summon a spirit which goes on to infect a number of history books there. You have to travel to each time period and kill the monsters there as you attempt to send the ghost back to his own book. These time periods include China during the Ming Dynasty, pirate skullduggery in the Caribbean and a castle from a nondescript medieval era. There are five weapons available, ranging from a fairly weak crossbow to a significantly more powerful homing plasma gun. ■

FACT

Although Ghoul Patrol was produced by LucasArts, the majority of development was actually handled by a Malaysian studio called Motion Pixel.

GOAL!

Year	1992
Publisher	Jaleco
Developer	Tose

SATISFIED WITH THE success of its two Goal! games on the NES, Jaleco decided to take the series 16-bit. Goal! (known as Super Goal! in Europe) offers just two modes: a one-off Exhibition match, or a Super Cup, which is a typical World Cup style tournament with groups of four followed by a knockout stage. There are 24 national teams in total to choose from, and you can select between four different formations: 4-3-3, 4-4-2, 3-5-2 and 'Sweeper' (which is basically 3-3-3 with an extra defender right at the back). Whereas both Goal! games on the NES use an isometric viewpoint, this SNES offering ditches those in favour of a more traditional side-on view. The collision detection and ball behaviour are questionable, though. ■

FACT

Here's a nerdy one for you: Goal! features both Scotland and England among its 24 teams, but the game's box instead shows the UK Union Jack flag, even though there's no UK team.

GODS

Year	1992
Publisher	Mindscape
Developer	Bitmap Brothers

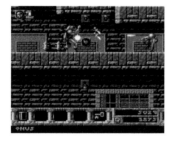

FOUR EVIL GUARDIANS have invaded the citadel of the gods. The gods say they'll reward any human who can stop them: step forward the game's nameless hero, who asks that for his reward he wants to be turned into a god too. Which is a bit of an awkward position to put them in, really. Gods was originally developed for the Amiga and Atari ST home computers before it was decided to bring the game to consoles too. At first glance it looks like your standard action platformer, but wading into each stage swinging away will only result in a swift death. Success here requires a more methodical pace, as you work your way through the oncoming enemies and figure out how to deal with the many traps facing you. ■

FACT

The EU cover art (which is the same as that on the home computer versions) was created by comic artist Simon Bisley. He was the inspiration for Simon Pegg's character Tim Bisley in cult TV sitcom *Spaced*.

GOOF TROOP

Year	1993
Publisher	Capcom
Developer	Capcom

RATHER THAN THE traditional platformer fare that cartoon licences tend to end up getting, Goof Troop is instead an adventure game with a Zelda-like viewpoint, in which everyone's favourite single father, Goofy, and his son Max explore Spoonerville Island. The pair have gone there on a fishing trip, but their plans have been spoiled by a pirate ship, which has kidnapped their neighbours Pete and PJ. It's up to either Goofy or Max – you get to choose who to control – to make their way to the ship by collecting various items to help solve the puzzles along the way. These include the likes of grappling hooks (to collect far away items), bells (to lure enemies towards traps) and boards to fill gaps in bridges. ■

FACT

Goof Troop was one of the first games designed by Shinji Mikami, who went on to direct the likes of Resident Evil, Dino Crisis, Resident Evil 4 and The Evil Within.

GP-1

Year | 1993
Publisher | Atlus
Developer | Atlus

THERE ARE OBVIOUSLY plenty of racing games on the SNES but not many of them focus on motorbikes. Atlus did its bit to correct this by releasing two bike-based racers, both similar in nature. The first lets you choose between six types of fictional bike – with names like MSR 500 and Cigavi – and race on 13 different courses spanning 12 countries (Spain gets two for some reason, though one of them is listed as just 'Europe' instead). You can either practice single races or take part in a Grand Prix style set-up where you qualify then race through each of the circuits in order as you attempt to finish with the most points. The game's handling is notably loose: players have to turn well in advance of corners. ■

FACT

Although GP-1 doesn't have any official licensing, the tracks are still based on real-life circuits. One of the Spain tracks, for example, has the same layout as Circuit de Catalunya.

GP-1: PART II

Year | 1994
Publisher | Atlus
Developer | Atlus

ATLUS' SECOND ATTEMPT at a motorcycle game actually made an effort to overhaul the engine entirely. Although both games make use of Mode 7 to rotate its courses, Part II makes the effect more noticeable by allowing you to see other parts of the track when a sharp turn would make these sections visible in real life. The number of circuits has also increased from 13 to 17, though bizarrely one of these new tracks is yet another Spanish one (simply called 'Mountain'). The GP mode is a little more detailed this time, too: now you can have rival racers who will challenge you to a bet before the race (though you don't have to take them up on it). Handling is improved too, which is nice. ■

FACT

The Japanese version (called GP-1 RS: Rapid Stream) has a slightly longer GP mode. It starts with four races in Japan before moving onto the normal 13-race world championship.

GRADIUS III

Year | 1991
Publisher | Konami
Developer | Konami

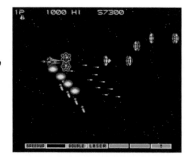

THE ONGOING EFFORTS to defeat the evil Bacterion Empire using a single spaceship called the Vic Viper continued with this third main entry in Konami's much-loved Gradius series. It's not an easy game, though the SNES port does at least let you continue when you die (the original arcade version was notorious for not offering continues). Players can choose from four set weapon configurations, or use the new Edit mode to choose which specific weapon upgrades they'd like to be able to earn. If the game isn't hard enough there's a cheat code to unlock a harder mode called Arcade mode, but you'll need to prove you're up to it first: you have to press the A button 16 times in one second to activate it(!). ■

FACT

In a sneaky twist, pausing the game and entering the famous Konami code actually causes your ship to self-destruct. Instead, you have to use the L and R buttons instead of Left and Right to get the real reward (a fully powered-up ship).

THE GREAT CIRCUS MYSTERY STARRING MICKEY & MINNIE

Year | 1994
Publisher | Capcom
Developer | Capcom

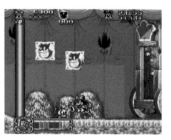

THE SECOND GAME in the Disney's Magical Quest trilogy (the first being Magical Quest, fittingly). Mickey and Minnie arrive at the circus for a day of frolics but instead they find an upset Goofy who tells them everyone in the circus has disappeared. Time to figure out what's going on. The Great Circus Mystery plays similarly to Magical Quest, with players – who can now choose to play as either Mickey or Minnie – able to don a variety of outfits and use their abilities. A sweeper outfit lets them suck enemies into a vacuum cleaner and spit them out as coins, a safari suit lets them climb walls and a cowboy outfit lets them jump higher and fire a cork gun at enemies. ■

FACT

The third Magical Quest game was released on the Super Famicom in Japan but didn't make it to the west. It didn't see an English-language release until it came to the Game Boy Advance in 2003.

THE GREAT WALDO SEARCH

Year	1993
Publisher	THQ
Developer	Radiance Software

QUITE POSSIBLY ONE of the shortest games ever made, The Great Waldo Search is based on the children's book of the same name (originally known as *Where's Wally? The Fantastic Journey* in the UK, where it was first released). The game consists of five stages, and in each you're tasked with finding just two things: Waldo and a scroll. Waldo's dog Woof is also hidden in each stage: finding him takes you to a brief mini-game where he flies a magic carpet collecting bones. Finish all five levels and the game's over: this can be done in a few minutes. There's also an Expert mode which stops the action occasionally to ask you to find something else (a red window, for example). ■

FACT

There have been a total of seven main Where's Wally / Waldo books, the most recent being *Where's Wally? The Incredible Paper Chase* in 2009.

GUNFORCE

Year	1992
Publisher	Irem
Developer	Bits Studios

THIS INTERESTING RUN 'n' gun game clearly takes its inspiration from Contra, and while it's certainly not as polished its easier difficulty may make it more appealing to those intimidated by Konami's notoriously hard game. The premise is similar: playing as a soldier from the elite world squadron known as GunForce, you're dropped onto an island and tasked with killing the hordes of enemy soldiers intent on destroying the earth. Along the way you can pick up various alternate weapons, ranging from a machine gun to a flamethrower and a bazooka. You'll also occasionally come across vehicles, like jeeps and helicopters, which you can ride through part of the stage: these control particularly janky, however, and they don't protect you in any way. ■

FACT

GunForce was also released in the arcades, but only in Japan. It got an arcade-only sequel (cleverly titled GunForce II), which did at least make it to North America.

HAGANE: THE FINAL CONFLICT

Year	1995
Publisher	Hudson Soft
Developer	CAProduction

AN INTERESTING ACTION platformer that borrows more than its fair share of ideas from Sega's Shinobi games. After the Fuma ninja clan was attacked and its holy grail stolen, only Hagane survived (albeit barely). A mysterious old man called Momochi salvages Hagane's brain and puts it in a cyborg's body, meaning that, yes, you get to play as a robot ninja. You're armed with four different types of weapon, which you can switch between at will: a sword, a grappling hook, grenades and shuriken throwing stars. Hagane is an extremely rare game in North America, where its release was limited. However, despite claims from some sources that it was exclusive to Blockbuster Video in the US, there's no actual evidence that this was the case. ■

FACT

CAProduction is a Japanese contract developer that regularly helps out with various projects. It had a hand in co-developing almost all of the Mario Party games.

HAL'S HOLE IN ONE GOLF

Year	1991
Publisher	HAL Laboratory
Developer	HAL Laboratory

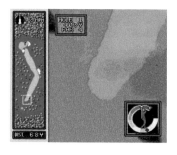

HOLE IN ONE Golf was the name of a series of golf titles HAL released on Japanese computers throughout the '80s. This SNES interpretation was the first to make it to the west, and it's a fun golf game if a little light on features. There's a single 18-hole course to play in a number of different modes: Stroke Play, Match Play, Tournament or a one-on-one match 'versus HAL' (which makes it sound like *2001: A Space Odyssey*). Each hole is introduced with a lovely Mode 7 flyby, though the actual gameplay is a strictly top down affair. If you sink a shot you're particularly proud of you can turn it into a 23-character password which can be entered later to watch a replay of it. ■

FACT

The Japanese version's called Jumbo Ozaki's Hole in One Golf. Jumbo Ozaki is Japan's most successful golfer: he featured in the world top 10 rankings for nearly 200 weeks.

HAMMERLOCK WRESTLING

Year	1994
Publisher	Jaleco
Developer	Jaleco

THIS TAKE ON professional wrestling offers an interesting visual style: the screen is split into three sections, with the actual gameplay taking place in the middle. The sections above and below it trigger manga-style cutscenes any time an action is performed (even something as simple as a punch or kick). While a very cool effect, this can initially be off-putting as the cutscene sections aren't locked and can often expand to show larger, more impressive art, shifting the actual game up or down the screen as a result. There are 12 fictional wrestlers to choose from, each with suitably terrible monikers including Baron Kaiser (who's clearly based on Hulk Hogan), Alpha Bozak, Sam Warhammer and possibly the worst name in video game history, Spud Marmoset. ■

FACT
The Japanese version of the game is called Tenryu Genichiro no Pro Wrestling Revolution. It includes Japanese wrestler Genichiro Tenryu and features branding from Japanese wrestling promotion Wrestle and Romance.

HANNA-BARBERA'S TURBO TOONS

Year	1994
Publisher	Entertainment International UK
Developer	Empire Interactive

AN INTERESTING TAKE on the racing genre that ditches cars in favour of Hanna-Barbera characters running around on foot instead. Players can choose from six different characters – Top Cat, Snagglepuss, Huckleberry Hound, Yogi Bear, Hong Kong Phooey and Quick Draw McGraw – and take part in 15 different tracks based on five different environments. It also features possibly the worst menu system seen in a game, right down to the fact that pressing the Start button on the title screen just takes you to a single race on a single track (the player has to instead press Select to get the main menu). Although Turbo Toons was planned for a North American release and was even rated by the ESRB, it ultimately only made it to European shores. ■

FACT
Turbo Toons began life as Cash Dash, a bespoke multiplayer game developed by Empire for use on the *Games World* TV show in the UK. Empire retained gameplay rights and adapted Cash Dash to make use of the Hanna-Barbera licence.

HARDBALL III

Year	1994
Publisher	Accolade
Developer	Accolade

THE HARDBALL GAMES are best known for appearing on home computers (and the Sega Genesis to an extent), but the third entry saw the series appear on Nintendo for the first and only time. Although it doesn't have the official MLB licence it does have the MLBPA one, meaning player names are real even if the teams and uniforms are generic. Possibly because of its home computer background, HardBall III offers some of the most extensive editing functionality in any 16-bit sports game: not only can you edit any player in the game, you can also edit team names, uniforms, even league and stadium names. There's also a logo editor in there, so if you aren't happy with the generic Toronto team you can rename them the Blue Jays and draw their actual branding in yourself. ■

FACT
There were six HardBall games in total, the last of which (HardBall 6, believe it or not) was the only one to feature polygonal graphics. All except the second and sixth game were released on the Sega Genesis.

HARLEY'S HUMONGOUS ADVENTURE

Year	1993
Publisher	Hi Tech Expressions
Developer	Visual Concepts

HARLEY'S A SCIENTIST who's perhaps gone a little too far with his latest experiment, a shrinking device. After a failed experiment in which he tried to shrink his rat, Harley accidentally shrunk himself instead and now has to make his way through his house and garden collecting the scattered parts of his broken machine. There's just one problem: all his previously failed mutation experiments are still hanging around, meaning he has to deal with a bunch of angry mutant bugs and fish. Even worse, the rat – which is still very much full size – is gathering weapons to teach Harley a lesson for trying to shrink it. The sprites in this quirky platformer are based on clay figures that have been digitised (similar to Goro in the original Mortal Kombat). ■

FACT

The game was originally funded by Electronic Arts, but eventually Hi Tech Expressions took over publishing duties. If you look closely at the box art you can still see the old 'EOA' logo on Harley's chest.

HARVEST MOON

Year	1997
Publisher	Natsume
Developer	Pack-In Video

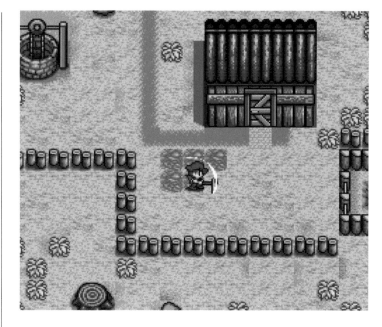

THESE DAYS THE idea of a farming simulator is fairly normal: the likes of Stardew Valley, Animal Crossing and (obviously) Farming Simulator give plenty of options for those gamers who crave a more slow-paced, cathartic time planting and sowing crops. Long before such agricultural entertainment became the norm, though, Harvest Moon brought it to an unsuspecting audience, kicking off a much-loved genre that continues to this day.

You play as Jack (the name can be changed), a young lad whose parents have decided to take a holiday together for two and a half years, and you're not invited (charming). They leave you at your grandfather's old farm, which is worse for wear: the land is filled with rocks and tree stumps, there isn't a single crop to be found and you don't have any animals. It's up to you to turn things around by growing crops, cleaning things up and turning the farm into a thriving business again, ultimately making something of your life… if you want to, that is.

The beauty of Harvest Moon is that there's no set path to success, and no specific objectives to meet. If you can't be bothered raising chickens and you'd rather concentrate on keeping your cows healthy and selling their milk for profit, you're more than welcome to do that. If you aren't interested in animals at all and just want to focus on growing a variety of crops from turnips to tomatoes, you can do that too. In fact,

FACT

Although there continue to be Harvest Moon games to this day, anything released from 2007 onwards is Harvest Moon by name only (since Natsume owns the title). The Story of Seasons series of games are believed to be the true successors to the pre-2007 games.

if you aren't even interested in the farm at all and would rather spend your time fishing up in the nearby mountains, that's a completely valid option too (though you may want to buy a fishing game instead if that's what you're into).

Then there's a completely separate metagame that's become one of the most loved features of Harvest Moon fans over the years: romance. There are a number of ladies in the nearby village who can be wooed and eventually wedded, and while the method used to attract them is perhaps a little off – you have to essentially walk into their house and read their diary to see what they like – the intention is good, at least. Probably. Eventually you're able to get married and then, should you so desire, have a child too.

All this freedom of choice eventually comes to a head, though, with the game's other main principle: you only get two and a half years to improve your farm or otherwise live your life however you see fit. After this, your parents will return and give you a score based on nine main criteria: money, marriage, children, the size of your house, the variety of crops being sold, number of cows and chickens, your relationship with your cows (steady on), farm development and befriending all five single women in town. Which is a bit rich when you consider they've been on a 30-month holiday sunning themselves while you've been sweating buckets digging up crops. ■

HEAD-ON SOCCER

Year	1995
Publisher	US Gold
Developer	US Gold

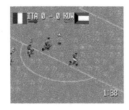

KNOWN AS FEVER Pitch Soccer in Europe, this arcade-style football game features 51 national teams from the obvious to the obscure (hello there Mali, Zambia and Kuwait), and offers Exhibition and Tournament modes. The main feature, though, is the star player system. Certain players will have stars above their head when you're controlling them, and pressing the A button will make them pull off a special move specific to them. This could be anything from the ability to jump tackles or hit extremely bendy shots, to the ability to turn the ball into an actual fireball and blast it into the net. Perhaps the sneakiest, though, is the diver: activate their skill at just the right time and they'll fall to the ground, potentially earning you a free kick or penalty. ■

FACT

If you live in Germany you may instead know this game as Mario Basler: Jetzt Geht's Los!, due to the presence of Werder Bremen winger Basler on the box. It means Here We Go!, if you're wondering.

HEBEREKE'S POPOITTO

Year	1995
Publisher	Sunsoft
Developer	Sunsoft

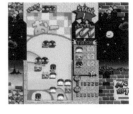

THE SECOND IN a pair of puzzle games released only in Japan and Europe and starring Sunsoft's mascot Hebe. Hebereke's Popoitto is a block-dropping game that looks similar to Puyo Puyo but acts more like Dr Mario instead. The aim is to drop coloured blobs in an attempt to line up four of the same colour, at which point they'll disappear. Each stage has a set of creatures called Poro-porous which are also colour-coded. If you can include them in your line they'll disappear too: the level is cleared when you get rid of all the Poro-porous (just like the viruses in Dr Mario). The twist, however, is that the Poro-porous have a habit of shuffling to the side every now and then, messing up your strategy. ■

FACT

The only game starring Hebe to ever make it to North America was Ufouria: The Saga, an NES title that was also Europe-only but came to the Wii Virtual Console in 2010.

HEBEREKE'S POPOON

Year	1994
Publisher	Sunsoft
Developer	Sunsoft

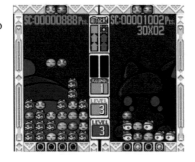

RELEASED BEFORE HEBEREKE'S Popoitto (thanks, alphabetical order), Hebereke's Popoon looks similar at first glance but has noticeably different rules and plays completely differently as a result. It's a lot closer to Puyo Puyo in terms of its physics: if you drop a piece sideways onto a single blob, the side hanging off the edge will split off and drop down. Although this is very Puyo-esque, players still have to form lines (rather than simply making the blobs touch), meaning it isn't quite a direct clone of Sega's puzzler. The game's main mode is a series of one-on-one battles against CPU opponents, each of whom has their own special abilities. They join your roster once they're defeated and can be selected for the next battle. ■

FACT

While many games have the classic Easy, Normal and Hard difficulty levels, Hebereke's Popoon goes a little off-beat and instead offers Octopus, Monkey, Amateur and Expert.

HIT THE ICE

Year	1993
Publisher	Taito
Developer	Taito

THIS ARCADE-STYLE ICE hockey game offers three-on-three action (well, two-on-two with goalies) and no rules whatsoever. There are six teams to choose from representing Toronto, Montreal, New York, LA, Chicago and Minneapolis and all of the players are completely fictional, though some have joke names based on real players (such as Wayne Greatman instead of Wayne Gretzky). Naturally, there are fights – which are played out in a basic one-on-one fighting game style – but they don't result in penalties: instead, the loser moves extremely slowly for a while. Hit the Ice was originally an arcade game, but something appeared to have been lost during the port to the SNES: what was a smooth, entertaining game before is a bit of a stuttery, flickering mess on Nintendo's console. ■

FACT

One of the Toronto players is named Tom Horyna: this is a reference to Tim Hortons, the much-loved coffee chain that started in Ontario in 1964. My Canadian wife made me mention this.

HOME ALONE

Year	1991
Publisher	THQ
Developer	Imagineering

THERE WERE NO fewer than six completely different games released to tie in with the hit children's movie *Home Alone*, all of which varied in quality from terrible to average. This SNES title is one of the better offerings, though it isn't actually based on the film itself. Instead, it's a sequel of sorts (before the actual sequel would arrive in cinemas a year later).

Following their stint behind bars after trying to rob Kevin McAllister's house in the movie, the Wet Bandits have done their time and are free men again. After arranging for Kevin's parents to be out of the house (it's not clear how they managed this), they decide to get revenge on Kevin by breaking into the massive McAllister house once again for a rematch. It's up to Kevin to round up all his family's valuables by searching around the house, then dumping them down the laundry chute into the basement, where a large vault is conveniently located.

FACT

Imagineering also developed the Game Boy version of Home Alone, which is still a separate game but the closest to the SNES version since it also involves finding valuables and sending them down the laundry chute.

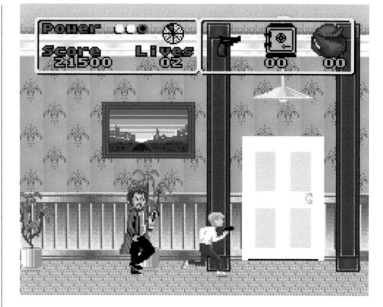

Along the way he has to avoid not only the Wet Bandits, but a bunch of other 'new Wet Bandit recruits', who are just generic-looking gangsters. Either the McAllisters have moved to a palace since the events of the movie or the game has vastly overestimated the size of their home: as well as four bedrooms and two bathrooms players also explore a dining room, lounge, kitchen, games room, rec room, second lounge, spare room, baby's room and gym (as well as the basement, which is swarming with killer rats and bats, because video games). ∎

HOME ALONE 2: LOST IN NEW YORK

Year	1992
Publisher	THQ
Developer	Imagineering

THE GAME BASED on the sequel to *Home Alone* tries its best to stick to the actual plot this time. Now stranded in New York City, Kevin has to first get out of the Plaza Hotel, whose entire staff is out to get him. Once out, he has to make his way across Central Park, avoiding the Sticky Bandits' attacks along the way, before arriving at his uncle's house and booby-trapping it for the final showdown. Well, not really final: after this you have to reach the roof of the house, climb down onto the streets below and leg it to the Rockefeller Center Christmas tree to find your relieved (yet still extremely negligent) parents. All nice in theory, but the game's clunkier than two robots wrestling. ∎

FACT

In its 1994 buyer's guide, American magazine *Electronic Gaming Monthly* gave the NES version of Home Alone 2 its annual award for the worst movie-to-game adaptation.

HOME IMPROVEMENT: POWER TOOL PURSUIT!

Year	1994
Publisher	Absolute Entertainment
Developer	Imagineering

WHEN POWER TOOL company Binford offers to do a deal with Tim 'The Toolman' Taylor to put his name on their new line of turbo-powered tools, Tim is naturally delighted. However, when he goes to reveal them on his TV show, he instead finds a ransom note. It's up to Tim to explore the TV studio and make his way through various other shows' sets – a prehistoric world, an ancient temple, a haunted castle and a space station – in order to gather his new tools. It eventually emerges that the evil fiend who sent Tim on this wild tool chase is… um, his own children. Which is a bit of a harsh thing to do when your old man's just trying to make a living. ∎

FACT

The game doesn't really have an instruction manual. When you open it up the pages are obscured by a large notice that reads: 'Real men don't need instructions.'

HOOK

Year	1992	
Publisher	Sony Imagesoft	
Developer	Ukiyotei	

FOUR DIFFERENT HOOK games were developed to cover an impressive 10 different platforms. The SNES version is similar to that released on the Mega Drive and Mega CD, and has Peter Pan – now an adult who's forgotten his past – running, jumping, flying and stabbing his way through Neverland in an attempt to find Captain Hook and rescue his kidnapped children.

Naturally, Peter being Peter, he can't just fly whenever he feels like it: he needs to find Tinkerbell – who's hanging around at different locations on each stage – and stand under her to gather enough pixie dust to fill his flight meter. The eventual aim is to make it to Pirate Town, board Captain Hook's ship and thwack his chops to get his kids back. ■

FACT

The *Hook* movie released to average reviews, but at the time of writing it's the sixth highest grossing pirate movie of all time, behind all five *Pirates of the Caribbean* movies.

HUNGRY DINOSAURS

Year	1995	
Publisher	Sunsoft	
Developer	Magical Company	

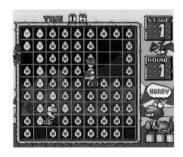

A MORE COLOURFUL take on the board game Othello, Hungry Dinosaurs shares the same basic rules at its core: you place coloured pieces – in this case, dinosaur eggs – on a board and can change your opponent's pieces to your own colour by surrounding them with your own. There are two major twists here, however, in an attempt to make things more interesting. Firstly, each player is controlling a dinosaur and both are running around the grid at the same time dropping eggs all over the place: this isn't turn-based like Othello is. Secondly, you have the ability to eat eggs for strategic purposes. It takes a lot longer to eat an egg than lay one, however, so doing so should only be a last resort. ■

FACT

Nintendo and Othello go way back. In 1978, Nintendo released Computer Othello in the arcades: this was an important game, because it was the first ever video game both developed and published by Nintendo.

THE HUMANS

Year	1993	
Publisher	GameTek	
Developer	Imagitec Design	

A PUZZLE PLATFORMER inspired to an extent by the success of Lemmings. That's not to say it's an identical game, however: there are some clear differences here. The most obvious is the fact that you control each of the game's caveman characters directly, rather than assigning them roles with a cursor. On their own the Humans only have a few abilities, primarily creating a human stepladder and picking up objects. It's this latter ability that opens up the game: by picking up various tools you can perform a variety of new skills. Grab a spear, for example, and you can use it as a pole vault to jump a gap, then turn back and throw it like a javelin so another Human can grab it and vault over too. ■

FACT

A sequel of sorts called The Humans: Meet the Ancestors was released by Deep Silver in 2009 for the PC and Nintendo DS. It attempted to capture the soul of the original but with upgraded graphics. It wasn't great, though.

THE HUNT FOR RED OCTOBER

Year	1993	
Publisher	Hi Tech Expressions	
Developer	Riedel Software Productions	

MUCH LIKE THE movie on which it's based, The Hunt for Red October sees you taking on the role of Soviet Captain Marko Ramius (aka Sean Connery not even trying to do a Russian accent) as he takes his prototype submarine the *Red October* and attempts to defect by reaching the United States. It doesn't quite follow the film to the letter, though: whereas in the movie Ramius does indeed eventually make his way to America, the game instead ends with a special mission in which you have to sail all the way back to the USSR and use your submarine to help democratic factions overthrow the Communist Party. Which is a bit of a kick in the teeth considering how hard you worked to get out of there. ■

FACT

Some missions have periscope sections where you gun down enemies from a first person perspective. Although they can be played with a normal controller, you can also use the Super Scope.

HURRICANES

Year	1994
Publisher	US Gold
Developer	Probe

OF ALL THE licenses to get a tie-in video game, it's probably safe to say *Hurricanes* – an animated collaboration between DiC Entertainment and Scottish Television about a multicultural football team – is among the

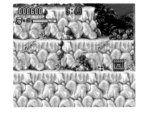

more unique examples. The Garkos Gorgons have challenged the Hurricanes to a charity match on the island of Garkos, and if they're late, they'll forfeit the victory. Cue a platforming adventure where your character runs around with a football at their feet. This ball can be kicked into enemies to defeat them, but if you miss a shot or otherwise lose the ball, you'll be defenceless for a while until a new ball spawns. Naturally, you don't get to actually play the final match: you face off against the Gorgon manager a total of three times then the game simply ends. ▪

FACT

The Hurricanes' manager is a no-nonsense Scot called Jack Stone. He's based on Jock Stein, the legendary manager who guided Celtic to win the European Cup in 1967, the first British team ever to do so.

HYPER V-BALL

Year	1994
Publisher	Mc O'River / Ubisoft
Developer	Video System

THIS IS THE sequel to Sega Mega Drive and TurboGrafx game Super Volleyball. It retains its predecessor's unique viewpoint: the game's played entirely side-on, meaning you can only move to the front and back of the court, not sideways. Although this obviously restricts the game's depth somewhat, it does at least make things more intuitive and easy to learn. There are three different leagues to choose from: Men's League, Women's League and Hyper League. The latter is a league for robots (as you do), allowing you to pull off special, super-powered moves. Hyper V-Ball is perhaps best known as Power Spikes II, its title on Neo Geo. The Neo Geo version is available to download on Switch, PS4 and Xbox One as part of the ACA Neo Geo series. ▪

FACT

This was the first of only two SNES games released by Video System in America under the bizarre name Mc O'River. Shortly after Aero Fighters launched, it decided to use Video System in the west too.

HYPERZONE

Year	1991
Publisher	HAL Laboratory
Developer	HAL Laboratory

HYPERZONE IS WHAT would have happened if F-Zero was a shoot 'em up. It's the year 2089, and the human race – having ignored environmental warnings – has now left Earth uninhabitable. The best place for them to

move to is a series of asteroid belts between Mars and Jupiter, but they're full of dumped nuclear waste and odd part-mechanical mutants. It's up to you to make your way along a 'safe' track that isn't covered in radiation and blast anything nasty in your way so you can clear things up in preparation for the human race's big move. Although not a racing game in the standard sense, your energy is constantly depleting so you have to keep moving fast to reach the next Power Zone and replenish it. ▪

FACT

HyperZone has a hidden 3D mode that was seemingly designed to work with shutter glasses (similar to Rad Racer on the NES). Since no glasses were ever released for the SNES the mode is a bit pointless.

THE IGNITION FACTOR

Year	1995
Publisher	Jaleco
Developer	Jaleco

THE FIREMEN IS generally considered one of the best SNES games to be released in Europe, but that doesn't mean North Americans were completely exempt from firefighting goodness. As

luck would have it, while Human was working on The Firemen, Jaleco was developing something comparable. The Ignition Factor uses the same viewpoint and has a similar aim: put out the fires, rescue trapped people. While The Firemen is a little more action-focused, though, The Ignition Factor tries to be a little more realistic: some flames can't be put out by your standard fire extinguisher, so you'll occasionally need to equip different ones to put out chemical or electrical fires. You only have a limited inventory too, so making sure you're armed with the right equipment is crucial in saving every life. ▪

FACT

Although The Firemen would never be officially released in North America, Europeans did at least get to play The Ignition Factor when it came to the Wii Virtual Console in 2011.

ILLUSION OF GAIA

Year	1994
Publisher	Nintendo
Developer	Quintet

RELEASED IN EUROPE as Illusion of Time, this RPG was published by Enix in Japan before Nintendo decided to take over and release it in the west. You play as young Will, the sole survivor of an expedition to the Tower of Babel that resulted in his father and a bunch of other townsfolk disappearing. With no recollection of what happened and the realisation that he can now move objects with his mind, Will gathers his pals to head out for the tower again to see if they can discover what happened. Rather than an experience system, Illusion of Gaia instead rewards players with a jewel each time they clear a room of enemies. These jewels can be applied to your characters to boost their attack, defence or health. ∎

FACT

The original Japanese version opens with Will and his friends at Sunday School at church. Given Nintendo's history of removing religious content from games, this was replaced with a normal school in the western version.

IMPERIUM

Year	1992
Publisher	Vic Tokai
Developer	Vic Tokai

DON'T YOU JUST hate it when your planet is invaded by the space fortress Zektron? If you've never experienced it, it won't be too far away (at the time of writing): according to Imperium it happens to Earth in 2027. You are the sole hero chosen to infiltrate Zektron and defeat the invaders, but you won't be doing it alone. Well, you technically will, but you'll be doing it inside a ruddy big mech called Imperium. Whereas most vertical scrolling shooters have a points system, Imperium instead gives you experience points. As you hit certain targets you unlock new weapons that can be switched between at will. You also have four speed settings, making Imperium a more customisable game than most shooters. ∎

FACT

Imperium is known as Mobile Armoured Dion in Japan: as you may expect, this also means the mech is called Dion instead. The game is by and large the same, but some stages have an extra layer of background detail in the Japanese release.

INCANTATION

Year	1996
Publisher	Titus Software
Developer	Titus Software

THE MAGIC KINGDOM (not to be confused with Disney's Magical Kingdom) is under threat from the evil wizard Necroman. He's stolen the Book of Sorcery, which gives him absolute power. Playing as a young magician, you have to make your way through the Magic Kingdom's various worlds (including an enchanted forest, cursed cliffs, mountains and swamps) before reaching Necroman's castle and attempting to finish him off for good. Other than its slightly annoying habit of frequently teleporting you to a bonus area, Incantation fails to conjure up anything truly innovative: it's a standard platformer with a jump button, an attack button and nothing else, and the only major feature of note is the ability to collect power-ups that let you fire different spells at enemies. ∎

FACT

The game's ending is as unremarkable as it gets. You're treated to a single screen of text saying: 'Thank you for defeating the evil wizard! We will always be grateful to you and hope that you will stop by and visit us again!!!'

THE INCREDIBLE CRASH DUMMIES

Year	1993
Publisher	LJN
Developer	Gray Matter

THE CRASH DUMMIES' creator Dr Zub has been kidnapped by the 'deranged dummy' Junkman, who wants to get his hands on the top-secret TORSO-9000 indestructible body. It's up to Slick to head out and get him back, even if it costs him an arm and a leg. The game consists of 16 stages, taking Slick through the crash test centre, a construction site and a military testing zone before he arrives at Junkman's Junk-Kastle. The most unique feature is Slick's energy, which isn't shown as an energy bar: he's the energy bar. Every time he takes a hit he loses a limb, until he's just a hopping torso with a head. Along the way you can collect screwdrivers that restore a limb though, so at least there's no arm done. ∎

FACT

Before crash test dummies became commonplace in the automotive industry, scientists used human and animal cadave to test the impact of car crashe instead. The moral issues with this were obvious, hence the use of dummies today.

THE INCREDIBLE HULK

Year	1993
Publisher	US Gold
Developer	Probe

INTELLIGENT SUPERVILLAIN THE Leader has decided it's time to take over the Earth, so he builds a huge fortress deep within a forest and assigns a huge army of robots to guard it. Aware that the Hulk will no doubt turn up to ruin his plans, he also enlists the help of the Abomination, Rhino, Absorbing Man and Tyrannus to put an end to the green menace. This action platformer naturally puts you in the oversized green feet of Mr Hulk, as you smash your way through countless robots and generally chuck scenery around. You can also collect tranquility pills, which transform you back to Bruce Banner: this may seem pointless, but in his smaller state Banner can crawl through small gaps and find hidden items. ■

FACT

There have been six games starring the Hulk in a lead role. The first was 1984 text adventure Questprobe Featuring Hulk, and the most recent (at the time of writing) was the tie-in game for the 2008 Incredible Hulk movie.

INDIANA JONES' GREATEST ADVENTURES

Year	1994
Publisher	JVC / LucasArts
Developer	Factor 5

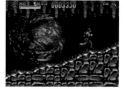

WHY MAKE A game based on an Indiana Jones movie when you can make one about all three? (There were only three movies at this point, and in many fans' hearts there still are.) Greatest Adventures guides player through the events of Raiders of the Lost Ark, Temple of Doom and Last Crusade, split into a total of 28 stages. While most of the game consists of typical side-scrolling action – armed with your fists and a whip, naturally, though guns and grenades can be picked up too – you'll occasionally be treated to some Mode 7 stages as Indy rides down a river on a rubber raft, fights Germans in a biplane and, of course, takes the iconic minecart ride that spawned countless video game imitators. ■

FACT

The game takes a few liberties along the way. When Donovan drinks the cup in Last Crusade's famous Holy Grail scene, instead of crumbling into dust he turns into a skeleton and becomes the game's final boss, throwing his head at you.

ININDO: WAY OF THE NINJA

Year	1993
Publisher	Koei
Developer	Koei

IN 1581, DEMONIC warlord Oda Nobunaga's army practically wiped out the Iga ninja clan. As one of the few remaining survivors, you have to travel around Japan, seeking help and building your strength so you can finally take on Nobunaga and get your revenge. Inindo is an interesting mix of traditional JRPG and a typical Koei strategy game. While much of the game consists of roaming around as the hero (you choose their name), visiting towns and getting involved in standard turn-based battles, at times you can also earn the trust of feudal lords and take part in larger-scale battles, which are more like turn-based strategy games in nature. The aim is to kill Nobunaga by 1601: if you don't manage that you've run out of time and the game is over. ■

FACT

A cutscene after the first dungeon changes the game significantly. If you see Nobunaga injured you'll follow the normal story (where you fight ninja and soldiers along the way), but if he's unharmed you'll go down the 'sorcerer' route, where you fight monsters instead.

INSPECTOR GADGET

Year	1993
Publisher	Hudson Soft
Developer	AIM

THE EVIL DR Claw has kidnapped Inspector Gadget's niece Penny, so it's up to the bumbling detective (who's actually not bumbling at all this time) to head out and save her. As you'd expect, the main gimmick in the Inspector Gadget game is the ability to use a wide variety of gizmos and whatnots in order to progress through each of the game's six stages. These generally come out of Gadget's hat and include a propeller, a bomb, a grappling hand, a lamp, a suction cup gun, a bow and arrow and – somewhat oddly – a little kamikaze man who jumps out and runs at enemies, blowing up in their face. In Ghouls 'n Ghosts style, taking a hit will reduce Gadget to his underwear. ■

FACT

This game marks only the second time you get to see Dr Claw's face (which is never seen in the cartoons). The first was an action figure that came with a sticker on the box, covering his face until it was opened.

INTERNATIONAL SUPERSTAR SOCCER

Year	1995
Publisher	Konami
Developer	Konami

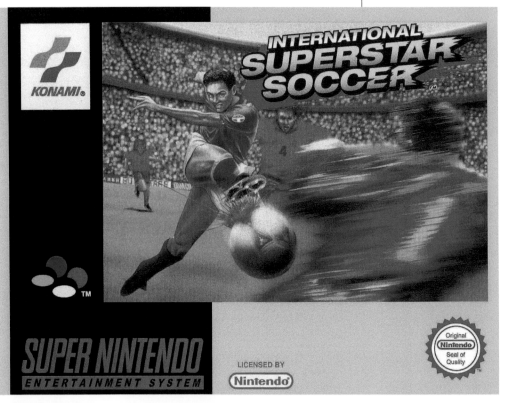

INTERNATIONAL SUPERSTAR SOCCER – better known among syllable-savers as ISS – may not have been Konami's first ever football game, but there's no denying it would become its most important. FIFA had already redefined the genre by the time it arrived on the SNES, so Konami did the most sensible thing in that situation: redefined it again.

At first glance it doesn't seem like it does anything too revolutionary. While FIFA's isometric camera view made it immediately noticeably different, Konami instead decided to go for a traditional side-on viewpoint similar to that used in many arcade and home console football games before it. The use of four buttons for passing, shooting, chipping and sprinting was more than most games, but certainly not the first game to go to that level of detail. The game modes, meanwhile – with the exception of its fun Scenario mode – are mostly the sort of thing you would have found in any other football title at the time: an International Cup (with a standard World Cup layout) and a World Series (which is just a big league) are the two main options.

Where it truly differed, then, was how the game actually felt when you were playing it. Character movement was flexible enough to let you dribble round opponents, but stiff enough – especially when sprinting – to still require a level of skill to master. Defending is effective

FACT

When the polygonal systems appeared, ISS split into two series. Konami's Major A studio worked on ISS 64 and its sequels, whereas its KCET studio made ISS Pro for the PlayStation. The latter is the series that would later become PES.

enough that pulling off a well-timed tackle or slide tackle is hugely satisfying, but has enough margin of error to ensure that a slip of concentration will result in an opponent skipping past you. Passing goes right to teammates' feet, but AI defenders generally position themselves well enough to make you work for good build-up play. Everything comes together to make ISS feel more like a real game of football than anything that had come before it. You can even sprint down the wing, reach the touchline and put a cross into the box for someone to catch with a header or overhead kick: something nearly impossible in most other offerings.

There are 26 international teams in the game, each with their own full rosters of players. Although player names are fake, fans of ISS – much like fans of the original FIFA – soon grew to love some of the more notable star players. The difference here was that in ISS some of these players looked visibly different from others in their team. Italy's Galfano is a clear homage to Robert Baggio, complete with ponytail. Colombia's Murillo is clearly supposed to be Carlos Valderrama, massive curly blonde afro and all. Whereas players could learn who the star men were in FIFA's teams, in ISS they could also spot them immediately.

ISS would eventually evolve (ahem) into the Pro Evolution Soccer series, which continues to this day, and what was the case in 1995 remains the case now: FIFA may be the most popular football game, but ISS/PES is the one that arguably plays the better game of football. ∎

INTERNATIONAL SUPERSTAR SOCCER DELUXE

Year	1995
Publisher	Konami
Developer	Konami

TRUE TO ITS name, Deluxe isn't an all-out sequel to the original ISS, it's more of an enhanced update. There are some new player animations, the commentator has new lines, there are more stadiums than before (eight instead of three) and there are new features like co-op and improved curve. There are now 36 teams to choose from (plus six hidden All-Star teams), and there are a bunch of new scenarios for players to take on. It's certainly the definitive version of the game on SNES – if only by a small degree – but it also wins the award for best use of the Konami code. Enter it on the title screen with the second controller and the referee and linesmen will be turned into dogs. ■

FACT

There were at least 10 bootlegged hacks of ISS Deluxe released in South American countries, with the teams and player names changed. These included Futebol Brasileiro 96, Fútbol Argentino 96, Fútbol Colombiano 96 and Peru's Fútbol Peruano 97.

INTERNATIONAL TENNIS TOUR

Year	1993
Publisher	Taito
Developer	Loriciel

THIS TENNIS GAME offers more game modes than you'd typically get from similar tennis titles at the time. As well as the standard exhibition and tournament modes (which can be played in either singles or doubles varieties), you can also take part in a Nations Cup, which is essentially a clone of the Davis Cup. There's also a Championship mode, which acts as a career mode: beginning at the bottom of the tennis rankings, you have to work your way through the 32 other players to reach the top. These opponents are fictional: the lowest ranked is Will Iston from Switzerland (who's ranked 50th), while the number one player is smiley American chap Dan Carter. A sizeable game, then, though its over-the-shoulder viewpoint can make it tricky to judge where shots will land on the other side of the court. ■

FACT

The Nations Cup may be an unofficial Davis Cup, but Loriciel actually released an officially licensed game called Davis Cup Tennis on the Mega Drive that same year.

THE IREM SKINS GAME

Year	1992
Publisher	Irem
Developer	Irem

THIS IS A port of Irem's arcade golf game Major Title 2: Tournament Leader, which focuses mainly on 'skins' golf: for the uninitiated, this means you play each hole for money and whoever has the most cash at the end wins. If virtual gambling isn't your thing you can also take part in the more standard Stroke Play, Match Play and Tournament modes. There are four golfers to choose from, with the rather impersonal names of Power Hitter (who has high drive and power stats), All-Around Player, Technician (high accuracy and back spin) and Magician (high hook and slice). Rather than setting your power and accuracy with a moving gauge as in most golf games, you choose your power manually and only have a gauge for accuracy. ■

FACT

The PGA Tour held an official Skins Game every year from 1983 to 2008. Although it was recognised by the PGA, it didn't count towards the players' official money list for that season.

THE ITCHY & SCRATCHY GAME

Year	1995
Publisher	Acclaim
Developer	Bits Studios

IT TAKES A bold move to make a Simpsons game that doesn't actually feature any of the Simpsons, but Itchy and Scratchy are popular enough characters to just about make it work. Playing as Itchy, the player has to face off against Scratchy in a series of enclosed stages. Each player has their own energy bar and the aim is to fully deplete Scratchy's before your own runs out. There's a wide variety of weapons to find, ranging from axes and bolt guns to flaming arrows and laser swords, all of which do harm to Scratchy in comical detail. Not too much detail, mind: a prototype of the cancelled Sega Mega Drive version later surfaced which showed that some 'death' animations were originally supposed to be a little more over the top. ■

FACT

Bart and Lisa were supposed to appear in between each stage, talking to each other on the couch while watching the show. Although these cutscenes were removed, the dialogue remains unused in the game's code.

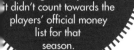

IZZY'S QUEST FOR THE OLYMPIC RINGS

Year	1995
Publisher	US Gold
Developer	Alexandria

WHEN LIFE GIVES you lemons, you do your very best to squeeze some sort of juice out of them. This was what US Gold attempted when making a game based on Izzy, the awful mascot for the 1996 Atlanta Olympic Games. The Eternal Flame needed to light the Olympic Torch has gone missing, but the problem is that Izzy lives in a different dimension (apparently). You have to help him find the five Olympic Rings in order to open the Reality Vortex, a portal that will teleport him to Atlanta so he can light the flame again. Cue an adequate platformer in which Izzy can morph into various shapes: most are Olympics-related (a javelin, hammer-thrower, archer, baseball player), while others aren't (a hang-glider, a rocket). ■

FACT

Izzy was originally introduced as Whatizit at the end of the 1992 Barcelona Olympics, then underwent a redesign. It didn't change much: he was referred to as 'the sperm in sneakers' by some newspapers.

J.R.R. TOLKIEN'S THE LORD OF THE RINGS, VOL. 1

Year	1994
Publisher	Interplay
Developer	Interplay

ONE OF THE risks that comes with taking on an adaptation of a lengthy piece of work is that you'd better be sure you're going to be able to finish the job. Interplay took such a gamble by taking its RPG based on *The Fellowship of the Ring* and splitting it into two parts. Starting off as Frodo, you eventually recruit the rest of the Fellowship, who can be controlled by other players using a multitap. The problem was that the game's length – which is extended through its many fetch quests – forced Interplay to end the story with the fight against the Balrog in the Mines of Moria. Wanted to see what happened next? Tough luck: Vol. 2 was never made. ■

FACT

Interplay had already tried this in 1990 with a home computer game for Amiga and PC. This was slightly more successful in that there was at least a Vol. 2 which covered *The Two Towers*. There was no Vol. 3.

JACK NICKLAUS GOLF

Year	1992
Publisher	Tradewest
Developer	Tradewest

INITIALLY RELEASED ON Amiga and PC in 1990 as Jack Nicklaus' Unlimited Golf & Course Design, this SNES port ditched the course designer element, leaving players with the two preset courses. These are Muirfield Village (a real course in Ohio owned by Nicklaus and named after the Scottish course where he won his first British Open) and The Bear's Track, a fictional course designed by Nicklaus. Each can be played in either skins or stroke play, and the game uses a standard three-press control system to set power and accuracy. It hasn't entirely shaken off its home computer roots, though: every time you hit a shot, the game takes an absolute age to redraw the course from your new viewpoint, making it an exercise in patience at times. ■

FACT

There's still a 'course designer' of sorts in the game, but it simply involves picking your favourite 18 holes from the two pre-existing courses and choosing what order to play them in.

JAMES BOND JR

Year	1992
Publisher	THQ
Developer	Gray Matter

YOU'D THINK IF you were James Bond's nephew you'd see all the trouble your uncle gets into and decide to leave it to him. Instead, James Bond Jr happily finds himself getting into all manner of adventures, including the three in this game. James has to stop Dr Derange from finding a Central American treasure, ride through Venice to stop Maximillion Cortex discovering a secret Da Vinci invention, then head to the Antarctic to face the evil S.C.U.M. Lord. The game's split into two different types: levels 1, 3, 5 and 7 are action platformers (complete with typically Bond-esque gizmos like rocket shoes and a snake-charming flute), while levels 2, 4 and 6 are vehicle-based shoot 'em ups in which James uses a minicopter, speedboat and jet respectively. ■

FACT

In the cartoon, James Bond Jr was voiced by Corey Burton, better known for voicing Shockwave in the original *Transformers* cartoon. He was also the voice of Dale in *Chip 'n Dale Rescue Rangers*, though obviously that was then squeakified.

JAMES POND 3: OPERATION STARFISH

Year	1993	
Publisher	Electronic Arts	
Developer	Millennium Interactive	

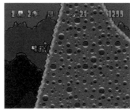

THE THIRD AND final game in the James Pond series, Operation Starfish sees our piscean protagonist travelling to the moon for a final confrontation with his arch-nemesis Dr Maybe. After learning the moon is made of the finest cheese, Dr Maybe puts together a crack team of rats to start mining it so he can become a world leader in the cheese industry and use the money to fund his other evil projects. Off goes James to the moon, then, where his special boots let him stick to the sloped floors and even run up walls with enough pace. He's also armed with a series of gadgets, ranging from spring boots to a fruit gun, which lets him fire food at enemies. ■

FACT

Continuing the theme of puns on popular franchise names (James Pond, Robocod), the original name for James Pond 3 was going to be Splash Gordon.

JAMMIT

Year	1994	
Publisher	GTE Interactive Media	
Developer	GTE Interactive Media	

A STREET BASKETBALL game that focuses strictly on one-on-one games. You get to choose between one of three fictional street players – defensive powerhouse Chill, long shooter Roxy and speedy Slade – and face off against the others in a series of different 'first to 21' matches, each offering slightly different rules. For example, Sweat rules mean there are no fouls, Slams Only means you only get points for dunks and Poison means if your score reaches exactly 20 it'll drop down to 10. Win a match of every type and you'll face off against a hidden final player called Judge who has high stats in every category. Which doesn't seem fair, frankly, but I'm reliably informed that's how business is done on the streets. ■

FACT

Developer GTE Interactive was a subsidiary of telecoms company GTE. When the telecoms industry was deregulated in 1996, GTE suffered heavily and closed down the studio in 1997, before the entire corporation folded in 2000.

JELLY BOY

Year	1995	
Publisher	Ocean Software	
Developer	Probe	

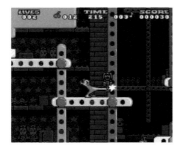

DON'T YOU HATE it when you wake up in an evil toy factory and need to get out? That's the fate that's befallen Jelly Boy, a blobby chap who now has to bribe the factory's elevator operator with six objects to escape. Jelly Boy's main gimmick is his ability to transform into various shapes: his standard attack sees a boxing glove pop out of his belly, while ducking literally turns him into a small duck. There are also power-ups littered around that let him pull off special transformations for a limited time: these include turning into a hammer to smash blocks, or a submarine so he can swim. Then there's the brick power-up, which turns him into… well, a brick. He just stays there until it wears off. ■

FACT

Jelly Boy shouldn't be confused with Game Freak's Smart Ball (found elsewhere in this book), which was named Jerry Boy in Japan. A sequel for that game called Jelly Boy 2 – they fixed the spelling – was in development but was never released.

JEOPARDY!

Year	1992	
Publisher	GameTek	
Developer	Imagineering	

THERE'S NO GREATER game show in America than answers-and-questions game *Jeopardy!*, so naturally most gaming systems got their own versions over the years. The SNES got no fewer than three, starting with this one. Featuring digitised versions of the studio, the theme music and even sound samples from host Alex Trebek, this was a fairly decent recreation of the show and included 3,500 questions covering categories as wide-ranging as Banned Books, Insect Trivia and Presidential Middle Names. As in the show, players take part in Jeopardy!, Double Jeopardy! and Final Jeopardy! rounds, and other features like the Daily Doubles are in there too. When it comes to answering questions you have to type in the answer, so you'd better be a good speller too. ■

FACT

Here's a sample question: 'There's a statue of him in Crystal City, Texas, spinach capital of the world.' The answer: 'Who is Popeye?'

JEOPARDY! DELUXE EDITION

Year	1994
Publisher	GameTek
Developer	GameTek

RINSED ALL 3,500 questions in the first Jeopardy! game? Well, you're in luck, because here's another 3,500 of the swines. Despite its Deluxe Edition moniker, this isn't massively different from the first game other than a few little changes here and there: the digitised photo of Alex Trebex between questions looks a bit better, the contestants have new avatars and, of course, there's a completely new set of questions. This time the categories include the likes of Patriot Songs, Magazines and Words That End With 'U'. Other than these changes, the game remains practically identical, so unless you've got a legitimate hatred for one of the avatars in one of the games, you can buy either, happy in the knowledge you aren't getting the inferior product. ■

FACT

Here's another sample question: 'In this system, a book on the history of art in the US would be found under 709.73.' Answer: 'What is the Dewey Decimal System?'

JEOPARDY! SPORTS EDITION

Year	1994
Publisher	GameTek
Developer	GameTek

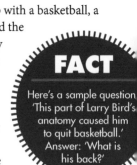

IF YOU LIKE the idea of playing Jeopardy! but are more into the likes of American football, hockey and baseball than ancient history and '50s television shows, the Sports Edition may be for you. As you may expect, the general game is identical to the Deluxe Edition, but once again the player avatars have been changed, this time to make the contestants suitably sporty: a chap with a basketball, a woman holding a pair of ice skates and the like. Naturally, the questions are solely focused on sports too, with categories including Baseball Equipment, Football Positions and Famous Yankees. So, if you know your Saskatchewan Roughriders from your Sacramento Goldminers (or even that they're Canadian Football League teams), this is the game for you. ■

FACT

Here's a sample question: 'This part of Larry Bird's anatomy caused him to quit basketball.' Answer: 'What is his back?'

THE JETSONS: INVASION OF THE PLANET PIRATES

Year	1994
Publisher	Taito
Developer	Sting Entertainment

THE FLINTSTONES WASN'T the only Hanna-Barbera property to be turned into a platform game by Taito: futuristic family show The Jetsons also got the same treatment. Playing as George Jetson, you have to get through nine stages in order to stop the intergalactic space pirate Zora carrying out his plan to raid the solar system of its natural resources. George is armed with the Pneumo Osmatic Precipitator (POP), which is essentially a fancy vacuum cleaner. This lets the player pull off a number of tricks that help keep the platforming interesting: not only can you suck up enemies and fire them at others, you can also use the POP to pick up blocks, stick to walls and breathe underwater. Very clever but, hey, that's the future for you. ■

FACT

Sting repurposed this game in Japan to tie in with manga series Yokai Buster Ruka. It's pretty much identical to the Jetsons but with different sprites.

JIM POWER: THE LOST DIMENSION IN 3D

Year	1993
Publisher	Electro Brain
Developer	Loriciel

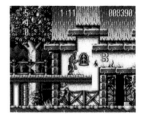

THIS IS A sequel of sorts to Loriciel's home computer game Jim Power in Mutant Planet, in that it's a new game but borrows a lot of material from the original. It's a notoriously difficult adventure in which you play as Jim Power, a special agent assigned to destroy an evil alien called Vaprak and prevent him from opening a rift to a fifth dimension that would allow his alien cronies to invade the Earth. As well as being known for its extreme difficulty, the game also comes bundled with a pair of 'NUOPTIX' 3D glasses, which have a clear right eye and a dark left eye (similar to the lens on sunglasses). When playing with the glasses on, the parallax scrolling (which is already pretty extreme) gives an extra illusion of depth. ■

FACT

If you don't have the glasses that come with the game, you don't really need them. Simply hold a pair of sunglasses to your face and make sure they cover only your left eye.

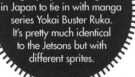

JIMMY CONNORS PRO TENNIS TOUR

Year	1992
Publisher	Ubisoft
Developer	Blue Byte

ONE OF THE more feature-heavy tennis games on the SNES, Ubisoft and Blue Byte's offering comes attached to the name of former world number one Jimmy Connors. The main game mode is the Tour option, in which you play as Connors himself as he takes on a series of tournaments each month in his calendar. There are 28 tournaments to choose from, including biggies like Wimbledon and the French Open. Whereas most tennis games offer grass, hard and clay surfaces, this goes further by adding indoor, desert and Antarctica(!) to the mix. It also has a surprisingly in-depth training mode – where five separate coaches talk you through different elements of the controls – and an Easy control scheme where the CPU moves your player and you just focus on the strokes. ■

FACT

At the time of writing, Connors still holds three all-time men's tennis records: the most [tit]les won (109), the most matches played (1,557) and the most matches won (1,274). Roger Federer is right behind him in all three categories, however.

JIMMY HOUSTON'S BASS TOURNAMENT USA

Year	1995
Publisher	American Sammy
Developer	American Sammy

IF THERE'S ANYTHING Jimmy Houston doesn't know about bass fishing, it's not worth knowing (or so I'm told). The two-time B.A.S.S. Angler of the Year lends his name to this SNES offering which features four real-life American lakes: Lake Santee Cooper in South Carolina, Lake Fork in Texas, Lake Winnipesaukee in New Hampshire and Lake Seminole in Florida. Each of these lakes has a number of different fishing spots you'll need to visit as you participate in a series of tournaments to try and catch the biggest bass. If it's official gear you're looking for – and why wouldn't it be – the game also has a license with Japanese fishing equipment manufacturer Shimano, with seven of its real-life rods and two of its reels available to choose from. ■

FACT

As well as being a pro angler, Jimmy Houston is also a long-time fishing TV host, having appeared on ESPN for an impressive 21 years. At the time of writing he can be found on NBC Sports.

JOE & MAC

Year	1992
Publisher	Data East
Developer	Data East

KNOWN AS JOE & Mac: Caveman Ninja or just Caveman Ninja depending on your region or format, this action platformer from Data East stars two prehistoric pals – I'll let you guess their names – as they attempt to rescue their tribe's women-folk from a gang of ne'er-do-well neanderthals. Initially armed with a club, Joe and Mac can also pick up various weapons along the way to help them, ranging from bones and boomerangs to fireballs and, best of all, big stone wheels that are tricky to aim but do lots of damage. As well as the standard single-player game and two-player games you'd get in most platformers, there's also a 2P Super Game option, where both Joe and Mac appear on-screen at the same time and can interact with each other. ■

FACT

In case you've always [wa]nted to be able to tell the [di]fference between them, [Jo]e is the one with green hair and Mac is the one with blue hair.

JOE & MAC 2: LOST IN THE TROPICS

Year	1994
Publisher	Data East
Developer	Data East

HERE'S A NICE and confusing fact for you: because Congo's Caper is known as Joe & Mac 2 in Japan, there was seemingly some indecision about how to number this one. As a result, the North American version is called Joe & Mac 2, whereas the European version is called Joe & Mac 3. Don't go buying them both, then, because they're the same game. They're a good game, mind you: this time the duo have to get back the Chief of Kali Village's crown, which has been stolen by a caveman called Grok. Animation has been noticeably improved over the previous game, and the scrolling is much smoother than that of its predecessor. You can now ride dinosaurs at times too, including a pteranodon, a plesiosaurus and a styracosaurus. ■

FACT

An officially licensed SNES cart containing Joe & Mac, Joe & Mac 2 and Congo's Caper was released by retro gaming specialists Retro-Bit in 2017.

JOHN MADDEN FOOTBALL

Year	1991
Publisher	Electronic Arts
Developer	Park Place Productions

ALL OF GAMING'S longest-running series have to start somewhere, and the Madden series… um, didn't start here. The first John Madden Football was released in 1988 for the Apple II, Commodore 64 and DOS PCs: its success led to a brand new game, also called John Madden Football, to be developed for the Sega Mega Drive / Genesis in 1990, followed by this SNES port a full year later. Rather than a straight copy of the Sega version, however, this SNES title stands on its own. Whereas the first Mega Drive title only had 16 teams to choose from, the SNES game contains all 28 teams in the NFL at the time: albeit with no licensing, which means no player names and no real team names or logos. Indeed, the only official licence here is that of Mr Madden himself: the legendary Hall of Fame coach and commentator appears before every game to give a run-down of each team's strengths and weaknesses so the player knows which areas of their offence or defence they should focus on. On the field itself, the game is a mixed bag: at its core there are many aspects that helped define future American football games. Running is intuitive and players can actually find and exploit gaps made by blockers. Passing, meanwhile, brings up a series of windows at the top of the screen which let you see where your receivers are and which ones are open. The issues lie with the SNES port specifically, which runs far less smoothly than its year-old Sega counterpart. ■

> ### FACT
> John Madden is a big fan of the turducken, a turkey stuffed with a duck stuffed with a chicken. He deemed it the 'official food of the 1997 All-Madden team'.

JOHN MADDEN FOOTBALL '93

Year	1992
Publisher	Electronic Arts
Developer	EA Canada

THE SECOND MADDEN game on SNES completely fixed the technical issues of its predecessor, meaning it finally played just as smoothly as its Mega Drive counterpart. This aside, Madden '93 is the same sort of thing, though there's  now the added bonus of 10 new 'Greats' teams covering some of Madden's favourite ever teams from history (including the 1984 San Francisco 49ers, the 1976 Oakland Raiders and the 1972 Miami Dolphins). These new teams also form the basis for the All-Time Greats mode, a 12-team playoff that includes all 10 of these teams, a Madden Greats team (which picks the best players from each) and a modern All-Madden team. As before, though, there are no player names, making it a tad tricky to figure out which legends are actually in each roster. ■

> ### FACT
> John Madden considers the Madden games an educational tool, a 'way for people to learn [American football] and participate in the game at a pretty sophisticated level'.

JUDGE DREDD

Year	1995
Publisher	Acclaim
Developer	Probe

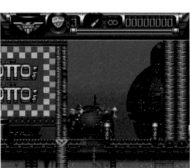

ANYONE FAMILIAR WITH the excellent SNES version of Alien 3 will immediately recognise elements of it in Judge Dredd, Acclaim's video game rendition of the notorious 1995 movie starring Sylvester Stallone. Each of the game's 12 stages gives Dredd a primary task and a secondary task, the progress of which can be checked on the terminals dotted around. Many of the enemies you defeat will hold their hands up in submission: you can choose to either kill them or arrest them for extra points. One of the more unique weapons is the Boing Bubble: this doesn't harm enemies but can trap their ghosts in a slimy floating capsule to help you make sure they're properly finished off. ■

> ### FACT
> Press Left, Up, X, Up, Right, Y during the copyright info screen and you'll get another screen telling you to 'say no to cheats'. Here you can press B & X to unlock auto health regain mode, and press A & Y to unlock a level skip.

THE JUNGLE BOOK

Year	1994
Publisher	Virgin Interactive
Developer	Virgin Interactive

ALTHOUGH DISNEY'S MUCH loved animated movie first hit cinemas back in 1967, it was given a home video re-release in 1991 in the US and 1994 in the UK. Following the success of games based on *Aladdin* and *The Lion King*, then, Virgin decided that the next Disney property to go through its platformer process would be *The Jungle Book*, given its newfound VHS popularity. The result is a fairly straightforward platform game, albeit one with lovely animation that seems inspired quite heavily by *Aladdin* (the climbing animations are identical, for example). Mowgli can attack enemies by throwing bananas at them, and throughout his journey will take on Kaa the snake and King Louie before his inevitable final battle with Shere Khan. ■

FACT

When I say the home video release of *The Jungle Book* was popular, I mean it. In 2002 it was revealed to be the best-selling video in UK history, with its 4.9 million sales beating out *Titanic* by around 100,000 copies.

JUNGLE STRIKE

Year	1995
Publisher	Electronic Arts
Developer	Gremlin Interactive

THE SEQUEL TO Desert Strike takes the action away from the Persian Gulf and moves it to North and South America. The first mission has you in Washington DC, protecting national monuments from a terrorist attack. Then it's off to a nondescript jungle to take on notorious drug lord Carlos Ortega, who's in cahoots with Ibn Kilbaba, the son of the first game's villain. After spending the majority of the game taking out Ortega's jungle fortress, rescuing hostages and ultimately capturing your two targets, the final mission brings you back to Washington as you try to take out four armoured trucks carrying nuclear weapons before they reach the White House. As well as your helicopter, some missions now let you control a motorbike, hovercraft and F-117 stealth plane. ■

FACT

The PC version of Jungle Strike adds an extra stage set in Alaska, where you have to take out a Russian called Ptofski who's taken control of a bunch of oil tankers.

JURASSIC PARK

Year	1993
Publisher	Ocean Software
Developer	Ocean Software

THERE WERE SEVEN completely different games made to celebrate the release of the monumental Hollywood blockbuster *Jurassic Park*. Sega created four of these for the Mega Drive, Master System / Game Gear, Mega CD and arcades. Ocean, meanwhile, got the rights to make games for non-Sega consoles and got to work creating three more: one for the NES and Game Boy, one for PC and Amiga, and this SNES effort. Playing as Dr Alan Grant, the game begins after things have already gone haywire and dinosaurs are already running around. You have free reign to explore Jurassic Park while you attempt to carry out six key objectives: power up the main generator to activate the motion sensors, secure the Visitor's Center from raptor attacks, stop some raptors escaping on a supply ship, destroy a group of underground raptor nests, find the communications room to radio for help then reach the helipad and escape the island.

FACT

An Ocean PR told *Super Play* magazine in 1993 that the game originally included the sound of bones crunching whenever a T-Rex ate Grant, but Nintendo said it was a bit too graphic so the sound was removed.

There are two main viewpoints during your adventure: park exploration takes place from an overhead view, but when you enter a building the action switches to a first-person perspective similar to something like Doom. These sections can be played using the SNES Mouse, should you so wish. There are seven different species of dinosaur roaming the island and each can harm you in different ways: the tiny compys, ostrich-like gallimimus and headbutting pachycephalosaurus will generally do minor damage, but the same can't be said for the lightning-fast raptors, the spitting dilophosaurs, the charging triceratops and, of course, the T-Rex. ■

JURASSIC PARK 2: THE CHAOS CONTINUES

Year	1995
Publisher	Ocean Software
Developer	Ocean Software

THIS HAS NOTHING to do with the actual second Jurassic Park movie, *The Lost World*: that didn't hit cinemas until 1997. Instead, this is an alternative sequel to the first film, set a year later. It sees Dr Alan Grant returning to the island with a tactical sergeant called Michael Wolfskin (who can be controlled by player two) and trying to stop the evil corporation BioSyn. They've sent in their own soldiers and scientists in an attempt to take over the island for their own nefarious purposes, so you have to make sure they don't succeed, by taking on six missions (which can be chosen at will). Whereas the first Jurassic Park game on the SNES was a mix of overhead and first-person sections, this sequel is a side-scroller. ■

FACT

It seems the T-Rex in Jurassic Park has more problems going on than you would expect. When you defeat it, it actually explodes for some reason.

JUSTICE LEAGUE TASK FORCE

Year	1995
Publisher	Acclaim
Developer	Blizzard

A ONE-ON-ONE FIGHTING game in the same vein as Street Fighter II (albeit one with a story mode) starring DC Comics characters. The story goes that supervillain Darkseid has blown up a military base on Earth, causing the Justice League to investigate. You control one of six characters – Batman, Superman, Aquaman, The Flash, Green Arrow or Wonder Woman – as they fight their way through other opponents before reaching Darkseid. Since there are only nine characters in the game, this means that while you do get to fight villains like Cheetah and Despero in story mode, most of your opponents are the other Justice League members. There's a convenient reason for that, though: they're actually android clones created by Darkseid. So that explains that. ■

FACT

The original Justice League consisted of Superman, Batman, Wonder Woman, The Flash, Green Lantern, Aquaman and Martian Manhunter.

KA-BLOOEY

Year	1992
Publisher	Kemco
Developer	Kemco

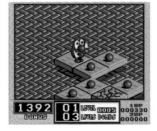

SOME MAY KNOW this game better as Bombuzal, which is its more common name: that's what it went by when it was originally released on the Amiga, Atari ST, Commodore 64 and DOS. It's a puzzle game set on a series of small islands where the aim is to detonate all the bombs on a stage without dying. To detonate a bomb you have to stand on it and light it: you can then only move one square away before it explodes. Complications include setting up chain reactions, cracked floors that can only be stepped on once, and larger bombs which have a wider blast radius and therefore can't be manually triggered. Ka-Blooey is one of the more difficult puzzle games to get into but it's ultimately rewarding once you get your head round it. ■

FACT

Kemco released a sequel of sorts on the PlayStation and Nintendo 64 in the late '90s. The PlayStation version starred Kid Klown (see over the page) while the N64 one starred a demolition expert called Charlie Blast.

KAWASAKI CARIBBEAN CHALLENGE

Year	1993
Publisher	GameTek
Developer	Park Place Productions

JAPANESE MANUFACTURER KAWASAKI is well known for its motorcycles, but it's no slouch when it comes to making jet skis too. Kawasaki Caribbean Challenge celebrates both vehicle lines by letting players choose one of three Ninja bikes – the ZX-6, ZX7R or ZX11 – or one of three jet skis – the 550SX, 650SX or 750SX – and take them out for a spin on three different tracks on Caribbean islands: Treasure Cay, Port Elizabeth and Wreckers Reef. The aim is to beat a qualifying time, which then gives you access to the main race. The motorbike racing is straightforward enough, but racing on a jet ski requires a little more skill because the course isn't so strictly designed, meaning you can hit the shore if you aren't paying attention. ■

FACT

N64 classic Wave Race 64 featured Kawasaki jet skis and advertising. The Wii Virtual Console version removed them due to an expired licence, but they were reinstated for the Wii U Virtual Console.

KAWASAKI SUPERBIKE CHALLENGE

Year	1995	
Publisher	Time Warner Interactive	
Developer	Domark	

DON'T BE FOOLED by the name: this has absolutely nothing to do with Caribbean Challenge other than the fact that Kawasaki features prominently in both games. Domark's offering – simply known as Kawasaki Superbikes in the EU – instead uses the same engine as its racing game F1 World Championship Edition, replacing its Formula One cars with Kawasaki bikes instead. There are 15 real-life circuits to race on here: while 14 of them (like the UK's Brands Hatch and Albacete in Spain) offer standard races, the final track – set in Japan's Suzuka Circuit – is instead an eight-hour endurance race. The SNES version uses sprite scaling to give the illusion of depth: while it's reasonably effective, the game is a little on the clunky side and the frame rate is low. ∎

FACT

Kawasaki was founded in 1896 but didn't start making motorbikes until the 1950s. The first ever bike made entirely of Kawasaki parts was the B8, which launched in Japan in 1982 and cost around $390 at the time.

KEN GRIFFEY JR PRESENTS MAJOR LEAGUE BASEBALL

Year	1994	
Publisher	Nintendo	
Developer	Software Creations	

WHILE SEGA HAPPILY licensed a slew of celebrity sportsmen for its Mega Drive / Genesis games, Nintendo tended not to. One exception is Ken Griffey Jr, whose name Nintendo would apply to no fewer than four games. This is the first, and as far as baseball games go it's pretty impressive. The MLB licence means every team name and logo are in there, and while their stadiums don't have official names many of them are still clearly based on the real thing: hit a home run in Toronto's Skydome-like stadium, for example, and you can see its restaurant. Player names are fake but inventive: each is based on a different theme. Colorado's players are named after horror movie makers, for example (G. Romero, B. Lugosi, T. Savini etc). ∎

FACT

As fun as it is, this game has more bugs than London Zoo's insect house. Players' home run totals can be wiped during a season, and in extreme cases entire season data can disappear.

KEN GRIFFEY JR'S WINNING RUN

Year	1996	
Publisher	Nintendo	
Developer	Rare	

THERE AREN'T MANY sporting moments iconic enough to inspire entire games, but that's the case here. The 'Winning Run' in question is Ken Griffey Jr's run from first base to home in the bottom of the 11th inning to win the 1995 American League Wild Card Playoffs. This time handled by Rare, Winning Run is visually very different from its predecessor, with digitised 3D models of players (similar to the technique Rare used for Donkey Kong Country). Once again, the team names are real but the player names aren't, and there's a bonus reward for anyone patient enough to complete a full 162-game season: four unlockable teams, including the upcoming 1998 expansion teams (the Tampa Bay Devil Rays and Arizona Diamondbacks), a Nintendo team and even a Nintendo 64 team. ∎

FACT

Ken Griffey Jr was the star player for the Seattle Mariners, which Nintendo's Hiroshi Yamauchi bought in 1992. In 2004 he gave the Mariners to Nintendo of America, who would own them until 2016.

KENDO RAGE

Year	1993	
Publisher	SETA	
Developer	SETA	

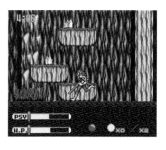

WHEN AMERICAN SCHOOLGIRL Jo's parents let her travel to Japan to study kendo, things don't go as she expected. Her sensei, calling himself Bob, gives her a talisman and explains that she has special psychic powers. Turns out it's up to Jo to use these newfound powers – as well as her kendo sword, obviously – to take out a bunch of monsters on her way to the kendo school. Similar in style to the Valis games, Kendo Rage is an action platformer where you can gather coloured balls to perform special attacks (such as firing a 'spirit shotgun' blast from your sword). If it looks anime-esque, you'd be right: an anime series based on Kendo Rage was released in Japan shortly after the game launched. ∎

FACT

In case killing monsters with a wooden sword gives you the urge to try kendo for yourself, the Kendo Rage manual includes the address for the Kendo Federation in Lomita, California.

KEVIN KEEGAN'S PLAYER MANAGER

Year	1993
Publisher	Imagineer
Developer	Anco

THIS SPIN-OFF OF the Kick Off games adds management to the mix, letting you not only play the game but also take control of things like transfers, finances and training. Endorsed by then Newcastle manager Kevin Keegan, its lengthy career mode has you starting as a brand new team in either the second or third division (your choice) in English football. The game's title comes into play more than you'd think: when you start off your player manager is 28 years old. When he retires at 37 you're no longer able to actually control matches and are limited to just the management side of things (until you buy your 'relative' a few seasons later). The manual is a must: the icon-based menus are among the most confusing in gaming. ■

FACT

Keegan was the recipient of probably the most boring driving ban in history. After being caught doing 36mph in a 30mph zone, he received enough penalty points on his licence to trigger a six-month ban.

KICK OFF

Year	1993
Publisher	Imagineer
Developer	Anco

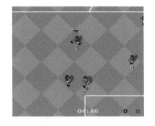

IF MANAGEMENT DOESN'T appeal to you and you just want a no-nonsense football game, but still want the extremely confusing menu icons to go with it, Kick Off has you covered. There are a number of different game modes, including an English League (with eight teams), an English Cup (with the same eight teams), a European League (with 16 European club teams) and an International Cup (with eight national teams). When originally created by Dino Dini the Kick Off series was noted for being a challenge to master, since the ball didn't stick to players' feet and had to be constantly controlled. Although this SNES version is programmed by the brilliantly named Steve Screech instead of Dini, this important feature remains: it wouldn't be Kick Off otherwise. ■

FACT

Even though plenty of SNES games start with the word Super in their name, it's actually the Mega Drive version of this one that's called Super Kick Off.

KICK OFF 3: EUROPEAN CHALLENGE

Year	1994
Publisher	Imagineer
Developer	Anco

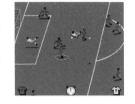

IT WOULD APPEAR that someone finally had a friendly word with Steve Screech, because Kick Off 3 ditches the horrible icon-based menu system of its predecessors in favour of text-based menus. There are a load more teams this time around: players can take part in full English, French, Spanish, German or Italian league campaigns with every major team in those leagues present. Player names are fake, but close enough to the real thing to make it possible to use the in-game editor or tweak them. Unusually, the game also ditches Kick Off's trademark overhead view in favour of a side-on viewpoint. It also offers a bunch of other European teams, though these include Rangers but not Celtic. As a Celtic supporter, therefore, I must selfishly say this game is terrible. ■

FACT

Although Kick Off is generally associated with Dino Dini, Steve Screech had arguably just as much to do with it. The original game was his idea, and while Dini designed and programmed it, Screech created the graphics, playtested it and fine-tuned it.

KID KLOWN IN CRAZY CHASE

Year	1994
Publisher	Kemco
Developer	Kemco

THE EVIL SPACE pirate Blackjack has kidnapped Princess Honey, and won't give her up until her old man, King Klown, steps down and declares him the new king. The king issues a royal decree asking for help and the only person to answer is the young, bumbling Kid Klown. Each of the game's five stages begins with a massive fuse being lit: you have to race against the fuse by running downhill, avoiding all manner of obstacles along the way, in an attempt to reach the bomb it's connected to and punt said bomb out of sight before the fuse runs out. This is a brief game but an entertaining one, as the various animations the player is 'treated' to when they mess up are certainly enough to elicit a few chuckles. ■

FACT

The game was re-released on the GBA in 2002 as simply Crazy Chase. It adds a bunch of extra stages but suffers from a significantly lower frame rate.

KILLER INSTINCT

Year	1995
Publisher	Nintendo
Developer	Rare

AS RARE WAS working on Donkey Kong Country, it was also dabbling with a prototype for a fighting game called Brute Force. When Nintendo's Ken Lobb saw it, it was quickly decided that this should be Rare's next release. Renamed Killer Instinct and designed as an arcade game first and foremost, the idea was to develop it using arcade hardware similar to Nintendo's upcoming 64-bit console, then port it to the console once it launched in late 1995: the hope was that by the time Nintendo's new system was out, the arcade version would be popular enough to make Killer Instinct an important exclusive. Sure enough, when the arcade game launched in October 1994, the attract mode regularly shouted: 'Available for your home in 1995, only on Nintendo Ultra 64.'

Things don't always work out like they're supposed to, though, and the Ultra 64 didn't make it to anyone's home in 1995. Instead, the console (now renamed the Nintendo 64) was delayed until well into 1996: June in Japan and September in North America, to be specific. In order to give fans something to tide them over until then, Rare instead got to work on a SNES version of Killer Instinct. The result would be an impressive SNES fighting game that may not have matched the arcade version pound-for-pound in the looks department, but still offered indisputably satisfying combat with a brilliant soundtrack.

What sets Killer Instinct apart from other fighting games is its combo system, which can essentially be as deep as the player wants it to be. Should they want to simply play the game Street Fighter II style, focusing on individual moves and pulling off the odd short combo here and there, they're more than welcome to do so. Anyone who takes the time to study the combo mechanics, however, will find a remarkably deep system that requires a fair deal of practice but can result in some jaw-dropping sequences. Combos are split into different types of moves called openers, auto-doubles, linkers and enders, and the player can chain these together in a variety of different ways to build their own combos. The larger the combo, the more excitable the announcer gets, all the way up to him hollering 'ULTRAAAAAA, ULTRAAAAAA' (a reference to Ultra 64) at the top of his lungs. In order to make sure these combos don't potentially last forever, skilled opponents can execute combo breakers at the right time to swiftly kill off a combo mid-flow.

Although Killer Instinct was never really made with the SNES in mind, and although some concessions had to be made – most notably when it came to background detail – in order to get such a groundbreaking arcade game running on Nintendo's 16-bit system, there can be no denying that most of those who owned the SNES version would happily declare it one of the best fighting games on the console. Rare had done it again, and as the Nintendo 64 era loomed, the UK developer had made it clear that it was going to be one of Nintendo's most important allies in the next generation. ∎

FACT

Rare actually made a SNES port of Killer Instinct 2 and developed it to completion, but Nintendo chose not to release it. Instead, the long-promised N64 version launched as Killer Instinct Gold.

KING ARTHUR & THE KNIGHTS OF JUSTICE

Year	1995
Publisher	Enix
Developer	Manley & Associates

THIS ACTION RPG is based on a now forgotten '90s animated series featuring one of the most ridiculous premises ever. King Arthur and the Knights of the Round Table have been kidnapped by the evil sorceress Morgana, so his wizard Merlin summons a team of 'warriors' from the future. These warriors are actually members of an American football team, led by a chap called Arthur King. Playing as Arthur, you have to choose two other teammates (who are controlled by the AI) and head off on your adventure. Each of the game's bosses is weak against one knight in particular, so it's in your best interest to return to the Round Table periodically and swap up your party. It's impossible to tell which knight is best suited to each boss, however. ■

FACT

There's a whole host of unused dialogue, sprites, animations, items and game maps left in the game's code, far more than in most other carts. This suggests the game was rushed to release it quckly.

KING ARTHUR'S WORLD

Year	1993
Publisher	Jaleco
Developer	Argonaut Games

A SORT OF cross between a strategy game and Lemmings, King Arthur's World has you guiding the titular monarch through 23 different stages as he leads a crusade against the enemies of the crown. The general aim is to get Arthur from one end of each stage to the other: he'll continue to walk in any direction you tell him to go, until he comes up against an enemy, who he'll then try to fight. You can accompany Arthur by summoning various different types of troops, from archers to mages to 'barrel men', who drop explosive barrels to blow things up. Although it's playable with a controller, it also supports the SNES mouse, which is particularly recommended for this game given its cursor-based nature. ■

FACT

King Arthur's World was the first SNES game to be encoded with Dolby Surround audio. Jaleco made a big deal o this in the manual, dedicating an entire page to essentially boasting, stating: 'Jaleco makes video game history.'

THE KING OF DRAGONS

Year	1994
Publisher	Capcom
Developer	Capcom

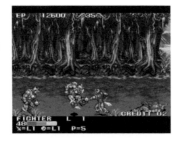

THE RED DRAGON Gildiss has taken over the kingdom of Malus, so it's up to a group of five heroes to kill it and its monster pals. The King of Dragons is a port of Capcom's arcade beat 'em up (well, slash 'em up) in which the player can choose between five distinct characters: an elf, a wizard, a fighter, a cleric and a dwarf. Each character has their own unique qualities: the dwarf, for example, is the strongest of the heroes but he's very slow, while the cleric is generally quite weak but levels up quickly. Whereas the arcade version allowed for simultaneous three-player adventuring, the SNES version drops this down to two (which, given Capcom's solo-only Final Fight port, is still decent). ■

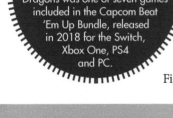

FACT

If you fancy trying this one out on modern systems, the arcade version of The King of Dragons was one of seven games included in the Capcom Beat 'Em Up Bundle, released in 2018 for the Switch, Xbox One, PS4 and PC.

KING OF THE MONSTERS

Year	1992
Publisher	Takara
Developer	Genki

ORIGINALLY RELEASED AS a Neo Geo arcade title in 1991, King of the Monsters would get a SNES adaptation a year later. Based on the 'kaiju' movies popular in Japan (such as Godzilla), King of the Monsters is a one-on-one fighting game in which players choose a giant monster and try to defeat another one, while inadvertently destroying the surrounding city in the process. Although the arcade version featured six monsters, the SNES one only includes four: the Godzilla-like Geon, the stone man Rocky, giant bug Beetle Mania and the suspiciously Ultraman-esque Astro Guy. The controls are clunky and the fighting is limited (leading to poor reviews at the time) but there's a charm to King of the Monsters that makes it possible to forgive some of this. ■

FACT

The two arcade characters dropped from the SNES version are Poison Ghost (a big green sludge monster made of toxic waste) and Woo, a huge gorilla in the King Kong vein.

KING OF THE MONSTERS 2

Year | 1994
Publisher | Takara
Developer | Takara

SET THREE YEARS after the events of the first game, King of the Monsters 2 sees only three monsters remaining after a huge massacre. An alien invasion has threatened to take over the Earth, so this time the monsters get to be the good guys. This time, instead of a one-on-one fighting game (though this is still available as a two-player mode), it's a side-scrolling beat 'em up where players fight their way through numerous aliens, with the occasional boss battle breaking things up. The playable monsters are enhanced versions of three of the original game's characters: Astro Guy is now Atomic Guy, Geon has become Super Geon and Woo – the gorilla who didn't make the cut in the first SNES game – is here as Cyber Woo. ∎

FACT

The arcade version's flyer was pretty dramatic. 'The monstrous battle is coming!', it stated, adding: 'Human beings no longer rule the Earth!'

KIRBY'S AVALANCHE

Year | 1995
Publisher | Nintendo
Developer | Compile / HAL Laboratory

IN LATE 1993, developer Compile released a Super Famicom version of its popular Puyo Puyo puzzle game called, appropriately, Super Puyo Puyo. Deciding that its anime characters may not appeal to western audiences, the game was given a complete makeover and had all its characters, backgrounds and music replaced with those from the Kirby universe. Kirby's Avalanche, then (known in Europe as Kirby's Ghost Trap), is essentially Puyo Puyo with a new story in which Kirby has to win a series of 'Avalanche' battles against former enemies on his way to a final showdown with King Dedede. Since this redesign included repurposing Super Puyo Puyo's cutscenes, this means Kirby engages in some smack talk with his opponents between each round: Kirby having dialogue is unusual for the series. ∎

FACT

Since Kirby's Avalanche was already based on the Japan-only Super Puyo Puyo, there was no reason to release it in Japan. This makes it the only Kirby game not to be released in that region.

KIRBY'S DREAM COURSE

Year | 1995
Publisher | Nintendo
Developer | HAL Laboratory

IF YOU'VE EVER wondered what mini golf would be like if the ball was Kirby, that's a strangely specific thing to be thinking about. Regardless, such a thing exists: Kirby's Dream Course turns HAL's popular pink podge into a golf ball and dumps him into 64 holes of increasing difficulty, each littered with enemies. You have to 'putt' Kirby into the enemies to defeat them, and when only one of them remains it'll turn into the hole. Keeping things interesting is Kirby's health: it's split into four sections and every time you take a shot he loses one. He gets one back every time he hits an enemy or lands the hole, though, so accuracy is crucial in keeping his energy topped up. ∎

FACT

Kirby's Dream Course was originally a straight mini golf game called Special Tee Shot that had nothing to do with Kirby. It later appeared as a download on the Japan-only Satellaview modem.

KIRBY'S DREAM LAND 3

Year | 1997
Publisher | Nintendo
Developer | HAL Laboratory

A FULL 14 months after the Nintendo 64 launched in North America, Nintendo finally released its final SNES game, drawing a line under its 16-bit output. Kirby's Dream Land 3 takes the Dream Land series away from the Game Boy for the first time and has Kirby trying to defeat the evil Dark Matter, who's shattered the rings of Dream Land and is going around possessing its residents. As well as his usual ability-stealing trick, Kirby can also summon his long-tongued blob pal Gooey as an AI helper, or ride a variety of animal pals (each with their own abilities) including Rick the Hamster, Coo the Owl and Kine the Ocean Sunfish. Not the most revolutionary game, but a pleasant end to the SNES's first-party library. ∎

FACT

This is one of 34 games that use the SA1 chip, a special enhancement chip included in the cartridge that triples the CPU's clock speed and adds a bunch of other features including faster RAM.

KIRBY SUPER STAR

Year	1996
Publisher	Nintendo
Developer	HAL Laboratory

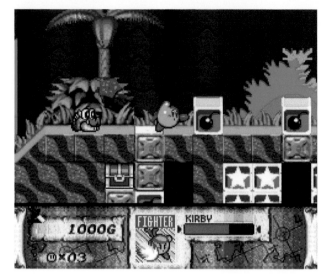

KNOWN AS KIRBY'S Fun Pak in Europe, this sizable compilation promises '8 games in one' on the box, but in reality offers six, seven or nine depending on your definition of what constitutes a 'full' game. In fairness, most are short adventures that wouldn't be long enough to release as standalone titles, but combined they make for a lengthy package. First up is Spring Breeze, which is a shorter remake of Kirby's Dream Land. Following that is Dyna Blade, where Kirby has to stop a giant bird destroying Dream Land's crops, while Gourmet Race offers a handful of foot races against King Dedede where scoring points is as important as finishing first. The Great Cave Offensive is arguably the best of the bunch: it's a Metroidvania style adventure where Kirby has to find 60 treasures, many of which are references to Nintendo games. Then there's two more standard platforming adventures in the shape of Revenge of Meta Knight

FACT

Kirby Super Star was going to have another game included called Kagero Mansion, where Kirby is in a haunted house and can't inhale enemies. It was scrapped for time reasons.

and Milky Way Wishes, the latter seeing Kirby collecting abilities and adding them to a permanent list. This is all rounded off with The Arena – which is essentially a large Boss Rush mode where you take on all 26 bosses in the game – and a couple of brief timing-based mini-games where Kirby has to attack an enemy with a samurai sword or punch a larger hole into a planet than his opponent. Combined, the various small offerings here make up an enjoyable overall package, making it the video game equivalent of those Kelloggs variety packs where you get a bunch of small boxes of cereal. ■

KNIGHTS OF THE ROUND

Year	1994
Publisher	Capcom
Developer	Capcom

SIMILAR IN STYLE to The King of Dragons, Knights of the Round is another medieval-themed arcade beat 'em up developed by Capcom. This time you get to choose between three noble sword-

wielding types, led by Arthur, as they head out on a quest to unite Britain by finding the Legendary Grail and in turn convincing the other lords and knights to accept Arthur as the new king. He's the most obvious choice to play as, especially since he's armed with Excalibur, but if you're something of a non-conformist you may prefer to play as Lancelot with his sabre, or Perceval, who carries a big battleaxe. One thing that sets Knights of the Round apart from most other beat 'em ups is its emphasis on blocking attacks, rather than just going in swinging. ■

FACT

When it comes to terrible jokes, they don't come much worse than the US magazine ads for Knights of the Round, which state: 'No knight club has ever seen this much action.'

KRUSTY'S SUPER FUN HOUSE

Year	1992
Publisher	Acclaim
Developer	Audiogenic

KRUSTY THE CLOWN'S fun house has been infested by rats! Rather than risk facing health and safety sanctions, he decides to instead risk proper criminal charges by hiring a small boy to kill the rats for him. Let me elaborate: this game

is a sort of reverse version of Lemmings where the aim is to kill all the rodents, not rescue them. You have to use blocks and other obstacles to create a path for the rats to follow that eventually leads them to one of Krusty's large extermination devices, each of which is controlled by a different Simpsons character: Bart, Homer, Corporal Punishment and Sideshow Mel. Easily one of the better 'dangerously irresponsible clown tortures live animals' games you'll play, and that's a hugely contested category. ■

FACT

There are two versions of the game on the SNES. They're more or less identical with one major change: the music in worlds 2 and 4 is totally different in each.

KYLE PETTY'S NO FEAR RACING

Year	1995
Publisher	William Entertainment
Developer	Leland Interactive Media

THIS STOCK CAR racing game features the likeness of Kyle Petty, a reasonably well-known NASCAR racer (at the time he'd finished 5th in back-to-back seasons, followed by 15th). It also includes a tie-in with No Fear, the edgy extreme sports clothing brand that was big at the time. As well as the option to pick a single race, there's a season mode where you race through 28 speedway tracks, including ones like Bristol and (the extremely foggy) Dover which are initially confusing to a British person until you realise they're circuits in Tennessee and Delaware respectively. If those aren't enough to keep you busy there's also a course creator, where you can make your own tracks and customise them by placing decals on them and choosing the background music. ◼

FACT

Kyle Petty's dad was Richard Petty, also known as The King, who was statistically the greatest driver in the history of NASCAR. Rock band Soundgarden once recorded a song called Kyle Petty, Son of Richard.

LAGOON

Year	1992
Publisher	Seika Corporation
Developer	Kemco

THERE'S A PROBLEM in Lakeland (the fictional country, not the chain of British kitchenware stores). What used to be an idyllic, fruitful land is now suffering from muddy water, which is polluting the rivers and lakes and causing some citizens to get sick and die. It's all the work of a warlock called Zerah, who's trying to resurrect an evil spirit and use it to take over the land. You play as Nasir, a young lad destined to be the Champion of Light, who heads out to save Lakeland and stop them having to drink bottled water all the time (I'm just speculating there). Although it's RPG-like in nature, Lagoon plays like a more dialogue-heavy Zelda game, with fights taking place in real-time instead of typical turn-based battling. ◼

FACT

Lagoon was originally released on the Sharp X68000 home computer in Japan, where it included animated cutscenes and a slightly different storyline which mixes around the order in which the game's objectives appear.

LAMBORGHINI AMERICAN CHALLENGE

Year	1993
Publisher	Titus Software
Developer	Titus Software

FRENCH STUDIO TITUS was mainly known for its home computer games, including the much-loved Crazy Cars series. Lamborghini American Challenge is essentially a Lambo-licensed port of Crazy Cars III, and has you taking part in various races across the US while placing wagers against your opponents. Money won can then be spent on upgrading your car: it's all very legally dubious, this underground racing scene. The SNES version supports the SNES Mouse and Super Scope: the former is simply an alternative control scheme, whereas the latter unlocks a special shooting mode, where the car drives automatically and you focus on gunning down other racers, as if racing for money wasn't quite illegal enough for you. ◼

FACT

The second Crazy Cars game was also given a licensed re-release, though this time it was a Ferrari tie-in called F40 Pursuit Simulator. It was only released on home computers.

LAST ACTION HERO

Year	1993
Publisher	Sony Imagesoft
Developer	Bits Studios

COLUMBIA PICTURES' ACTION comedy movie *Last Action Hero* may not have been as successful as hoped – that's what happens when you release a week after *Jurassic Park* – but that didn't mean it was spared the inevitable video game tie-ins anyway. In this action platformer you allegedly play as Arnold Schwarzenneger's character Jack Slater (he looks nothing like Arnie) as he pursues evil-doer Benedict in an attempt to retrieve a magical movie ticket that will send them back to the cinematic world where they belong. There are seven stages in total, two of which ditch the side-scrolling routine and give you a top-down car chase instead. One thing it doesn't have, however, is the Shakespeare level seen in the NES version. ◼

FACT

Last Action Hero was the first movie to be advertised in space, when Columbia paid NASA $500,000 to put the film's logo on the fuselage of a rocket. Judging by the box office, though, not many aliens bought tickets.

THE LAWNMOWER MAN

Year	1993
Publisher	THQ
Developer	Sales Curve Interactive

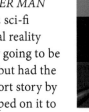

THE LAWNMOWER MAN was a strange 1992 sci-fi movie about virtual reality that was originally going to be called Cyber God but had the name of a 1975 short story by Stephen King slapped on it to try and boost hype. The SNES video game tie-in is actually a sequel of sorts, following on from the events of the film and putting you in control of either Pierce Brosnan's character Dr Angelo or his friend Carla as they try to put an end to secret agency The Shop and its head honcho the Doomplayer. The game jumps between standard 2D action platforming sections and third-person sections in the VR world, where you zoom through polygonal landscapes at high speed. The manual promised a second game: it didn't happen. ■

FACT

Stephen King was so annoyed that the film had nothing to do with his book that he sued New Line Cinema to take his name off the poster. The courts agreed and King was paid $2.5 million in a settlement.

LEGEND

Year	1994
Publisher	Seika Corporation
Developer	Arcade Zone

AFTER TERRORISING THE kingdom of Sellech for a thousand years, the evil dictator Beldor was eventually overthrown, his soul sealed away. Peace and harmony prospered until Clovis, the king of Sellech's dodgy son, decided he wanted to use the power of Beldor's soul to take over the kingdom. Now it's up to two knights named Kaor and Igor to wander through Sellech, booting lumps out of everything they come across, in order to reach Clovis and smack him around the chops. Legend is a somewhat underrated beat 'em up, with solid combat and decent sprite work. Elements of the design are odd though: while your hero moves extremely slowly, you can perform a jumping attack that shoots you quickly across the screen. This means you end up jumping more than walking. ■

FACT

Developer Arcade Zone consisted of just two people: Carlo Perconti and Lyes Belaidouni. When you beat the game you're presented with a photo of the pair sporting some impressively 1994 haircuts.

THE LEGEND OF THE MYSTICAL NINJA

Year	1992
Publisher	Konami
Developer	Konami

KONAMI'S GANBARE GOEMON series of games started in the arcades in 1986 and saw a few Famicom games in its early days, but it wasn't until the series moved to 16-bit gaming that Konami finally decided to bring it to the west with The Legend of the Mystical Ninja, the fifth major Goemon release. Not that anyone in America or Europe were supposed to know him by that name at the time, mind you: Goemon and his partner Ebisumaru had their names changed for the western release of the game to the slightly less mystical Kid Ying and Dr Yang. The story in this version goes that Ying and Yang (sigh) have to find a missing ghost princess and return her to the town of Horo-Horo, otherwise the 'Dragonbeast' will unleash a plague on the land. Each of the game's nine stages (or

FACT

A couple of Game Boy games aside, Goemon did briefly return to western consoles in two Nintendo 64 games (where he was called Goemon this time). Of the 23 main Ganbare Goemon releases, though, only five got English-language versions.

Warlock Zones, as they're known here) are split into two sections: the first is a top-down, Zelda style adventure where you explore each location – a haunted graveyard, an amusement park, a ninja castle and so on – while chatting to NPCs and taking part in a variety of mini-games. Then it's onto the second section, which consists of a side-scrolling platforming stage. While subsequent 16-bit sequels remained exclusive to Japan, The Legend of the Mystical Ninja's bizarre sense of humour gave it something of a cult following and it continues to impress those who stumble upon it and discover it to this day. ■

THE LEGEND OF ZELDA: A LINK TO THE PAST

Year	1992
Publisher	Nintendo
Developer	Nintendo

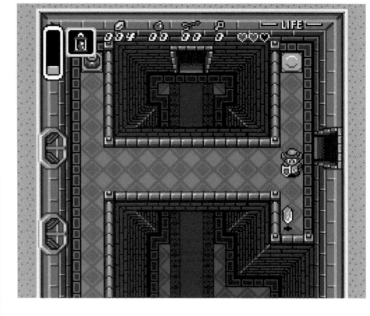

AFTER WOWING NES owners the world over with The Legend of Zelda, Nintendo followed it up by taking things in a completely different direction with Zelda II. While its RPG-style, side-scrolling combat was enjoyed by many, it was still generally agreed that the first game had been the most revolutionary and engrossing of the two. When it came to the series' debut on the SNES, then, there was probably many a sigh of relief when it emerged that the third Zelda game would be going back to the top-down action that made the original so adored.

A Link to the Past once again puts players in the boots of Link (albeit a different Link… look, it's a long story) and opens with him receiving a telepathic message from Princess Zelda asking him to rescue her from the dungeon of Hyrule Castle. After freeing her, the pair learn from a priest that an evil warlock called Agahnim plans to break a centuries-old seal that's been holding the even-more-evil Ganon prisoner. It's up to Link to head out and retrieve the magical pendants of Courage, Wisdom and Power in order to prove that he's worthy to wield the Master Sword, the only thing strong enough to defeat Agahnim.

It's a fairly straightforward story, then, but what makes A Link to the Past so impressive for those playing it for the first time is the way that it fools you into thinking you're approaching the end and then reveals that actually, no, this is a far bigger adventure than you expected. After

FACT

Link wasn't originally going to be going solo in this adventure. In a 1989 discussion with Dragon Quest creator Yuji Horii, Shigeru Miyamoto reveals that he wanted Zelda III to have a party of heroes including Link, a girl and a magic user.

gathering all three pendants, getting the Master Sword and defeating Agahnim, Link is sent to the Dark World, a parallel dimension to Hyrule. Here he's given a new, even bigger quest: find and rescue the seven maidens imprisoned in the Dark World's dungeons and use their power to access Ganon's Tower to put an end to Agahnim once and for all.

Such an enormous adventure was unprecedented at the time. Up until that point the biggest SNES cartridge held 4Mb, but A Link to the Past was given a shiny new 8Mb cartridge in order to fit everything in there. It was worth it, though, because nobody had played anything quite so grandiose. The world map was significantly larger than that in previous Zelda games, and the various atmospheric effects – the shimmering water, the light splitting through the trees in the forest, the way the rainfall in the opening sequence can still be heard (albeit muffled) when you enter the castle – all combined to make one of the most immersive experiences to date. Rounding all this off is the magnificent soundtrack by long-time Nintendo composer Koji Kondo. Many of the Zelda series' most recognisable themes – Kakariko Village, Zelda's Lullaby, Ganondorf's theme, the Fairy Cave – made their debuts in A Link to the Past, and the fact they returned for countless subsequent games is a testament to their quality. A Link to the Past may have been surpassed by its successors in terms of size, depth and graphical fidelity, but when it comes to initial impact few games in the series can hold a candle to it. ∎

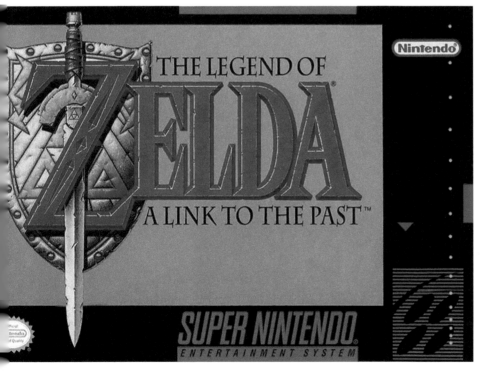

LEMMINGS

Year	1992
Publisher	Sunsoft
Developer	Psygnosis

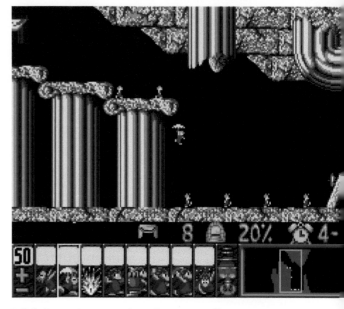

THERE ARE FEWER puzzle games more well-loved and well-known than Lemmings. The creation of Scottish developer DMA Design and originally released on Amiga home computers, Lemmings hit the perfect combination of taking simple, easy to learn mechanics and putting them in situations that were increasingly complex and tough to overcome. Players are put in charge of a group of tiny, mindless rodents who keep walking forwards until they hit a wall (at which point they turn round) or die in some manner. It's up to you to guide the Lemmings to the exit on each stage by assigning them certain roles: Climber (climbs any walls it walks into), Floater (uses an umbrella to avoid dying from high falls), Bomber (explodes, dying but taking part of the scenery with it), Blocker (stops Lemmings from getting past it), Builder (creates a small diagonal bridge), Basher (punches a horizontal tunnel through a wall), Miner (the same, but diagonal) and Digger (same again, but straight down).

FACT

Some console versions of Lemmings (Mega Drive, Game Boy Color and PlayStation) also included the Oh No! More Lemmings expansion pack, which added another 100 levels.

While Lemmings was released on practically every system at the time (and countless others since), reaction to the each port generally depends on one criterion: whether it has mouse support. Those versions that have to be played with a controller can become tricky in later stages where quick and accurate selection is a must, but unfortunately the SNES version of Lemmings launched around six or seven months before the SNES Mouse was released, meaning it doesn't support the peripheral. It does, however, include five extra difficult 'Sunsoft Special' stages exclusive to the SNES version. ■

LEMMINGS 2: THE TRIBES

Year	1994
Publisher	Psygnosis
Developer	Psygnosis

THE SEQUEL TO Lemmings ramped up the variety by quite some degree. This time the game's 120 levels are split into groups of 10 themed stages, each represented by a different 'tribe': Circus, Beach, Polar,

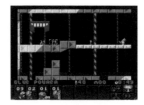

Highland, Space, Caveman, Classic, Outdoor, Medieval, Egyptian, Sports and Shadow. Each tribe has its own range of skills, meaning the Egyptian tribe has a magic carpet ability, the Polar tribe lets you turn a Lemming into a skier, and the Sports tribe can have a pole vaulter.

In all there are 51 different skills (some are in multiple tribes), giving the game more depth but also making it significantly less accessible to new players. On the bright side, the SNES Mouse is supported this time, at least making it easier in that regard. ■

FACT

A series of 12 'tribe pins' were included with some versions of Lemmings 2, Holiday Lemmings and 3D Lemmings. Each copy only got one random pin and they're now generally sold individually on eBay for big money, so getting a full set can be very expensive.

LESTER THE UNLIKELY

Year	1994
Publisher	DTMC
Developer	Visual Concepts

THIS STRANGE PLATFORMER has you playing as Lester, who's pretty much the early '90s stereotype of a teen nerd. While reading the latest issue of the *Super Duper Hero Squad* comic, he falls asleep next to

a cargo crate and ends up on a ship, which is then scuttled, leaving him stranded on a desert island. It's up to Lester to try to find a way off the island. For the first half of the game, Lester's animations sum up his character to an almost comical degree: he gingerly kicks at enemies, stands with his shoulders slumped and runs with his arms flailing. Then, when he saves a bikini-clad tribesgirl about halfway through, he gets a thank-you kiss and his animations become more heroic from that point on. ■

FACT

Programmer Brian Greenstone isn't too proud of Lester. On the website of his Pangea Software studio, he writes: 'Lester was a game I never liked. Don't wanna talk about it.'

LETHAL ENFORCERS

Year	1994
Publisher	Konami
Developer	Konami

ARCADES AND LIGHT gun games go together like loud children and annoyed passengers, and Lethal Enforcers was one of the noisiest kids around. An arcade staple in the early '90s, Konami decided to port it to home consoles a couple of years later. It's a five-stage shooting gallery where you play as a cop tasked with gunning down a slew of criminals and terrorists. Rather than supporting the Super Scope, the SNES version of Lethal Enforcers instead comes with the Justifier, a bright blue handgun designed to let players gun down criminals without worrying about any sniper rifle nonsense. You could also use a normal controller to move a cursor, but if player two felt left out they could send away to Konami for a second, pink Justifier. ■

FACT

In one of the more trivial examples of Nintendo censorship, the second stage is known as Chinatown Assault on all systems except the SNES, where it's been renamed Downtown Assault.

LIBERTY OR DEATH

Year	1994
Publisher	Koei
Developer	Koei

ONE OF KOEI'S many historical simulation games, Liberty or Death retells the events of the American Revolutionary War in lengthy, number-crunching detail. Players can choose to be on either the side of the American Continental Army or the British Army, taking on the role of George Washington or Thomas Gage respectively. Every turn (which represents two weeks) has you making a number of decisions, from basic stuff like setting your army's spending budget to more specific choices such as bribing enemy generals, holding parades to become more popular or dealing with independent militia units. Inevitably, this all eventually leads to battles, which are turn-based strategy skirmishes taking place on hexagonal battlefields. The ultimate aim is to defeat all enemy troops and claim America for your nation. ■

FACT

The PC version of Liberty or Death doesn't force you to play either Washington or Gage: you can instead choose to be Artemas Ward, Charles Lee, Sir Henry Clinton or William Howe should you so desire. It's basically Smash Bros for historians.

LETHAL WEAPON

Year	1992
Publisher	Ocean Software
Developer	Ocean Software

   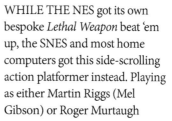 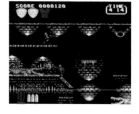

WHILE THE NES got its own bespoke *Lethal Weapon* beat 'em up, the SNES and most home computers got this side-scrolling action platformer instead. Playing as either Martin Riggs (Mel Gibson) or Roger Murtaugh (Danny Glover), you get to choose between four different missions: infiltrate a racketeering gang's ship and steal their money, stop terrorists from planting bombs on the subway, prevent another huge bomb going off in a shopping mall and rescue their friend Leo Getz (Joe Pesci), who's being held hostage in an office complex. You can take on the missions in any order, but beat them all and you'll unlock the fifth and final one, where you have to stop a corrupt ex-police sergeant who's developed special ammo that penetrates bulletproof vests. ■

FACT

The final mission is based on *Lethal Weapon 3*, which had just been released and sees Riggs and Murtaugh tracking a former lieutenant turned arms smuggler whose gang uses armour-piercing bullets.

THE LION KING

Year	1994
Publisher	Virgin Interactive
Developer	Westwood Studios

THE HUGE SUCCESS of Virgin Interactive's Mega Drive version of Aladdin meant the publisher would take on Disney's next cinematic release, *The Lion King*. Whereas the SNES version of Aladdin was a completely different game developed by Capcom, this time all formats were handled by Virgin. Playing as Simba, you essentially make your way through the plot of the movie over the course of 10 stages, the final four of which put you in the shoes (well, paws) of Simba as an adult. Among the more notable stages are the colourful Can't Wait to be King level where you swing on monkeys and bounce off giraffe heads, and the Stampede stage where the iconic wildebeest chase is recreated in a third-person viewpoint with Simba running into the screen. ■

FACT

The SNES version of The Lion King and Mega Drive version of Aladdin were re-released together on Switch, PS4, Xbox One and PC in late 2019 as Disney Classics: Aladdin and the Lion King.

LOCK ON

Year	1993
Publisher	Vic Tokai
Developer	Copya System

LOCK ON IS the sequel to the Mega Drive game Air Diver: indeed, in Europe and Japan it's known as Super Air Diver instead. You play as the gloriously named Jake Steel, a hotshot pilot for the United Nations who takes part in a number of missions in order to bring down an evil warlord. You get to choose between four real-world planes: the F-14D Super Tomcat, the Mitsubishi FS-X, the A-10A Thunderbolt II and the Panavia Tornado IDS. Combat is more user-friendly than most other dogfighting games: the scenery underneath you whips past in Mode 7 and you simply need to focus on gunning down enemies with your guns and various missiles. You also have a stock of flares that you can fire to prevent heat-seeking missiles hitting you. ■

FACT

A sequel called Super Air Diver 2 was released in Japan, and lets players fly either an F-15E Strike Eagle or a Mirage 2000. It was planned for a US release as Lock On 2 but was scrapped.

LOONEY TUNES B-BALL

Year	1995
Publisher	Sunsoft
Developer	Sculptured Software

A COUPLE OF years before *Space Jam* did it, Sunsoft dumped Bugs Bunny and chums onto basketball courts and insisted they shoot some hoops. Looney Tunes B-Ball – or Looney Tunes Basketball in Europe, because apparently Europeans wouldn't be able to figure out what B-Ball means – lets players create their own two-man team from a roster of eight: Bugs Bunny, Daffy Duck, Elmer Fudd, Wile E. Coyote, the Tasmanian Devil, Yosemite Sam, Sylvester the Cat and Marvin the Martian. Gameplay is similar to NBA Jam: not just because it's two-on-two but because there are plenty of over-the-top dunks in there too. There's also a 'wacky meter', which can be adjusted in the settings and affects the frequency of zany obstacles and power-ups appearing. ■

FACT

If you're wondering why Lola Bunny isn't in this game, it's because, as previously stated, it launched a couple of years before *Space Jam*. Lola was actually an original character created specifically for that movie.

THE LOST VIKINGS

Year	1993
Publisher	Interplay
Developer	Silicon & Synapse

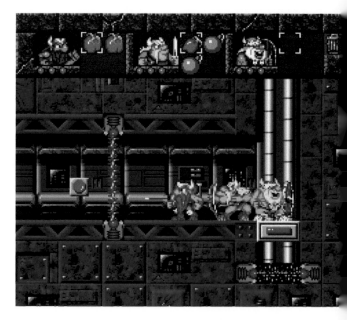

ERIK THE SWIFT, Baleog the Fierce and Olaf the Stout are in way over their Norse heads. The trio have been abducted from their village by an alien called Tomator, who needs some Earthlings for his intergalactic zoo and reckons this bearded trio fits the bill. It's up to the three to work together to figure out how to escape Tomator's massive spaceship and make their way back to their home village to be reunited with their families. When I say 'work together', I mean it: the entire core of The Lost Vikings' puzzle-based platforming revolves around the fact that each Viking has specific abilities, all of which are needed in order to get to the exit on each stage. Erik is the only member of the group who can jump, and his faster running speed makes him valuable during moments where time is limited. Baleog is the only armed Viking: his sword lets him take out close enemies, while his bow and arrow is useful for hitting switches that are otherwise impossible to reach. Meanwhile, Olaf has a shield which can not only be used to block dangers (lasers, fire and the like) but also lets him float slowly down from high drops should the need arise. The combination of all three characters' skills – you can freely swap butween them at any point – makes The Lost Vikings one of the best examples of how when everyone's playing to their strengths, teamwork can very much make the dream work. ■

FACT

The Lost Vikings was added to Blizzard's Battle. net platform as a free download for those with a US account. It's still active at the time of writing.

THE LOST VIKINGS 2

Year	1997
Publisher	Interplay
Developer	Blizzard Entertainment

SET A YEAR after the events of the first game, The Lost Vikings 2 sees Erik, Baleog and Olaf once again captured by Tomator, but this time it goes wrong and the trio are sent through time: though not before dismantling one of Tomator's robot guards and stealing some of its parts. These robot parts give them extra skills on top of what they had before: Erik can now double-jump, Baleog has a telescopic arm and Olaf can both shrink and pull off super farts that make him float upwards (look, nobody said they were classy). Two new characters are also introduced later on: Fang is a werewolf who can jump, climb walls and slash enemies, and Scorch is a dragon who can fly and shoot fireballs. ◼

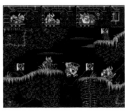

FACT

The Lost Vikings 2 also launched on the PlayStation, Saturn and PC. These versions featured pre-rendered CG sprites, much like Donkey Kong Country, as well as voice acting, but were essentially the same game.

LUCKY LUKE

Year	1997
Publisher	Infogrames
Developer	Infogrames

LUCKY LUKE IS a popular Belgian comic series that's been running since 1946. Set in the Wild West, it's a humorous telling of the adventures of Lucky Luke, a sharpshooting cowboy. This SNES adaptation has Luke trying to apprehend his most well-known rivals, the Dalton Brothers. Luke has to make his way through towns, mines, jails, saloons and trains in search of Averell, William, Jack and Joe Dalton, while also carrying out various sub-quests for other townsfolk. It's an action platformer with a relatively slow pace, but that's not to say it isn't entertaining: there are still plenty of bad guys ready to be filled with lead. Breaking up the action are a series of bonus mini-games – including one where you arm-wrestle your horse, because, why not? ◼

FACT

After starting the comic in 1946, mononymous Belgian artist Morris teamed up with Asterix co-creator René Goscinny in 1955. The pair created *Lucky Luke* comics until Goscinny's death 22 years later. It continues on to this day, however.

LUFIA & THE FORTRESS OF DOOM

Year	1993
Publisher	Taito
Developer	Neverland

NINETY-NINE YEARS AGO, the Sinistrals – a group of four evil forces representing Chaos, Destruction, Terror and Death – descended on the world and spread their dark powers across the land. It was all looking fairly grim until a team of heroes led by Maxim vanquished the Sinistrals, seemingly for good (you play this battle in the game's prologue). Now they're back, though, and with those original warriors long gone, nothing can stand in their way. Nothing, that is, except for your hero – you name him at the start – who's a descendent of Maxim. Accompanied by his best friend Lufia (who has a bit of a thing for him), and eventually joined by top soldier Aguro and half-elf Jerin, he sets off to give the Sinistrals a second smackdown. ◼

FACT

A Sega Genesis port of Lufia was planned for December '94, and was then delayed until Spring 1995, with a magazine ad declaring: 'It's worth the wait!' Turns out it wasn't, because it was eventually cancelled altogether.

LUFIA II: RISE OF THE SINISTRALS

Year	1996
Publisher	Natsume
Developer	Neverland

THE FIRST LUFIA game was well received, but its opening prologue, showing the end of a massive battle against the Sinistrals that took place 99 years before the rest of the game, had fans curious to know more.

Rather than a sequel, then, Lufia II is a prequel that tells the full story of Maxim and his party, their first encounter with the Sinistrals and all the events leading up to the start of the first game. While Lufia II is still an RPG at its core there are some rogue-like elements in there too thanks to the Ancient Cave, a 99-floor dungeon that randomly generates its layout every time you enter. Since the first Lufia wasn't released in Europe, Lufia II is simply known as Lufia there. ◼

FACT

Lufia II was remade for the Nintendo DS under the name Lufia: Curse of the Sinistrals. It ditches the turn-based RPG elements altogether and battles take place in real time.

MACS

Year | 1993
Publisher | US Army
Developer | Sculptured Software

WHEN IT COMES to specialist software, you don't get more specialist than MACS, which stands for Multipurpose Arcade Combat Simulator. Commissioned by the US Army, it's a bespoke light gun game designed to help recruits improve their shooting skills. Rather than using a standard Nintendo gun like the Zapper or Super Scope, however, MACS came with an actual replica M16 rifle (a Jäger AP 74, specifically) that had been modified to act like a light gun. The game itself is an extremely basic shooting exercise where targets appear at various locations on the screen. Players are then given feedback on their steady position, aiming, breath control, trigger squeeze and shot location. It's not clear how accurate or useful the software actually was. ■

FACT

There are three known variants of the MACS cartridge: the initial MACS version 1.1e, MACS Moving Target Simulator and the last known version, MACS Basic Rifle Marksmanship Program version 1994.

MADDEN NFL 94

Year | 1993
Publisher | Electronic Arts
Developer | Visual Concepts

THE THIRD MADDEN game on SNES (after John Madden Football and John Madden Football '93) was the first to get the official NFL licence, hence the addition of the league's name to the series title from this point on. As well as all 28 NFL teams from the 1993 season, the game also includes 13 'All-Time' teams featuring the best players in certain teams' histories, as well as 38 classic teams from previous Super Bowls (such as the 1972 Miami Dolphins and the 1980 Philadelphia Eagles). While undoubtedly a welcome feature, it was dampened a little by the fact that despite now having the NFL licence the series still didn't have a players' licence, meaning players were still represented by only their numbers. ■

FACT

The first batches of the game shipped with an error that switched the rosters (well, the player numbers) of the New York Jets and New York Giants.

MADDEN NFL 95

Year | 1994
Publisher | Electronic Arts
Developer | Visual Concepts

THE 1995 INSTALMENT of Madden is an interesting one in that it gives with one hand and takes away with the other (though mainly the latter). Since Madden had joined the *NFL on Fox* team shortly before the game launched, Madden NFL 95 includes that show's iconic theme as well as Fox Sports banners hanging up at the endzone. However, all the classic All-Time and Super Bowl teams are removed, leaving players with the standard 28 teams and the usual All-Madden team. To add further insult to injury, the Mega Drive version finally received actual player names for the first time, but SNES owners had to continue to do without them this time around, with players on the Nintendo version still represented by their jersey numbers instead. ■

FACT

Although their league debut was still a full season away, NFL expansion teams the Carolina Panthers and Jacksonville Jaguars could be unlocked.

MADDEN NFL 96

Year | 1995
Publisher | Electronic Arts
Developer | Tiburon Entertainment

MADDEN 96 SEES the SNES finally get real player names. Also new to the '96 edition is the ability to create your own player and take part in a series of training drill mini-games. The Panthers and Jaguars become proper, standard teams (as opposed to the hidden unlockables in Madden 95) and the AI is improved to allow for special situations (like spiking the ball to stop the clock and making quick snaps during two-minute drills). Classic teams return, with every team getting its own classic equivalent when you win the Super Bowl with them (or unlock them with a cheat code). Since the Panthers, Jaguars and All-Madden teams don't have classic teams, they instead unlock a free agent team, and teams consisting of EA Sports and Tiburon developers. ■

FACT

Visual Concepts, who had developed the SNES versions of Madden 94 and 95, moved on to work on a PlayStation version of Madden 96. It was eventually cancelled because EA didn't consider it good enough.

MADDEN NFL 97

Year | 1996
Publisher | Electronic Arts
Developer | Tiburon Entertainment

WITH THE MADDEN series finally making its way to the next generation of consoles following a false start the previous year, EA's attention was focused mainly on the PlayStation and Saturn versions of Madden 97 rather than the 16-bit ones. That's not to say the SNES Madden 97 was completely without merit, however: the teams and rosters had been updated to reflect the 1996 season (including the removal of this writer's beloved Cleveland Browns and their replacement with the Baltimore Ravens). A salary cap was introduced when trading players, and a new array of hidden classic teams were added, this time going as far back as 1952 (for the Detroit Lions). On the field, however, it was beginning to become clear that notable changes were thin on the ground. ■

FACT

The Browns may have gone, but their spirit remained as the Ravens' classic team. Since this was the Ravens' first season, their classic team was instead the 1986 Browns.

MADDEN NFL 98

Year | 1997
Publisher | THQ
Developer | Tiburon Entertainment

IF IT WASN'T already clear that EA's focus was now fully on the polygonal systems, the fact it handed publication duties for the SNES and Genesis versions of Madden 98 to THQ should have been the final proof. The tweaks continued, though: for the first time since Madden 94 all the classic teams were available from the start without the need to unlock them through gameplay or with cheat codes. A new Super Bowl mode was also included, which let players recreate any Super Bowl from 1988 to 1997 using the teams that were involved in those years. Ultimately, though, Madden NFL 98 will be remembered more for being the seventh and final SNES Madden game rather than for any specific features it included. ■

FACT

The Houston Oilers moved to Tennessee at the end of the 1996 season, but while in real life they became the Tennessee Oilers for a couple of years (until they were renamed the Titans), here they're the Memphis Oilers.

MAGIC BOY

Year | 1996
Publisher | JVC
Developer | Empire Software

HEWLETT IS A young wizard's apprentice who's messed up a tad: he's accidentally turned his master into a blue elephant, and transformed every other animal within 100 miles into a monster. You have to play through 32 platforming stages (as well as 32 bonus ones), capturing all the animals you meet along the way. You do this by firing your magic wand at enemies, which stuns them. While in this stunned state you can walk over them to put them in your magic bag, after which you can press a button to dump them into little cells at the bottom of the screen. Dumping multiple enemies at once nets you bonus points, but they can only stay in your bag for so long before they get free and instantly kill you. ■

FACT

Magic Boy was originally released for home computers. The game was identical but the plot was different: Hewlett had accidentally opened a hidden trapdoor and released his master's collection of crazed animals.

MAGIC SWORD

Year | 1992
Publisher | Capcom
Developer | Minakuchi Engineering

ORIGINALLY RELEASED AS an arcade game in 1990, Magic Sword was eventually ported to the SNES a couple of years later as a slightly downgraded but no less enjoyable adventure. Playing as a 'mysterious warrior' (named Alan the Brave in the Japanese version), you have to fight your way to the top of Drockmar Keep, a 50-floor tower filled with monsters and bosses, in order to reach and defeat the evil Lord Drockmar, keeper of the Black Orb. Magic Sword is a side-scrolling hack 'n' slash affair where carving down countless enemies is the order of the day. Occasionally you'll come across keys which open locked doors: these rescue helper warriors (there are eight in total) who will accompany you on your quest and provide extra firepower until their health runs out. ■

FACT

Much like Final Fight, the arcade version of Magic Sword featured two-player co-op gameplay, which was removed from the SNES version for performance reasons.

THE MAGICAL QUEST STARRING MICKEY MOUSE

Year	1992
Publisher	Capcom
Developer	Capcom

THE FIRST GAME in Capcom's Magic Quest trilogy and the best known of the three. Mickey Mouse, Donald Duck, Goofy and Pluto are playing catch in the park when Goofy – the big lunk – throws the ball too hard and smacks Mickey on the head with it. The ball bounces off into the distance and Pluto goes running after it, so Goofy heads off to get Pluto back. After the pair fail to return Mickey decides to go and find them, but ends up falling off a cliff and landing in a magical land where a wizard informs him that Pluto's been dognapped by the world's evil ruler, Emperor Pete. If you think this isn't going to end in a rescue mission, you don't know your platformers. At first Mickey can jump on enemies' heads, and also has the ability to grab blocks and stunned bad guys and give them a little spinny throw. As you clear each stage, however, you're given a trio of new outfits that you can change between at will to get different powers. The first of these is the wizard's costume, which lets Mickey fire bolts of energy, swim underwater and control magic carpets. Then comes the firefighter's costume, which lets him fire a huge stream of water that takes out enemies, pushes blocks and extinguishes fires (obviously). Finally, once you find Goofy you're given the mountaineer's costume, which arms Mickey with a grappling hook and lets him grab and swing from certain objects. And no, we never find out what Donald's been doing all this time. ∎

MANCHESTER UNITED CHAMPIONSHIP SOCCER

Year	1995
Publisher	Ocean Software
Developer	Krisalis Software

ROTHERHAM-BASED STUDIO KRISALIS had actually developed no fewer than five other Manchester United video games before making its way to the SNES with this sixth and final title. As well as offering players the option between an isometric and vertical viewpoint, the game includes a total of 72 teams: all 22 squads from the 1994–95 FA Premier League season, a bunch of other top European teams and six all-star teams consisting of the best English, French, German, Spanish, European and all-time players. Although Manchester United is the only team in the game with accurate player names, the rest are close enough that there's no trouble telling who's who: in the Liverpool squad, for example, Robbie Fowler and Ian Rush are called Robbie Fowl and Ian Rash. ∎

MARIO IS MISSING!

Year	1993
Publisher	The Software Toolworks
Developer	The Software Toolworks

BOWSER AND HIS army of Koopas have invaded Earth (as in the actual one), using a portal system to steal various ancient artefacts from all around the world. Why? So Bowser can sell them, spend the money on a load of hairdryers from a shopping channel and use them to melt Antarctica, flooding the planet. Seriously. Along the way Mario's been kidnapped too, so it's up to Luigi to use the portals to visit 15 real-world cities, defeat the Koopas there to recover the three pieces of stolen loot in each city then return them to their respective Information Booths. You then have to find Yoshi, who'll help you unblock the portal to return to Bowser's Castle, ready to travel to another city. ∎

The Chinese can boast, they're on the Pacific's west coast.

MARIO PAINT

Year	1992
Publisher	Nintendo
Developer	Nintendo R&D1 / Intelligent Systems

ALTHOUGH THE MOUSE controller was first invented in the 1960s and numerous mouse devices were released throughout the '70s and early '80s, it didn't start seeing common use until the arrival of the Macintosh 128K in 1984. As such, the mouse – at least in terms of its life as a well-known input device – was still less than a decade old when Nintendo decided it wanted in on the point-and-click action. The SNES Mouse (or Super Famicom Mouse in Japan) was born in 1992, and accompanying it was the game it was designed for: Mario Paint.

Although the title makes it clear where the key focus lies, painting is only one of a number of features offered in Mario Paint. Naturally, though, it's still the most prominent mode and the one players access first when they start the game by clicking on Mario on the title screen. Initially presented with a blank canvas, players are armed with a number of basic tools with which they can create their masterpiece. There's a pencil which comes in three different sizes, an airbrush, a straight line tool, an eraser, a paint can and various other tools that wouldn't look out of place in similar basic art packages on home computers at the time. If you're looking for a little more flair, you can apply different textures to your ink, like a rainbow effect or a heart pattern. There are also

75 stamps you can apply to the page, ranging from Super Mario World sprites to animals, transport and the like. If you aren't happy with the stamps on offer, you can create up to 15 custom stamps using a Special Stamp creator that gives you a 16x16 grid to fill in. You don't have to limit yourself to static images, either: a basic animation package is also included, giving you the ability to create basic looping animations four, six or nine frames in length.

Aside from the painting and animating side of things, Mario Paint's other major mode – and arguably the one that fans look back on most fondly decades later – is its music composer, which lets players make their own basic tunes by placing icons representing different instruments on a large staff. Although it has its limitations – you can only make songs up to 24 measures in length and there's no ability to assign flat or sharp notes – the ease at which players could compose music ensured it was still much loved. Finally, rounding things off was an actual game, Gnat Attack. It puts players in control of a gloved hand brandishing a fly swatter, which they then use to kill a variety of bugs that fly across the screen.

Given that these days there are far more advanced image editing suites readily available for free on your phone or computer, it may be difficult for younger gamers to see the appeal of Mario Paint. In a pre-Windows 95 world, however, this was the first experience with a mouse for many people, and in that sense its importance can't be denied. ∎

FACT

Mario Paint was made available for download in Japan through Nintendo's Satellaview system. Renamed Mario Paint: BS Edition (don't laugh), it added controller support for those without a mouse.

MARIO'S EARLY YEARS! FUN WITH LETTERS

Year	1994	
Publisher	The Software Toolworks	
Developer	The Software Toolworks	

CALIFORNIAN DEVELOPER THE Software Toolworks – previously best known for its Mavis Beacon Teaches Typing software – arranged a deal with Nintendo in the early '90s to create a range of educational titles starring Mario called the Mario Discovery series. As well as Mario is Missing! and Mario's Time Machine the series also included three Mario's Early Years! games, each designed to help young children learn various things. Fun With Letters gives players seven different mini-games, each offering a variation on learning phonics. Each mini-game is generally extremely basic, and is accompanied by a young narrator who reads out words and pronounces sounds for the player so they can listen to and understand them. Some of the sprites and music are recreations of those in Super Mario World. ■

FACT

Mario got his own pair of 'Teaches Typing' games but The Software Toolworks had nothing to do with them: they were developed by Interplay.

MARIO'S EARLY YEARS! FUN WITH NUMBERS

Year	1994	
Publisher	The Software Toolworks	
Developer	The Software Toolworks	

MUCH LIKE FUN with Letters, Fun with Numbers offers another seven mini-games, this time designed to help young children with basic numeracy skills. These include picking bags of peanuts for an elephant, opening the right numbered hotel room doors and counting objects in a kitchen. Despite the game's title, not all the mini-games are to do with numbers: one shows players a series of objects and asks players to choose the odd one out, while another has Mario picking specific shapes to build a train. Most games have Luigi sleeping at the bottom of the screen: players can freely practice clicking on shapes until they're ready to wake Luigi up, at which point the actual mini-game begins. ■

FACT

The Software Toolworks consulted with child development specialists, educational research experts and speech and language teachers to make sure the Mario's Early Years! games were actually beneficial to children's learning.

MARIO'S EARLY YEARS! PRESCHOOL FUN

Year	1994	
Publisher	The Software Toolworks	
Developer	The Software Toolworks	

THE LAST OF the Mario's Early Years! games does away with the pretence of a themed compilation and simply gives six random mini-games gathered under the umbrella of 'things that will appeal to really young kids'. There are six activities to choose from here: a classroom with Princess Toadstool where objects can be counted, an 'opposite world' where you're given a series of opposites and have to choose the right one (e.g. 'choose the opposite of hot'), a farm where you choose animals based on their noises, a circus that asks you to find specific shapes, one where you help Luigi draw a picture by finding shapes and a weird one where you get to touch parts of Mario's body to make him wiggle them. ■

FACT

Another educational game not developed by The Software Toolworks is Mario's Game Gallery, which launched for PC in 1995. It's notable for being the first ever game in which Mario is voiced by Charles Martinet.

MARIO'S TIME MACHINE

Year	1993	
Publisher	The Software Toolworks	
Developer	The Software Toolworks	

A SEQUEL OF sorts to Mario is Missing!, Mario's Time Machine has a similar vibe but this time returns Mario to the lead role, relegating Luigi once again. Bowser's created a machine called the Timulator which lets him go back in time to steal historical artefacts and put them in his museum, so Mario has to use the Timulator to give them back to their rightful owners. Each item is associated with a historical person, and is accompanied by a short essay about that person with some blanks in it. The aim is to travel to the right time period, speak to local townsfolk to learn more about the person then fill in the blanks. Complete the essay and you'll be able to give the artefact back to the person in question. ■

FACT

The time travelling element consists of an odd Mode 7 mini-game where Mario collects mushrooms while riding a jet ski. It seems someone wanted some actual action in there somewhere.

MARK DAVIS' THE FISHING MASTER

Year	1995
Publisher	Natsume
Developer	Natsume

ONE OF THE most difficult fishing games created, The Fishing Master has something of a cult following among some fans of the sport for its attention to detail and its realism (after all, most other fishing games have you catching fish every five minutes). Before players are able to catch anything here, they have to take into account their location on the lake – including the streams and rivers that lead into it – as well as their lure, their rod, their boat and even what sort of hat they wear to keep the sun out of their eyes. After casting a line there's an extremely brief window of time between a fish biting and swimming off, so unless you have exactly the right choice of lure and location you need superhuman reaction times. ■

FACT
Arkansas-born Mark Davis a three-time B.A.S.S. Angler of the Year and one of only two people to win both that award and the Bassmasters Classic tournament in the same year.

MARKO'S MAGIC FOOTBALL

Year	1995
Publisher	Acclaim
Developer	Domark

IF YOU'VE ALREADY read the entry for The Adventures of Kid Kleets (aka Soccer Kid) you may feel a little déjà vu with this one. Marko's Magic Football features very similar gameplay mechanics: it's a platformer where your hero is armed (well, legged) with a football that he can kick at enemies or jump on to use as a trampoline to reach higher areas. At least the plot is more detailed in this one: Marko is a young lad who stumbles upon a plot by evil toymaker Colonel Brown, who's developed a special slime that can transform people into sludge mutants. After his ball comes into contact with the slime it becomes magical, so Marko decides to take his magic football(™) and use it to put a stop to his nefarious scheme. ■

FACT
The game was designed by Domark co-founder Mark Strachan, who'd originally called it Mark's Football Game until subtly changing the character's name.

MARVEL SUPER HEROES IN WAR OF THE GEMS

Year	1996
Publisher	Capcom
Developer	Capcom

MORE THAN TWO decades before Avengers: Infinity War hit cinemas, the SNES was already telling the story of Thanos and his Infinity Gauntlet. In this telling of the story, the Infinity Gems have been scattered across the Earth so Adam Warlock calls on Captain America, Iron Man, Spider-Man, Hulk and Wolverine to find them before Thanos gets his hands (well, his glove) on them. War of the Gems is an interesting cross between a beat 'em up and a one-on-one fighting game: while you wander along each stage beating up numerous enemies, the action is locked to a single 2D plane and combat very much feels more like a Street Fighter than a Final Fight. When you find an Infinity Gem you can use its power to help you in the next stage. ■

FACT
The first Infinity Gem (known as Infinity Stones in the Marvel movies) appeared in a Marvel comic in 1972, where it was called Soul Gem. It wasn't until a 1976 Captain Marvel comic that it was revealed there are six Soul Gems, each with different powers.

MARY SHELLEY'S FRANKENSTEIN

Year	1994
Publisher	Sony Imagesoft
Developer	Bits Studios

PRODUCED BY FRANCIS Ford Coppola as a companion movie to Bram Stoker's Dracula, the 1994 Frankenstein movie was nowhere near as successful despite fantastic performances from Kenneth Branagh as Dr Frankenstein and Robert De Niro as his monster. Nevertheless, the inevitable video game tie-in is your typical action platformer in which the monster makes his way through the streets of Ingolstadt in Bavaria, an underground crypt, the woodlands, the Frankenstein mansion, the Arctic and finally a Russian ship as he seeks a final confrontation with the man who gave him life. The game's ending omits some key details: the monster holds his dying creator's hand, then you're simply shown a fire and the credits: presumably explaining that both Frankenstein and his monster were burnt to death would be too much. ■

FACT
The film's original screenwriter Frank Darabont was unhappy with the way his script was interpreted, calling it 'the best script I ever wrote and the worst movie I've ever seen'.

THE MASK

Year	1995
Publisher	Black Pearl Software
Developer	Black Pearl Software

1994 WAS JIM Carrey's year. Although the Canadian comic had been starring in movies for more than a decade, it was '94 and the release of the holy trinity of *Ace Ventura*, *Dumb & Dumber* and *The Mask* that cemented him as one of Hollywood's top funny men. The SNES version of The Mask tries to capture just some of that comedy by letting you play as Carrey's character Stanley Ipkiss as he tries to make his way across town to the Coco Bongo Club in order to confront and defeat local crime boss Dorian Tyrel. In his way are Dorian's countless thugs, who can be defeated with a variety of comic Mask-like moves, ranging from a giant boxing glove to an over-the-top array of machine guns. ■

FACT

The game took longer than expected to make, eventually releasing nearly a year and a half after the movie. As a result, a carnival level was scrapped, as was a Mega Drive port.

MATH BLASTER: EPISODE 1

Year	1994
Publisher	Davidson & Associates
Developer	Western Technologies

THIS EDUCATIONAL GAME has you travelling through space in pursuit of the alien who kidnapped Spot, your trusty robot friend, after he was nabbed while carrying out repair work on your ship. Your journey consists of three different types of mission: in Trash Zapper, you're given a maths problem and have to shoot the numbered object that corresponds to the right answer. In Platform Chase you have to collect drops of water to change the number on your suit so that it lets you pass through electrified barriers. Then, in the Final Battle, you have to figure out the answers to more maths problems and fly through the appropriately numbered vents on the enemy's ship. As far as educational games go, this one's fun: there's some actual gameplay in there. ■

FACT

Before you get snarky at the title, there actually was an Episode 2. It was only released on home computers, though.

MAUI MALLARD IN COLD SHADOW

Year	1996
Publisher	Nintendo
Developer	Eurocom

IF YOU WANT to release a game based on one of the world's most popular cartoon characters, dressing them up as a new character and never referring to them by their real name is an interesting way to go about it. Maui Mallard does this by putting players in control of a 'quack detective' while refusing to mention at any point – not on the box, in the game or in the manual – that he's actually Donald Duck (at least not in the North American version). The game itself is a competent enough platformer in which Don… um, Maui Mallard, armed with a gun that fires different types of bugs, heads to a tropical island to try and recover its missing Shabuhm Shabuhm idol. ■

FACT

It seems other regions realised how silly it was to have a Donald Duck game that doesn't namecheck the hero. In Europe, the game's called Donald in Maui Mallard.

MECAROBOT GOLF

Year	1993
Publisher	Toho
Developer	Toho

IF IT'S GOLF games with backstories about discrimination you're looking for Mecarobot Golf is the one for you. After a group of engineers create an amazing golf-playing robot called Eagle, golf pros join forces and ban Eagle from taking part in any tournaments. To get round this, the engineers' rich sponsor buys a golf course for Eagle, calling it the Hyper Golf Club. As a curious golfer, you've been invited to the Hyper Golf Club to take part in a match against Eagle to determine once and for all whether man or machine is better at golf. Therein lies the game's main problem, however: despite its Ultraman-style robot featuring prominently on the game's packaging, you can't actually play as a robot: only against it as a human. ■

FACT

The Japanese version of the game is much less odd. It's called Nobuo Serizawa Birdie Try and features Japanese pro golfer Serizawa instead of Eagle.

MECHWARRIOR

Year | 1993
Publisher | Activision
Developer | Beam Software

IT'S THE YEAR 3027. Ten years have passed since Herras Ragen's mum, dad and sister were killed by renegade mercenary cartel the Dark Wing Lance, and now it's time for revenge. As a freelance MechWarrior, your aim is to take on numerous jobs, defeating enemies and using your reward money to upgrade and buy new mechs, as you continue to search for clues to bring you closer to the Dark Wing Lance. Set in the universe of wargaming franchise BattleTech, MechWarrior features impressive-looking Mode 7 combat from a first-person perspective, but suffers from clunky combat and most of the weapons being ineffective (indeed, the first person you speak to in the game tells you to focus on buying homing missiles for a reason). ■

FACT
Whereas the PC version of MechWarrior included mechs taken from the BattleTech board games, the eight mechs in the SNES version are completely new creations.

MECHWARRIOR 3050

Year | 1995
Publisher | Activision
Developer | Tiburon Entertainment

DON'T WORRY, THE SNES didn't miss out on 3,048 other MechWarrior sequels before getting this one. Set during the Clan Invasion storyline in the BattleTech universe, MechWarrior 3050 has you playing as a Clan Wolf MechWarrior carrying out a variety of missions assigned to you by Galaxy Commander Conal Ward (who's accidentally named Colonel Ward in the game). Whereas the first MechWarrior game was a first-person combat affair, this second effort goes for a third-person isometric viewpoint, making it look and feel a lot like a mech-powered version of EA's Desert Strike. There's a potential reason for this: developer Tiburon was set up in 1994 by former members of Visual Concepts, who had previously worked on the SNES version of Desert Strike. ■

FACT
The game's missions take place in the wrong chronological order, according to BattleTech canon. For example, in the accepted timeline, the first mission actually takes place a year and a half after the third one.

MEGA-LO-MANIA

Year | 1994
Publisher | Virgin Interactive
Developer | Sensible Software

ALTHOUGH ITS IMPACT had been slightly lessened by the time it made it to the SNES, when Mega-Lo-Mania was originally released on the Commodore Amiga in 1991 it was praised for ideas that were considered revolutionary. It offered real-time strategy gameplay a year before Dune II made it popular, and featured a research-based 'technology tree' before Civilization did it (and is in fact considered by many to be the first game to do so). The game takes place on a new planet that's recently been formed, a planet fortunate enough to be blessed with intelligent life. Planets need a god, however, so four different demigods – Scarlet, Caesar, Oberon and Madcap – decide to set up shop in an attempt to claim the right to oversee this new world. The game consists of 28 different islands, which essentially serve as battlegrounds of varying sizes. After choosing an island you choose which sector of it to defend and are given 100 unarmed men.

FACT
Mega-Lo-Mania 2 was in development for a while, and even appeared as a three-part developer diary in Amiga Power magazine before it was ultimately scrapped.

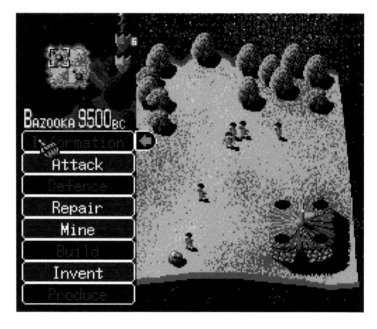

The aim is to use these men to research increasingly advanced technology in order to help them attack other armies, defend themselves and mine resources. The 28 islands are split into different epochs of time, each consisting of three islands. The first epoch is set in the year 9500 BC and conquering all three islands will move you onto the next (3000 BC) and so on until you reach the tenth and final epoch, which is set in 2001 AD, has a single island and has your men firing lasers at each other. ■

MEGA MAN 7

Year	1995
Publisher	Capcom
Developer	Capcom

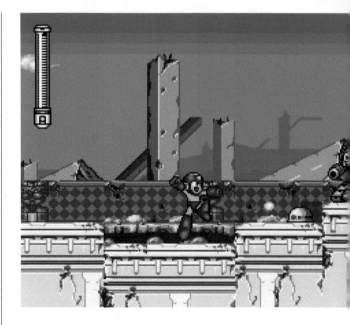

ALTHOUGH CAPCOM HAD tried to breathe new life into Mega Man with Mega Man X (see the opposite page), it still wasn't done with the main Mega Man series, which had already seen no fewer than six popular instalments on the NES. The SNES would only get a single new entry, but it's an entertaining enough Mega Man game nevertheless and gave fans a 16-bit taste of the traditional gameplay they'd enjoyed on Nintendo's 8-bit system. It's set six months after the events of Mega Man 6, with the evil Dr Wily locked up in jail. Naturally, you can't keep a bad doctor down, and Wily's got a trick up his sleeve: four robot masters programmed to find and rescue him if they go for six months without any instructions (wonder why he didn't just make it three months). Mega Man heads out once again to put a stop to Wily's wily scheme, but there's a new robot on the block too: the mysterious Bass, who appears to be

> ### FACT
> Shade Man is a robot master designed to look like a vampire, and he comes with a hidden Easter egg. Hold down the B button while selecting his stage and the music will be replaced with a new version of the theme from Ghouls 'n Ghosts.

an ally but may be hiding a secret (let's face it, they always are). Anyone who's played any of the previous Mega Man games will know what to expect from Mega Man 7: once again there are eight robot masters to defeat and gain abilities from, though this time not all eight are available from the beginning of the game. You're initially only presented with four – Burst Man, Cloud Man, Junk Man and Freeze Man – and only once you defeat them all are Spring Man, Slash Man, Shade Man and Turbo Man then introduced. ■

MEGA MAN SOCCER

Year	1994
Publisher	Capcom
Developer	Sun L

WHEN YOU THINK of Mega Man, you obviously think of football. Well, someone did at least, which explains how we ended up with the bizarre Mega Man Soccer, a football game consisting entirely of characters from the Mega Man series. Set after the events of Mega Man 4, the game opens with Mega Man watching football on TV, only for the match to be infiltrated by Dr Wily and his robot army (which I think is cause for abandonment under FIFA rules). Outraged, Mega Man heads out to teach Wily a lesson… um, by joining in and playing football too. Matches are 8-a-side affairs and generally play in a relatively reserved manner: although there are no fouls and there are walls around the pitch to keep the ball in, the action is still generally quite modest for what could have been a chaotic game. The only exception is the occasional power shot, which makes

> ### FACT
> Perhaps indicating how rushed it was, Mega Man Soccer has an ending but it isn't actually accessible in the game: you have to use a cheat cartridge to view it.

use of a character's special ability to unleash a strong shot the goalie will struggle to save. As well as Exhibition, League and Tournament modes there's also the Capcom Championship: this starts you off with a team of eight Mega Mans (Mega Men?) and has you playing against a series of robot master teams. Just like in the main Mega Man series, you can choose which order you face them in, and each time you beat a team the robot master joins your squad, meaning by the time you face Dr Wily in the final you've got a who's who of Mega Man characters in your team. ■

MEGA MAN X

Year	1994
Publisher	Capcom
Developer	Capcom

WITH SIX MEGA Man games released on the NES, the series' development team felt change was needed for the blue bomber's 16-bit debut. Rather than churn out the same old story – Dr Wily coming back with more robot masters, so it's up to Mega Man to save the day and so on – it was decided that the SNES Mega Man would be set 100 years later and feature a new villain, a slightly darker tone and, most notably, a new hero. Whereas the tradition for each new game had generally been that lead artist Keiji Inafune would work on the Mega Man design while his protégé Hayato Kaji would work on other characters, Inafune decided to freshen things up by swapping the roles around, putting Kaji in control of the new hero's look instead. Initially the pair created Zero, a slick new robot clad in red, as the candidate to become the new hero, but Inafune got cold feet and feared a fan backlash so Zero was relegated to a secondary role and instead the hero X was created. Essentially a new and improved Mega Man, X is the most advanced robot in the world with human-like intelligence and free will. Unfortunately, after Dr Light buried him for 30 years to let him run a lengthy diagnosis process, X was discovered by another doctor and cloned, leading to a new race of smart robots called Reploids. The problem

FACT

If you follow an extremely elaborate series of instructions you can unlock the ability to throw fireballs like Ryu from Street Fighter II. You even need to do the fireball motion to perform them.

was that the aforementioned free will element meant some Reploids chose to become criminals: these ones were dubbed Mavericks. It's up to X and Zero (who's a Maverick Hunter) to defeat the Mavericks and take down Sigma, an advanced and very dangerous Maverick.

In case it wasn't clear, there's a lot more plot in Mega Man X than were was in previous Mega Man games. This highlights the development team's desire to make more than just another Mega Man game: this is a proper story with a lot more to it than just gunning down enemies. Granted, there's still a lot of that in there too, and you do still have to take down a series of particularly dangerous robots, though this time they aren't robot masters as such and don't follow the traditional 'Something Man' naming scheme. Instead, X has to face off against eight Mavericks, each based on robotic animals: Chill Penguin, Spark Mandrill, Armored Armadillo, Launch Octopus, Boomer Kuwanger, Sting Chameleon, Storm Eagle and Flame Mammoth. Despite the change in style, the central mechanic remains the same: defeat one of the Mavericks to acquire their weapon, which will inevitably be extremely effective against one of the other Mavericks. Despite it still containing some similarities to the main series, though, there's one issue that some critics did raise: Mega Man X is slightly less challenging than the NES games. Not enough to make it on a par with a Kirby game or anything, but enough to make typical Mega Man masochists at the time raise an eyebrow. ■

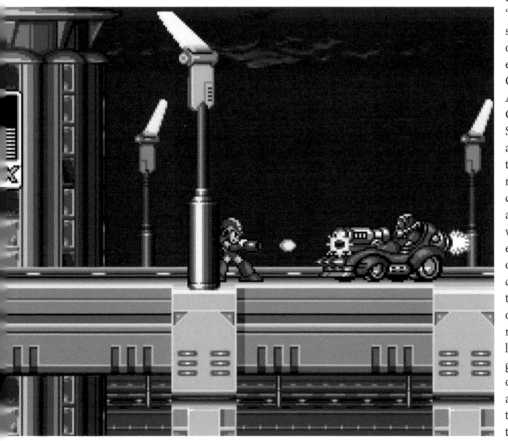

MEGA MAN X2

Year	1995
Publisher	Capcom
Developer	Capcom

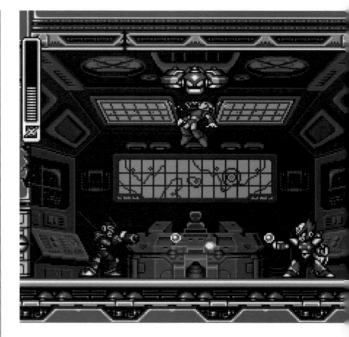

IT WOULDN'T BE a Mega Man game without a bunch of sequels (unless it's Mega Man Soccer) and so, sure enough, a year after Mega Man X came its successor. As well as confusing the people who wrongly thought the X was a Roman numeral 10, Mega Man X2 continues the first game's plot, kicking things off six months later. After defeating Sigma and cementing himself as a top-tier Maverick Hunter, X has essentially painted a big bullseye on his backside. Three powerful Mavericks called Serges, Agile and Violen form a group called the X-Hunters and decide to dedicate their efforts to taking X out, setting up a base on the North Pole (because, why not). Before he can reach them, X has to take on another eight Mavericks, who once again are based on animals: Wheel Gator, Bubble Crab, Flame Stag, Morph Moth, Magna Centipede, Crystal Snail, Overdrive Ostrich and Wire Sponge. On top of that, this time you also have to try

and find Zero's three body parts – because in case it isn't clear, he didn't do too well in the last game – with the plot changing depending on whether you manage to get them all before the final confrontations. Ultimately, Mega Man X2 is another strong adventure that doesn't offer much new in terms of gameplay mechanics: other than the ability to occasionally control vehicles (like a mech or a hovercycle), it plays pretty much like Mega Man X. In that sense, then, it isn't really too different from the main series after all. ■

MEGA MAN X3

Year	1996
Publisher	Capcom
Developer	Minakuchi Engineering

WITH X AND Zero having seemingly put an end to the Maverick crisis once and for all, a Reploid scientist named Dr Doppler seals the deal with his Neuro Computer, which stops Reploids turning into Mavericks. The utopian Dopple Town is established, where Reploids come from miles around to live. A few months later though, without warning, huge swathes of Reploids become Mavericks again and, apparently led by Doppler, start attacking the Maverick Hunter headquarters. It soon emerges that the evil Sigma has returned but in virus form, infecting Doppler and causing him to generally act a bit of a prat. If you smell another excuse to fight eight more animal-themed Mavericks then you're very good at this. This time X will have to square off against Blast Hornet, Blizzard Buffalo, Tunnel Rhino, Volt Catfish, Crush Crawfish, Neon Tiger, Gravity Beetle and the brilliantly named Toxic Seahorse. Mega Man X3 has one major new gameplay feature, the

ability to call on Zero to help you whenever you need him. By accessing a communications submenu while playing, you can summon Zero and play as him for most of the game, with some exceptions (he can't take part in boss or sub-boss fights, for example). The catch is that if Zero dies, he's dead for good and you can't summon him again for the rest of the game, so it's in your best interests to keep him nice and shiny for the duration of your adventure so he's always there if you ever need him. ■

METAL COMBAT: FALCON'S REVENGE

Year	1993
Publisher	Nintendo
Developer	Intelligent Systems

METAL COMBAT IS the sequel to Battle Clash, Nintendo's Super Scope exclusive gun combat game. Just like its predecessor, it consists of a number of epic one-on-one battles against a variety of aliens inside giant mechs. Playing as either the first game's hero Mike Anderson or a mysterious new pilot named Carol Eugene, you take control of a mech of your own and use its chargeable energy guns to take down each massive opponent. There are 10 different types of enemy 'ST' (Standing Tank) to battle, each with their own weak points that must be identified and exploited. There's also a two-player battle mode, in which one player uses the Super Scope as normal while player two chooses their favourite enemy ST and uses a standard controller. ■

FACT

The game constantly refers to you as 'Partner', but a hidden cheat lets you change this. Plug in a controller and enter L, A, B, on the title screen and you're taken to a screen that lets you enter your name.

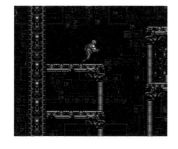

METAL MORPH

Year	1994
Publisher	FCI
Developer	Origin Systems

EARTH HAS MADE contact with aliens in another dimension called Otherside. After creating a hypergate linking the two locations, it's decided that Metal Morph – a man made of liquid metal – is the only one who can safely pass through it. Once he does, though, he's ambushed by Othersidian aliens who take him to a lab to study him so they can figure out how to pass through the portal and attack Earth. Seemingly inspired heavily by the T-1000 in *Terminator 2*, Metal Morph is a part platformer, part shoot 'em up in which your hero can transform into a liquid metal puddle at will. The shooting sections take place from a third-person perspective behind your ship and make copious use of Mode 7 effects. ■

FACT

Metal Morph's original name was going to be Cyber Morph. When Atari released a game called Cybermorph for the Jaguar in 1993, the name was changed.

METAL MARINES

Year	1993
Publisher	Namco
Developer	Namco

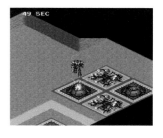

IF YOU'RE READING this book in 2115, I hope you're doing it in an underground bunker, because according to Metal Marines that's the year the great Antimatter War nearly destroyed the planet (something to do with each country's stockpiled supplies of antimatter weapons all being triggered at once). The game takes place two years later, where you play as a member of the Space Colonies Allied Forces. While colonists were off looking for a new planet to live in, Earth was taken over by the evil Zorgeuf and his army, so you need to go back and teach him a lesson. This is an isometric strategy game in which each side is based on their own island, and you can only see sections of your opponent's island by attacking them. ■

FACT

The game's title refers to your main unit, the Metal Marine: a massive 50ft high mech that can wander around, attacking enemy units with its gun, axe and electric whip.

METAL WARRIORS

Year	1995
Publisher	Konami
Developer	LucasArts

FOR THREE YEARS, the United Earth Government has been at war with the evil dictator Venkar Amon and his Dark Axis military. The only thing stopping him from taking over is the Metal Warriors, a group of freedom fighters in huge mechs. This action platformer has you playing as one of these Metal Warriors, a chap named Lieutenant Stone, as you take on nine missions designed to finally end the war with the Dark Axis. There are six mech types in the game, each armed with their melee weapon and special abilities, though you can also collect power-ups that add extra weapons like rocket launchers. If your mech is about to be destroyed you can leave it and run around, exposed, in search of a new one. ■

FACT

Nintendo wanted to publish Metal Warriors (under its original name of Battledroids). However, the launch of the PlayStation led to Nintendo switching focus to N64 development and Konami picked the game up instead.

MICHAEL ANDRETTI'S INDY CAR CHALLENGE

Year	1994
Publisher	Bullet-Proof Software
Developer	Genki

ROUGHLY BASED ON the 1994 PPG Indy Car World Series, this technically impressive racing game features all 16 tracks from that season, although the lack of official licensing means each track name is based on its location rather than its actual moniker in real life (for example, the Race America track is instead called Elkhart Lake). All the racer names are fake too, despite the presence of Michael Andretti, who finished fourth in the real-life 1994 season. Instead, Andretti simply appears before the start of each race to give advice. As in advice on the upcoming track, I mean: he doesn't recommend shares to invest in or anything. Somewhat unusually for its era, the game includes the option to view a replay of your race with two camera angles. ■

FACT

Michael Andretti is the son of another racing legend, Mario Andretti. As luck would have it, EA released Mario Andretti Racing for the Mega Drive in the same year.

MICHAEL JORDAN: CHAOS IN THE WINDY CITY

Year	1994
Publisher	Electronic Arts
Developer	Electronic Arts

AFTER TURNING UP for practice for an all-star charity game basketball legend Michael Jordan discovers his teammates have been kidnapped by the evil doctor Max Cranium. Cue one of the oddest licensed platformers on the SNES, in which His Airness makes his way through 24 stages throwing basketballs at enemies. Along the way he'll encounter special balls that give him extra powers: a fire ball, freeze ball or bowling ball, for example. Occasionally you'll also come across basketball nets conveniently standing there. By dunking a ball into these you'll trigger different effects, ranging from a level checkpoint to blowing up every enemy on the screen. Jordan recorded a handful of voice samples for the game, including the phrase 'time out' which plays every time you pause. ■

FACT

One of the balls you can collect is a baseball, which acts like a boomerang. It's a reference to Jordan's brief stint as a Minor League Baseball player in 1994.

MICKEY MANIA: THE TIMELESS ADVENTURES OF MICKEY MOUSE

Year	1994
Publisher	Sony Imagesoft
Developer	Traveller's Tales

MICKEY MANIA WAS originally supposed to be a celebration of 65 years of Mickey Mouse, but this plan was scrapped when the reality hit that this would mean only six months of development time. Still, it does go some way to explaining why the game is what it is: a celebration of Mickey's animated history. Playing as modern-day Mickey, you have to make your way through six classic animated shorts, beginning with his black-and-white 1928 debut in *Steamboat Willie* and proceeding through *The Mad Doctor* (1933), *Moose Hunters* (1937), *Lonesome Ghosts* (1937), *Mickey and the Beanstalk* (1947) and *The Prince and the Pauper* (1990). Along the way, you'll bump into cameo appearances from the Mickeys who featured in each short, as well as many other little references and Easter eggs.

FACT

A sequel to Mickey Mania was started soon after its release, but the studio only got as far as a basic prototype based on the *Two Gun Mickey* cartoon before moving on to work on a *Toy Story* game instead.

Despite being an entertaining platformer, Mickey Mania is also notorious for being one of the few games released on both the SNES and Mega Drive / Genesis that's significantly better on Sega's console. Not only does the SNES version include loading times not present in the Mega Drive game, it's also missing the hidden hurricane bonus level based on *The Band Concert*. This wasn't due to any technical reasons: according to the game's designer and programmer Jon Burton, the level was created at the very last minute, and after he put it into the Mega Drive game he realised there was just no time left to add it to the SNES version too. ■

MICKEY'S ULTIMATE CHALLENGE

Year	1994
Publisher	Hi Tech Expressions
Developer	Designer Software

WHILE READING A fairy tale book in bed, Mickey falls asleep and ends up in the fantasy town of Beanswick. He has to take on five different challenges, each hosted by a different character: sorting floating books in alphabetical order by jumping on them, moving potions around on a giant board, dusting portraits in matching pairs, playing pipes in the correct order and guessing which tools are in Goofy's toolbox. Each time you beat a challenge you're given an item that will help one of the other characters: give all the items to their correct owners and you'll be given five magic beans which can be used to climb a beanstalk and wake a giant via one of the most overused mini-games in gaming, the sliding puzzle. ∎

FACT

The beanstalk plot is based on *Mickey and the Beanstalk*, which was originally one of the two tales in Disney's movie *Fun and Fancy Free*.

MICRO MACHINES

Year	1994
Publisher	Ocean Software
Developer	Codemasters

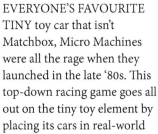

EVERYONE'S FAVOURITE TINY toy car that isn't Matchbox, Micro Machines were all the rage when they launched in the late '80s. This top-down racing game goes all out on the tiny toy element by placing its cars in real-world tracks that look like they were created by a child for their Micro Machines to race on. There are nine different types of vehicle, each with their own environment: jeeps on a breakfast table, sports cars on a school desk, 'warriors' in a garage, dune buggies in a sandpit, F1 cars on a pool table, powerboats in a bathtub, helicopters in the garden, tanks in the bedroom and RuffTrux (larger jeeps) in the backyard. The game supports up to four players with the use of a multitap. ∎

FACT

Micro Machines toys were so popular that toy shops were flooded with imitators. That led to the slogan: 'Remember, if it doesn't say Micro Machines it's not the real thing.'

MICRO MACHINES 2: TURBO TOURNAMENT

Year	1996
Publisher	Ocean Software
Developer	Merit Studios

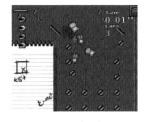

THE SEQUEL TO Micro Machines offers more of the same, with 16 different types of vehicle: convertibles, 4x4s, supercars, off-roaders, dumper trucks, rally cars, sports cars, hovercrafts, dragsters, beach buggies, ATVs, F1 cars, helicopters, monster trucks, bugs and power boats. There are 27 brand new tracks too, and while some of the environments are similar to those in the previous game – dinner tables, workbenches and the like – there are some new ones too, like a pinball table and a garden pond. The game once again supports up to four players, and also features a cameo from Violet Berlin, the co-host of UK children's video game TV show *Bad Influence!*, who was added to the game after visiting developer Codemasters to report on it. ∎

FACT

The Micro Machines slogan was borrowed by other toy manufacturers. When the release of *Jurassic Park* led to countless nameless dinosaur toys, Kenner used the slogan: 'If it doesn't say Jurassic Park, it's extinct.'

MIGHT AND MAGIC II: GATES TO ANOTHER WORLD

Year	1993
Publisher	Elite Systems
Developer	Iguana Entertainment

THIS IS THE sequel to Might and Magic: Secret of the Inner Sanctum, which was released on NES as well as on a bunch of home computers. Players put together a party of six characters – be that the ones offered at the start of the game or completely new ones you create before heading off – and try to save the world of CRON (Central Research Observational Nacelle) from being fired into the sun. As well as your squad of six, you can also recruit 'hirelings', which can boost the party size up to eight. While Might and Magic II was generally well regarded on other systems, the SNES version had numerous bugs, including broken spells and some items costing 10 times what they should. ∎

FACT

Might and Magic II had many elements changed to suit Nintendo's family friendly policy. Most notably, the Slaughtered Lamb pub (a reference to *An American Werewolf in London*) became Norm's Bar (a reference to *Cheers*).

MIGHT AND MAGIC III: ISLES OF TERRA

Year	1995
Publisher	FCI
Developer	Iguana Entertainment

THE THIRD MIGHT and Magic game takes seven pages of the manual to explain the plot, so let's just say it's about tracking down and defeating the evil Sheltem in his homeworld of Terra. The SNES version of Might and Magic III makes an attempt to play more like the home computer versions, but struggles to do so: mainly because its icon-based interface was designed with a mouse in mind, rather than a controller (that said, the game does have support for the SNES Mouse). Like its predecessors it suffers from some fairly heavy Nintendo-based censorship but it's even more comic this time around, most notably in the case of a fountain that contains a statue of a nude woman who's now wearing a bright pink bikini. ■

FACT

At the time of writing there have been 10 main games in the Might and Magic series, the latest being 2014's Might and Magic X: Legacy on PC and Mac.

MIGHTY MORPHIN POWER RANGERS

Year	1994
Publisher	Bandai
Developer	Natsume

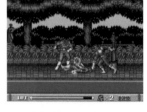

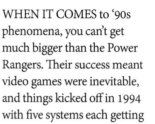

WHEN IT COMES to '90s phenomena, you can't get much bigger than the Power Rangers. Their success meant video games were inevitable, and things kicked off in 1994 with five systems each getting their own completely different game. While Sega made Power Rangers games for the Mega Drive, Mega CD and Game Gear, Bandai instead got the rights to make SNES and Game Boy titles. The SNES one is a side-scrolling action game where you fight your way through seven stages as any one of the five main Power Rangers. Each stage has three sections: one in your street clothes, one in your Ranger costume, and a boss fight. The final two stages have you fighting as the Megazord, the Power Rangers' mech. ■

FACT

The Power Rangers sections in the TV show were actually redubbed fight scenes from *Kyoryu Sentai Zyuranger*, the 16th instalment in the Super Sentai franchise in Japan.

MIGHTY MORPHIN POWER RANGERS: THE FIGHTING EDITION

Year	1995
Publisher	Bandai
Developer	Natsume

THE STANDARD POWER Rangers fight scenes were all well and good, but the best bit in each episode was when the team combined their powers to summon a giant mech. The Fighting Edition is a Street Fighter style one-on-one fighting game which focuses primarily on these moments, meaning the standard Power Rangers in their human form are nowhere to be found.

There are eight characters in total here: four heroes (Thunder Megazord, Ninja Megazord, Shogun Megazord and Mega Tigerzord) and four villains (Lip Syncher, Goldar, Lord Zedd and Silver Horns). The story mode's final boss is Ivan Ooze from the *Power Rangers* movie, who can be unlocked in the Fighting (versus) and Trial (survival) modes when you beat the game on Hard. ■

FACT

Not good enough to beat it on Hard? Not to worry: you can unlock Ivan Ooze by highlighting any character in Fighting mode and pressing X, Y and Start together.

MIGHTY MORPHIN POWER RANGERS: THE MOVIE

Year	1995
Publisher	Bandai
Developer	Natsume

THE *POWER RANGERS* movie saw the team fighting the evil Ivan Ooze – a third-rate Freddy Krueger cosplayer – who ruled the Earth 6,000 years ago and has been dug up to give it another go. Much like the first SNES Power Rangers game, this is another side-scrolling action game where the aim is to pummel countless members of the Putty Patrol before reaching a boss fight, though this time you can transform into your Ranger suit at any time by collecting energy icons. Because the movie only had one villain, the first five stages' bosses are instead bad guys from the TV show. The sixth is a completely original character, and only in the seventh and final stage do you face off against Ooze himself. ■

FACT

Ivan Ooze was played by Paul Freeman. He starred in Raiders of the Lost Ark as Bellog the evil archaeologist who tried to steal Indiana Jones' work and dies when the Ark of the Covenant opens.

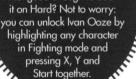

THE MIRACLE PIANO TEACHING SYSTEM

Year	1991
Publisher	The Software Toolworks
Developer	The Software Toolworks

PIANO LESSONS CAN cost a small fortune, so what if you could learn to play the piano at a fraction of the price by replacing your teacher with a machine? That was the logic behind the Miracle Piano Teaching System, a product released for the SNES (as well as the NES, Sega Genesis, PC and Amiga) that came bundled with a 49-key full sized MIDI keyboard. After plugging the Miracle into your console and inserting the cartridge, you can work your way through hundreds of lessons on the screen, getting instant feedback as you play. The game itself doesn't actually generate any sound (other than a metronome in some lessons): all the music comes through the keyboard's speakers itself, which means you can use it as a separate instrument. ■

FACT

The Miracle's $500 price point meant it didn't sell quite as well as hoped. Some of the NES ones were recalled, had the Nintendo logos removed and were converted for PC use.

MOHAWK & HEADPHONE JACK

Year	1996
Publisher	THQ
Developer	Black Pearl Software

IF YOU'RE LOOKING for the SNES game most likely to make you nauseous, look no further. Mohawk & Headphone Jack is set on the 'Party Planet' of M17X, which is populated by the carefree Morfs. One evil Morf called General Headslot creates an underground army of robot soldiers to take over, so it's up to Mohawk and his best friend (which is a pair of headphones) to save the day. The game's 14 stages are at least straightforward in terms of your goal: you have to collect a certain number of CDs to open the exit. The twist (literally) is that each stage is circular in design and can be spun around at a high speed: this, combined with its psychedelic art style, means only those with a strong stomach need apply. ■

FACT

The game came with a pre-paid phone card, which let you call its premium rate hotline and get $5 worth of tips for free. Presumably it was one of those pre-recorded ones that takes ages to get to the point.

MLBPA BASEBALL

Year	1994
Publisher	Electronic Arts
Developer	Visual Concepts

WITH ALL THESE baseball games doing the rounds on the SNES, it was only a matter of time before EA Sports got involved too. Its take doesn't have the MLB licence but, as the name states, does include the MLBPA licence: this means all the player names are correct, even if some of the team names had to be replaced. For example, the California Angels were renamed Anaheim (coincidentally, they became the Anaheim Angels in 1997). As decent as the game is, it's the Japanese version, Fighting Baseball, that's better known online thanks to its completely fictional roster made up of terrible sounding Japanese attempts at American names, like Sleve McDichael, Ted Balloon, Andy Pmith, Elvis Crushel and the infamous Bobson Dugnutt. ■

FACT

Although it doesn't have authentic team names, the game does have authentic stadium chants, including the Atlanta Braves' controversial tomahawk chop.

MONOPOLY

Year	1992
Publisher	Parker Brothers
Developer	Sculptured Software

AS PROBABLY THE world's most famous board game, Monopoly needs no introduction (except that one I just did). This SNES interpretation keeps things relatively simple, which works in its favour: although it includes little animations of things like properties being bought and your pieces moving to each space, it keeps them brief enough to ensure they don't become an annoyance in a game that can often last a number of hours. Up to eight players can take part, any of which can be CPU-controlled. Conveniently, then, there are eight AI opponents, each with their own stereotypical personalities: these include the likes of a butler called Jeeves, a gangster called Paulie, a hillbilly called Billy Bob and a gold-digger 'lady in red' type called Amanda. ■

FACT

Since it was originally created in 1935, more than $3 trillion of fake Monopoly money has been printed.

MORTAL KOMBAT

Year	1993
Publisher	Acclaim
Developer	Sculptured Software

A GREAT FIGHTER is nothing without a great rival to push them to their limits. Bruce Lee said that, you know. Okay, he didn't. The point remains, though: competition breeds success. Would Coke have been so well marketed and globally popular if it didn't have Pepsi breathing down its neck? Would McDonalds sell an estimated 50 million burgers a day if Burger King wasn't encouraging it to keep improving? And would Street Fighter II have evolved into its even better Turbo and Super versions were it not for the imposing presence of Mortal Kombat? Hopefully not, or this intro was a waste of time.

Originally released in arcades in October 1992, Mortal Kombat quickly gained popularity (and notoriety) for two main reasons. Firstly, it was visually striking: Midway's decision to ditch hand-drawn sprites and instead use digitised photos of real life martial artists gave the game a grittier, more realistic look. It wasn't the first fighting game to use digitised sprites: Atari's Pit Fighter had done the same thing a couple of years before, for example. For some reason, though – maybe the renewed interest in fighting games caused by Street Fighter II – this time it really resonated with players and before long you'd struggle to find an arcade that didn't have at least one Mortal Kombat machine.

Of course, the realistic character sprites weren't the main reason for Mortal Kombat's success. The reason

gamers queued up at arcades to play it (and the reason it stoked so much controversy) was its gory violence, which was much more graphic than most games that had come before it. Certain moves like jab flurries and uppercuts saw blood splashing all over the place, but it was the infamous 'Fatalities' that took things to another level. After defeating an opponent and being commanded to 'finish him', players could input a secret command to kill their enemy in a suitably grotesque manner: punching their head off, setting them on fire, tearing their heart out and the like. The most notorious Fatality belonged to Sub Zero, who would tear his opponent's head clean off with the spinal cord still attached. Such sights would have been questionable at the best of times in the early '90s, but the fact the characters looked so realistic led to national outrage.

FACT

The home versions launched in the US on 13 September 1993. The day was dubbed Mortal Monday and a slew of TV commercials aired promoting the date in advance.

Given Nintendo's family-friendly image, Mortal Kombat had to be heavily censored for its inevitable SNES port. All the blood was recoloured to look like sweat, and the gory Fatalities were replaced with much tamer ones (although, oddly, the ones that set opponents on fire and reduced them to skeletons were still considered okay). The move helped Nintendo claim the moral high ground, especially when a US congressional hearing on violent video games was held just months after the home versions of Mortal Kombat were released. Financially, however, it wasn't the best move: the Sega Mega Drive / Genesis version had a 'blood code' that kept all the gore intact, and as a result it sold five times as many copies as the SNES one. ■

MORTAL KOMBAT II

Year	1994
Publisher	Acclaim
Developer	Sculptured Software

THE CONTROVERSY SURROUNDING Mortal Kombat and similar games like it led to the establishment of the ESRB, a ratings board that let the video games industry regulate its own content and give each game an age rating. This was enough to convince Nintendo to cool it with the censorship – though you'd imagine Mortal Kombat's dismal SNES sales played a part too – and so Mortal Kombat II arrived on the SNES all-singing, all-dancing and all-bleeding. As well as increasing the number of playable characters from seven to 12, each fighter was also given multiple Fatalities, literally doubling down on the violence.

New fighter Jax, for example, can use his brute strength to either crush his opponent's head with a powerful double slap, or tear their arms off and toss them to the ground. Somewhat ironically – and presumably a deliberate tongue-in-cheek jibe at the controversy surrounding the first game – the biggest additions to Mortal Kombat II are its new, anti-violent finishing moves, Babalities and Friendships. The former do what they say on the tin, turning your opponent into a tiny baby, but it's the latter that allowed the development team to get a little more creative with its comedic ways of resolving the fight amicably. These include Jax cutting out some paper dolls, Johnny Cage presenting his foe with a signed photo, Liu Kang busting out his finest disco dancing moves and Scorpion pulling out a smaller Scorpion action figure with the caption 'buy a Scorpion doll!'. ∎

FACT

Mortal Kombat II has a trio of hidden fighters to find and ght against: grey ninja Smoke, green female ninja Jade and silhouette ninja Noob Saibot (whose name is based on the surnames of creators Ed Boon and John Tobias).

MORTAL KOMBAT 3

Year	1995
Publisher	Williams Entertainment
Developer	Sculptured Software

WHILE MORTAL KOMBAT II upped the ante slightly with more characters and a wider variety of finishing moves, the general combat was more or less identical. Mortal Kombat 3 changes things by introducing a few new tweaks designed to game a faster pace, as a response to arcade players complaining that there was too much defensive play going on. The addition of a new run button lets players briefly dash at opponents, forcing them to engage in combat instead of just keeping their distance. On top of that, a new combo system gives each character a selection of preset combination techniques that let experts ensure that once they caught their opponent, they would be able to keep hold of them for a while. Outside of standard combat, another two new types of finishing move have been added: Mercy gives your opponent a tiny sliver of energy back so they can continue the fight, whereas Animalities (which can only be performed after granting Mercy) turn your character into an animal which then mauls your foe to death in an appropriately gory manner.

The new 15-character roster includes new faces like robot assassins Cyrax and Sektor, riot cop Stryker and Sheeva, a four-armed female fighter who's the first stop-motion character in the series to actually be playable (rather than a boss). Not all the changes were met with universal praise, however: although the return of Sonya Blade and Kano – both of whom were missing from MK II – was welcome, fan favourites like Scorpion and Johnny Cage were ditched. ∎

FACT

The actors who played Liu Kang, Sonya Blade, Shang sung and Sub Zero (among hers) left their contracts with Midway after a dispute over royalties, so they were replaced with new actors in MK3.

MR DO!

Year	1996
Publisher	Black Pearl Software
Developer	C-Lab

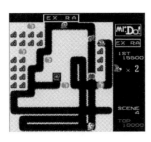

ALTHOUGH CONSIDERED SIMILAR to Dig Dug, Mr Do! actually launched in Japanese arcades around the same time, both making their debuts in 1982. Playing as a clown called Mr Do, you work your way through a series of single-screen stages consisting of cherries and enemies, with the goal being to clear the stage of either. Dotted around each level are apples, which can be dropped on enemies' heads if you remove the ground from under them (though your timing needs to be good, and you have to be careful not to crush yourself instead). Mr Do is also armed with a 'power ball', which when thrown will bounce around the stage until it hits something. The SNES port includes a new Battle mode, where two players share the same stage. ■

FACT

Mr Do! was one of the first arcade games to be made available as a conversion kit. This let arcade owners convert one of their older machines into a Mr Do! one for much less than buying a completely new machine.

MR NUTZ

Year	1993
Publisher	Ocean Software
Developer	Ocean Software

IF YOU THOUGHT global warming was a problem, you should try global cooling on for size. An evil Yeti is trying to cocoon the entire world in ice and snow, in order to create a new frozen kingdom. 'Not on my watch,' says heroic squirrel Mr Nutz – or at least he would if he could talk – and so off he heads to save the day and keep the world feeling roasty toasty (so he's the one to blame, climate change activists). Having a hip and happening 'Z' in the title isn't enough to make Mr Nutz any more than a straightforward, if entertaining platformer: as well as jumping on enemies' heads to defeat them, he can also collect and throw acorns at them or use his tail as a weapon. ■

FACT

Mr Nutz was created by French designer Philippe Dessoly. He was originally toying with the idea of making the hero a dolphin, parrot or turtle, until his wife suggested that he go with a squirrel instead.

MS PAC-MAN

Year	1996
Publisher	Williams Entertainment
Developer	Digital Eclipse

IT COULD BE argued that Ms Pac-Man is a better game than the original. It's got four different mazes whereas Pac-Man only had one, and the fact that the bonus fruit moves around is a fun little twist. The SNES port by Digital Eclipse is authentic enough but there are a few tweaks. Firstly, because the original game was played with a vertical orientation, the SNES game instead scrolls upwards. There are also extra stages to play on top of the arcade ones, split into Small, Big and Strange categories. There's now a speed boost that can be toggled with the A or B button, and a new co-op mode in which two players play at the same time (player two is Pac-Man). ■

FACT

The original name for the arcade game was going to be Miss Pac-Man, until someone pointed out that in the third cinematic she and Pac-Man have a baby. To avoid any controversy about them having a child out of wedlock, the name was changed.

MUSYA

Year	1992
Publisher	SETA
Developer	Jorudan

DESCRIBED ON THE packaging as 'the classic Japanese tale of horror', Musya tells the tale of Imoto, a pikeman who's somehow managed to survive an enormous battle. Seeking refuge in a nearby mountain village, he passes out as soon as he gets there. When Imoto wakes, the mayor tells him that his daughter Shizuka has been kidnapped and held prisoner in an abyss, and if she isn't rescued a gateway to the demon world will open. Playing as (a presumably exhausted) Imoto, you have to enter the abyss and rescue Shizuka by using your trusty pike to ward off the various enemies that approach. Nintendo once again requested the western versions be changed, though in this case it's perhaps for the best: a tanuki character in the game has enormous testicles. ■

FACT

Other censorship for the western version included the removal of 'manji' symbols, which are entirely harmless but look similar to swastikas.

NATSUME CHAMPIONSHIP WRESTLING

Year	1994
Publisher	Natsume
Developer	Natsume

THIS GRAPPLING GAME is based on Natsume's licensed Japanese title, All Japan Pro Wrestling Dash: World's Strongest Tag Team. Although this version has no licences to speak of, its 12 playable wrestlers are still based on real-life wrestlers like Kenta Kobashi, Stan Hansen, Terry Gordy and Dr Death Steve Williams. It's noticeably more detailed than most wrestling games of its era: there are over 50 moves and a fairly deep energy system which consists of six separate life bars which can heal over time. There are exhibition matches and round robin tournaments available, but the two most important modes are Championship Tournament and Champion Tag Match, which see you defeating every other wrestler or tag team in the game in order to claim the Triple Crown championship. ■

FACT

All Japan Pro Wrestling (or [Z]en Nihon Puroresu as it was [pr]eviously known in Japan) has [be]en active for nearly 50 years. It was first set up in 1972 by iconic Japanese wrestler Giant Baba.

NBA ALL-STAR CHALLENGE

Year	1992
Publisher	LJN
Developer	Beam Software

IF YOU'RE LOOKING for a basketball game that doesn't actually have any team-based basketball in it, NBA All-Star Challenge is the one for you. There are four different events on offer here, the most notable being one-on-one basketball against an opponent, which can be played as an exhibition match or in a tournament. Then there's a free-throw competition (where you have to score as many as possible), a three-point contest and H-O-R-S-E (where you have to match your opponent's shot or gain a letter). All 27 NBA teams are officially licensed here, but they're each only represented by a single player. While this does mean there are plenty of superstars like Jordan, Ewing, Olajuwon, Bird and Barkley, the stars who played alongside them aren't in here. ■

FACT

A sequel called NBA All-Star Challenge 2 was released on the Game Boy. It replaces H-O-R-S-E with a similar 'accuracy shootout' event, and adds a slam dunk contest.

NBA GIVE 'N GO

Year	1995
Publisher	Konami
Developer	Konami

THIS PORT OF Konami's massively underrated basketball arcade game Run and Gun offers probably the largest sprites you'll ever see in a 16-bit team sports game. With the camera set at the end of the court and positioned fairly low, as players approach the bottom of the screen they get truly massive. Whereas Run and Gun was entirely unlicensed, Give 'n Go has the full NBA licence, including team logos and players. As well as an arcade mode, which features minimal rules (only the shot clock and out of bounds are called), you can get a little more serious and play through a season: either 6, 28, 52 or the full 82 games in length. There's also a playoffs mode should you wish to just cut to the chase. ■

FACT

[D]espite the official licence, [th]e game's missing Shaquille [O]'Neal and Charles Barkley. [Bo]th players bought their name [a]nd license from the NBA, meaning separate deals were needed to get them in games.

NBA HANGTIME

Year	1996
Publisher	Midway Games
Developer	Funcom

AFTER THE RELEASE of the second NBA Jam game Tournament Edition, the NBA Jam name was acquired by Acclaim, who went on to create NBA Jam Extreme with a completely new development studio. Meanwhile, the actual team at Midway who'd created NBA Jam released its 'true' spiritual sequel, NBA Hangtime. Fans of NBA Jam could immediately tell: the game looks and plays very similarly, with a couple of new features added to keep things interesting. Alley-oops and double dunks (where you start a dunk then pass to your partner who's also dunking) let you build team fire, while a create-a-player mode lets you make your own bizarre-looking players. At the end of each game you're given a trivia question: get it right and you earn more attribute points for your created player. ■

FACT

Players can enter codes on the 'tonight's matchup' screen for some fun secrets, including the ability to play on a city, jungle or rooftop court.

NBA JAM

Year	1994
Publisher	Acclaim
Developer	Iguana Entertainment

MIDWAY'S NBA JAM wasn't the first arcade basketball game to offer two-on-two action with no rules: Midway itself had already done it years earlier with Arch Rivals. What made NBA Jam stand out were three things: its digitised players, its ridiculous dunks and the fact it was just so much more fun to play than anything that had come before it. Hot on the heels of Mortal Kombat's success in arcades the previous year, Midway decided to use the same digitisation technique to make each of NBA Jam's 54 players – all 27 NBA teams are present, with two players representing each – look just like their real-life counterparts. That's not to say that they behave like them, of course: players can pull off insane dunks that often involve leaping 50 feet into the air before slamming the ball home (and on very rare occasions, shattering the backboard).

If a player scores three times in a row,

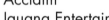

FACT

Michael Jordan wasn't in the game for licensing reasons, and Gary Payton didn't make the cut. After the pair contacted Midway, a special version of the arcade game was sent to them with an extra team containing Payton and Jordan.

they'll go 'on fire', making their dunks even more ridiculous. Publishing duties for the SNES version were taken over by Acclaim, and it plays a commendably authentic game of NBA Jam, although the players are less detailed and harder to identify purely by looking at their face. One notable feature carried over to the SNES version is the secret characters who can be unlocked with cheat codes. The likes of funk legend George Clinton, NFL player Warren Moon and even Bill Clinton and Al Gore can be summoned to play for your chosen team. ∎

NBA JAM TOURNAMENT EDITION

Year	1995
Publisher	Acclaim
Developer	Iguana Entertainment

THIS UPDATE TO NBA Jam adds a whole slew of new features. Most teams now have three players in their roster instead of two, with the player able to make substitutions after each quarter. What's more, winning the Tournament mode (by beating every team in the game) will unlock expanded rosters, giving most teams five players to choose from. A new Rookies team is also included, offering a variety of new players who were picked in the 1994 NBA Draft, including Jason Kidd and Grant Hill. An optional new hotspot rule is available: this puts random spots on the court with different points values: if you take a shot from these spots you can score up to nine points. For many, however, the best addition to the Tournament Edition is the vastly increased number of hidden characters. If players thought Bill Clinton and Al Gore were impressive in the first game,

FACT

NBA Jam's lead designer Mark Turmell confirmed years later that, as a big Detroit Pistons fan, he secretly added code to the game that would make the Bulls miss last-second shots any time they played against the Pistons.

they weren't prepared for what was on offer here: not only did Clinton and Gore return – along with all the other hidden characters from the first game – but they were also accompanied by the likes of Hillary Clinton, Prince Charles, all three members of the Beastie Boys, legendary former player Larry Bird and even hip hop duo Jazzy Jeff and the 'Fresh Prince' himself, Will Smith. Best of all, though, was the option to unlock a handful of NBA team mascots as playables, including Benny the (Chicago) Bull, Hugo the (Charlotte) Hornet and Crunch, the Phoenix Suns gorilla. ∎

NBA LIVE 95

Year	1994
Publisher	Electronic Arts
Developer	Electronic Arts

THE SUCCESS OF FIFA International Soccer's isometric viewpoint led EA to decide to implement it for its basketball series too. NBA Live 95, the first game in the NBA Live series, was the first to use a modified version of the FIFA engine, giving players a better view of the court. It also added some new gameplay features that would become standards for the NBA Live series going forwards, including the addition of a speed boost to give your player a little extra zip when he needs it. Although the SNES version played similarly to the Sega Mega Drive / Genesis one, it did have one notable disadvantage: whereas the Mega Drive rosters were based on the 1994–95 rosters, the SNES version used the older 1993–94 rosters instead. ■

FACT

Charles Barkley doesn't appear in NBA Live 95 for licensing reasons. More recently, EA's refused to allow his likeness to be used in the NBA 2K games, because 2K Sports won't pay money to retired players from historic squads.

NBA LIVE 96

Year	1995
Publisher	Electronic Arts
Developer	Electronic Arts

NBA LIVE 96 was the first game in the series to appear on the PlayStation, but EA wasn't ready to ditch the 16-bit era just yet. The big addition here was the inclusion of the two new expansion teams, the Toronto Raptors and the Vancouver Grizzlies. However, because there was a lockout in the real-life NBA during the off-season, neither team's roster was confirmed by the time EA was ready to ship the game. Instead, players have to do a draft to add players to each team: you can either do an automatic one that pulls players from other teams, or a manual one. Because every player that ended up in the actual Raptors and Grizzlies teams is in the game, you can get accurate rosters with a manual draft. ■

FACT

The game's player creation feature let you sneakily unlock some players not featured in the game. Stats for the likes of Michael Jordan, Larry Bird and even Charles Barkley would appear if you created players with their surnames.

NBA LIVE 97

Year	1996
Publisher	Electronic Arts
Developer	Electronic Arts

THE THIRD GAME in the NBA Live series was more about minor refinements rather than massive new features (at least when it came to the 16-bit versions). New additions to NBA Live 97 included reverse layups and dunks, manual steal controls and a new 'player lock' feature that let you choose one player and retain control of them throughout the entire game (instead of controlling whoever has the ball). The big headline here, however, was the new option to play 2-on-2 or 3-on-3 games using one half of the court. Since these were simply one-off games with no tournaments to speak of, however, they were mainly only useful for practice purposes. Updated rosters and slightly larger player sprites aside then, not much to write home about this year. ■

FACT

Unbeknownst to most gamers, Shaquille O'Neal had exclusivity deal with EA to use his likeness in NBA games. EA made a point of this by proudly declaring on the back of the box that 'NBA Live has Shaq!'.

NBA LIVE 98

Year	1997
Publisher	THQ / EA
Developer	Tiertex

WITH THE POLYGONAL generation now very much in full swing, gamers still clinging to 16-bit consoles were beginning to see ever-diminishing returns in terms of new features in their annual sports games. NBA Live 98, the last game in the series to release on the SNES, was the perfect evidence of this: its only new feature of any note was a new three-point contest mini-game. Other minor changes included an All-Star game appearing midway through the season mode, the ability to practice with your team on the court with no opposition, and tweaked trading functionality that took player ratings into account. It was fair to say, however, that EA's attention was elsewhere by this point, and the handful of SNES owners who hadn't made the jump to 3D paid the price. ■

FACT

The NBA Live series was renamed in 2010, when EA completed NBA Elite 11. Completed, that is, but not released: the game was so bad that EA pulled it at the last minute and didn't make another basketball game until NBA Live 14.

NBA SHOWDOWN

Year	1993
Publisher	Electronic Arts
Developer	Electronic Arts

NBA SHOWDOWN WAS the fifth and final game in the NBA Playoff series (which included Lakers vs Celtics, Bulls vs Lakers, Team USA Basketball and Bulls vs Blazers). As such, it was the last EA NBA game to feature a side-on viewpoint, before the studio moved on to the NBA Live series and its isometric camera the following year. Whereas previous games in the series only included the 16 teams that had made it to the NBA Playoffs, NBA Showdown is the first to include all 27 teams in the 1993 NBA season (plus an extra All-Star team). It also includes signature dunk animations for certain players, such as Shaq's gorilla dunk, Shawn Kemp's bounce-ball slam and Harold Miner's around-the-world slam. ■

FACT

Had this game followed the previous two games in being named after the previous year's NBA Finals, it would have been called Bulls vs Suns. However, the fact that the Suns' Charles Barkley isn't in the game may have changed these plans.

NCAA BASKETBALL

Year	1992
Publisher	HAL Laboratory / Nintendo
Developer	Sculptured Software

WHILE MOST BASKETBALL games of the era focused on trying to get the NBA licence, Nintendo and Sculptured Software instead opted to go down the college basketball route instead, securing the NCAA brand. There are 44 teams in NCAA Basketball, covering five different NCAA conferences: the ACC, the Big East, the SEC, the Big 8 and the SWC. The game also has a unique perspective: instead of a fixed camera, the action takes place on a rotating court thanks to the use of Mode 7 effects. Because the NCAA is relatively unknown outside of North America, the European game is instead called World League Basketball and features 60 fictional teams based on world cities, such as the London Royals, the Brussels Chocolateers and the somewhat questionable Ecuador Bananamen. ■

FACT

The Japanese version of the game, Super Dunk Shot, contains fake NBA teams with comically altered logos. Examples include the Chicago Bills, Detroit Pistols and Boston Celeries.

NCAA FINAL FOUR BASKETBALL

Year	1995
Publisher	Mindscape
Developer	Bitmasters

NINTENDO AND SCULPTURED Software weren't the only ones to release an NCAA basketball game on the SNES. Mindscape's effort tries to do things a little differently, but despite some of its more interesting features – such as its impressively smooth player animations – its clunky controls let it down somewhat. Whereas Nintendo's game offers 44 teams, Final Four instead gives players 64 of the top Division 1-A teams to choose from. Despite having such a sizeable helping of squads, it still isn't perfect: while the game prominently features the logo of the 1995 NCAA Final Four in Seattle, some of the smaller teams who actually qualified for the earlier stages of the tournament (such as the Chattanooga Mocs) aren't among the 64 teams here. ■

FACT

At the time of writing, the North Carolina Tar Heels have appeared in the most NCAA Final Fours (20 times). Spare a thought, though, for the BYU Cougars, who've appeared in the NCAA Tournament 29 times and never reached the Final Four.

NCAA FOOTBALL

Year	1994
Publisher	Mindscape
Developer	The Software Toolworks

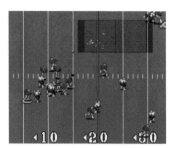

LONG BEFORE EA secured the NCAA football licence, Mindscape decided to give it a go. There are 40 teams to choose from here, though given there were well over 100 Division 1-A teams at the time that means a lot of big names don't make the cut (sorry Ohio State, Notre Dame and Michigan fans, your teams aren't represented here). The options are fairly limited: players can take part in an exhibition game or a four-game tournament, and for each game they can set the quarter length to 5, 10 or 15 minutes and choose fair, rainy or snowy weather. The major issue players had was the extremely easy CPU and the lack of difficulty options, meaning once you'd learnt how to outsmart the AI it was nearly impossible to lose. ■

FACT

No NCAA game (this one included) has ever included real player names. That's because it's against NCAA rules to use a player's name or image to market a third-party product.

NEWMAN/HAAS INDYCAR FEATURING NIGEL MANSELL

Year | 1994
Publisher | Acclaim
Developer | Gremlin Interactive

A SEQUEL OF sorts to Nigel Mansell's World Championship (see page 138), using that game's first-person viewpoint. While its predecessor was focused on Formula One racing, this one is instead based on the 1994 IndyCar season, which Mansell took part in (he finished in 8th place overall, if you're asking). There are a total of 15 tracks to play through in the order they appeared in the 1994 season: although in reality there were 16 races, the Indianapolis 500 race technically doesn't count because it was sanctioned by the USAC. The season mode has 12 drivers competing for the highest points total across all 15 races: all the other racer names are fake with the exception of Mario Andretti, who was also racing for Newman/Haas that year. ■

FACT

A.J. Foyt, Al Under Sr and Rick Mears are the most successful Indy 500 racers, having each won the famous race four times.

NFL FOOTBALL

Year | 1993
Publisher | Konami
Developer | Park Place Productions

KONAMI'S ONLY ATTEMPT at a SNES American football game is a visually impressive one, even if it doesn't offer much in the way of features. Although it features all 28 NFL teams playing at the time, the fact it only has the NFL licence and not the NFLPA one means there are no real player names here. There's also no season mode: you can only play an exhibition game or take part in the playoffs. There are two playbooks to choose from, though: a standard one designed for all teams, or a bespoke one for your team. Easily the most impressive aspect of NFL Football, however, is its use of Mode 7 to spin the field around and zoom in during the more dramatic moments. ■

FACT

This is not to be confused with NFL Football on the NES, which was published by LJN and developed by Atlus, and has nothing to do with this one.

NFL QUARTERBACK CLUB

Year | 1994
Publisher | LJN
Developer | Iguana Entertainment

THE NFL QUARTERBACK Club games outdid even Madden when it came to features. This first entry splits the game into three sections: QB Challenge, Play NFL and Simulation. QB Challenge has you choosing from 19 of the NFL's best quarterbacks and taking on four events – read and recognition, accuracy, obstacle course and distance – to see who's the best. You can also create your own quarterback, whose stats increase depending on how well you do. Play NFL does as you'd expect, offering exhibition, playoff and season modes. Finally, Simulation gives the player 30 scenarios from NFL history and asks you to win the game, so if you've always wanted to affect the result of the 1957 Western Conference final you're in luck. ■

FACT

The quarterbacks featured include the likes of Troy Aikman, John Elway, Boomer Esiason, Bernie Kosar, Dan Marino, Brett Favre and Steve Young.

NFL QUARTERBACK CLUB 96

Year | 1995
Publisher | Acclaim
Developer | Iguana Entertainment

THE SECOND QUARTERBACK Club was more of an evolution than a revolution, but enough tweaks were made to ensure it was now the best game in the series by default. For starters, the NFL's two expansion teams that year, the Jacksonville Jaguars and the Carolina Panthers, were added to the 28 already available. There are now 20 quarterbacks to choose from in QB Challenge, including stars like Drew Bledsoe, Randall Cunningham, Jim Everett, Jim Kelly and Warren Moon. The Simulation mode now has 50 classic scenarios to choose from (rather than the previous game's 30), and players can now set their own custom scenarios too. On the field, new moves like the up-and-over dive and the ability to call over 50 audibles from the line of scrimmage enhanced the game's depth. ■

FACT

The manual makes the rather unfortunate claim that if your friends are still arguing over which American football game is best, 'NFL Quarterback Club 96 ends the discussion with a concussion'.

NHLPA HOCKEY 93

Year	1992
Publisher	Electronic Arts
Developer	Electronic Arts

THE FIRST GAME in EA's ice hockey series was NHL Hockey (known as EA Hockey in Europe), which released exclusively on the Sega Mega Drive / Genesis in 1991. NHL Hockey was so well received that a sequel was inevitable, and this time the SNES got in on the action too. The NHL wasn't playing ball (well, playing puck) this time though, hence the use of the NHLPA licence instead: this meant real player names, but generic team names (the Pittsburgh Penguins became simply Pittsburgh, for example). What sets NHLPA Hockey and its predecessor apart from the other ice hockey games that came before is its sense of momentum and speed. Players legitimately feel like they're skating on ice: they take a while to build up to a high speed and take just as long to slow down again. While this would be considered a recipe for disaster if not handled properly, in NHLPA Hockey it's perfectly tuned to add to the chaos that regularly unfolds. The ability to poke check is one thing, but the dedicated body check move – which unleashes a burst of speed to help you slam into your opponent – is one of the most satisfying feelings you'll find in a game of any era. Even better, it occasionally triggers a brief fight, which lets you smack your opponent around the chops for daring to share a rink with you. Despite its lack of pizazz by today's standards, no modern ice hockey game can match this one for overall feel and general satisfaction. ∎

FACT

Although the team names in NHLPA Hockey 93 aren't the official ones, that didn't stop EA adding the NHL's two expansion teams, the Tampa Bay Lightning and the Ottawa Senators (albeit as simply Tampa Bay and Ottawa).

NHL 94

Year	1993
Publisher	Electronic Arts
Developer	Electronic Arts

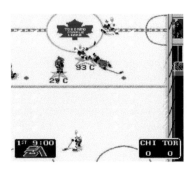

AFTER SITTING OUT the second game, the NHL got involved again for the third entry in EA's hockey series. Given that the original NHL Hockey didn't include player names, this meant NHL 94 was the first game in the series to feature the full shebang: real teams, real logos and real players. Other new additions to the game include 'one-timer' shots (where your player hits a powerful slapshot without needing to take a touch first), penalty shots, support for up to five players and the two new expansion teams, the Florida Panthers and the Mighty Ducks of Anaheim. All this shiny new stuff came at a price, however: the NHL insisted that as part of its return, fighting had to be removed from the game. ∎

FACT

NHL 14 on Xbox 360 and PS3 included an NHL 94 Anniversary mode, which changed the camera angle, controls and presentation to match those of NHL 94.

NHL 95

Year	1994
Publisher	Electronic Arts
Developer	Visual Concepts

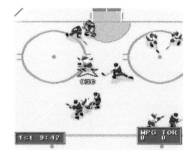

WITH THE FULL NHL and NHLPA licences nailed down, it was time to start the inevitable process of annual improvements. First up for NHL 95 was the addition of a proper season mode for the first time. Previous games only allowed you to take part in exhibition games or the playoffs, but this time you could take part in a full 84-game season, with the Stanley Cup awarded to the team that came out on top at the end. You could now also trade players between teams, or create your own future stars. The SNES version was met with criticism by some, however, because the Sega Mega Drive / Genesis version had even more new features such as fake shots and drop passes, but they weren't present here. ∎

FACT

Kevin Smith's movie *Mallrats* has a scene where a character plays NHL All-Star Hockey for the Sega Saturn. Smith was a huge fan of EA's NHL games but had to use Sega's game for sponsor reasons, so he used EA's sound effects instead.

NHL 96

Year	1995
Publisher	Electronic Arts
Developer	High Score Productions

BECAUSE SOME IMPROVEMENTS had been left out of the SNES version of NHL 95, it was a no-brainer that they'd be added to NHL 96 as an easy win for the developers. Sure enough, fake shots, drop passes and the ability to lie down on the ice to block shots were touted on the back of the NHL 96 as fancy new features, even though Sega fans got them the year before. At least this time the other new additions were present on both systems: new moves like quick stops and the 'spin-o-rama' gave the player new offensive possibilities, while new five-minute major penalties punished extreme behaviour. Best of all, however, was the return of fighting, which came as the result of a seriously determined plea from EA. ■

FACT

NHL 96 also had its presentation tweaked. An elaborate Stanley Cup ceremony was now your reward for toughing out a full season, and stadiums could now blare out 2 Unlimited's *Get Ready for This* to pump up the crowd.

NHL 97

Year	1996
Publisher	Electronic Arts
Developer	Black Pearl Software

AS WAS THE case with the Madden series and the NBA series, so too was the fate of the NHL series. The arrival of the PlayStation and Saturn generation meant the focus shifted away from the 16-bit NHL games, with fewer notable updates each year. The biggest feature in NHL 97, then, is the simple updating of each team's rosters to keep them up-to-date with the most recent NHL season. Also new is a coaching menu that lets you apply different strategies to each line. Eagled-eyed players could probably tell new features were thin on the ground because the back of the box promised things that had already been added the year before (including, yes, fake shots and drop passes), as well as vague things like 'improved gameplay'. ■

FACT

Once again, SNES owners were denied Sega-only features. The Mega Drive version added national teams, signature moves for certain players and new puck-shooting mini-games.

NHL 98

Year	1997
Publisher	THQ
Developer	Electronic Arts

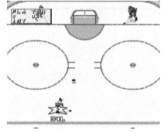

THE NHL SERIES went out (perhaps understandably) with more of a whimper than a bang on the SNES, with NHL 98's new features offering welcome but ultimately negligible changes. Players could now choose two different game speeds, and players could go on hot and cold streaks, affecting their stats to an extent. Goalies could be switched automatically and the game's AI was made more aware of specific penalties such as the two-line pass rule. The SNES version also finally got the three national teams (USA, Canada and Europe) that were added to the Sega version the year before, meaning that at least both versions went into the sunset on equal footing for once. And when you think about it, that's what life is all about. Or something. ■

FACT

Since the first game on the Sega Mega Drive, EA's NHL series has featured on 21 different systems, ranging from the PS4 and Xbox One to the Game Boy Color and Game Gear.

NHL STANLEY CUP

Year	1993
Publisher	Nintendo
Developer	Sculptured Software

FOLLOWING THE CRITICAL success of Nintendo and Sculptured Software's NCAA Basketball, the pair teamed up again to see what they could do with ice hockey. The result was NHL Stanley Cup, a game that featured the full NHL licence but not the NHLPA licence (which, as you'll know by now if you've been reading this book in order, means no real player names). Like its basketball effort, Stanley Cup uses Mode 7 graphics to create a pseudo-3D effect. With all 26 teams included, a full season mode and features that it took EA's series years to add – fake shots, hip checks, and the like – the result was a game that may not have been the best hockey experience on the SNES, but was certainly the most unique. ■

FACT

The European version of the game, Super Hockey, contains 26 entirely fictional teams with names like the Oslo Vikings, Madrid Bulls, Toronto Rams and New York Skyline.

NICKELODEON GUTS

Year	1994
Publisher	Viacom New Media
Developer	Viacom New Media

GUTS WAS NICKELODEON'S attempt at making a children's version of *American Gladiators*, with young contestants competing in various events in order to take on the Aggro Crag, a giant glowing mountain. The SNES exclusive video game version consists of six different events, but in reality they only comprise two different play styles. Slam Dunk, Spirals and Attack all have you jumping off a large platform with a bungee cord and bouncing up to throw a ball into a target of some sort, whereas Basic Training, Tornado Run and the aforementioned Aggro Crag are all side-scrolling events with deliberately awkward controls. Beat your opponent when all's said and done and you'll be awarded with a piece of the Aggro Crag, just like in the show. ■

> **FACT**
>
> A total of 160 episodes of *Guts* were filmed in total. Spin-off versions included *Global Guts* (where contestants came from different countries) and *My Family's Got Guts* (where families competed as teams).

NIGEL MANSELL'S WORLD CHAMPIONSHIP

Year	1993
Publisher	GameTek
Developer	Gremlin Graphics

THIS F1 GAME is based on the 1992 Formula One season which, coincidentally, Nigel Mansell won. The game is played in a first-person perspective similar to Sega's Super Monaco GP, and each of the 11 other racers you face off against in a season have their real names: Berger, Schumacher, Hakkinen, Alesi and the like. Naturally, you play as Mansell himself, though you can change your name if you want (but not your face, which is either good or bad depending on whether you have a thing for moustaches). One of the game's more interesting features is Mansell's Advice, where you choose a track and as you race along it Mansell appears at the top of the screen to recommend what speed you should be hitting each turn at. ■

> **FACT**
>
> The US version of the game is called Nigel Mansell's World Championship Racing just in case the big photo of the car on the box didn't make it obvious what it was about.

NINJA GAIDEN TRILOGY

Year	1995
Publisher	Tecmo
Developer	Tecmo

RETRO COMPILATIONS WERE still relatively uncommon in the 16-bit era, mainly because there hadn't been too many console generations before it. When they did emerge, though, fans were keen to see how these old games had been improved: Super Mario All-Stars was the perfect example of this sort of thing done right (see page 197). Ninja Gaiden Trilogy is an interesting one and is remembered more for what it doesn't do than what it does. It gathers all three Ninja Gaiden games released on the NES and presents them in one useful package, adding a password system for those who want to dip in and out. It also includes newly updated versions of the games' memorable cutscenes, making use of the SNES's improved palette support to give extra detail to each of them. Somewhat oddly, though, this is where the list of improvements ends: when it comes to the actual gameplay all three entries in the series are provided in their NES forms. That isn't to say they're identical ports, mind you: there have been some very minor visual tweaks, mainly in terms of colours. Ryu's sprite now has black outlines instead of the odd brown ones he had on the NES, for example. Unless you stood both the NES and SNES versions side-by-side, however, you'd struggle to be able to tell them apart. Other small changes include the addition of infinite continues in Ninja Gaiden III (like the first two already had), and tiny tweaks to the dialogue. ■

> **FACT**
>
> Ninja Gaiden was rebooted for the Xbox in 2004. The original NES trilogy could be unlocked in this reboot, albeit as their Ninja Gaiden Trilogy versions.

THE NINJA WARRIORS

Year	1994
Publisher	Taito
Developer	Natsume

DESPITE SHARING THE same name as Taito's 1987 arcade game The Ninja Warriors, this SNES title is actually a sequel (hence its name in the EU, Ninja Warriors: The New Generation). Set in a dystopian future, it has you controlling one of three robot ninjas – the speedy Kamaitachi, who's armed with sickles on chains, the balanced female robot Kunoici who has knives and swords, and the powerful but slow Ninja, who has a nunchaku and a terrible name – as they take on… let me check my notes here… a mutant dwarf dictator called Banglar the Tyrant. It's a side-scrolling beat 'em up where you pummel a steady stream of enemies, all while charging a power meter that lets you unleash a huge attack. ■

FACT

A reboot called The Ninja Saviors: Return of the Warriors was released on the Switch in 2019. It adds two new characters and includes co-op play for the first time.

NO ESCAPE

Year	1994
Publisher	Sony Imagesoft
Developer	Bits Studios

WHEN YOU CONSIDER that movie tie-ins are generally associated with bad quality games, it would take something particularly special to be considered one of the worst. Step forward No Escape, based on the sci-fi movie of the same name starring Ray Liotta and Lance Henriksen. Playing as Liotta's character John Robbins, you find yourself serving life imprisonment on an island inhabited by cannibals, and decide it's time to escape (despite the title making it clear that's not really on the cards). Bits Studios' interpretation of the movie is a barely functioning action platformer in which you're immediately swamped by a massive group of fast enemies and can only survive by running away, straight into a bunch of traps that appear out of nowhere. It was roundly panned by critics. ■

FACT

Ray Liotta's character only smiles four times during the entirety of the No Escape movie. Which is roughly four times more than anyone playing the game.

NOBUNAGA'S AMBITION

Year	1993
Publisher	Koei
Developer	Koei

GIVEN THAT THE SNES was home to a large number of historical simulations developed and published by Koei, it makes sense that it would also receive one of its most popular ones, despite its age. Nobunaga's Ambition was seven years old by the time it made its way to Nintendo's 16-bit system, having originally launched on Japanese PCs in 1986 and a number of subsequent systems. Like the other versions, it's set during Japan's Sengoku period (around 1467–1603) and is a strategy game in which you play as either Oda Nobunaga or one of Japan's other daimyos (feudal lords) as you try to unify Japan by taking over every fiefdom. It may be an old game, but it was still praised by strategy fans regardless. ■

FACT

The game's manual promotes the upcoming release of Genghis Khan II, with the somewhat questionable explanation that 'you're one awesome Mongol by the name of Genghis Khan'.

NOBUNAGA'S AMBITION: LORD OF DARKNESS

Year	1994
Publisher	Koei
Developer	Koei

DECIDING TO SKIP Nobunaga's Ambition II, Koei opted to jump straight to 1990's Lord of Darkness (originally known as Nobunaga's Ambition: Records of the Generals) for its next SNES port. While other games in the series – and indeed many other Koei games – tend to have a generous number of scenarios to choose from, there are just two here. The first, called The Warring States, is set in 1555 and sees Nobunaga as a minor daimyo, just finding his feet as ruler of the weak state of Owari. The second, the catchily named Nobunaga Surrounded by his Enemies, is set in 1571 and has the now powerful Nobunaga finding himself the prime target of daimyo forces of at least five other states. ■

FACT

The succession of power in Japan in this era is summed up by this popular Japanese phrase: 'Nobunaga pounds the national rice cake, (Toyotomi) Hideyoshi kneads it and (Tokugawa) Ieyasu sits down and eats it.'

NOLAN RYAN'S BASEBALL

Year	1992
Publisher	Romstar
Developer	Affect

ONE OF THE earliest SNES games to be officially endorsed by a sportsperson, Nolan Ryan's Baseball is, unsurprisingly, named after Texas Rangers pitcher Nolan Ryan. Unfortunately for baseball fans, Ryan's name is the only real one in the game: this was originally a Japanese game called Super Stadium and it didn't pick up any licences during its travels westward. As such, there are no real player names (other than Ryan) and no real team names. In fact, there are barely team names at all: there's only a single league with 14 teams each given single-letter names: R Team, V Team, L Team and so on. At the end of the day, all players needed to know was that the T Team was the one with Nolan Ryan in it. ■

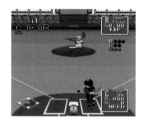

FACT

Nolan Ryan holds the MLB record for the longest career, having taken part in 27 seasons. He started in September 1966 and played his last game in September 1993.

OBITUS

Year	1994
Publisher	Bullet-Proof Software
Developer	Psygnosis

MEDIEVAL HISTORY LECTURER Wil Mason isn't having the best of days. While driving through Wales (Snowdonia, to be precise) his car breaks down, so he heads to a nearby abandoned tower to seek shelter from the storm. After falling asleep, Wil wakes up to find himself in a completely new world called FalconWood. As Wil, you have to figure out what's going on and how to get back home. Obitus is an RPG that's mainly played from a first-person perspective, but occasionally switches to a side-scrolling view when you're exploring certain buildings. While its pseudo-3D graphics are impressive (especially when moving between screens in the woods), the game received criticism for its nearly identical scenery, making it hard to navigate and figure out where you've been. ■

FACT

The original Amiga version of Obitus had sections that were too dark to navigate unless you had a torch. Since the PC version only supported up to 16 colours, these sections were left fully lit, making that version easier.

NOSFERATU

Year	1995
Publisher	SETA
Developer	SETA

NOSFERATU WAS STUCK in development hell for a while: previews of what seemed to be a near-complete version of the game were seen in magazines in 1991. Still, SETA persevered, and Nosferatu finally launched years later. You play as Kyle, a young chap whose girlfriend Erin has been captured by Nosferatu, so he's headed to the vampire's castle to defeat him and rescue her. The game can best be described as a horror version of Prince of Persia: Kyle's movements are very slow and deliberate, which means that overcoming your own momentum can sometimes be just as challenging as overcoming the various monsters roaming the castle. Combat is more involved than in Prince of Persia, though: Kyle is armed with an array of punches, kicks and tackles. ■

FACT

The original 1922 movie Nosferatu was an adaptation of Bram Stoker's Dracula. However, the Stoker estate refuse permission for the names to be used: as such, Dracula became Count Orlok and the word 'vampire' became Nosferatu.

OGRE BATTLE: THE MARCH OF THE BLACK QUEEN

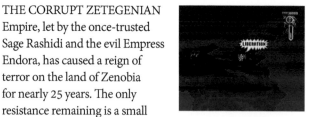

Year	1995
Publisher	Enix
Developer	Quest

THE CORRUPT ZETEGENIAN Empire, let by the once-trusted Sage Rashidi and the evil Empress Endora, has caused a reign of terror on the land of Zenobia for nearly 25 years. The only resistance remaining is a small group of rebels who are vastly outnumbered by the Empire's forces. Rumour has it, though, that there's a great wizard called Warren who may be able to help. Ogre Battle is a real-time tactical RPG that was previously highly sought after due to its limited release (though it was later ported to the Wii Virtual Console, where Europe also got it for the first time). Apparently its designer Yasumi Matsuno was inspired by the Yugoslav Wars of the early 1990s, which if I recall were fairly light on wizards. ■

FACT

Both Ogre Battle and The March of the Black Queen are titles of songs from Queen's second album. The sequel, Tactics Ogre: Let Us Cling Together, is also named after a Queen song.

OLYMPIC SUMMER GAMES

Year | 1996
Publisher | US Gold
Developer | Black Pearl Software

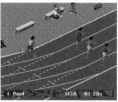

THE OFFICIAL VIDEO game of the Atlanta 1996 Olympic Games, this was also the third and final official Olympics game published by US Gold (after 1992's Sega-only Olympic Gold and 1994's Winter Olympics). There are 10 events to choose from here, the majority of which are your standard track and field affairs: 100m sprint, 110m hurdles, pole vault, long jump, triple jump, high jump, javelin, discus, archery and skeet shooting. The majority of events use the tried and tested control method of bashing buttons – the A and B buttons, in this case – to build speed or power, meaning while the game is far from revolutionary it's at least easy enough for newcomers to get to grips with without too much effort. ■

FACT
The 1996 Olympic Games was won by the USA, who gathered a total of 44 gold medals (Russia were second with 26). As for Great Britain? Um… 36th. But still, it's the taking part that counts.

ON THE BALL

Year | 1992
Publisher | Taito
Developer | Taito

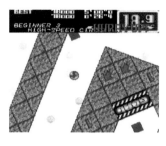

DESCRIBED BY TAITO as 'a hypersensation ball race against time', On the Ball is a SNES port of the studio's 1989 arcade game Cameltry. Those familiar with the bonus stage in the original Sonic the Hedgehog will have a good idea of what's going on in this one: the aim is to guide a marble through a series of mazes by rotating the screen. As you make your way through progressively more complicated levels, you'll have to cope with dead ends, walls that need to be broken through and obstacles on the course that can reduce your already strict time limit if you bump into them. Should the need arise you can also shake the screen by pressing the B button: this makes the ball jump. ■

FACT
A new version of On the Ball was released for the DS in 2007, under the name Labyrinth. The arcade original was also included in Taito Legends 2 on PS2, Xbox and PC.

OPERATION EUROPE: PATH TO VICTORY

Year | 1994
Publisher | Koei
Developer | Koei

THERE AREN'T MANY games that let you play as Adolf Hitler, but Operation Europe can make such a claim. Another of Koei's historical simulations, it's similar in style to the likes of Nobunaga's Ambition and Liberty or Death but this time takes place during the events of the Second World War. There are six scenarios to choose from: the occupation of France in 1940, the North African War in 1942, the fierce battles at Kursk in 1943, the storming of Normandy in 1944, the Battle of the Bulge in 1944 and the fight for Berlin in 1945. In each of these scenarios, players can choose to play as either the Allied or Axis side, with a selection of different commanders available in each scenario (including, yes, Hitler). ■

FACT
Although the vast majority of the commanders are real people, a few are fictional. One US commander, Sanders, is believed to be based on Sgt Chip Saunders from the TV show Combat! which aired on ABC in the '60s.

OPERATION LOGIC BOMB

Year | 1993
Publisher | Jaleco
Developer | Jaleco

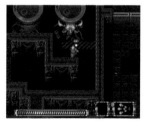

THIS TOP-DOWN ACTION game is a sequel to the Game Boy game Fortified Zone (it's actually Fortified Zone 3, since the second game was released exclusively in Japan). Players take control of Agent Logan, a special soldier who's been fitted with bioelectronic implants that give him 'superior strength, reflexes and analytical abilities'. A research lab working on a teleporter has accidentally ripped the dimensional fabric of space and time, and monsters are now running rampant, so it's up to Agent Logan to make his way through the lab, gunning down all the creatures he comes across. Starting off with a basic machine gun and triple cannon, on your travels you'll eventually come across a homing missile launcher, a laser and a flamethrower. ■

FACT
If you're confused about the title, a 'logic bomb' is a piece of malicious code that's intentionally left in a software system that can be triggered when required. Which doesn't help much, really.

OPERATION THUNDERBOLT

Year	1994
Publisher	Taito
Developer	Aisystem Tokyo

THE SEQUEL TO light gun classic Operation Wolf, Operation Thunderbolt offers similar on-rails action. After a group of hijackers force a passenger jet to land in the Bintazi People's Republic, the Republic's evil dictator General Abul Bazarre makes a demand on TV: free his comrades in prison in France and Germany, or the hostages on the plane will be killed. Playing as one of six green berets, you have to take on eight different missions as you shoot your way through Bazarre's forces while trying to resolve the hostage situation. Although the game can be played with a standard SNES controller, players can also choose to use the Super Scope or the SNES Mouse, both of which offer far speedier cursor movement in busy moments. ■

FACT

In other versions, the plane lands in Kalubya. This sounds suspiciously close to Libya, where an actual hijacking landed in 1976 to refuel before flying to Uganda. The name of the rescue mission carried out by Israeli forces? Operation Thunderbolt.

OSCAR

Year	1996
Publisher	Titus Software
Developer	Flair Software

OSCAR IS A… creature of some sort (a mouse? It's not made clear) who's found himself trapped in a movie theatre. The only way he can escape is to enter each of the four movies playing there, and turn them into award-winning productions by finding the numerous Oscar-like trophies dotted around each stage. This is a standard platform game that's livened up by the four themed worlds based on movie genres: horror, cartoon, western and, um… prehistoric. Oscar can find a yo-yo on his travels, which he can use to both attack enemies and swing from overhead platforms. An odd Game Boy power-up exclusive to the SNES version transforms the screen into that trademark pea soup green associated with the original Game Boy's display. ■

FACT

Oscar was re-released on the Nintendo DSi's online DSiWare store in 2010, along with three new sequels: Oscar in Toyland, Oscar in Toyland 2 and Oscar's World Tour.

OUT TO LUNCH

Year	1993
Publisher	Mindscape
Developer	Mindscape

PIERRE LE CHEF is a world renowned culinary expert, but his ingredients have escaped so he has to go and get them back. This platformer features 48 levels, spread across six different countries: Switzerland, Greece, the West Indies, Mexico, China and France. The aim is to collect the various ingredients wandering around by capturing them in his net (stunning them first with bags of flour is optional) then dropping them into a large cage in each level. Collect enough ingredients and the stage is complete. Out to Lunch is an entertaining enough little platform game, but some issue must be raised at the fact that it makes no effort to explain why such a respected chef is allowed to cook using vegetables that are clearly alive. ■

FACT

As well as capturing his ingredients, Pierre also has to defeat bacteria and insects. Because eating a tomato with a face on it is fine as long as flies haven't gone near it.

OUTLANDER

Year	1993
Publisher	Mindscape
Developer	Mindscape

AFTER MAKING ITS Mad Max game for the NES, Mindscape decided to start working on a SNES adaptation of its sequel *The Road Warrior*. However, the licence was lost during development, meaning a swift name change was necessary. Thus Outlander was born. The game consists of two different play styles that you alternate between. At first you'll be driving across the country, armed with a front-facing machine gun and a shotgun (the latter of which can be fired out of your window to take out enemies that approach from the side). As you enter towns you'll need to get out of your car, at which point the game switches to a side-on action game as you kill enemies while gathering vital food, petrol and ammunition. ■

FACT

Outlander was also released on the Sega Genesis, but there were some differences between the two versions. Most notably the driving sections in the Sega version had a first-person viewpoint instead.

PAC-ATTACK

Year	1993
Publisher	Namco
Developer	Namco

IN 1993 NAMCO decided to resurrect Pac-Man, who hadn't starred in a major game since Pac-Mania in 1987. The result was a series of new Pac-Man games, starting with Pac-Attack: a block-dropping puzzler similar to Tetris, where various shapes fall from the sky and the player has to rotate and drop them to form lines. The twist is that some of the squares that make up these shapes contain ghosts, and others contain Pac-Man. When a piece containing Pac-Man is dropped on the board, he'll head off and eat any ghosts that are in his path. Eat enough and you'll fill a meter that causes a fairy to remove all the ghosts, allowing for a massive chain reaction as the gaps are filled in by the remaining blocks. ■

FACT

Pac-Attack is actually a remake of another Namco game called Cosmo Gang the Puzzle. This arcade and Super Famicom title is basically identical except Pac-Man and the ghosts are blue balls and aliens.

PAC-IN-TIME

Year	1994
Publisher	Namco
Developer	Kalisto Entertainment

THIS PAC-MAN PLATFORMER (or Pac-former if you will) is actually based on Kalisto's Amiga and PC game Fury of the Furries, which was about a small round fluffy creature that could transform into four different forms. In this take, the hero is now a young Pac-Man (who's been sent back in time by an evil witch), and he gains his new abilities by jumping through large coloured rings. The yellow ring lets Pac-Man throw fireballs that can kill enemies, while the red one gives him a sledgehammer that can be used to destroy parts of the scenery. The blue ring gives him the ability to swim underwater, while the green one gives him a magic rope that lets him grapple to nearby walls and ceilings and swing around. ■

FACT

The game's intro sequence introduces the Pac-Man family, during which it refers to Ms Pac-Man as Mrs Pac-Man. Either this was a mistake or the pair decided to make it official.

PAC-MAN 2: THE NEW ADVENTURES

Year	1994
Publisher	Namco
Developer	Namco

THE MAIN EVENT in Namco's attempt to breathe new life into Pac-Man was the first ever numbered sequel to the original game. Despite it having the bold name of Pac-Man 2, however, this plays nothing like the maze-munching mirth the character is known for. Instead, it's an interesting take on the point-and-click adventure genre, which tries to do some unique things with varied results. Whereas other point-and-clicks have you selecting where on the screen you want your character to move, in Pac-Man 2 you don't actually have any direct control over Pac-Man. Instead, you're more of an observer with two ways of interacting with the game. The first is to point at areas of interest and press the Y button: this makes you shout 'LOOK!' at Pac-Man in an attempt to get him to notice (and hopefully interact with) key items. The second is your slingshot, which you can use to fire at various objects and characters: for example, you can knock an apple out of a tree so Pac-Man can eat it. The hero's emotions also play a crucial role: Pac-Man goes through some serious mood swings and much of the game is about trying to get him in the right frame of mind. It isn't always about making him happy, either: if he's too happy he has the tendency to become a little carefree and ignore your requests. Although this hands-off interface can lead to its fair share of frustration, the result is a SNES game that can truly call itself unique. ■

FACT

Should you still be craving some actual arcade-style Pac-Man action, Pac-Man can stumble upon two cartridges in the game which unlock retro versions of Pac-Man and Ms Pac-Man.

PACKY AND MARLON

Year	1995
Publisher	Raya Systems
Developer	Wave Quest

 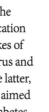

ANOTHER ENTRY IN the Raya Systems health education series that includes the likes of Bronkie the Bronchiasaurus and Captain Novolin. Like the latter, Packy and Marlon is also aimed at children with type 1 diabetes and attempts to educate them on the condition. Packy and Marlon are two diabetic elephant children who are at summer camp at the diabetes-friendly Camp Wa-Kee. Unfortunately, the camp has been invaded by rats who've stolen all the food and medical supplies, so it's up to the pair to get everything back and teach those rats a lesson, all while making sure they continue to take their insulin and that their blood glucose levels remain healthy. Sadly, there was no sequel aimed at educating camp owners on how to prevent vermin infestations. ∎

FACT

Stanford University's research on Packy and Marlon suggested diabetic kids who played it were four times less likely to need urgent care visits than those playing a different game. Unless that game was Bronkie the Bronchiasaurus, obviously.

THE PAGEMASTER

Year	1994
Publisher	Fox Interactive
Developer	Probe

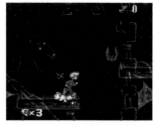

THE PAGEMASTER, OTHERWISE known as the Macaulay Culkin movie nobody remembers, was a disaster at the box office. Still, this is one of the gambles you take when you make a video game based on a movie, and as such the game tie-in for *The Pagemaster* happily made its way onto store shelves regardless (where it was pretty much ignored there too). Playing as young Richard Tyler, you find yourself trapped in a magical library where everything is animated. The only way you can leave is by collecting eight library cards and rescuing his newfound book friends Horror, Adventure and Fantasy. As well as the standard 2D platforming fare there's also a 3D bonus stage where you fly around in a giant book collecting gold tokens. ∎

FACT

Just how badly did *The Pagemaster* movie do? The total budget was $34 million, but it only grossed $13.7 million in cinemas.

PALADIN'S QUEST

Year	1993
Publisher	Enix
Developer	Copya System

CHEZNI IS VERY much the '90s RPG version of Harry Potter. After great magic potential is found in him, his mum grudgingly sends him off to magic school, where he becomes top of the class. He's got a bit of the devil in him though (not literally), and as part of a dare he accidentally activates an ancient machine called the Dal Green, which destroys the magic school. It's up to Chezni to destroy the Dal Green while preventing it from falling into the hands of Zaygos, a young dictator who wants it to take over the world. This RPG features first-person turn-based battles similar to Enix's Dragon Quest games, but there's a twist: any time you cast a magic spell you actually lose health. ∎

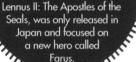

FACT

In Japan, Paladin's Quest was called Lennus: Memories of an Ancient Machine. Its sequel, Lennus II: The Apostles of the Seals, was only released in Japan and focused on a new hero called Farus.

PAPERBOY 2

Year	1991
Publisher	Mindscape
Developer	Tengen

WHEREAS THE FIRST Paperboy was a hit both in the arcades and at home, its sequel was designed exclusively for consoles and computers. Like the original, the aim is to deliver papers by throwing them at the houses in your local neighbourhood. A number of improvements have been made to keep things fresh, including the ability to now play as a Papergirl should you wish. This time you aren't just delivering papers to one side of the street: you'll have to regularly cross the road and deliver to both sides. There's also a greater variety of house types now, ranging from haunted houses and mansions to kids' clubhouses. Because all children love a good browse of *The Guardian* every now and then. ∎

FACT

Toys-to-life game Lego Dimensions has a Midway Games level pack, part of which has you wandering up the street from Paperboy destroying various cars and objects.

PARODIUS: NON-SENSE FANTASY

Year	1992
Publisher	Konami
Developer	Konami

THIS PARODY OF Gradius – hence the name – was originally released in arcades before making its way to the likes of the NES, PC Engine and SNES (although the latter version didn't make it to the US). Playing as either the Vic Viper from Gradius, the ship from TwinBee, Konami's penguin mascot Pentarou or a flying octopus, you face off against all manner of odd enemies, ranging from a pirate ship with a cat's head attached to it, to an enormous 200-foot Las Vegas dancing girl. The SNES version contains an extra stage set in a traditional Japanese bathhouse, as well as a special mode oddly named Lollipop where you respawn immediately after dying (instead of restarting at the last checkpoint). ■

FACT

There were six games in the Parodius series. This was the second: others include Jikkyo Oshaberi Parodius on the PlayStation and the dubiously named arcade game Sexy Parodius.

THE PEACE KEEPERS

Year	1994
Publisher	Jaleco
Developer	Jaleco

ALTHOUGH YOU WOULDN'T know it by its name, The Peace Keepers is the third and final game in Jaleco's trilogy of beat 'em ups that started with Rival Turf! and continued with Brawl Brothers. This time the plot surrounds the notorious Deutschland Moldavia corporation and its mysterious genetic experiments. You play as one of four people affected by DM's work: a former test subject called Flynn who can turn into a muscular superhero, a woman called Echo whose grandfather was murdered by a DM worker, a soldier called Al who wants to know why one of his squadmates was acting differently after a DM test, and a huge muscle man called Prokop who's searching for his kidnapped sister. Oddly, the US version removed most of the music from the Japanese game. ■

FACT

You can unlock two more playable characters: the previous game's hero Rick Norton (aka Hack) and a yellow robot called Orbot. To get them right away, turn on the SNES and hold L, R, A and Start until the title screen appears.

PGA EUROPEAN TOUR

Year	1996
Publisher	Electronic Arts
Developer	Polygames

THIS SPIN-OFF FROM the main PGA Tour Golf series focuses on, you guessed it, European competitions. There are five courses in the game, letting you play all 18 holes on the Real Club Valderrama in Spain, the Golf Club Crans-sur-Sierre in Switzerland, Le Golf National in Paris and a pair of English courses: the Wentworth Club in Surrey and the Forest of Arden Hotel in the West Midlands. After creating your own player, you can compete against 10 real-life pros including Seve Ballesteros, Bernhard Langer, Ian Woosnam, Sandy Lyle and Colin Montgomerie. They can join you on the course and you can watch them hit their shots, but you can't control them. By which I mean you can't play as them, not that they're maniacs. ■

FACT

The SNES version supports the TeeV Golf, an elaborate golf club controller that used infrared beams to track the position of your swing.

PGA TOUR 96

Year	1996
Publisher	Electronic Arts
Developer	Polygames

AFTER THE ORIGINAL PGA Tour Golf launched on the SNES, Nintendo fans were shunned from subsequent entries. They weren't allowed back into the world of golfing goodness until this, the fourth main game in the series. There are eight courses here: Avenel (known these days as Potomac), Las Colinas in Spain, River Highlands in Connecticut, Sawgrass in Florida, Scottsdale in Arizona, Southwind in Memphis, Summerlin in Las Vegas and The Woodlands in Texas. As with its European spin-off opposite, there are digitised versions of 10 non-playable pros to compete against, including Fuzzy Zoeller, Davis Love III and Craig Stadler. The SNES version is notorious for its putting, which generates a (thankfully optional) 3D grid that takes a lifetime to render and has to redraw every time you rotate it. ■

FACT

This was also the first PGA Tour game to make it to the PlayStation, but because of the need to create each course in a polygonal form there are only three in this version.

PGA TOUR GOLF

Year	1992
Publisher	Electronic Arts
Developer	Sterling Silver Software

IT'S NOT OFTEN that you can make a case for an earlier entry in a series being better than later instalments, but fans of the original PGA Tour Golf could probably put together a reasonable argument. Unlike its successors (see the previous page), which featured more courses but presented them with a static camera, the four courses on offer here make use of Mode 7 so you can track the ball's progress once you've hit it. It's an impressive effect and certainly flashier than the games that followed. The courses on offer in this one are Sawgrass (Florida), Avenel (Potomac), the PGA West Stadium (California) and Eagle Trace (Florida). Although there are no pros to compete against, they do appear in a flyby of each hole to give advice. ■

FACT

How soon we turn: the original Amiga version was re-released in 1994 with a bunch of new courses, and what was previously critically acclaimed was now widely panned for having aged badly.

PHALANX

Year	1992
Publisher	Kemco
Developer	Kemco

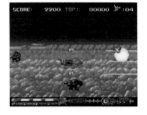

PHALANX IS PERHAPS better known for its bizarre cover – which features a confused old hillbilly playing the banjo while a spaceship flies past overhead – than the game itself. That's not to say the game isn't worth a look: set in 2279, it has you playing as Wink Baufield, a space pilot sent to an alien planet called Delia to investigate the disappearance of a group of researchers. Whatever's happened, it's caused a bunch of alien fighters to all want to kill you, so it's shooty time. Phalanx has a gimmick that makes it different from other shoot 'em ups of the era: rather than replacing your weapon when you collect a new one, you can store up to three at a time and switch between them. ■

FACT

The cover was the idea of two advertisers, Matt Guss and Keith Campbell. Guss explains: 'Keith could have done some predictable spaceship shooting bullshit […] or create a story that would make people stop and think about it.'

PHANTOM 2040

Year	1995
Publisher	Viacom New Media
Developer	Viacom New Media

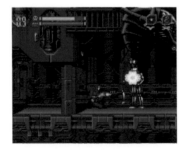

PHANTOM 2020 WAS a cult animated series that only lasted 35 episodes despite wide critical praise. Halfway through its run this action platformer was released, which borrows parts of the storyline from numerous episodes to make its own Frankenstein's monster of a plot. Playing as college student Kit Walker Jr, aka the 24th Phantom, you have to make your way through seven stages fighting enemies and using your 'inductance rope' as a grapple hook to reach higher areas. At various times in the game you'll be given different options on what to do next: depending on what you choose the story will change. The result of this is that Phantom 2040 has no fewer than 20 different endings, of which only four are considered 'good'. ■

FACT

If you're able to choose which version of the game to play, get the North American one. It gives you the option of a 'complete' or 'summarised' storyline, whereas the EU version only offers a summarised one.

PIECES

Year	1994
Publisher	Atlus
Developer	Prism Kikaku

ALL THOSE HOURS spent as a child putting together jigsaws can finally be put to good use in Pieces, an interesting competitive jigsaw 'em up game. Playing against either the CPU or up to four other human players, the aim is to put together a set number of jigsaws before your opponent(s) can. As you correctly place pieces you'll build up a power meter, which can be spent on power-ups that trigger a wide range of actions, from showing you where each piece goes for a limited time to removing pieces from your opponent's jigsaw. Playing with the standard SNES controller is a perfectly acceptable way to enjoy Pieces, but should you so desire you can also crack out the SNES Mouse and play using that instead. ■

FACT

Pieces got a sequel of sorts in 2002 in the form of Jigsaw Madness on the PlayStation. By that point developer Prism Kikaku had changed its name to Nippon Ichi Software.

PILOTWINGS

Year | 1991
Publisher | Nintendo
Developer | Nintendo EAD

ALTHOUGH F-ZERO WAS one of the first games designed to showcase the power and visual spectacle of Mode 7 to new (and potential) SNES owners, it's fair to say that Pilotwings was probably the most revolutionary, at least from a console side of things. Flight simulators were nothing new to home computers, but the genre had yet to truly crack consoles, partly because they tended to be too complicated and partly because the NES and chums weren't really powerful enough to provide a realistic recreation of flight. Step forward Pilotwings, which took a traditionally impenetrable genre for console gamers and made it accessible in a way that hadn't been seen before.

Naturally, its major selling point was its graphical splendour. Pilotwings uses Mode 7 in a similar way to F-Zero, by using a large sprite as the 'ground' and rotating and scaling it underneath the player's static aircraft to give the impression that they're flying over it. The result is a pretty convincing illusion of a fully 3D game, and one that runs significantly smoother than most other 3D flight sims on home computers at the time (since Mode 7 is efficient enough to allow games to run at a full 60 frames per second). F-Zero may have been the game you would show off to your friends, but Pilotwings was the one that felt the most immersive.

FACT

In its prototype stage, Pilotwings was called Dragonfly and had you controlling an actual dragonfly as it flew around shooting enemies. Nearer to release another Dragonfly prototype was shown which looked more like the Pilotwings we know today.

Just as important as how it looked, however, was how it played. Pilotwings presents players with a number of increasingly challenging missions that generally revolve around four methods of flight: a light plane, a rocket belt, a hang glider and skydiving. Each discipline has its own control method and brings with it its own unique challenges: the light plane's momentum means movements have to be planned in advance, the rocket belt has a limited supply of fuel, the hang glider requires you to find and ride wind currents to stay airborne and skydiving has the whole slamming into the ground thing to worry about.

The game's split into a series of licence tests, each consisting of a handful of events. Each event grades you on your performance, breaking it down to a variety of different factors (be it accuracy, speed or how well you performed a specific requirement for that event). The maximum for each event is 100 points and if you can score enough combined points across all events to hit a certain target, you'll get your licence and move onto the next set. It isn't without its secrets, either: land on certain special targets and you'll unlock special bonus events, like controlling a man with wings as he jumps on a series of trampolines, or trying to help a penguin dive into a pool. Things properly kick off during the last stage, where the action switches to a top-down view without warning and you suddenly have to take part in a hostage rescue mission while flying a combat helicopter as enemies fire a barrage of missiles at you from the ground. ∎

PINBALL DREAMS

Year	1994
Publisher	GameTek
Developer	Spidersoft

LONG BEFORE SWEDISH studio DICE was making Battlefield games for EA, it was known as Digital Illusions and was making pinball games. Pinball Dreams originally launched on the Amiga in 1992 and a couple of years later was ported to the SNES by Spidersoft. It consists of four fictional pinball tables, each with their own distinct theme. Ignition is a space-themed table, where you have to perform various tasks to launch a rocket and explore planets. Steel Wheel has an Old West theme and focuses on old steam trains. Graveyard (called Nightmare in some other versions) is a typical horror-themed table. Finally there's Beat Box, which is based on the pop music industry and has you trying to release singles, videos, LPs and movies while going on tour. ∎

FACT

The renaming of the Nightmare table to Graveyard isn't a case of censorship for once. The actual table says Graveyard in every version of the game, but was wrongly called Nightmare on most main menus. The SNES version is actually a fix, then.

PINBALL FANTASIES

Year	1995
Publisher	GameTek
Developer	Spidersoft

  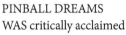 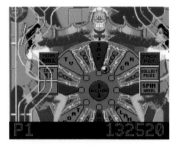

PINBALL DREAMS WAS critically acclaimed (mainly on home computers) so not-yet-DICE got to work on a sequel, which Spidersoft again duly ported to the SNES. There are another four tables to choose from here, each once again offering its own distinct vibe. Party Land is based on a theme park and has players trying to light the letters to spell out PARTY and CRAZY for big points. Speed Devils is a racing-themed table where hitting various targets will make you overtake rival cars. Billion Dollar Gameshow is a spoof of TV gameshows where you try to win prizes by shooting the ramps. Finally, Stones N Bones is the token creepy table, this time based on a haunted house. The SNES port was criticised for its choppy scrolling. ∎

FACT

A number of further sequels were launched on other formats. Spidersoft was given the nod to make its own PC game, Pinball Dreams II, while DICE worked on the true threequel, Pinball Illusions.

PINK GOES TO HOLLYWOOD

Year	1993
Publisher	TecMagik
Developer	Altron

PRESUMABLY SICK OF being known for his TV cartoons, the Pink Panther decides to go to Hollywood to audition for a big movie role. There's just one problem: Inspector Clouseau is hell-bent on ruining his big break. Starting from a central hub called Honey I Shrunk the Pink (where our hero is tiny), from here you can access a number of other stages, most of which have various movie themes and all of which have terrible names that barely pass as puns. There's a Robin Hood stage called Pinkinhood, a pirate stage called Pinkbeard, a stage set in the jungle called Jungle Pink and so on. One odd feature is toll booths: these require coins that, once inserted, build a bridge or summon a magic carpet. ∎

FACT

Of course, the Pink Panther had already been a Hollywood star of sorts many years earlier, having originally appeared in the animated intros of the live action Pink Panther movies.

PINOCCHIO

Year	1996
Publisher	Disney Interactive
Developer	Virgin Interactive

ALTHOUGH MOST RETRO gamers tend to hold up Aladdin (the Sega version), The Jungle Book and The Lion King as a sort of holy trinity of Virgin Interactive platformers, many tend to forget that a fourth game was released during the 16-bit era's final days. Pinocchio has the same high quality of animation as the three Virgin games that came before it, and retells the story of the movie over the course of nine levels. Players will guide Pinocchio to school, escape from Stromboli's show, escape (again) from Pleasure Island, find Monstro the whale and eventually escape (yet again) from inside its guts. Despite maintaining the high visual standards of Virgin's other Disney-licensed platform games, it was criticised for being more awkward to control. ∎

FACT

The manual's top tips feel like life lessons instead: 'Always choose the path of truth, be brave enough to stand up to the bad guys no matter what, and be selfless by helping others, even when all seems lost.'

THE PIRATES OF DARK WATER

Year	1994
Publisher	Sunsoft
Developer	Sunsoft

THE PIRATES OF Dark Water was a short-lived Hanna-Barbera series that started as a five-part miniseries in 1991 then got a further 21 episodes before it was cancelled in 1993. That didn't stop Sunsoft making an entertaining tie-in a year later, in which young pirate Ren has to find 13 ancient treasures to stop his planet Mer being overcome with an evil substance called Dark Water. The game is a side-scrolling beat 'em up in the style of Final Fight, with players able to choose from Ren or his two crewmates: the fortune-hunting rogue Ioz – who's strong, slow and only in it for the treasure – and Tula, the quick-but-weak ecomancer whose 'skills are as dazzling as her beauty' (look, it was a different time). ■

FACT

Ren's talking monkey-bird pal Niddler was originally voiced by Roddy McDowall but was taken over by Frank Welker. Welker went on to star in *Futurama* where he once again played the hero's animal sidekick, this time called Nibbler.

PITFALL: THE MAYAN ADVENTURE

Year	1994
Publisher	Activision
Developer	Redline Games

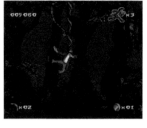

THE ORIGINAL PITFALL! was one of the pioneers of the platforming genre. Two sequels followed, but after all that running and jumping took its toll, their hero, Pitfall Harry, took early retirement. The apple doesn't fall too far from the tree, however, so enter his son Pitfall Harry Jr in this beautifully animated platformer. His old man's been kidnapped by an evil Mayan warrior spirit named Zakelua, so it's up to Harry Jr to explore the jungles of Central America to find him, while overcoming the numerous traps, creatures and enemies that stand in his way. The game's fantastic character animation was the result of Activision's collaboration with Kroyer Films, the animation studio responsible for movies like *Ferngully: The Last Rainforest*. ■

FACT

A near-perfect recreation of the original Atari 2600 Pitfall! is hidden in the game. To unlock it quickly, press Select, A six times, Select then Start on the title screen.

PIT-FIGHTER

Year	1994
Publisher	THQ
Developer	Atari Games

WHEN IT LAUNCHED in arcades in 1990, Pit-Fighter was a revelation. As one of the first games to use digitised actors as sprites (long before Mortal Kombat did it), this gritty underground fighting game looked unlike anything else. It was fun, too: playing as either wrestler Buzz, kickboxer Ty or karate black belt Kato, you had to make your way through a series of mean and moody opponents, surrounded by a crowd all too happy to push you back into the action if you try to escape. Then it came to the SNES and everything went wrong: the sprites became tiny, the crowd didn't do anything and the combat had been so badly implemented that it was nearly impossible to beat even the first opponent. One of the worst ports ever. ■

FACT

A sequel to Pit-Fighter was considered 75 per cent complete and featured three new heroes including a 'roller queen' called Tanya.

PLOK

Year	1993
Publisher	Tradewest
Developer	Software Creations

PLOK IS A fan of flags. His favourite flag is a big square one with a picture of his face on it, but one day it's stolen. Little does Plok know that the theft of his flag is a decoy to lure him away from Akrillic so it can be taken over by fleas. It's time to throw hands… literally, in this case. Plok has the ability to detach his limbs and fire them at his enemies. Though this decreases his mobility a little, he gets them back quickly so it's fine. That said, there are some puzzle sections in the game where Plok has to, for example, hold down a switch or two with some of his limbs, temporarily leaving him with less to work with. ■

FACT

Plok was designed by the legendary Pickford brothers, who still own the rights to the character and continue to make a webcomic about him to this day.

POCKY & ROCKY

Year	1993
Publisher	Natsume
Developer	Natsume

POCKY IS A young shrine maiden who's approached one day by a raccoon called Rocky. Rocky is a part of a group of 'Nopino Goblins' and the other Goblins have gone crazy, so Pocky – who's cured them of insanity before – decides to team up with Rocky to find out what's going on. This is a whimsical shooting game where you can play as either Pocky, Rocky or both in co-op mode. Pocky can throw amulets at distant enemies, or use her wand to attack at close range. Rocky, meanwhile, throws leaves instead, or uses his tail to bat away approaching bad guys. There are six stages in total, culminating in a battle with the evil Black Mantle, who's the one responsible for the Goblins' insanity. ■

FACT

If it feels like the ending was just spoiled for you, bear in mind the Japanese title is Mysterious Ghost World: The Riddle of the Black Mantle, so it's not supposed to be a huge secret.

POCKY & ROCKY 2

Year	1994
Publisher	Natsume
Developer	Natsume

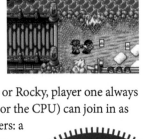

THE SEQUEL TO Pocky & Rocky has the duo teaming up again to rescue a princess who's been kidnapped by a bunch of demons, under the command of a mysterious enemy called Impy. This time, instead of being able to play as either Pocky or Rocky, player one always controls Pocky. A second player (or the CPU) can join in as Rocky or one of two new characters: a huge man called Bomber Bob who throws spiked balls, and a young ninja girl fittingly called Little Ninja. Pocky can throw her partner at enemies to do great damage, which seems cruel but there you go. Along the way you'll come across four other characters who join your team, and player two can switch to them should they so wish. ■

FACT

Although it's called Pocky & Rocky 2, this is actually the third game in the series. The first game, KiKi KaiKai, was only released in Japan in 1986 and has Sayo-chan (Pocky) using her scrolls and wand to defeat rogue spirits.

POP'N TWINBEE

Year	1993
Publisher	Palcom
Developer	Konamo

ALTHOUGH THE TWINBEE series was popular in Japan, only a few TwinBee titles made it to the west. This Europe-only release is the sixth in the series, and has cute spaceship TwinBee flying over Donburi Island to try and stop Dr Mardock, a once kind scientist who suffered a bump on the head and is now trying to take over the world with an army of Acorn Men. TwinBee (and its pink companion WinBee, if a second player wants to join in) can shoot enemies in the sky and bomb those on the ground. Along the way, coloured bells can be collected: these give a range of upgrades, from mini TwinBee helpers to another shot of your Chibi Blaster, which fills the screen with tiny clone ships. ■

FACT

The Options screen has a special 'Couple' mode: this directs most enemy attacks towards player one, in case you want to play with your partner but they don't have much gaming experience.

POP'N TWINBEE: RAINBOW BELL ADVENTURES

Year	1994
Publisher	Konami
Developer	Konami

UNTIL THIS POINT the TwinBee series had consisted mainly of vertical shoot 'em ups. Rainbow Bell Adventures was Konami's first attempt to move TwinBee and pals to a different genre: in this case, an action platformer. Players control either TwinBee, WinBee or their green pal GwinBee as they run through over 30 stages split across seven worlds in an attempt to rescue Princess Melora from the evil scientist Dr Warmon, by recovering the seven Rainbow Bells that bring peace to the universe. While at its core this is a standard action platformer, players can also charge their jumps and attacks by holding each button, and – as in the shoot 'em ups – collect different coloured bells for power-ups. ■

FACT

There have been more than 15 TwinBee games released over the years. The most recent at the time of writing was 2013's Line GoGo! TwinBee a shoot 'em up for iOS and Android devices.

POPULOUS

Year	1991
Publisher	Acclaim
Developer	Bullfrog Productions

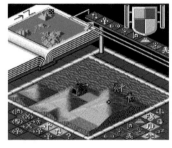

WHEN IT FIRST launched on the Commodore Amiga in 1989, Populous was one of the first god games ever created. The brainchild of designer Peter Molyneux, it puts players in the role of a god overseeing their own little population of people on an island. There's a problem, though: on the same island lives another group of people, and they have a different god, so there's only one solution: a holy war. Each of the 500 levels can be manipulated by the player in a number of different ways: you can raise and lower the land to flatten it (so your followers can build on it), make suggestions to your followers and create a variety of natural disasters such as earthquakes, swamps and volcano eruptions. ■

FACT

The team at Bullfrog created a basic Populous map out of Lego in order to help them prototype the game. Molyneux says it didn't help much, but gave the media something to write about. Like I just did, so thanks Pete.

POPULOUS II: TRIALS OF THE OLYMPIAN GODS

Year	1993
Publisher	Imagineer
Developer	Bullfrog Productions

THE SEQUEL TO Populous focused specifically on Greek mythology, rather than random nameless gods. Playing as one of Zeus's many demigod children, you have to prove yourself by defeating 16 other Greek deities over a series of 48 stages until you face off against Zeus himself. Populus II was far more detailed than its predecessor and offered many more abilities (29 compared to the original's eight). These include a deadly fungus outbreak, lightning storms, baptismal fonts (which can convert enemy followers to your side) and the ability to summon a number of 'heroes', such as Achilles, Odysseus, Herakles or Adonis. Unlike the original, the SNES version of Populous II also supports the SNES Mouse, which makes navigating the game's numerous menus so much easier. ■

FACT

The next Populous sequel didn't come until 1998. Populous: The Beginning on PC and PlayStation had you playing as a shaman who can directly command her followers to build and attack, rather than simply influence them.

PORKY PIG'S HAUNTED HOLIDAY

Year	1995
Publisher	Acclaim
Developer	Phoenix Interactive Entertainment

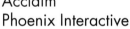

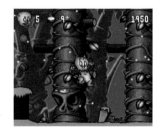

PORKY PIG HAS earned a well-deserved rest, and with only one more sleep to go he's pretty ruddy excited about it. The problem is, that night he has a nightmare and has to escape six terrifying locations – the haunted woods, Dry Gulch Town, Atlantis, the abandoned mines, the Alps and a haunted castle – before he can finally wake up and go on holiday. This platformer is notable for its dynamic weather system, which means the weather is random every time you play: one moment it could be raining, the next it could be snowing. Other than this, the game is fairly nondescript as far as platform games go. ■

FACT

Porky Pig's first appearance is in *I Haven't Got a Hat* on March 1935. On that same date, the seventh monarch of Siam abdicated the throne. Coincidence? Yup, probably.

POWER DRIVE

Year	1994
Publisher	Rage Software
Developer	US Gold

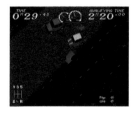

NOT TO BE confused with Bally Midway's 1987 monster truck arcade game of the same name, Power Drive is a racing game that focuses on rally racing. You take part in time trial and head-to-head races across eight different tracks: Arizona, Australia, Corsica, Finland, Kenya, Sweden and two in Great Britain (one on tarmac, one on snow). As you progress you'll earn prize money which can then be spent on unlocking new cars, of which there are six officially licensed ones: Austin Mini Cooper S, Fiat Cinquecento, Ford Escort RS Cosworth, Renault Clio 1, Toyota Celica GT-Four and Vauxhall Astra III. The handling can take a little getting used to, but once you get a feel for its powerslides it's a surprisingly compelling racer. ■

FACT

There was a US version of Power Drive planned but it was ultimately cancelled. It was also developed for the Mega Drive / Genesis but it too was scrapped as a physical release, only appearing as a download on the Sega Channel.

POWER INSTINCT

Year	1994
Publisher	Atlus
Developer	Atlus

A MORE LIGHT-HEARTED take on the one-on-one fighting game genre, Power Instinct tells the story of Oume Goketsuji, the 78-year-old head of her clan and the ruler of Oumeworld. Every five years the clan holds a fighting tournament to see who the new ruler should be, and every five years Oume wins again, but can things change this time? There are eight fighters to choose from here, ranging from Angela, a huge Italian strongwoman, to Thin Nen, a Shaolin Monk with an obscene love for women and money. The combat is what you'd expect from a Street Fighter clone, but not many Street Fighter clones can claim to star an old woman who throws her teeth at her opponents and can transform into a younger, rainbow-throwing woman at will. ∎

FACT

Power Instinct is the first entry in the Goketsuji Ichizoku (Goketsuji Family) series of fighting games in Japan. There are six games in total, the majority of which only launched in Japan.

POWER MOVES

Year	1993
Publisher	Kaneko
Developer	Kaneko

YET ANOTHER ONE-ON-ONE fighting game coming in the wake of Street Fighter, although to Power Moves' credit there are some interesting touches in this one. The single-player mode has you playing as single character, Joe, as he fights his way through the other seven fighters on his way to the final battle against a chap called Ranker. You get to choose the order you fight each opponent, and each time you win Joe's stats will increase, meaning by the time you reach Ranker you'll be much stronger than when you started. The combat is also enhanced with the ability to move between two different planes: it's similar to Fatal Fury in this way to an extent, but more intuitive because you simply move up and down instead of leaping over. ∎

FACT

The badly written box gets a little confused, stating: 'This exciting action adventure game recreates the fury and explosiveness of international boxing.'

POWER PIGGS OF THE DARK AGE

Year	1996
Publisher	Titus Software
Developer	Radical Entertainment

BY LOOKING AT it you'd swear Power Piggs was based on yet another animated series designed to be the next *Teenage Mutant Ninja Turtles*, but in reality it's an entirely original idea designed for this SNES exclusive. You play as Bruno, a Pigg who runs a doughnut shop and is forced to act when the evil Wizzard of Wolf invades his home town. The game plays similarly to the Sega Mega Driver version of Aladdin, as Bruno is armed with both a sword and jelly doughnuts which act exactly like Aladdin's sword and apples respectively. Although the name and title screen seem to suggest there were originally supposed to be three playable heroes, Bruno is the sole pork-tagonist here. I think that pun just about works. ∎

FACT

Enter the password Grunt, Bruno, Grunt, Lotta to access a hidden shoot 'em up called Bad Guys From Space II where the enemies are the digitised faces of one of the programmers and his pals.

POWER RANGERS ZEO: BATTLE RACERS

Year	1996
Publisher	Bandai
Developer	Natsume

THE FOURTH AND final Power Rangers game on the SNES is a Mario Kart clone based on the Zeo generation of *Power Rangers*, which was the fourth season of the TV show. As well as all five Zeo Rangers, players can also choose to race as the Gold Ranger or one of three enemies: King Mondo, a Cog or the Cog Ace (who's a hidden unlockable). The game features Mode 7 tracks similar to Super Mario Kart, but rather than placing power-ups on the track it simply gives the player five blaster shots to use when they see fit. There are 17 tracks to choose from (including a hidden Sky Course track) and six battle tracks, where two players can take part in combat either with or without blasters. ∎

FACT

The mysterious Gold Ranger was originally supposed to be later revealed as Ryan from Saban's other superhero show VR Troopers, with the plan being to merge both shows into the same universe. This plan fell through, though.

POWERMONGER

Year	1993
Publisher	Imagineer
Developer	Bullfrog Productions

USING THE SAME engine as Populous, Powermonger asks what would happen if Populous was a war game. Instead of a god, then, here you play as a king whose land was ravaged by a storm and has to start all over on a new land with a few followers. There you'll encounter various armies led by different warlords, but you've been through a lot so you're ready to fight. Since you aren't a god, you can't raise land or perform natural disasters: instead you get to directly instruct your small army. The game's map is made up of 195 different levels, but you don't have to play them all: you start at the top-left corner of the map and only need to make a path down to the bottom-right. ■

FACT

The home computer versions of Powermonger got an expansion pack that changed the setting to the First World War.

PREHISTORIK MAN

Year	1996
Publisher	Titus Software
Developer	Titus Software

PREHISTORIK MAN IS the third game in the Prehistorik series by French developer Titus (the original Prehistorik and Prehistorik 2 were only released on home computers). It's technically a SNES-exclusive remake of the second game, but one that improves on it in all aspects, from graphics to controls to plot (in that there actually is one now). You play as Sam, a caveman who's been asked by his chief to head out and get some food for the village after their supplies were stolen in the middle of the night by dinosaurs. Armed with your trusty club (you can find other weapons like axes and spears later), you have to explore each of the 23 stages and gather as much food as possible. ■

FACT

At the end of each stage the chief will rate your haul. He doesn't hold back either: bring him less than 20 per cent of the food on a stage and he'll call it 'damned pathetic'.

PRIMAL RAGE

Year	1995
Publisher	Time Warner Interactive
Developer	Bitmasters

BY THE MID '90s there were so many one-on-one fighting games that it would take something pretty different to stand out. Enter Primal Rage, a fighter with a unique selling point: it's got stop-motion dinosaurs in it. It's not set in prehistoric times as you may expect, it's actually set in the future. A giant meteor strike has ravaged the Earth, all but killing off the human race except for a handful of 'lucky' survivors. Over time the human race reverts back to Stone Age levels of development, while Urth (as they call it) suddenly becomes host to seven prehistoric beasts who rise from the planet's crust. Each of the dinos ends up with a clan of followers who worship them like gods, so inevitably this results in a mass brawl, where all seven battle for dominance of the Urth. As you fight each opponent your tiny followers will run around you, trying to support you. If you're in a particularly nasty mood, you can eat some worshippers to regain some health. (It's what they would have wanted. Probably.) The characters were created using a similar technique to Goro in

FACT

Although the SNES version is practically feature complete it did have one weapon removed: Chaos's 'Golden Shower', in which he pees acid on his opponent until they dissolve to a skeleton.

Mortal Kombat: when working on the initial arcade version the original development team at Atari Games created flexible model figures of each dinosaur, photographed them performing each move in a stop-motion style, then digitised them into sprites. Although the effect isn't quite as pronounced in the SNES version because of the smaller sprites and drop in detail, it still gives the game a unique look compared to most other fighters of the era. ■

PRINCE OF PERSIA

Year	1992
Publisher	Konami
Developer	Arsys Software

EVERY NOW AND then a game comes along that pushes the limits of what's considered graphically possible. Prince of Persia was one such game when it was originally released in 1989, thanks to its incredible character animation. Although its designer Jordan Mechner had used a similar technique in his previous game Karateka, for some reason it was the release of Prince of Persia that made most gamers sit up and take notice. Mechner filmed footage of his brother performing various running, jumping and combat moves, then drew over each frame of the footage (a process called rotoscoping). This led to sprites that moved in a lifelike manner, since they essentially were a real person underneath. It helped that the game was compelling too: playing as an unnamed prince who's been thrown into a dungeon by the evil Jaffar, you have 120 minutes to escape the dungeon, defeat Jaffar and rescue the princess before she's forced to marry him or be killed. While practically every port of Prince of Persia was identical in all but graphical fidelity, the SNES version is

FACT

Unlike other versions of the game, the SNES version actually allows you to keep playing after the timer runs out. This leads to a 'bad' ending, where the prince escapes but the princess is already gone.

more of a remake, with completely redrawn sprites (albeit still using the same reference animations), new music and longer, more difficult levels: hence the 120-minute time limit, which is only 60 minutes in other versions of the game. Along the way the Prince must avoid traps, engage in battles with Jaffar's guards and even confront his own doppelganger who escapes from a magic mirror at one point. ∎

PRINCE OF PERSIA 2: THE SHADOW AND THE FLAME

Year	1996
Publisher	Titus Software
Developer	Titus Software

ELEVEN DAYS AFTER the events of the first game, the prince is set to marry the princess. When he arrives at the palace, though, he instantly transforms into a beggar, at which point someone who looks just like the prince orders the guards to kill him. Jaffar's back, you see, and he's disguised himself as the prince to seize the throne. Having escaped on a ship, you're now exiled on a foreign island and have to figure out how to get back to the palace and save the day. Prince of Persia 2 is a more fantastical take on the format, with the likes of reanimated skeleton enemies, magic carpets and flying horses making an appearance. While the SNES port of the original was arguably the best version of the game, the SNES sequel is missing stages (including the last one). ∎

FACT

The game ends on a cliffhanger, with an evil witch watching the prince and princess in a crystal ball. This was supposed to be addressed in Prince of Persia 3 but that was never made.

PRO QUARTERBACK

Year	1992
Publisher	Tradewest
Developer	Tradewest

OF ALL THE American football games on the SNES, Pro Quarterback is… well, it's one of them. Offering 27 playable teams (not 26, as the box claims), it features neither the NFL or NFLPA licence which means no official team names, no logos and no real players. That said, the team colours do match what was being worn in the NFL that season, so if you choose to play as Cleveland you'll still get brown jerseys and orange helmets. Pro Quarterback makes use of Mode 7 to provide a more 3D view of the field, but whereas Mode 7 is usually handled fairly smoothly the number of characters on-screen takes its toll and the frame rate is pretty poor as a result. ∎

FACT

Pro Quarterback comes with a rather serious-looking warning on the back of the box, in big red letters. 'Warning,' it reads, 'this game is too real.' Something to be aware of.

PRO SPORT HOCKEY

Year	1994
Publisher	Jaleco
Developer	Tose

AS WELL AS releasing Pro Sport Hockey on the NES (cheap plug: read about it in the *NES Encyclopedia*), Jaleco also developed a 16-bit version designed to take full advantage of the SNES hardware. Much like its 8-bit sibling, the game features the NHLPA licence, which means that even though the teams don't have their logos, they do at least have full rosters. Players can take part in a full 84-game season, though the divisions are a little odd: split into four groups of six teams, they're called the Smile Divison, Noble Division, Anger Division and Panic Division for some unknown reason.
Another interesting quirk is the option to turn on 'home luck' in the options, which leads to calls that favour the home side more. ■

FACT

here's an odd myth online at turning off fatigue in the ame makes it impossible to core because the goalies never get tired. This is false.

P.T.O. PACIFIC THEATER OF OPERATIONS

Year	1993
Publisher	Koei
Developer	Koei

THIS SECOND WORLD War strategy game focuses on the conflict between America and Japan in the Pacific Ocean theatre, as well as their respective allies. There are nine scenarios you can choose to take part in as either the allied or axis forces. The first, Negotiations Breakdown, is the most complex, starting in 1941 and lasting until the end of the war. Others focus on specific battles: the attack on Pearl Harbor, the battle of the Coral Sea, the battle at Midway, the battles of the Solomon Islands, the battles in the South Pacific, the assault on the Marianas, the battle for the Philippines and the Okinawa offensive. There are 250 historical ships in the game, and the maps are historically accurate. ■

FACT

Although you can rewrite history to an extent in P.T.O. some events outwith your control happen like they did in real life. For example, Italy is no longer a member of the Axis in 1943.

P.T.O. II: PACIFIC THEATER OF OPERATIONS

Year	1995
Publisher	Koei
Developer	Koei

THE SEQUEL TO P.T.O. contains another 10 scenarios, once again focusing on the conflict between America and Japan. This time there are three longer 'campaign' scenarios to choose from (entitled The Brink of War 1941, Counter Offensive 1942 and Approaching V-Day 1944), as well as seven smaller ones based on Pearl Harbor, the Southern Operation, the battle of Midway, the US-Australia plan, Operation A-GO, the battle at Leyte and the 'final days'. The latter is particularly challenging if you choose to play as the axis: with allied forces outnumbering the Japanese in huge numbers, your forces become suicidal as the scenario progresses and all pressure lies on your battleship *Yamato* to turn things around.
Spoiler: it didn't. ■

FACT

A third P.T.O. game was released in Japan for the ₁Station but didn't make it to the ₁t (partly due to a huge argument ith China over how Japan was represented in the game). P.T.O. IV did get an English language PS2 release, though.

PUSHOVER

Year	1992
Publisher	Ocean Software
Developer	Red Rat Software

G. I. ANT is a soldier ant who's been asked by his pal Captain Rat to recover some bundles of cash that he's dropped down an ant hill. This particular ant hill must be a fairly big one because it contains 100 levels split over nine separate worlds. The aim is to clear each level by toppling all its dominos to open an exit door. There's a catch, though: you have to topple every domino with a single push, and the last domino to be toppled has to be the specific 'trigger' domino with three red stripes on it. Along the way you'll encounter new types of domino that do different things when they're hit: some split into two, others explode, while others disappear. ■

FACT

Other versions of Pushover have a sponsorship with British crisp snack Quavers, and the plot is to instead head down the ant hill to retrieve Quavers mascot Colin Curly's lost crisps.

PUTTY SQUAD

Year	1994
Publisher	Ocean Software
Developer	System 3

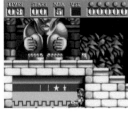

THE SEQUEL TO Super Putty is perhaps famous less for being on the SNES, and more for being cancelled on everything else. The Amiga and Mega Drive versions were even complete enough to be sent to magazines for review purposes before they were pulled. As such, only the SNES version was released, meaning Nintendo owners were the only ones able to guide Putty through 14 stages in search of a number of M.I.A. putties who've been captured and imprisoned. As in its predecessor, Putty can stretch into numerous shapes (letting him punch enemies and reach distant platforms), and can also flop down into a 'puddle' to absorb power-ups. He can also summon his former enemy Dweezil the cat, who can help out with more gizmos. ■

FACT

Putty Squad did eventually make it onto more systems. The Amiga version was made available for download on System 3's website in 2013, and launched for purchase on all major systems that same year.

RACE DRIVIN'

Year	1992
Publisher	THQ
Developer	Imagineering

RACE DRIVIN' AND its predecessor Hard Drivin' were considered revolutionary in arcades because they offered '3D' racing experiences using extremely simple polygonal graphics that were nevertheless impressive at the time. The SNES version launched a year before Star Fox turned up with the Super FX chip, meaning Imagineering had to come up with polygonal graphics on Nintendo's system without any additional 3D chips. The result is impressive, as long as you only look at screenshots: in motion the frame rate is so terrible – easily in the single figures – that it's nearly impossible to play with any degree of accuracy. A noble attempt at recreating this influential stunt-based driving game, but the SNES just wasn't up to it yet at this point. ■

FACT

Race Drivin' didn't mess around when it came to arcade cabinets. It included a force-feedback wheel, an ignition key, a four-speed gearstick and even a clutch pedal.

Q*BERT 3

Year	1992
Publisher	NTVIC
Developer	Realtime Associates

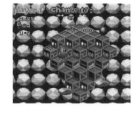

GOTTLIEB'S FOUL-MOUTHED ORANGE hop-monster made his arcade debut in 1982, and a decade later made his way to the SNES. Despite the 10 years of difference, Q*bert 3 isn't massively different to the original in terms of its basic principles: the game's still got an isometric grid of cubes and the aim is still to colour all the cubes by jumping on them while avoiding enemies. And yes, Q*bert does still let loose with a string of (censored) obscenities whenever he dies. One thing the SNES version does do is offer stages with a different layout (as opposed to the standard pyramid in the arcade game), and mixes things up with different background and cube designs. ■

FACT

If you're wondering what happened to Q*bert 2, it didn't exist (though there were a couple of spin-offs with different names). It's said that Q*bert 2 was planned for the Game Boy but the eventual Game Boy game that launched was simply called Q*bert.

RADICAL REX

Year	1994
Publisher	Activision
Developer	Laser Beam Entertainment

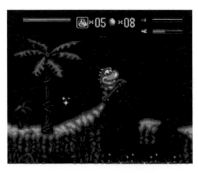

IF YOU EVER needed a character who summed up the mid '90s, Radical Rex is the one for you. He's a dinosaur – *Jurassic Park* made them cool again a year prior – he rides a skateboard and he's even got 'Radical' in his name (not to mention the fact that the box claims he's 'too hip to be extinct'). Rex has to make his way through 10 stages to rescue his girlfriend Rexanne from an evil warlock called Sethron, but to do so he has to fight (and, indeed, shred) his way through a bunch of other dinosaurs and monsters. Though he can breathe fire and perform a roar attack that clears the screen, Rex's main gimmick is his ability to ride his skateboard through parts of each stage. ■

FACT

The box is painful to read. 'Check Rex thrashin' on his board,' it suggests, 'sportin' his flame breath, bustin' out with killer jump-kicks, swingin' on vines and blastin' out screen-shaking roars. Excellent!' Quite.

RAIDEN TRAD

Year	1992
Publisher	Electro Brain
Developer	Micronics

IT MAY BE hard to believe but by 2090 we'll have achieved world peace, according to Raiden. Unfortunately, peace on Earth doesn't mean peace outside of it, so when an alien force known as the Carnass (the Crystals in other versions)

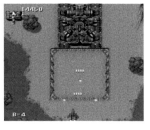

attacks, the planet doesn't know what's hit it. As the pilot of the new innerspace fighter bomber Raiden, it's up to you to fill the Carnass full of lead and save the remaining population of what is now a rather flame-grilled Earth. Raiden Trad is a SNES port of the 1990 arcade game, where players can power up their ship with two different types of shot – wide shot and laser – and up to eight levels of power. The SNES version is notorious for its jerky scrolling. ■

FACT

The name Raiden Trad comes from the SNES version's Japanese title, Raiden Densetsu. Whereas most games translate Densetsu as 'Legend' (as in Zelda no Densetsu), it can also mean 'Tradition'.

RAMPART

Year	1992
Publisher	Electronic Arts
Developer	Bitmasters

THIS 1990 ATARI arcade game got a relatively faithful SNES version a couple of years later. It's an early version of the tower defence genre, albeit one that offers a more hands-on approach. The game is split

into two different phases: the first has you choosing a castle on a shore, placing some cannons and using those cannons to blow up approaching enemy ships. After a while you're told to cease fire and the second phase begins, where you use randomly chosen blocks to repair any damage caused by enemy fire and (if you have time) acquire extra castles by building walls around those too. The aim is to keep going until either you destroy every ship, or the building phase ends without any of your castles having a complete wall. ■

FACT

Rampart was included in Midway Arcade Treasures on the GameCube, PS2, Xbox and PSP, as well as Midway Arcade Origins on the Xbox 360 and PS3.

RANMA ½: HARD BATTLE

Year	1993
Publisher	DTMC
Developer	Atelier Double

KNOWN AS SIMPLY Ranma ½ in the EU (presumably because there's no such thing as a hard battle for us tough types), this is a one-on-one fighting game based on the Ranma ½ anime and

manga, which tells the story of a young lad called Ranma who's an expert martial artist but is afflicted with a curse (some would say a blessing) which transforms him into a girl any time he's splashed with cold water. The game features 10 playable characters, including Ranma himself (in both male and female forms), his dad Genma (who's only available in his giant panda form… don't ask) and his potential fiancée Akane. It's less complex than most other fighting games on the SNES, because there are only two attack buttons. ■

FACT

There are 38 volumes of the Ranma ½ manga, which ran from 1987 to 1996. They were translated to English by Viz Media, who sells them in 2-in-1 collections, meaning you'd 'only' need to buy 19 books to get the whole story.

RAP JAM: VOLUME ONE

Year	1995
Publisher	Mandingo Entertainment
Developer	Motown Software

IT'S ALWAYS A bold move to name your game Volume One if you don't yet have a guarantee it's going to be successful enough to warrant a sequel. That said, how could Rap Jam fail? It's an urban

basketball game that can be played one-on-one, two-on-two or three-on-three, with no fouls and plenty of contact allowed. It's NBA Jam, basically. What's more, players can choose from some of rap and hip-hop's finest to play on their teams: Coolio, House of Pain, LL Cool J, Naughty by Nature, Onyx, Public Enemy, Queen Latifah, Warren G and Yo-Yo are all available as playable characters. Unfortunately, while it's unarguable that they all know how to rap, they didn't know how to jam: the game was panned and Volume Two became Straight Outta the Question. ■

FACT

The idea of rappers playing basketball may not have been too terrible: NBA 2K13 included a Celebrity All-Stars team with the likes of Bow Wow, Chamillionaire and Sean Kingston in the roster.

REALM

Year	1996
Publisher	Titus Software
Developer	Titus Software

THERE ARE PLENTY of games that take place in the future, but the year 5069 could maybe be considered overkill. Regardless, Realm has you playing as a teenage super cyborg called Biomech, who takes it upon himself to save the world from an alien invasion that threatens to completely destroy the entire planet. To do this you have to travel to the world's four 'realms' (which are really just a forest, a cave, a city on the sea and an airship) and free them of alien rule, before reaching the fifth and final level: a tunnel that leads to a giant cyborg boss. Realm is notable for offering players a large number of weapons, though most have limited ammo and you can only carry two at once. ∎

FACT

If you think Realm is a fairly boring title you should probably track down the PC version instead, which has the much more badass (and SEO-friendly) title of Alien Terminator.

RELIEF PITCHER

Year	1994
Publisher	Left Field Productions
Developer	Left Field Productions

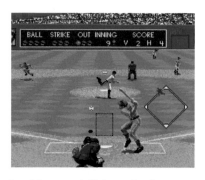

RELIEF PITCHER WAS originally an arcade game released by Atari. There are four fictional teams to choose from – the Boston Bashers, the Houston Dusters, the Los Angeles Speeders and the questionably named Chicago Strokers – and each has their own signature strength (the Bashers, for example, specialise in power hits). Although you can still bat in this game, the focus is clearly on pitching, with a series of gauges that control your accuracy and speed, similar to a golf game. You can choose to play a single exhibition game from the start, or take on the 'season' mode, which sees you coming on as a relief pitcher in the 9th inning of 12 different games to try and close them down. ∎

FACT

Relief Pitcher's play-by-play commentary was recorded by Jack Buck, who was best known for announcing games for the St Louis Cardinals.

REDLINE F-1 RACER

Year	1993
Publisher	Absolute Entertainment
Developer	Absolute Entertainment

KNOWN AS AGURI Suzuki F-1 Super Driving in Japan and Europe, Redline is a Formula One game based on the 1992 F1 season. All 16 tracks from that season feature here in the same order, and there are two bonus tracks too: a USA circuit and an oval. The season mode is obviously the main feature here: as well as qualifying heats and the races themselves you also get to tinker with your car's tyres, suspension, brakes, wings and the like. The other racers' names are real (even though there doesn't appear to be an official FIA Formula One licence), and as well as the season mode you also get to take part in a one-on-one race against Aguri Suzuki himself. ∎

FACT

It's fair to say that Aguri Suzuki was only a decent F1 racer at best. His greatest ever result was a 3rd place finish at the Japanese Grand Prix in 1990 and his highest position in an F1 season was 12th that same year.

THE REN & STIMPY SHOW: BUCKEROO$!

Year	1993
Publisher	THQ
Developer	Imagineering

THE HUGE POPULARITY of Nickelodeon's *Ren & Stimpy Show* led to THQ securing the rights to make video games, which it then did with gusto. It made seven over the course of two years, four of which made it to the SNES. Buckeroo$! (which was also released on the NES) has you playing through three episodes of the show, each consisting of several levels (the game rotates between them to keep things fresh). The first episode, Robin Hoek, is set in Logwood Forest and tasks Ren with rescuing Maid Moron. In Out West, Ren has to make his way through a Wild West town to find Mr Horse. Finally, in Space Madness, you play as Stimpy and have to stop your spaceship crashing onto Earth. ∎

FACT

There were a total of 78 episodes of *The Ren & Stimpy Show*, consisting of 150 segments in total. It spanned from August 1991 to December 1995, with an unused episode airing on MTV in late 1996.

THE REN & STIMPY SHOW: FIRE DOGS

Year | 1994
Publisher | THQ
Developer | Argonaut Games

FIRE DOGS HAS the most limited gameplay of the four Ren & Stimpy games on the SNES, but there's a reason for that: it was a rental exclusive at Blockbuster Video (although ex-rental copies were sold after the game had run its course). It consists of two separate sections: the first has you playing as Stimpy as he explores a fire station looking for the items he needs for his fire engine. Get them all before time runs out and you'll move on to the second section, where Ren and Stimpy head to the scene of a fire and have to use a safety net to catch all the items being thrown out of the building. Beat this and you'll repeat the process four more times, one for each weekday. ■

FACT

A more mature version of Ren & Stimpy called *Adult Party Cartoon* launched on Spike TV in 2003, but only lasted for three episodes before it was cancelled due to negative feedback.

THE REN & STIMPY SHOW: TIME WARP

Year | 1994
Publisher | THQ
Developer | Sculptured Software

TIME WARP WAS the final Ren & Stimpy game released on the SNES (and, indeed, the last of THQ's seven-game run). Ren & Stimpy need 47 million proofs of purchase of Gritty Kitty Litter to buy a time machine from Muddy Mudskipper, so off they head to collect them. Fret not, because about 20 minutes into the game a train with a shipment of 47 million bags of Gritty Kitty is destroyed. With their new time machine, the pair travel back to three previous Ren & Stimpy episodes: the horror-themed Haunted House, the zoo in Monkey See, Monkey Don't and the nature show Untamed World. The time travel sections are viewed from the cockpit: you have to blow holes through walls to fly through them and reach the next area. ■

FACT

Stimpy was voiced by Billy West, who's also known for voicing a wide variety of other cartoon legends like Fry from *Futurama*, the red M&M, Bugs Bunny in *Space Jam* and Nickelodeon's *Doug*.

THE REN & STIMPY SHOW: VEEDIOTS!

Year | 1993
Publisher | THQ
Developer | Gray Matter

OF ALL THE Ren & Stimpy game plots, Veediots! has easily the weakest: Ren & Stimpy are stuck in their TV show and want to get out. This is little more than an excuse for another platformer with another set of levels based on actual episodes of the TV show. In The Boy Who Cried Rat, you play as Ren, who's dressed up as a mouse and has to avoid Stimpy in his mouse catcher role. Then there's In the Army, where Ren has to make his way through three battlefields without getting blown to bits. This is followed by Stimpy's Invention, where Stimpy has to find seven pieces of his Happy Helmet. Finally, Marooned! has Space Cadet Stimpy trapped inside an alien's digestive system. ■

FACT

There are few days more monumental to the history of cartoons than 11 August 1991. On that day, the first three Nicktoons cartoons – *Ren & Stimpy*, *Rugrats* and *Doug* – all aired for the first time.

REVOLUTION X

Year | 1995
Publisher | Acclaim
Developer | Software Creations

THIS LIGHTGUN SHOOTER uses the same engine as the Terminator 2 arcade game but this time it revolves around rock gods Aerosmith. It's set in the year 1996, where a corrupt government and military forces have formed the New Order Nation. The NON have banned all youth culture, so when Aerosmith are performing a gig one night they swoop in and capture them. It's up to you, armed with a machine gun and a weapon that fires CD bombs, to head out and save music by destroying the NON's bases in the Amazon jungle, the Middle East and the Pacific Rim. The game's soundtrack naturally consists of looped Aerosmith music, and the band themselves pop up in a few brief cameos. ■

FACT

Although the arcade version of Revolution X was well-received, the home versions were panned. This led to a planned sequel featuring Public Enemy to be scrapped.

REX RONAN: EXPERIMENTAL SURGEON

Year	1994
Publisher	Raya Systems
Developer	Sculptured Software

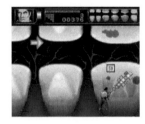

THE SECOND OF Raya's four health-based educational games on SNES is arguably the most interesting idea. Whereas Captain Novolin and Packy and Marlon focused on diabetes and Bronkie looked at asthma, Rex Ronan is designed more to warn children rather than help them with an existing condition. Specifically, it's about smoking, as Rex shrinks himself to a microscopic size and enters the body of a smoker (who works for a tobacco company and is now dying after years of smoking). Starting in the mouth, you have to remove all the tar, nicotine and precancerous cells from the man's body to save his life, all while learning about the dangers of smoking in the process. Beware, though: the evil tobacco company has sent microbots to kill Rex. ■

FACT

Although some experimental treatments go on to see widespread use in the medical industry, the process of doctors shrinking themselves to a millimetre in height to fire lasers at teeth didn't quite take off.

RIDDICK BOWE BOXING

Year	1994
Publisher	Extreme Entertainment Group
Developer	Malibu Interactive

FANS OF BOXING games on other platforms will quickly recognise Riddick Bowe Boxing as a reskinned version of Mega Drive titles Evander Holyfield's Real Deal Boxing and Greatest Heavyweights, featuring more cartoon-like designs for the boxers. Players can create their own boxer from scratch and, starting at number 25 in the rankings, work your way up the ladder – taking on opponents and increasing your stats along the way – until you reach the top and face off against Riddick Bowe himself for a title fight. The game was also released in Mexico and some southwest states in the US under the name Chavez, with Bowe replaced by Mexican boxer Julio César Chávez and adverts added for brands like Pepsi and Pizza Hut. ■

FACT

Bowe beat Evander Holyfield for the undisputed heavyweight title in 1992, but lost it in a rematch the following year. That second match was delayed after the seventh round when a parachutist dropped onto the ropes.

RISE OF THE PHOENIX

Year	1995
Publisher	Koei
Developer	Koei

YET ANOTHER HISTORICAL simulation from Koei, Rise of the Phoenix takes place in ancient China in the 3rd century BC and tells the story of the Chu-Han Contention between Liu Bang and Xiang Yu (which I'm sure you don't need me to tell you about, since we all know it well). You can play as either Liu Bang or Xiang Yu: the former can make allies easily due to his charisma but isn't the smartest tool in the shed, whereas the latter is a highly skilled politician but has all the personality of a grapefruit. There are four scenarios to choose from, each focusing on different parts of the conflict, and if it's all too much to take in you can just have two AI opponents face off against each other instead. ■

FACT

In real life, Liu Bang and Xiang Yu called a truce and signed the Treaty of Hong Canal, which divided China into east and west. A few months later, Liu Bang went back on his word and attacked Xiang Yu, who killed himself after suffering defeat.

RISE OF THE ROBOTS

Year	1994
Publisher	Acclaim
Developer	Probe

FEWER GAMES IN history have received as much hype as Rise of the Robots. Promising the most advanced level of artificial intelligence ever seen in a fighting game, a soundtrack by Brian May and a fighting engine that would 'have one over on Street Fighter II', only one of those ended up happening and it was the one that made Queen fans happy. Players control ECO35-2, a human-like cyborg who has to fight six other droids at robotics company Electrocorp. It got a multi-million pound marketing campaign, a novelisation and was going to get toys and a movie… but the problem was, the game itself was roundly hammered by critics and gamers alike for its terrible controls and its unnecessary difficulty spikes. ■

FACT

Although most people disliked it, Rise of the Robots still got a sequel. Rise 2: Resurrection launched on PC, PlayStation and Saturn in 1996, but it was another critical and financial disaster.

RIVAL TURF!

Year	1992
Publisher	Jaleco
Developer	Jaleco

THE FIRST GAME in Jaleco's Rushing Beat trilogy, which continues with Brawl Brothers and The Peace Keepers, Rival Turf! tells the story of Jack Flak, whose girlfriend Heather has been kidnapped by the Street Kings gang, led by a chap called Big Al. Accompanied by his policeman chum Oozie Nelson, the pair head off to get Heather back. The pair are similar to Final Fight characters in some respects: Jack is the Cody of the pair, with his well-rounded moves, whereas Big Al is the Haggar, due to his sheer size and his ability to perform wrestling moves. This was also the first game in the series to introduce the 'angry' mode, which gives you temporary invincibility and extra power if you find yourself on the wrong end of a beatdown. ■

FACT

The Japanese version (known as Rushing Beat) is a little more blunt when it comes to defeated enemies. In the US version a red X appears over their icon when you beat them, but in the Japanese version it's the symbol for death instead.

ROAD RIOT 4WD

Year	1992
Publisher	THQ
Developer	Equilibrium

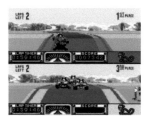

THIS RALLY-BASED RACING game was originally released in arcades by Atari. That version performed significantly smoother than this SNES port, which does the best with what it has. Players race in dune buggies equipped with machine guns, which is far from safe but I suppose that's where the 'Riot' element comes into it. After taking part in an initial training race, you're presented with a map showing 11 other tracks dotted all over the world, taking in the likes of Antarctica, the Swiss Alps, Saudi Arabia, Africa and Ohio. Each track has its own 'host' – which is essentially an excuse to show a stereotypical cartoon of a person from that region – and the aim is to beat that host's three-car team to move onto the next race. ■

FACT

Atari had created an arcade sequel called Road Riot's Revenge and even got to the stage where cabinets had been made for it, but it was ultimately never released.

ROAD RUNNER'S DEATH VALLEY RALLY

Year	1992
Publisher	Sunsoft
Developer	Sunsoft

OF ALL THE Looney Tunes cartoons, it could be argued that the concept of the Road Runner was probably the one best suited to video games. Playing as the titular bird, you have to make your way through 15 levels split across five locations – the desert, a construction site, a train, a mine and Mars – while trying to avoid Wile E. Coyote, who has a different Acme contraption in each stage. One minute he's trying to fire himself at you with a giant catapult, the next he's swinging a wrecking ball at you. The game was known simply as Looney Tunes: Road Runner in Europe, perhaps in case children didn't know Death Valley is a real place and thought the title was more sinister than it actually was. ■

FACT

A sequel to Death Valley Rally was around 50 per cent complete when Sunsoft shut down its US offices. Some near-finished games like Speedy Gonzales were acquired by Acclaim, but those that needed more work were scrapped.

ROBOCOP 3

Year	1992
Publisher	Ocean Software
Developer	Ocean Software

NOTORIOUS MEGA-CORPORATION OCP is trying to clear the streets of Old Detroit so they can build the shiny new Delta City. The problem is, they're doing it with Rehab Officers, who are storming in and kicking poverty-stricken families out of their homes. Deciding he's had enough of such heartless behaviour, RoboCop decides it's up to him to… um, kill as many Rehab Officers as he can lay his targeting system on. RoboCop 3 is a straightforward run 'n' gun game, albeit one where you can't run (a walk 'n' gun game, then). In some stages RoboCop will activate his gyropack, a large jetpack that lets him fly through the sky taking out enemies. These sections take the form of top-down, vertical scrolling shoot 'em up levels. ■

FACT

The first version of RoboCop 3 was developed for the Amiga, but work began a full year and a half before the film was released. The team wasted weeks designing a bike for RoboCop when they heard about his 'gyrocycle', not realising it was a jetpack.

ROBOCOP VS THE TERMINATOR

Year	1993
Publisher	Virgin Interactive
Developer	Interplay

ALTHOUGH BOTH *ROBOCOP* and *The Terminator* were released in the '80s, their sequels in 1990 and 1992 respectively ensured that both remained the most popular action movie franchises throughout the early '90s. As such, despite their decade of origin, a SNES game combining the two was the most '90s crossover you can get. (Except for that time someone made Pogs based on the O.J. Simpson trial. Seriously). This wouldn't be allowed to include the Terminator if it didn't have a massively confusing time-travel story, so here goes: in the future, John Connor's resistance forces learn that the technology in RoboCop was one of the early foundations for what would become Skynet. A resistance soldier called Flo is sent back to the present day to kill RoboCop, but then Skynet sends some Terminators back to kill Flo, so RoboCop helps her kill the Terminators.

FACT

There was also going to be an NES version of the game, where the Terminators and an evil clone of RoboCop are sent back to kill both John Connor and RoboCop. Although it was finished, it was never released.

Look, the important thing is that this is an action platformer where you play as RoboCop and the aim is simply to kill everything that moves. That said, there's an interesting twist at one point where RoboCop is captured, disassembled and used to build Skynet. He then rebuilds himself in the future, where you have to destroy Skynet itself. Interestingly, the SNES and Mega Drive versions of RoboCop vs the Terminator have different plots and are significantly different games: the Sega version (which was developed by Virgin Games) has lashings of gore throughout, whereas in the SNES version your enemies simply explode instead. ■

ROBOTREK

Year	1994
Publisher	Enix
Developer	Quintet

WHAT IF *POKÉMON* was about robots instead? It may be something like Robotrek, an Enix RPG where the hero (whose name you choose) doesn't personally get involved in battles himself, but sends his android chums into fights on his behalf. The young lad in question lives in the small, usually idyllic town of Rococo, which has been infiltrated by a rogue band of pirates calling themselves The Hackers. The Hackers are looking for an invention that belonged to the hero's genius father, so it's up to said hero and up to three robots to figure out what's going on. Each robot is fully customisable, from their appearance and name to their moves and abilities, and as in Pokémon, you can switch between your three robots during battles. ■

FACT

Robotrek is designed to be a comedy game. Just in case that wasn't entirely clear, the game was named Slapstick in Japan.

ROCK N' ROLL RACING

Year	1993
Publisher	Interplay
Developer	Silicon & Synapse

A SEQUEL TO RPM Racing (see page 164), Rock n' Roll Racing improves on its predecessor in practically every way. It's played in an isometric viewpoint, where four cars compete against each other while armed with missiles, landmines and the like. Each race nets you some prize money, which can be spent on upgrading your car or buying new weapons. Rock n' Roll Racing would be a great little racing game regardless, but it's made even better by its impressive rock soundtrack, which consists of SNES versions of the likes of Steppenwolf's *Born to be Wild*, Black Sabbath's *Paranoid* and Deep Purple's *Highway Star* (among others). Olaf from The Lost Vikings is a hidden character (highlight Snake on the character select screen, hold down L, R and Select, then press Left, Right). ■

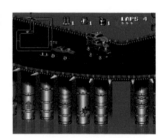

FACT

A 3D remake of the game called Motor Rock was released on Steam in 2013. Blizzard (who Silicon & Synapse became) doesn't take kindly to people stealing its ideas, and the game lasted a week before it was pulled from Steam.

THE ROCKETEER

Year	1992
Publisher	IGS
Developer	NovaLogic

WHEREAS THE NES adaptation of Disney's modestly-received superhero movie was a straightforward action platformer, the SNES game is a port of NovaLogic's PC game, which instead consisted of a series of mini-games. Unfortunately, the first of these – where you take part in a biplane race against two other pilots – gained notoriety as one of the hardest first levels in any game, partly thanks to the fact that the best way to control the plane is to study the tiny chase cam on the bottom of the screen. Subsequent stages involve having a shootout with enemies in a hangar, another race (this time with your actual rocket pack), and a fistfight atop a Zeppelin. It gets better, then, but the damage is done early. ∎

FACT

Don't just take my word for it: after the game was released, US magazine Electronic Gaming Monthly awarded it the Worst Movie-to-Game of 1992 in its annual awards.

ROCKO'S MODERN LIFE: SPUNKY'S DANGEROUS DAY

Year	1994
Publisher	Viacom New Media
Developer	Viacom New Media

EVERYONE LOVES AN escort mission in a game (citation needed), so that's probably why this tie-in based on the much-loved Nickelodeon cartoon series *Rocko's Modern Life* consists entirely of them. Rocko's dog Spunky has a habit of wandering off in search for stuff, so in order to make sure he's safe Rocko has to follow along, interacting with obstacles and defeating enemies to clear the way. There are four stages in total: Sand in Your Navel is set at the beach, Trash-O-Madness is set at the Hill-O-Stench garbage dump, Ice Scream is set in Rocko's neighbourhood in O-Town and Unbalanced Load is set in the Laundryland laundromat. It's not really clear why Rocko doesn't just pick Spunky up, given that he's walking alongside him most of the time. ∎

FACT

After *Rocko's Modern Life* was cancelled and its creator Joe Murray moved on to other projects, its creative director Stephen Hillenburg and many other staff members started work on *SpongeBob SquarePants*.

ROCKY RODENT

Year	1993
Publisher	Irem
Developer	Irem

THE UMPTEENTH DUDE-WITH-A-TUDE animal mascot platformer inspired by Sonic the Hedgehog, Rocky Rodent is a rat-like chap with an unhealthy knack for eating everything he comes across. After he swallows a restaurant's protection money, the mob kidnaps the restaurant owner's daughter Melody. Rocky's told that if he rescues Melody he can have all the food he wants, so off he trots. Rocky's main gimmick is his ability to change his hair into four different styles, with each style giving different powers. A red mohawk lets him pick up enemies and climb walls, a blue mohawk can be thrown like a boomerang, a green ponytail can act like a grappling hook and a whip, and a spring-shaped blonde rinse lets him bounce upside-down. ∎

FACT

The game ends on a weak note, with the mob boss saying he's impressed by Rocky's hair and asking him to be his right-hand man. Rocky refuses and the mob boss simply leaves.

ROGER CLEMENS' MVP BASEBALL

Year	1992
Publisher	LJN
Developer	Sculptured Software

ALTHOUGH THIS EARLY SNES baseball game doesn't have either the MLB or MLBPA licences, it does at least try its best with what it has. All 26 teams are still present, though their nicknames have been changed. Some of these make sense: the Cleveland Indians become the Cleveland Tomahawks, while the Baltimore Orioles become the Eagles. Others, however, seem fairly random, such as the Boston Red Sox becoming the Boston Crabs. Elsewhere, player names are fake too (except for Clemens), but some of the more notable players have names that make sense through word association. Mark McGwire and Jose Canseco, for example, are both called Bash because when they played with the Oakland Athletics they were given the nickname the Bash Brothers. ∎

FACT

Roger Clemens won seven Cy Young awards during his career, more than any other pitcher in baseball history. These are given to the best pitcher of the year in an MLB season.

ROMANCE OF THE THREE KINGDOMS II

Year	1992
Publisher	Koei
Developer	Koei

 ✓ ●✗

OF ALL OF Koei's historical simulations (and there are a lot, as you'll know if you've been reading this book in order), the Romance of the Three Kingdom series is among its most popular. They're based on the 14th century

Chinese novel of the same name, which tells the story of the Three Kingdoms period in Chinese history which took place from 169–280 AD. The second game in the series offers six different scenarios which roughly lay out each territory's leader and their allegiances as they were at that part in the novel, though once you start playing, things obviously stop following the same course. The aim is to take control of all 41 provinces on the map and conquer China as a result. ■

FACT

If you're looking for a sneaky way to get an edge, keep capturing province 10 over and over again. The game is programmed to give you high quality war spoils when you capture it, so by repeating this you'll get loads of vital charms, books and weapons.

ROMANCE OF THE THREE KINGDOMS III: DRAGON OF DESTINY

Year	1993
Publisher	Koei
Developer	Koei

 ✓ ●✗

THE GOOD THING about the Romance of the Three Kingdoms book – at least as far as Koei is concerned – is that it's 800,000 words long (about four and a half times the size of this book). That means plenty of scope for sequels for the games, and sure enough this third entry effortlessly introduces six brand new scenarios covering more key moments in the Three Kingdoms era. This time there are now 46 cities in China that have to be conquered in order to win the game, and there are a bunch of new rulers too (33 of them, compared to 27 in the second game). If you aren't happy with any of them, you can create your own. ■

FACT

The book is considered one of the four great classical novels of Chinese literature. The others are *Water Margin*, *Journey to the West* and Bruce Lee's autobiography. Just kidding, it's *Dream of the Red Chamber*.

ROMANCE OF THE THREE KINGDOMS IV: WALL OF FIRE

Year	1995
Publisher	Koei
Developer	Koei

 ✓ ✗

THOSE THREE KINGDOMS certainly love getting a good wooing, because they're back for more of the old romance in this fourth instalment. Yet again, you get to choose from

six new scenarios, including when Dong Zhuo seized control of Luoyang in 189 AD, to that pivotal moment we all remember so well when Liu Bei sought shelter in Xinya in 201 AD. This time there are 450 male and female officers to choose from, and you can create up to 108 characters of your own, on the off-chance you have absolutely no regard for historical accuracy and would like to see Michael J. Fox take over Xiangyang. Other new features include the ability to form temporary alliances and summon barbarians to raid enemy land. ■

FACT

At the time of writing, the fourteenth(!) Romance of the Three Kingdoms game is due to release on PC and PS4 in 2020.

RPM RACING

Year	1991
Publisher	Interplay
Developer	Silicon & Synapse

✓ ●✗

THE PREDECESSOR TO Rock n' Roll Racing is significantly less graphically impressive, but it can be forgiven for this because it's one of the first games released for the SNES. In fact, Blizzard Entertainment (which was

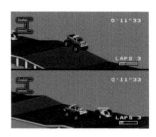

Silicon & Synapse at the time) once claimed that RPM Racing was 'the first American-developed game for the Super Nintendo'. Its season mode consists of 24 different chapters, each offering a selection of different tracks to race on. You don't have to race every track to move onto the next chapter, you simply have to earn enough money to afford the qualification fee. There are three types of terrain in the game – tarmac, dirt and ice – with each being more slippery than the last, and if you aren't happy with the tracks in the game you can create your own. ■

FACT

You may think RPM stands for the usual 'revolutions per minute' often used in racing terminology. You'd be wrong, it's actually Radical Psycho Machine, according to this game.

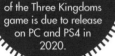

R-TYPE III: THE THIRD LIGHTNING

Year	1994
Publisher	Jaleco
Developer	Tamtex

THE BYDO EMPIRE, previously thought to have been destroyed, has returned to have another crack at taking over the Earth. Only one thing stands in their way: you, in your fancy new R90 fighter

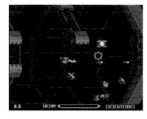

ship. R-Type III should be immediately familiar to fans of its predecessors but there are a few new additions to keep things interesting. On a technical level, the slowdown that plagued Super R-Type is all but gone. Your Force – the iconic glowing sphere from other R-Type games that attaches to your ship – now comes in three flavours: the typical Round Force, the Shadow Force (which can be retrieved faster) and Cyclone Force (which doesn't shoot when it's detached but does more damage when it hits enemies). ■

FACT

Retro specialists Retro-Bit released a collector's box called R-Type Returns in 2018, which includes Super R-Type and R-Type III on a single SNES cartridge and a bunch of other physical goodies.

RUN SABER

Year	1993
Publisher	Atlus
Developer	Hori Electric

WITH ITS GIANT curving sword swipes, its angled slopes and the ability to climb up walls, Run Saber clearly takes its influences from Capcom's Strider (there are worse games to imitate, of course). It's

set in 2998, where the Earth's resources are running low due to pollution. A scientist called Dr Bruford came up with a 'solution' to clear the pollution with radioactive energy, but it turns out he was doing it to mutate the Earth's population and turn them into his slaves. It's up to two cyborgs – Allen the Thunder Saber and Sheena the Ice Saber – to take out the mutants and foil Dr Bruford's evil plan. Along the way you'll come across a third saber, Kurtz the Fire Saber, who's become corrupt and must be defeated too. ■

FACT

The boss at the end of the fifth stage used to be a beautiful 100-foot woman in a pink dress who fired lasers at the player. Since Nintendo was uneasy about violence against women her sprite was changed to a skeleton woman, which was fine.

SAILOR MOON

Year	1994
Publisher	Bandai
Developer	Arc System Works

WHILE IT TOOK a while for anime to properly make an impact in the west, some regions were slowly starting to see some exposure in the early '90s. France was one of the pioneers of

this: much like it got Dragon Ball before most other countries, it was also one of the first to get dubbed versions of Sailor Moon: and, just as with Dragon Ball, it got its own localised version of a Japanese Sailor Moon game. This is the French version of Bishoujo Senshi Sailor Moon, a Super Famicom beat 'em up in which Usagi (known as Bunny Rivière in France) and her fellow Sailor Soldiers travel to the Arctic Circle to try and find the Dark Kingdom's base. ■

FACT

The author of this book's Canadian wife loved Sailor Moon so much growing up that we named our daughter Serena, which was Usagi's name in the original English dub. So don't mess with her.

SAMURAI SHODOWN

Year	1994
Publisher	Takara
Developer	Takara

ANOTHER TOP QUALITY arcade fighter from the studio behind the likes of Fatal Fury and The King of Fighters, Samurai Shodown was the first of SNK's one-on-one fighting games to focus on

weapons-based combat. Set in the late 1700s, it offers a roster of 12 characters (plus a boss who can be unlocked in versus mode), with moody ronin Haohmaru being the 'Ryu' of the group. Given the difference in power between the SNES and SNK's Neo-Geo arcade hardware, Samurai Shodown had to be significantly pared down for Nintendo's system. The arcade version's impressive scaling effects which dynamically zoom in and out of the action had to be removed. The SNES version at least has a full roster, though: the Mega Drive and Mega CD versions are missing a character. ■

FACT

Some of the more violent pre- and post-fight dialogue was censored for the SNES version. For example, the arcade version's 'Now in this scene, I rip open your belly' was changed to 'Now in this scene you cry like a baby'.

SATURDAY NIGHT SLAM MASTERS

Year	1994
Publisher	Capcom
Developer	Capcom

WHAT IF STREET Fighter II was a wrestling game? The answer, quite simply, is Saturday Night Slam Masters, a Capcom arcade wrestler with eight weird and wonderful fighters all looking to prove their dominance in the ring. Played in either one-on-one or tag team battle modes (the latter adds the two boss characters, bringing the roster up to 10), players have to wear their opponent's energy down then pin them for the win. Although Final Fight's Mike Haggar is one of the playable characters, he isn't actually the main hero: that would be Biff Slamkovich, a Ukrainian Ultimate Warrior lookalike who hates anyone who says wrestling is fake. Other characters include Mexican luchador El Stingray, enormous English fighter Titanic Tim and questionable Dominican man-beast King Rasta Mon. ■

FACT

Slam Masters' place in the Final Fight timeline depends on your region. The Japanese version states that it takes place before Haggar becomes the mayor of Metro City, whereas the western version calls him the 'former mayor of Metro City'.

SCOOBY-DOO MYSTERY

Year	1995
Publisher	Acclaim
Developer	Argonaut Software

A PLATFORMER BASED on Scooby-Doo would have been all well and good, but given that the cartoons are all about solving mysteries it makes sense that this is an adventure game instead. The game consists of four separate mysteries at suitably spooky locations – a shipwreck, an amusement park, a swamp and a mansion – and the aim is to search each area with Shaggy and Scooby to earn enough 'clue points' to let you build a trap that will capture the monster (so that Fred can, of course, pull their mask off). Along the way you'll have to dodge various creepy creatures: bumping into them will increase your fright meter, but you can get Scooby Snacks from Daphne to reduce it every now and then. ■

FACT

Scooby-Doo was voiced by Don Messick from his first appearance in 1969 right up until this game in 1995. This was his last performance as Scooby before his death in 1997.

SEAQUEST DSV

Year	1995
Publisher	Malibu Games
Developer	Sculptured Software

SEAQUEST DSV WAS a relatively short-lived TV series about a deep submergence vehicle in the future that went on missions for the equivalent of the United Nations (Sea Trek, in other words). The video game tie-in consists of two different play styles: an isometric overworld section where you explore the ocean quadrant taking on low-level combat and awaiting missions, and a side-scrolling section where you take on the missions themselves. The latter sections are more involved, requiring you to choose from a variety of vehicles including the Crab (a mining and recovery craft), the Stinger (a one-person attack sub) and the Sea Truck (a large vessel designed for transporting lots of people). You can also control their hyper-intelligent dolphin Darwin. ■

FACT

The show was plagued with disputes between the cast and production crew. Lead actor Roy Scheider left after season two and was replaced by Michael Ironside, but the show was cancelled 13 episodes into the third season.

SECRET OF EVERMORE

Year	1995
Publisher	Square
Developer	Square

DESPITE ITS TITLE and the fact it shares many of its mechanics, Secret of Evermore has nothing to do with Secret of Mana. It's a completely separate adventure in which a young boy and his dog (both of whom you name) stumble on a laboratory in an abandoned mansion. After the dog gets curious and nibbles on some cables, the pair are transported to Evermore, a strange world consisting of four major areas. These each relate to different historical eras: prehistoric times, ancient Rome and Egypt, medieval England and space in the future. As an odd twist, your dog's appearance changes in each of these eras (to a wolf, greyhound, poodle and robot dog respectively). Combat is real-time, but attacks must be recharged to do full damage. ■

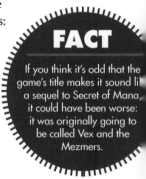

FACT

If you think it's odd that the game's title makes it sound like a sequel to Secret of Mana, it could have been worse: it was originally going to be called Vex and the Mezmers.

SECRET OF MANA

Year	1993
Publisher	Square
Developer	Square

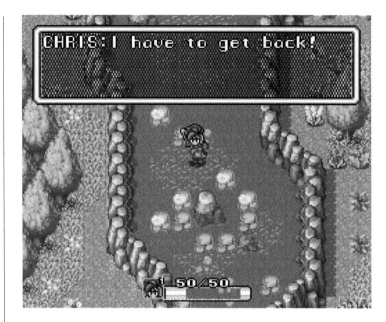

THE MANA SERIES (known in Japan as Seiken Densetsu, or The Legend of the Sacred Sword) originally started off as a Final Fantasy spin-off with Final Fantasy Adventure on the Game Boy. After this, Square decided to ditch the Final Fantasy training wheels and make the series its own standalone body, naming the second game Secret of Mana. This SNES RPG follows the adventures of a young lad called Randi – who isn't named in the original SNES release – who teams up with a girl named Primm and a sprite called Popoi to try and stop an ageing sorcerer called Thanatos possessing the body of a warrior called Dyluck (who Primm loves) and taking over the world. Secret of Mana was notable for offering co-operative multiplayer, something that was rare at the time and continues to be so to this day. While players can obviously go through the adventure on their own with Primm and Popoi accompanying as AI helpers, you can instead choose to have either or (with a multitap) both of them controlled by your friends, making it a two-player or three-player adventure. The combat system also got some praise: rather than the turn-based battles fans of Square's games are used to, Secret of Mana's battle system is a real-time affair: though you do still have to charge attacks to make sure they do the most power, you can move around the screen in an attempt to defend yourself from enemy attacks. ■

> **FACT**
>
> The Mana trilogy was re-released on the Switch in 2019. It contains the Game Boy title [Fin]al Fantasy Adventure, Secret of [M]ana and Trials of Mana (which [h]ad only been released on the Super Famicom, making this its first official English translation).

SECRET OF THE STARS

Year	1995
Publisher	Tecmo
Developer	Tecmo

SADLY NOT A documentary about the hidden lives of Hollywood A-listers, but a Tecmo RPG about a lad called Ray and his quest to defeat the Evil Lord Homncruse, who wants to take over the world. Bet you saw that coming. Ray and his four friends have to become Aqutallion warriors, a group of five who combined can stop Homncruse. Before they do this, though, your four fellow Aqutallions each have to find a temple and undergo a trial there to gain a special power (Ray already has one). Only once all five have their powers can they save the day. Along the way you can temporarily enlist the Kustera, eleven other characters who can fight in the Aqutallions' place while they work towards powering up. ■

> **FACT**
>
> [T]ecmo makes no bones about [the] fact it isn't an RPG developer [o]n the game's box. 'You know [Te]cmo for creating unequalled sports games', it confesses, [b]efore adding that this Secret [o]f the Stars is 'a whole new ball game'.

SENSIBLE SOCCER: EUROPEAN CHAMPIONS

Year	1992
Publisher	Renegade Software
Developer	Sensible Software

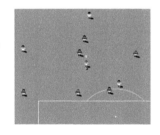

ALTHOUGH THE 16-BIT era would begin the FIFA vs International Superstar Soccer / PES debate, for many it was a fairly pointless argument because Sensible Soccer was always top of the football gaming league. Focusing less on realism and more on speed and swerve, the game lovingly referred to as Sensi by its fans was praised for years as the most fun football game. Although the original Amiga version was also called European Champions, this SNES port is actually based on the sequel, Sensible Soccer 92/93. There are 40 national teams and 64 club teams to choose from, all of which are European, but the player names are tweaked slightly (Giggs becomes Goggs) and the team names are fake (Celtic and Rangers are Glaswegian and Glasgow respectively). ■

> **FACT**
>
> The team at Sensible Software came up with the idea for the first Sensible Soccer when they were messing around with sprites from Mega Lo Mania and decided to make a football game with them.

SENSIBLE SOCCER: INTERNATIONAL EDITION

Year	1994
Publisher	Sony Imagesoft
Developer	Sensible Software

ALTHOUGH THE FIRST Sensible Soccer on SNES was only released in Europe, the fact that the World Cup was held in the USA in 1994 convinced Sensible and Sony Imagesoft to release the second game in North America (under the name Championship Soccer 94), just in case the twelve Americans who cared about football at that point fancied playing it. As the International Edition name suggests, this edition – it's more of an update than a true sequel to European Champions – focuses more on national competitions, with the number of teams increased from 40 to 51, including all the non-European teams who qualified for the World Cup. Naturally, there's also the option to play that very tournament, and even swap out any of the teams for those who didn't qualify (particularly useful for Scotland and England fans). The same 64 European club teams are also included, but there's a major difference now: all the club and player names are correct (accompanied by a large disclaimer at the start of the game making it clear that it isn't 'connected with or endorsed or approved by any player, team or organisation'. This change only applies to the European version, sadly: the US release goes in the opposite direction and makes the names completely different. Whereas Ryan Giggs was called Goggs in the last game and is now Giggs in the EU version of this one, in the North American version he's been named Jircalau. Which is slightly tweaked. ∎

FACT

The next game, Sensible World of Soccer, was only released on computers and added a management element. It was going to be published by Virgin Games, but they wanted to call it Virgin Soccer so Sensible backed down.

SHADOWRUN

Year	1993
Publisher	Data East
Developer	Beam Software

LOOSELY BASED ON the popular tabletop RPG of the same name, Shadowrun is set in Seattle in the year 2050 and tells the story of Jake Armitage, a chap who's been gunned down in the streets but has lived to tell the tale. At least, he would if he could remember the tale in the first place. Waking up in the morgue with amnesia, Jake has to find out who tried to kill him and figure out what's going on quick, because chances are the people who wanted him dead still quite fancy the idea. Shadowrun has an isometric viewpoint, and players switch between controlling Jake and controlling a hand pointer that lets them interact with people and objects in the world. Despite critical praise, it sold poorly. ∎

FACT

Shadowrun also came to the Mega Drive and Mega CD but were both completely different. The Mega Drive version was an open-world game, while the Mega CD one was an interactive novel only released in Japan.

SHANGHAI II: DRAGON'S EYE

Year	1993
Publisher	Activision
Developer	Hot-B

MANY KNOW MAHJONG solitaire by its alternative name of Shanghai solitaire, but few may realise that the Shanghai name was actually created and trademarked by Activision (in much the same way that Picross is Nintendo's trademarked name for nonograms). There may be countless mahjong solitaire games out there, then, but only Activision is legally allowed to call them Shanghai. This SNES title is the first official sequel and features 13 different tile layouts: the standard one, and one based for each of the animals in the Chinese zodiac (dog, dragon, rat and so on). If the traditional mahjong tiles confuse you, there are also 11 tile designs to choose from, including national flags, sports and road signs, many of which have unique animations when you clear them. ∎

FACT

A study at Radboud University in the Netherlands looked at 10 million random games of Shanghai using the standard 'turtle' layout and estimated that around 3 per cent of games are impossible to beat.

SHAQ FU

Year	1994
Publisher	Electronic Arts
Developer	Delphine Software

WHILE IN JAPAN for a charity basketball game, Shaquille O'Neal pops into a dojo and eventually finds himself entering a portal to the Second World, another dimension where the evil Sett Ra is planning to perform an ancient ritual that involves killing a young lad called Nezu. It's up to Shaq to save the day, by doing what he does best. What's that? Basketball? Oh. No, not that. Kicking people. Shaq Fu is a one-on-one fighting game that's notorious for being one of the worst games ever made (which is a little unfair, because it's nowhere near the worst). Although the main story mode only lets you play as Shaq, there's also an arcade-style Duel mode that lets you choose any of the game's seven fighters. ■

FACT

In case one helping of Shaq Fu wasn't enough, O'Neal also released a rap album called Shaq Fu: Da Return to help promote the game. It reached number 67 in the US charts.

SHIEN'S REVENGE

Year	1994
Publisher	Vic Tokai
Developer	Almanic

SHIEN WAS A ninja fighting in a huge war when suddenly a time portal opened up and his girlfriend Aska was kidnapped. Deciding the war can take care of itself, Shien heads into the tunnel and finds himself travelling through time, killing countless enemies along the way. Throughout the game you'll visit sixteenth century Japan, twenty-first century South America and fifth century BC Greece before finally reaching a castle for the final battle. Played using either the controller or a SNES Mouse, Shien's Revenge uses a cursor that doubles as two attacks in one. Not only can it be used to throw shurikens at distant enemies, it can also be swiped sideways to slash at close foes. ■

FACT

The characters in Shien's Revenge were designed by Go Nagai, the manga artist who's best known for creating cult mangas like *Cutie Honey* and *Devilman*.

SIDE POCKET

Year	1993
Publisher	Data East
Developer	Iguana Entertainment

 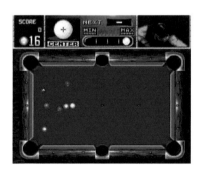

SIDE POCKET IS a pool game and not, as the title may imply, a game about where a bachelor keeps his mints. Although it was originally released in arcades before spawning an accurate NES port, this SNES version is something of a reimagining with improved visuals, a new jazz soundtrack and a revamped version of the main mode, Pocket Game. Here you're given 16 balls and, starting in Los Angeles, have to continue to build your score by potting balls (with bonus points for doing it in sequence) until you earn enough points to move on to Las Vegas, San Francisco, New York and finally Atlantic City. If straight pool isn't your thing there's also a Trick Shot mode where you're given 19 different setups that have to be cleared with one shot. ■

FACT

Side Pocket got two sequels on other systems, though the second was renamed Minnesota Fats: Pool Legend and the third was only released in Japan.

SIMANT

Year	1993
Publisher	Maxis Software
Developer	Tomcat System

  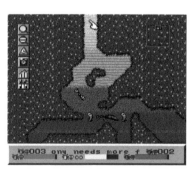

AFTER ENJOYING HUGE success with the home computer versions of SimCity and SimEarth (see over the page), all eyes were on designer Will Wright to see what his next idea would be. The obvious guess would be something even bigger, like SimUniverse, so eyebrows were raised when he instead made SimAnt, which has you playing as a black ant who's part of a colony in a house's back garden. Unlike the previous Sim games this one had a final goal: drive out the red ants, then take over the house and drive out its residents too. The game consists of two main views: a side-on view where you can view and expand your colony underground, and a top-down view when you're exploring on the surface. The SNES version has an exclusive Scenario mode with eight levels. ■

FACT

Will Wright once said that the way real ants respond to pheromone trails was one of the inspirations for the way characters act in his biggest success, The Sims.

SIMCITY

Year	1991
Publisher	Nintendo
Developer	Maxis / Nintendo

POPULAR COMPUTER GAMES are often ported over to video game consoles, and most of the time they lose something in the process. Whether it's the controls, the performance, the number of features or just the general change in a game's feel when it's ported over by a new team, it's uncommon for a game that was originally designed for PC or Mac to still feel like a perfect fit on a console once the developer has taken its round peg and chiselled pieces off it to fit it into a square hole (or a rectangular cartridge slot, if you really want to commit to this metaphor). SimCity is one of those extremely rare examples of a computer game that not only kept its magic on console, but actually offered even more than its PC equivalent.

The general concept is the same. Starting off with a small landform, you're initially armed with little more than some water, some brown fields and some green forests. Oh, and some money, which can be used to start laying the groundwork for a small city. Starting off with a power plant – either coal which is cheaper but highly polluting, or nuclear which is non-polluting but prone to meltdowns later – you can then start adding zones. Add a residential zone and houses will start getting built, while commercial zones give them somewhere to shop and industrial zones

give them somewhere to work. On top of all this you have to build infrastructure like roads and rail, as well as other key buildings like police and fire stations, stadiums, airports and parks in order to help keep your city thriving and safe.

The success of the SNES version may have been due to the involvement of Nintendo's own EAD division, who worked with Maxis to ensure the game met typical console sensibilities. While it shared many of the same features as the computer versions, its goal was made less open-ended. Players could still of course build their city to their heart's content, but the SNES version also added milestones for the player to aim towards. Some of these were purely for status' sake: as you continue to build your city and your population grows, the city's definition changes from a village to a town (once it hits 2,000 people), to a city (10,000), capital (50,000), metropolis (100,000) and megalopolis (500,000). Other milestones added new special buildings that could be built to further improve your city: these include zoos, amusement parks, casinos, libraries, banks and windmills. And of course, this being a Nintendo game, you can get a Mario statue for your city too.

As well as being able to create a city from scratch in the game's main mode, there's also a Scenario mode which offers six pre-existing cities with their own dilemmas, be that an earthquake in San Francisco, crime in Detroit, flooding in Rio or a monster attack in Tokyo (by Bowser, naturally). Clear all six and you'll unlock two SNES-exclusive ones: Las Vegas following an alien attack, and the challenging Freeland map, which has no rivers. ∎

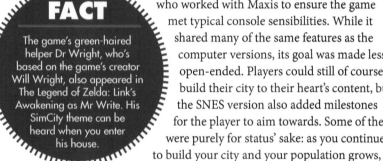

FACT

The game's green-haired helper Dr Wright, who's based on the game's creator Will Wright, also appeared in The Legend of Zelda: Link's Awakening as Mr Write. His SimCity theme can be heard when you enter his house.

SIMCITY 2000

Year	1996
Publisher	THQ
Developer	Black Pearl Software

THE SEQUEL TO SimCity ditched the overhead view and instead went for an isometric one, which transformed the game's sense of scale: whereas commercial zones used to simply be differently coloured squares, now they were depicted by massive skyscrapers and the like. The SNES port, however, was the opposite of the SimCity port in nearly every way. Whereas SimCity was a SNES launch title, offered extra features and was ported over with Nintendo's help to ensure it still worked as a console game, SimCity 2000 did the inverse. It launched near the end of the SNES's life, removed a number of the PC version's features – no volcanoes, no riots, no difficulty settings, fewer scenarios, etc. – and was criticised for having an awkward control system that hadn't been optimised for consoles. ∎

FACT

The PC version of SimCity 2000 had some spin-offs that let you import your cities and explore them in 3D. SimCopter had you flying around your city taking on missions, while Streets of SimCity was a racing game that let you drive around your city.

SIMEARTH

Year	1993
Publisher	FCI
Developer	Tomcat System

IF CREATING YOUR own metropolis in SimCity felt a little complicated, SimEarth – Will Wright's second game – is rocket science by comparison. Rather than being in charge of a city, this time you're in control of the entire planet and have to evolve it over millions (and billions) of years. Players can monitor and influence things like atmospheric gases, continental drift and overall temperature, and can also place basic lifeforms with the aim of evolving their species through their respect life classes until they reach intelligent life. The game's eight scenarios are suitably complex too: the first puts you on a planet consisting entirely of water, and you have to figure out how to create land so you can eventually create fire and therefore form an eventual civilisation. ∎

FACT

SimEarth's manual explains how the game follows the Gaia Theory, which suggests the development of life forms changes the environment of a planet. And if that goes over your head, don't worry: there's a *Simpsons* game up next.

THE SIMPSONS: BART'S NIGHTMARE

Year	1992
Publisher	Acclaim
Developer	Sculptured Software

BART SIMPSON MAY be 'an underachiever and proud of it' (as an early *Simpsons* catchphrase used to go), but there have been times when he's been known to genuinely try at school. During a rare late-night studying session, Bart falls asleep at his desk and starts dreaming of a fantasy version of Springfield where eight pages of his homework are fluttering around. Bart needs to gather as many pages as possible before he wakes up: the more he gets, the better his school grade.

Bart's Nightmare opens with a hub world, which is an endless strip of street in Springfield. Bart has to avoid taking damage here (too much and he'll wake up) while looking for pages. Once he finds one, jumping on it will take you a pair of randomly chosen coloured doors. There are five of these, each leading to a different mini-game that rewards players with one or two pages upon completion. The green door has Bart turning into a large green Godzilla-like creature who has to destroy the attacking army, climb the Springfield State Building and fight King Homer. The orange door is an Indiana Jones clone where Bart has to jump between stone columns. The yellow door puts Bart in an Itchy & Scratchy episode, where he has to survive being attacked by the pair. The purple door is set in Bart's bloodstream and has him using a pump to destroy germs. Finally, the blue door hides a shoot 'em up where the player controls Bartman flying through the sky with his slingshot. ∎

FACT

The late Bill Williams was one of the developers who worked on Bart's Nightmare. He became so annoyed at the level of corporate interference messing with its development that he nicknamed it Bill's Nightmare and quit the games industry.

SINK OR SWIM

Year	1994
Publisher	Titus Software
Developer	Zeppelin Games

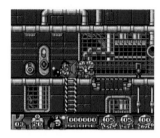

THE *SS LUCIFER* has sprung a leak (well, that's what happens when you name your boat that), and it's only a matter of time before it sinks. Playing as the heroic Kevin, you have to travel to each of the ship's 100 areas in your little yellow submarine and save the passengers running around in a panic. Sink or Swim is similar to Lemmings in that the passengers don't have a mind of their own: they'll just continue walking in a straight line until they hit an obstacle. The aim, then, is to guide them to each stage's exit using switches, bombs, dinghies and other tricks to keep them out of trouble. On some stages the water level is constantly rising too, as if simply rescuing them wasn't hard enough. ■

FACT

The Amiga version of the game gives Kevin's full name as Kevin Codner. The cover also says the game 'stars Dim Passengers', which may be a reference to Kim Basinger.

SKYBLAZER

Year	1994
Publisher	Sony Imagesoft
Developer	Ukiyotei

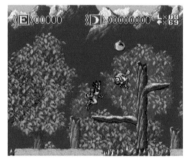

ARGUABLY SOMETHING OF a hidden gem, Skyblazer was developed by the same team behind the SNES version of Hook and shares a similar art style and feel, but with none of the restrictions a movie licence places on it. You play as Sky, the last descendant of the Mystic Pantheon, who has to free the young sorceress Arianna from the evil lord of war Ashura (hey, just because it isn't a licensed game doesn't mean the story's original). There are 17 levels in total to play through, and while the vast majority of the game is side-scrolling there are some interesting Mode 7 effects, including one stage where you ascend a rotating tower and another which is set from behind you and has you flying through rings in a similar way to Pilotwings. ■

FACT

One of the tips in the manual is very profound: 'Be patient and use your head. Remember, even the most heroic fool is still just a fool.'

SKULJAGGER: REVOLT OF THE WESTICANS

Year	1992
Publisher	American Softworks
Developer	Realtime Associates

OF ALL THE pirate-themed bubblegum-blowing games out there, Skuljagger is certainly among the best. You play as Storm Jaxon, an enslaved citizen who steals the magical sword belonging to the evil Skuljagger and decides to use it to help start a revolution that will repel Skuljagger's army and free him and his fellow Westicans. Naturally, the big man's not happy with this, so he sends his crew of Kiltish troops to defeat you. You have to fight your way through 21 stages in order to find and kill Skuljagger. As already noted, one of the game's more unusual mechanics is the power-up system which consists of four different flavours of bubblegum. Each flavour gives a different ability: cherry ones, for example, let you fly if you keep inflating the bubble by pressing A. ■

FACT

Skuljagger's instruction manual is one of the most impressive ones in the SNES library. It's an 80-page book filled with illustrations and lore.

SMART BALL

Year	1992
Publisher	Sony Imagesoft
Developer	Game Freak

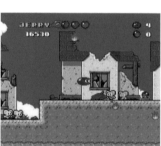

FIVE YEARS BEFORE Pokémon arrived on the scene, its creators Satoshi Tajiri and Ken Sugimori were just starting out with their development studio Game Freak. Smart Ball was Game Freak's second game (following odd NES puzzler Mendel Palace) and has players controlling Jerry Bean, a prince who's been transformed into a blob by a witch on the orders of his jealous brother Tom (yes, as in Tom and Jerry), who quite fancies being the king himself. Being a blob, Jerry can stick to walls and can also stretch to reach higher platforms. His blobbiness does mean he can't kill enemies by jumping on their heads, but he can at least jump onto them then squish down over them to defeat them that way. ■

FACT

Smart Ball's Japanese title was Jerry Boy, and a sequel called Jerry Boy 2 was cancelled. It's not clear if this title (and the character's name Jerry Bean) is the result of the Japanese language replacing the letter L with R.

SMASH TENNIS

Year	1994
Publisher	Virgin Interactive
Developer	Namco

THE PREDECESSOR TO Namco's Smash Court Tennis series, Smash Tennis was known as Super Family Tennis before it was renamed for Europe. It offers 20 characters to choose from: 12 men and 8 women. On the court, the game plays extremely well with players able to hit hard, soft and lob balls with a great degree of accuracy. Easily the most enjoyable aspect of the game, though, is the selection of courts available: as well as the standard arenas with grass, clay and hard surfaces, you can also play at a resort, a lodge, a Japanese shrine, at the beach or on a mountain top. The scenery is interactive too: hit a tree at the beach with the ball and a coconut will fall out and hit a spectator on the head. ■

FACT

Smash Tennis was followed by seven Smash Court Tennis games. The second featured a bunch of Namco characters as hidden players, including Reiko from Ridge Racer Type 4, Yoshimitsu and Heihachi from Tekken, and Pac-Man.

THE SMURFS

Year	1994
Publisher	Infogrames
Developer	Infogrames

THE FIRST OF two SNES Smurfs games that were only released in Europe, The Smurfs has you playing as a generic Smurf as he tries to rescue Jocky Smurf, Greedy Smurf, Brainy Smurf and Smurfette from the clutches of Gargamel. It's a fairly straightforward platformer in which you collect sarsaparilla leaves for extra lives and raspberries to replenish your energy. The first stage is something of an odd introduction to the game, as you have to make your way out of the Smurf Village, but since practically everything in this game harms you it's not uncommon for you to die at the hands of a fellow Smurf, which seems to go slightly against the generally peaceful and friendly Smurf narrative. ■

FACT

The back of the box is no use, explaining that you 'have to smurf the Angry Smurfs before smurfing the mountain by sled, then smurfing the maze of mine galleries, smurfing on the back of a stork and finally smurf Gargamel! Good smurf!'

THE SMURFS TRAVEL THE WORLD

Year	1996
Publisher	Infogrames
Developer	Infogrames

THE NINTH AND final season of *The Smurfs* TV show introduced the idea of a magic crystal that let them travel around the world. While many agreed the show had finally smurfed the shark, it didn't stop Infogrames using the idea for a platformer. Smurfette has accidentally broken the magic crystal, so now she and Inquisitive Smurf (you can play as either) have to travel to various locations – the jungles of South America, the North Pole, the deserts of North America, the villages of Africa, the outback in Australia and a temple in Asia – and find the shards of crystal in each so they can head back to their village and repair it. Critical reception varied: some thought it was 'smurf' while others felt it was 'smurf'. ■

FACT

Inquisitive Smurf only appears in this game. He's probably supposed to be Nosey Smurf, but why he's called this isn't really clear.

SNOW WHITE IN HAPPILY EVER AFTER

Year	1994
Publisher	American Softworks
Developer	Imagitec Design

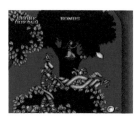

DON'T GET TOO excited, Disney fans: you haven't just discovered a hidden gem you didn't know about. This is based on *Happily Ever After*, the animated movie from defunct production company Filmation which starred Irene Cara (aka Coco from *Fame*) as Snow White. The Queen's equally evil wizard brother Lord Maliss has cast evil spells throughout the kingdom in an attempt to get to Snow White, so it's up to old Whiters and her 'Shadowman' protector (don't ask) to make their way through eight stages, reach Lord Maliss and defeat him in his dragon form. Despite this being a Snow White game, the Shadowman is the default character: players have to go into the options menu to switch to Snow White each time they play the game. ■

FACT

Happily Ever After was originally an NES game but it was canned after the movie was a dismal flop. A prototype cartridge of the complete NES game was discovered and shared online in 2016.

SOCCER KID

Year	1994
Publisher	Ocean Software
Developer	Krisalis Software

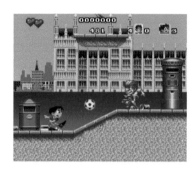

KNOWN AS THE Adventures of Kid Kleats in North America (because giving up the word 'football' apparently wasn't good enough), Soccer Kid tells the story of a young chap who decides to save the day when an alien called Scab steals the World Cup during the USA 94 final. During its escape, Scab's ship was hit by a meteor and the World Cup split into five pieces, so Soccer Kid has to travel to England, Italy, Russia, Japan and the US to collect them. Much like Marko's Magic Football, this is a platformer where your hero is armed with a football. You can kick it at enemies, chip it to collect items high in the air, and bounce off it to gain extra height on your jumps. ■

FACT

Soccer Kid was originally known as Football Kid (that's more like it), and early magazine previews in the summer of 1992 showed a completely different USA stage set in the desert.

SONIC BLAST MAN

Year	1992
Publisher	Taito
Developer	ITL / Zuntata

SONIC BLAST MAN was originally a 'test your strength' style arcade machine in which players had to punch a huge red pad to try and do as much damage as possible in five separate situations: attacking a giant crab, stopping an asteroid hitting the Earth and so on. Naturally, Taito wasn't about to start selling giant punching bags to SNES owners, so the home version of Sonic Blast Man was completely different, instead offering fairly standard side-scrolling beat 'em up action in the style of Final Fight. There are five stages, with names ranging from the straightforward 'Defeat the Villains and Save the Town' and 'Destroy the Factory' to the slightly sillier 'Exterminate the Hideous Thing that has Risen from the Sewage'. ■

FACT

On 14 March 1996 Taito agreed to recall all its Sonic Blast Man arcade machines and was ordered to pay $50,000 in damages after around 70 reported instances of players getting injured by punching it, the majority of which were fractured arms and wrists.

SONIC BLAST MAN II

Year	1994
Publisher	Taito
Developer	ITL / Taito

THE SNES SEQUEL to Sonic Blast Man once again opts to go down the beat 'em up route, but makes sure to improve every element along the way. Yafu, a self-proclaimed omniscient being from a distant planet, has declared that Earth is due to be destroyed. Time for Sonic Blast Man to save the day, but this time he's not alone. You can now choose to play as either the man himself, a cybernoid superhero called Captain Choyear or Sonia the Sonic Blast Girl. Each has their own unique moves and fighting style, adding a little variety to proceedings. While the first game was single-player only, the addition of these two new characters also makes co-op play possible for two players. ■

FACT

UK heavyweight boxers Gary Mason and Frank Bruno played the arcade version of Sonic Blast Man in separate episodes of UK TV show *GamesMaster*. Mason's three punches hit a total of 331 tons of power, whereas Bruno's hit 430 tons.

SOS

Year	1994
Publisher	Vic Tokai
Developer	Human Entertainment

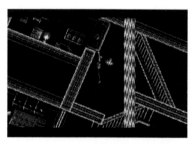

THERE'S NOTHING QUITE like SOS in 16-bit gaming. Designed to be played in an hour, the game takes place on the *Lady Crithania*, a cruise ship that's hit by a massive wave and tips over. You have roughly 60 minutes to rescue as many people as you can and get off the ship before it sinks. There are four separate characters to choose from: a young architect called Capris, a counsellor called Redwin, a crewman called Luke and an older doctor chap called Jeffrey. Each has their own loved ones on the boat with them, and each character has up to five endings depending on how many people they saved and whether their loved one was among the survivors.

FACT

The game's called Septentrion in Japan. A sequel called Septentrion: Out of the Blue was released on the PlayStation in 1999, but this one doesn't have a one-hour time limit.

SOUL BLAZER

Year	1992
Publisher	Enix
Developer	Quintet

THIS ACTION RPG developed by the team behind Actraiser has an interesting twist: the further you get into the game, the more you rebuild the world you're exploring. The evil spirit Deathtoll has destroyed every village and living creature in the Freil Empire, and captured their souls for good measure. As you explore each of the game's dungeons and defeat the monsters and their lairs you'll get opportunities to free these souls, which in turn makes one of the village's buildings and its residents appear again. This helps you eventually rebuild the once empty village into a thriving community of grateful residents, some of whom in turn have new quests for you. It's a clever way of handling how your player progresses through their adventure. ◾

FACT

Some consider Soul Blazer to be part of an unofficial trilogy of Quintet RPGs along with Illusion of Gaia and Terranigma. All three were designed by Tomoyoshi Miyazaki.

SPACE ACE

Year	1994
Publisher	Absolute Entertainment
Developer	Entertainment International

THE ARCADE VERSION of Space Ace was a sci-fi sequel to Dragon's Lair which used the same laserdisc technology to give players an interactive cartoon to play through. Since the SNES obviously couldn't read laserdiscs, a completely different Space Ace game was made for Nintendo's system. Rather than just a video sequence with button prompts, then, this is an isometric platformer where the hero Dexter has to rescue his sidekick Kimberly from the evil Commander Borf. The problem was that despite being a different game, it still wants to feel like the arcade version, which means countless instances of enemies appearing out of nowhere and killing you. This leads to a gruelling trial-and-error situation where you replay stages countless times until you learn exactly where you need to move. ◾

FACT

These days you don't need to spend a fortune dying over and over in the arcade version of Space Ace. It's included as part of the Dragon's Lair Trilogy on PS4 and Switch, so now you can die over and over for a single fee.

SPACE FOOTBALL: ONE ON ONE

Year	1992
Publisher	Triffix
Developer	Bits Studios

ROCKET LEAGUE? PAH, Space Football was doing it more than two decades earlier (albeit not as well). Taking place on a variety of arenas across the galaxy, Space Football puts you in control of a spaceship and tasks you with grabbing hold of a hovering ball and firing it into your net before your opponent can do the same. The twist is that once you grab the ball you can't just fly it into the net: you only have four seconds to fire it off again otherwise it'll explode. Each arena contains a bunch of obstacles designed to hinder your progress, which is probably just as well because the gun each player gets to try and stop their opponent is close to useless. ◾

FACT

These armchair quarterbacks go 400 miles per hour,' enthuses the game's packaging in an attempt to convince players that it isn't in fact quite a sluggish game. 'Race across the fields of play at hypersonic speed', indeed.

SPACE INVADERS

Year	1997
Publisher	Nintendo
Developer	Taito

THIS BEWILDERING RELEASE which came near the end of the SNES's life is an authentic recreation of the original 1978 arcade version of Space Invaders with no extra gizmos or gameplay mechanics added. Players can choose to play using any of the four colour styles used in the cabinets back in the day: the original black-and-white 1978 version, the version used in the Deluxe model (which was still black-and-white but superimposed the game onto a colour background), the cellophane version (which ran the game over coloured strips of cellophane to give the cheap appearance of colour) and full colour. The only new addition is a split-screen mode where two players can play separate games at the same time instead of having to take turns. ◾

FACT

If you're looking for a more modern take on Space Invaders, 2008's Space Invaders Extreme on DS and Xbox 360 is an incredible psychedelic revamp with a pumping soundtrack which integrates itself with the action on the screen.

SPACE MEGAFORCE

Year	1992
Publisher	Toho
Developer	Compile

KNOWN AS SUPER Aleste in Europe and Japan, Space Megaforce is one of the more technically accomplished shoot 'em ups on the SNES, regularly filling the screen with bullets and enemies but rarely showing any sign of slowdown. It's set in 2048 and has you piloting the Super Aleste ship as you head off on a mission to enter and destroy a giant mechanical sphere that's arrived from space and started destroying many of the Earth's major cities. Uniquely, if you don't have time to play through the main game, there's a Short Game option which only gives you four stages (as opposed to the 12 of the main game) and lets you mainly focus on getting the highest score possible. ■

FACT

If all the action is getting too much for you, the options screen has a setting called Break Time which gives you a large Mode 7 sprite from the game and lets you rotate and zoom into it to your heart's content.

SPANKY'S QUEST

Year	1992
Publisher	Natsume
Developer	Natsume

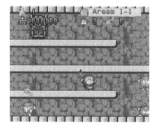

SPANKY THE MONKEY – why are you laughing? – has been trapped in a giant tower by a witch, who's also decided to transform the fruit in his knapsack into giant, living, fruity enemies. In order to escape, he has to make his way out of the witch's six towers while avoiding the numerous baddies along the way. Spanky's unique form of attack is a magic transforming ball, which he throws in a steep upward arc. After throwing the ball you can press a button to turn it into a baseball, doing minor damage, but if you jump up and juggle the ball with your head you can change its colour, making it transform into a group of footballs, a volleyball or a shower of basketballs. ■

FACT

Although it's hard to beat a title like Spanky's Quest, the Japanese version does at least have a more unique name. It translates to Monkey Reflections: The Adventures of Mr Jiro.

SPARKSTER

Year	1994
Publisher	Konami
Developer	Konami

NOT TO BE confused with the Mega Drive game also named Sparkster (which is a sequel to the Sega-only Rocket Knight Adventures), this SNES affair is a completely different adventure. You play as the heroic opossum knight Sparkster as he heads out to rescue Princess Flora from Generalissimo Lioness, who's also planning on destroying Sparkster's home planet (she's got her fingers in a lot of pies, this one). Sparkster isn't your typical opossum in a suit, though: and yes, you can get typical ones. He's armed with a special sword that can fire blasts of energy at opponents, and a rocket pack that can be charged to let him zoom across the screen. He's also got a new roll-dash move, which doesn't feature in the Sega games. ■

FACT

Sparkster lost his parents in a war and was adopted by a descendant of the Rocket Knights, who trained him to become one too. That's an *X Factor* backstory if ever you've heard one.

SPAWN: THE VIDEO GAME

Year	1995
Publisher	Acclaim
Developer	Ukiyotei

ORIGINALLY CREATED BY writer and artist Todd McFarlane, Spawn is an anti-hero with a constant dilemma hanging over him: his powers were given to him by the lord of darkness, Malebolgia, and once they run out his soul will become Malebolgia's possession for eternity. In this SNES action platformer, Spawn is trying to stop a renegade hero called The Mad One, who plans on killing Malebolgia with a magical orb containing the souls of 13 children, including Spawn's own stepdaughter. True to the character's backstory, Spawn tends to use punches and kicks instead of any special powers, and when the player does decide to use any his energy will be depleted. Defeat a boss, though, and they'll drop a little spawn logo that replenishes it. ■

FACT

Spawn's popularity has spawned (ahem) five other video games, as well as guest appearances as a playable fighter in Soulcalibur II and Mortal Kombat 11.

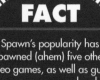

SPECTRE

Year	1994
Publisher	Cybersoft
Developer	Synergistic Software

THIS COLLECT 'EM up features first-person vector graphics similar to Atari's 1980 arcade game Battlezone. The focus here, however, is less on combat – though it's certainly a large part of the game – and more on collecting the yellow flags dotted around each level. Trying to prevent you from doing this are a bunch of enemy vehicles, each armed to the teeth and trying to deplete your energy. You can take them out with your cannon and grenades, while using your jump ability to avoid being hit. If it all gets too much you can use your hyperspace to teleport to a different part of the stage, but this is a last resort: it uses a lot of energy and may still dump you in an enemy-heavy area. ◾

FACT

Spectre was remade in 2010 as Spectre 3D and made available to download on iOS devices. It includes multiplayer support for up to 16 players.

SPEED RACER IN MY MOST DANGEROUS ADVENTURES

Year	1994
Publisher	Accolade
Developer	Radical Entertainment

SPEED RACER WAS one of the few anime series that made it to American TV long before anime because as popular as it is today: it actually first appeared on US screens in the late 1960s. An attempt to revive the brand in the early '90s led to a new animated series, merchandise and this SNES game, where Speed Racer has to rescue his girlfriend Trixie from Captain Terror. He does this by taking part in a series of races (because Speed Racer) as well as some side-scrolling action platformer sections. The racing sections make use of Mode 7 graphics in a way similar to Super Mario Kart and F-Zero, but with a severely reduced frame rate that was more acceptable then but may make it difficult for modern gamers. ◾

FACT

Speed Racer was created by Tatsuo Yoshida in 1966. Yoshida formed the anime studio Tatsunoko Productions, which later featured in Wii crossover fighting game Tatsunoko vs Capcom.

SPEEDY GONZALES: LOS GATOS BANDITOS

Year	1995
Publisher	Sunsoft
Developer	Majesco Entertainment

A GROUP OF friendly, peace-loving mice in a small Mexican town were having fun at a fiesta when Los Gatos Banditos – a trio of feline bandits led by Sylvester the Cat – arrived and kidnapped them all. All, that is, except for Slowpoke Rodriguez, who's able to call on Speedy Gonzales for help. Speedy has to make his way through seven worlds, trying to rescue as many mice as he can. This game was arguably the closest SNES players could get to Sonic on their system, because Speedy's momentum and the sloped platforms made everything feel a lot like the Mega Drive Sonic games. Indeed, a popular SNES bootleg called Sonic 4 was actually this game with Speedy and the mice replaced with Sonic and Mario. ◾

FACT

One of the switches in the sixth world was programmed with some odd coding that doesn't affect the actual game running on a real SNES, but causes emulators to freeze. ¡Toma, piratas!

SPIDER-MAN

Year	1995
Publisher	LJN
Developer	Western Technologies

THE SNES WAS home to a few Spider-Man games, as you'll see over the page. This particular one was based on the popular 1994 animated series, and has a bunch of Spidey's former nemeses (more than 15, in fact) breaking out of the Ravencroft Institute. Cue a side-scrolling action game where the web-slinger has to track down and defeat Dr Octopus, the Green Goblin, Alistair Smythe, Vulture, Mysterio, Scorpion, Rhino, Venom and the others before they combine their forces and destroy New York. Along your journey through the likes of the Empire State University lab, the Brooklyn Bridge, Coney Island and J. Jonah Jameson's penthouse, you'll be able to call on the members of the Fantastic Four for help from time to time. ◾

FACT

The 1994 Spider-Man animated series ran for five seasons, chalking up a total of 65 episodes before Fox Kids decided to put a big glass over it and throw it into the garden.

SPIDER-MAN AND VENOM: MAXIMUM CARNAGE

Year	1994
Publisher	LJN
Developer	Software Creations

CLETUS KASADY MAY have been safely tucked away in Ravencroft, but the symbiote inside him had different ideas. Transforming into the awesome Carnage, he breaks out of the institution along with his fellow inmate Shriek, and the pair quickly grow in numbers when they meet up with Doppelganger, Demogoblin and Carrion. It's up to Spider-Man and Venom to put their differences aside and team up to defeat this quintuplet of chaos before the entire city is destroyed. Maximum Carnage is a side-scrolling beat 'em up where players start off as Spider-Man but soon reach stages where they get to swap over to Venom should they so desire. Scattered throughout the game are icons representing other superheroes: Black Cat, Captain America, Cloak, Dagger, Deathlok, Firestar, Iron Fist and Morbius. Collect these and you can call on them to help you out when

FACT

The soundtrack was written by American rock band Green Jelly (most 'famous' for their song *Three Little Pigs*) and converted into the SNES's music format. Their album *333* features the title theme as its first track.

you're in a bit of a pickle. Based on their allegiances, some of these superheroes will act differently depending on who summoned them. Spider-Man and Venom can also call on each other, because teamwork makes the dream work and all. The game is based on the 14-part *Maximum Carnage* comic series, and animated versions of panels from the actual comics appear in the game's cutscenes. Thankfully though, it doesn't share the comic's odd ending, where Spidey and Venom get a device from Stark Industries which projects love and hope into Carnage, leaving him confused and giving Venom a chance to tackle him into an electric generator. ■

SPIDER-MAN AND THE X-MEN IN ARCADE'S REVENGE

Year	1992
Publisher	LJN
Developer	Software Creations

THE FIRST SPIDER-MAN game released on the SNES had its fair share of problems behind the scenes, with Software Creations' producer Richard Kay once revealing in an interview with *Retro Gamer* magazine that development was going so badly that 'Acclaim were screaming at us and threatening litigation' if it wasn't fixed. With three different teams ultimately working together on the game it's something of a miracle that it ended up being a half-decent adventure. It opens with Spider-Man defusing a series of bombs located inside and outside an abandoned building. Once this slightly lengthy task is over Spider discovers that the evil Arcade has captured four of the X-Men and imprisoned them in his deadly amusement park. You get to play as each of the X-Men as they each have to clear a couple of bespoke stages, before Spider-

FACT

Software Creations was due to develop the home versions of Mortal Kombat, but the fall-out over Arcade's Revenge led to Acclaim giving the deal to Sculptured Software and Probe instead. Kay says it cost him a potential $40 million in royalties.

Man eventually teams up with them to take on Arcade in the final showdown. The stages are varied enough: Cyclops has to explore a minecart rollercoaster, complete with numerous instances where he has to jump into carts to proceed. Storm has been trapped in an underwater maze and must fire lightning bolts at hatches to raise the water level so she can reach the exit on the ceiling. Gambit finds himself in a cave with a giant spiked ball rolling after him: if he can escape that he has to face off against the Black Queen. Finally, Wolverine has been dumped into a circus-themed playhouse, with toy soldier enemies and jack-in-the-boxes firing machine guns at him. ■

SPINDIZZY WORLDS

Year	1992
Publisher	ASCII Entertainment / Activision
Developer	ASCII Entertainment

THIS IS A sequel to Spindizzy, an action puzzle game released in 1986 for home computers. You control a spinning top, which according to the game's original Amiga release is called GERALD (Geographical Environmental Reconnaissance And Landmapping Device). As its name suggests, GERALD has to explore a star system consisting of a number of planets, so they can be mapped before they're destroyed.

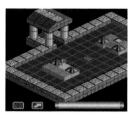

The game is played from an isometric viewpoint, but you can toggle the camera between 90-degree turns so you can see behind walls and the like. GERALD has no abilities other than moving around, so you have to make use of the environment and the game's reliance on momentum-based physics: for example, hitting bumps at high speed to help him jump over gaps. ∎

FACT

Spindizzy's creator Paul Shirley despised the SNES version of the sequel, once saying in an interview: 'This port was an absolute disaster, I disown it.' It took him years of legal action to get royalty payments.

SPIROU

Year	1995
Publisher	Infogrames
Developer	Infogrames

JOINING THE REST of Infogrames' sizeable roster of SNES platformers based on popular French and Belgian comics (*Asterix*, *The Smurfs*, *Tintin*, *Lucky Luke*), Spirou is based on French cartoonist Rob-Vel's long-running *Spirou & Fantasio* series. It opens in a scientific research symposium in New York, with Spirou's pal Count Champignac about to give a speech on a groundbreaking discovery. Before he can, he's kidnapped by the evil robot Cyanide. Off goes Spirou to track her down and rescue the Count before Cyanide can use his inventions to turn the world's population into robot slaves. Like most other Infogrames platformers on the SNES, Spirou is beautifully animated and designed but has a relatively high difficulty level with some cheap deaths that are hard to avoid if you don't know they're coming. ∎

FACT

Spirou & Fantasio started way back in 1938 as part of the first issue of *Le Journal de Spirou*, an eight-page French magazine containing short stories and serial comics.

THE SPORTING NEWS: POWER BASEBALL

Year	1995
Publisher	Hudson Soft
Developer	Now Production

POWER BASEBALL IS associated with the long-running 'Bible of Baseball', the *Sporting News*, and contains the MLBPA logo, which – if you've been paying attention throughout this book – means the team names and logos

aren't official but all the player names are. It's a fairly unremarkable baseball game except for one strange but brilliant addition: as well as the option to play in a dome or a standard ballpark, you can also play in a 'dream field', which is a baseball park built into a cornfield. This is a reference to the 1989 movie *Field of Dreams*, where Kevin Costner builds a baseball park into his cornfield only to see the ghosts of former players (and his father) turning up to play. ∎

FACT

The *Sporting News* published its first edition on 7 March 1886 at a price of cents. In December 2012 the al print edition was published and it became a website only, which continues to this day.

SPORTS ILLUSTRATED: CHAMPIONSHIP FOOTBALL & BASEBALL

Year	1994
Publisher	Malibu Games
Developer	Malibu Games

ANOTHER SNES GAME named after a magazine? How spoiled we are. As the title suggests, this *Sports Illustrated* branded game is actually two games in one, offering both American football (which is played with an isometric viewpoint) and baseball. Neither sport is blessed with official licensing, so there are no team logos and no real player names. Oddly, many of the American football teams' colour schemes carry over to the baseball mode, so if you play baseball as Cleveland the players will be wearing the orange of the American football team. European fans of American sports were screwed over on this one: it was released in PAL regions as All-American Championship Football, ditching not only the *Sports Illustrated* brand but also the entire baseball section of the game. ∎

FACT

Sports Illustrated was first published in August 1954 and became (in)famous for its annual swimsuit edition. In 1983 it became the first American weekly magazine to be printed in full colour.

STAR FOX

Year	1993
Publisher	Nintendo
Developer	Nintendo EAD / Argonaut

SHIELD

HEY!! DON'T BE SO G-G-GREEDY!!

POLYGONAL GAMES HAD appeared from time to time in the past, most notably in the arcades with games like Hard Drivin' and Winning Run, but it wasn't until Sega's Virtua Racing appeared in 1992 that gamers began to believe that polygons could be the future of gaming. None of the home consoles at the time could come close to matching Virtua Racing's unique look: although Mode 7 gave the SNES the ability to perform a pseudo-3D effect by rotating a large sprite, it was just an optical illusion in a sense and wasn't true 3D. Enter British developer Argonaut, who showed Nintendo a demo of their polygonal Amiga game Starglider running on an NES and later a prototype SNES. Argonaut told Nintendo it could make even more impressive polygonal graphics if it was allowed to design custom hardware to let the SNES better handle 3D. Nintendo agreed, and the Super FX chip was born.

The Super FX could be used for advanced 2D graphics effects like sprite scaling and stretching that went well beyond what Mode 7 could do: this was how games like Yoshi's Island made use of it. By far its most exciting feature, though, was the ability to render hundreds of 3D polygons at a time, making rudimentary 3D games possible on the SNES. It was this feature that led to the birth of Star Fox (or Starwing in Europe), the first Super FX game.

Star Fox follows the adventures of Fox McCloud and the rest of the Star Fox team, a group

FACT

Star Fox was inspired by Shigeru Miyamoto's love for the Fushimi Inari-taisha shrine in Kyoto, which includes around 1,000 torii gates (like the gates you fly under in the first stage) and numerous statues of foxes.

of elite mercenaries for hire who are employed by General Pepper to find and defeat Andross, an evil scientist who was banished to the planet Venom and now threatens to destroy the entire Lylat System of planets. Fox and his crew take one of three routes – each representing a different difficulty level and each offering a different set of stages – shooting their way through countless hordes of Andross's forces, including some truly impressive bosses.

Although the visual gimmickry is clearly one of the reasons Star Fox was such a success at the time, it's the story and characters that ensured it would become the start of a series that continues to be loved by fans to this day. If Super Metroid was Nintendo's version of *Alien*, then Star Fox is Miyamoto's *Star Wars*. Fox is Luke Skywalker: the strong, fatherless, white-shirted hero who happens to also be an expert pilot. Falco is Han Solo: a cocky, arrogant pilot who doesn't want anyone getting in his way but deep down still cares about the team. Peppy is Chewbacca: the loyal and reliable wingman who knows his way around a spanner. And Slippy is C-3PO, the comic relief who clearly loves his team and is loved in return, even though he's a bumbling numpty. Together, the four form a team that – much like the heroes in *Star Wars* – can clearly kick sizeable helpings of rump, but more importantly share a bond that many players can relate to and become attached to as a result. ∎

Revolutionary Super FX Micro Chip Creates Special Effects Like Never Before!

STAR TREK: DEEP SPACE NINE – CROSSROADS OF TIME

Year	1995
Publisher	Playmates
Developer	Novotrade

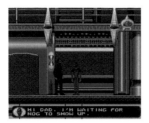

THE FOURTH SERIES in the *Star Trek* universe, *Deep Space Nine* had its fans but also its fair share of critics, who complained the pace was too plodding. The same could be said of its SNES tie-in, which looks impressive but is rather slow at times. It consists of five missions – with the suitably exciting names of Saboteurs, Pursuit, Nest of Vipers, Mysterious Time Attack and Finale – which switch between two game styles: 'adventure' (where you move around the Deep Space Nine, talking to various characters to advance the plot) and 'action' (where you get to set phasers to 'pew pew'). For the most part you play as Commander Sisko, but at times you'll take control of Dr Bashir, Major Kira and Odo. ■

FACT

There were 176 episodes of *Deep Space Nine* spanning seven seasons. If you have to watch one, watch The Magnificent Ferengi, which stars Iggy Pop as a Vorta.

STAR TREK: STARFLEET ACADEMY – STARSHIP BRIDGE SIMULATOR

Year	1994
Publisher	Interplay
Developer	Paramount Interactive

ALL GREAT CAPTAINS have to learn their trade somewhere, and that's where the Starfleet Academy comes in. Starship Bridge Simulator does what it says on the box: it puts you in the nifty uniform of a Starfleet Cadet and lets you take on 20 simulated missions, making your way through your sophomore, junior and senior years and eventually graduating. There are five different vessels in the game: a Federation Science Vessel, Federation Light Cruiser, Federation Heavy Cruiser, Romulan Vessel and Klingon Vessel. The simulator missions choose a vessel for you, but there are also Combat Training and two-player duel modes that let you choose any one. Beat all 20 missions and you'll take on the infamous and unbeatable *Kobayashi Maru* test. ■

FACT

The *Kobayashi Maru* is actually beatable with some skullduggery. A cheat code lets you play as classic Star Trek characters. Play as Kirk and hail the Klingons and they'll escort you to safety, letting you complete the test without being destroyed.

STAR TREK: THE NEXT GENERATION – FUTURE'S PAST

Year	1994
Publisher	Spectrum Holobyte
Developer	Spectrum Holobyte

THE ONLY SNES *Star Trek* game based on *The Next Generation* revolves around the Integrated Field Derandomizer, a mysterious machine that lets whoever uses it reshape matter and energy. There are three main gameplay styles in *Future's Past*: the first lets you wander around the bridge, visit various stations and sit at the conn to decide where to travel next. The second is space combat, which takes place from a top-down perspective. Finally, there are away team missions where you can beam a team down to a planet to explore. While you can choose major characters for this – Picard, Riker, Troi, Worf, Dr Crusher, La Forge, Data and the like – you can also choose some red shirts to go along too to make sure your top-rankers don't die. ■

FACT

One of the red shirts is named Ed Semrad after the editor of *Electronic Gaming Monthly* magazine. EGM gave the game 7.5 out of 10 saying it was 'boring at times', so that didn't really work out.

STARGATE

Year	1995
Publisher	Acclaim
Developer	Probe

ALTHOUGH MOST KNOW *Stargate* for its numerous TV series, in particular the much-loved *Stargate SG-1*, none of them existed at this point. Instead, the SNES game is based on the 1994 movie that started the whole franchise off. Players control Colonel Jack O'Neill (played by Kurt Russell in the movie) as he tries to defeat the villain Ra, free the Abydonian slaves and collect all the hieroglyphs needed to assemble the Stargate address that will help his crew return to Earth. Most of the game consists of standard action platforming gameplay, where O'Neill uses his machine gun and grenades to take out various enemies. Occasionally, though, there are Mode 7 stages where O'Neill flies a glider, presumably because all SNES platformers need to have a Mode 7 level by law. ■

FACT

Although it was popular enough to lead to the TV shows, the *Stargate* movie was famously despised by movie critic Roger Ebert, who wrote: 'The movie *Ed Wood*, about the worst director of all time, was made to prepare us for *Stargate*.'

STEEL TALONS

Year	1993	
Publisher	Left Field Productions	
Developer	Panoramic	

STEEL TALONS IS a helicopter combat game which originally hit the arcades in 1991 courtesy of Atari. The arcade version made use of basic polygons to create a 3D environment and the SNES version attempts to do the same (though without the Super FX chip, the polygons are extremely limited and the frame rate is noticeably slower). There are 14 missions to take on, all of which generally consist of shooting all the targets before they shoot you. The missions place in four different locations – woodlands, a desert, a riverside and mountains – and there are numerous weather conditions including clear, clouds, night, dusk, fog, haze and smoke. The Select button lets you switch the viewpoint from behind the helicopter to first-person inside the cockpit. ■

FACT

The Mega Drive version attempts to properly recreate the arcade game by using more polygons. The result was an even slower game, with the frame rate sometimes hitting as low as just 5 fps.

STERLING SHARPE: END 2 END

Year	1995	
Publisher	Jaleco	
Developer	Tose	

WHEN IT COMES to bad timing, there are fewer better examples than Sterling Sharpe: End 2 End. Sharpe was an incredible wide receiver for the Green Bay Packers, appearing in five Pro Bowl all-star games in seven seasons. Things were looking great until, in December 1994, Sharpe received a bad neck injury that cut his career short and caused early retirement. Three months later, his SNES game – which had obviously been in development for a while – was awkwardly released. To be fair though, the game was the least remarkable thing about this story: it's a basic Madden clone with no team or player licensing, and was criticised for not even having a season mode to its name. Its oddly suggestive name. ■

FACT

Sterling Sharpe become an analyst for the NFL Network after his injury, which is somewhat fitting because he appears before each match in End 2 End and gives his verdict on each team.

STONE PROTECTORS

Year	1994	
Publisher	Kemco	
Developer	Eurocom	

THE TROLL DOLL craze of the early '90s had one major issue: not a lot of boys were buying them. Various companies tried (and failed) to remedy this, with things like Teenage Mutant Ninja Turtles troll dolls doing the rounds. One particularly notable failure was Stone Protectors, which could only muster a roundly ignored 13-episode animated series, two mediocre toy lines and this SNES game before it went back under its rock. The game itself is decent enough: it's a beat 'em up in which the player can choose between the five Stone Protectors – that's Cornelius, Clifford, Chester, Angus and Maxwell, in case you'd forgotten – as they fight through 10 stages to find the final piece of a magical crystal before the evil Zok gets it. ■

FACT

As well as the game, the cartoon and the action figures, other similarly failed products designed to promote Stone Protectors included a board game and a comic book that lasted four issues.

STREET COMBAT

Year	1993	
Publisher	Irem	
Developer	Opus Corporation	

ALTHOUGH PUBLISHER DTMC brought Ranma ½: Hard Battle to the west, Irem – who owned the first Ranma ½ game on the Super Famicom – wasn't so confident the brand would do well in America. So, it took Ranma ½: Chonai Gekitohen and completely reskinned it, redrawing all of the characters and most of the stages and naming it Street Combat. The main hero Ranma was replaced by a blonde superhero called Steven, and instead of Ranma's male and female forms you could choose Steven with or without a robot suit. None of this redesign made up for the fact that the game was average, and putting 'Street' in the title only meant that 26 years later it would appear in a book right next to its vastly superior inspiration. ■

FACT

Most games run at 256x240 resolution, while a few run in a hi-res 512x448 mode. Street Combat runs at 256x448 meaning it was stretched vertically. This leads to a horrible interlaced effect when played on a TV.

STREET FIGHTER II: THE WORLD WARRIOR

Year	1992
Publisher	Capcom
Developer	Capcom

IF YOU FLICK through this book you'll see that the SNES was home to a slew of one-on-one fighting games. It wasn't a one-off, either: the Mega Drive and arcades were too, and so too has every major system since. It's no exaggeration to say the reason for this all boils down to a single game: Street Fighter II. Of course, there were one-on-one fighting games before Street Fighter II – including, well, the first Street Fighter – but the genre may as well be split into two eras: BC (Before Chun-Li) and AD (Anno Dhalsim).

Originally making its way into Japanese arcades in March 1991, Capcom's groundbreaking fighter gave players a choice of eight 'world warriors', fighters travelling the globe and taking on others, each with their own reasons and motivations for taking part. These eight fighters are as key an element of Street Fighter II's success as any other: you would struggle to find any other fighting game – even Mortal Kombat – where you could find a lapsed gamer who hadn't touched a controller in 20 years and still have them able to identify the entire roster by name.

There's Ryu, the lone warrior in constant pursuit of self-improvement. Ken, his former training partner and the outspoken yang to Ryu's reserved yin. Guile, the American army hero with the impossibly flat hair. Chun-Li, the Chinese Interpol agent trying to avenge her dead father. Blanka, a Brazilian jungle monster with a hidden past.

FACT

A ridiculous 200,000 Street Fighter II and Champion Edition cabinets were produced, bringing in total coin revenue of $2.3 billion by 1995. This means the average Street Fighter II cabinet was played more than 46,000 times in its lifetime.

Zangief, a Russian wrestler built like the back of a Moscow tram. E. Honda, a Japanese sumo wrestler who fights in a public bathhouse in Tokyo. And finally, Dhalsim, the Indian yoga master known for his stretchy limbs and fire-breathing antics.

Not only are these eight fighters immediately recognisable by gamers of a certain era, their special moves are too. Ryu and Ken's Hadoken fireballs and Dragon Punch are obviously the most famous, but the Sonic Boom, Spinning Bird Kick, Yoga Fire, Hundred Hand Slap, Spinning Piledriver and Blanka's electricity are as iconic as the fighters they belong to. Again, Street Fighter II wasn't the first fighting game to introduce character-specific special moves, but it was the first to make them such an integral part of the game design that they became the rulebook going forwards. Ask someone to do the 'fireball motion' in a fighting game and they immediately know you want them to sweep the D-Pad or stick in a quarter-circle from down to towards their opponent.

Then, of course, there were the boss characters. Defeat the other standard fighters and you'd gain access to four mythical, non-playable fighters: American boxer Balrog, Spanish cage fighter Vega, huge Thai kickboxer Sagat and the evil warlord M. Bison. Even though there was no way to play as them, their personalities and movesets became engrained just as deeply in players' minds. The success of Street Fighter II, both in arcades and with the exceptional SNES port, would lead to a number of updates and sequels. None of these were quite as momentous and important to the history of gaming, however, than this original release. ■

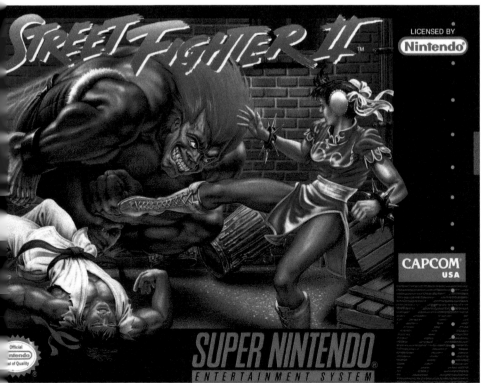

STREET FIGHTER II TURBO: HYPER FIGHTING

Year	1993
Publisher	Capcom
Developer	Capcom

THE ASTRONOMICAL SUCCESS of Street Fighter II had Capcom scrambling to capitalise with follow-ups. The arcade release of Champion Edition made the four boss characters playable and let players use the same fighter (meaning both could be unoriginal and choose Ken). This was followed with Street Fighter II Turbo: Hyper Fighting, which was ported to the SNES six months later. Turbo adds the same features introduced in the Champion Edition (the ability to play as the bosses and the option to have versus matches with the same characters) and added another key feature: speed settings. The main menu's new Turbo option let players set a speed of up to four stars, making the game far more fast-paced. While this meant reaction times obviously needed to be better than usual, it also meant players had to be able to pull off special move inputs quicker.

> ### FACT
> If you want to make the game unplayable, press Down, R, Up, L, Y, B on the second controller as the Capcom logo fades at the start. You can now increase the Turbo setting up to 10 stars instead of the usual four.

Changes were made to the general gameplay too. With the exception of Guile and the four bosses, everyone else got at least one new special move to keep things interesting. Ryu and Ken could now pull off their hurricane kicks in mid-air, Dhalsim could now teleport and – perhaps most interesting of all – Chun-Li could now throw fireballs, filling a key gap in her fighting style. Other changes specific to the SNES version include the reinstatement of a barrel-breaking bonus game that didn't feature in the SNES original, improved endings for each character and a Normal mode, which let players enjoy the Champion Edition with none of the speed shenanigans. ■

STREET FIGHTER ALPHA 2

Year	1996
Publisher	Nintendo
Developer	Capcom

AS EACH ITERATION of Street Fighter II was released, the question from the fans became louder: 'This is all well and good, but where's Street Fighter 3?' Capcom eventually responded by trolling its fans slightly: a new Street Fighter was indeed announced, but it was to be a prequel rather than a sequel. Street Fighter Alpha was set between the events of the first two Street Fighter games and included younger versions of Ryu, Chun-Li, Bison and Sagat along with returning characters from the original Street Fighter and a bunch of new faces. Alpha 2 was more of an update than a proper sequel: the game's roster was increased to 18 with Zangief and Dhalsim making their returns among other newcomers, including Final Fight boss character Rolento and Japanese schoolgirl Sakura. The release of a port of Alpha 2 on the SNES was

> ### FACT
> Street Fighter III did eventually appear in late 1996, but it too annoyed some of the hardcore fans by ditching every Street Fighter II character except for Ryu and Ken.

met with surprise by some: the arcade version looked significantly better than the Street Fighter II series and there were genuine questions as to whether the SNES hardware – now entering its twilight years – would be able to handle it. The answer was a diplomatic 'yes, sort of'. The core game is faithfully represented, with all 18 characters present and accounted for, but voices and other speech is muffled. The biggest sticking point, however, is the presence of a noticeable pause of a few seconds between the word 'Fight' appearing and a round actually beginning: this is down to the game loading sounds onto the SNES's sound chip. ■

STREET HOCKEY 95

Year	1994
Publisher	GTE Interactive Media
Developer	GTE Interactive Media

THIS WAS THE second of GTE's ill-fated Street Sports series, following urban basketball game Jammit. It plays like an ice hockey game, except it takes place on the streets and the players are wearing rollerblades. There are nine frankly silly characters to choose from, each of whom are digitised versions of some presumably ashamed actors. Examples include the purple-clad Lars, who is apparently a 'shred dog' and a 'puck stuffer', and Baruk, who looks like a Sacha Baron Cohen character and is a 'sweat head' and 'whackrobat'. There are five game modes to play, entitled Fat Point, Rush, Whack, Crammit and Hot Puck. And if you know what any of that means, I need your help selling some old Kris Kross cassettes. ◼

FACT

The box states that you can 'get enough air to show up on radar' and 'combine a knee stop with a no-look pass, if you can hang'. And let's face it, who can't.

STREET RACER

Year	1994
Publisher	Ubisoft
Developer	Vivid Image

UBISOFT'S ANSWER TO Mario Kart has its fair share of interesting quirks. There are no power-ups: instead, each racer can punch to either side, and occasionally trigger a special move unique to them. The eight playable racers are fairly stereotypical, including the likes of German war pilot Helmut, Australian teenager Surf Sister, the Japanese Sumo-san and the questionable Suzulu, an African racer who practices voodoo. As well as the standard Mode 7 racing you'd expect from a Mario Kart challenger, Street Racer has two unique modes: Rumble puts all eight drivers in a Destruction Derby style bowl and tasks them with knocking the others off the arena, while Soccer is a (bad) precursor to Rocket League, where everyone competes to grab a ball and drive it into a goal. ◼

FACT

Street Racer claims to be the first karting game to support four players. Oddly though, the split-screen used consists of four thin horizontal sections, rather than four corners.

STRIKE GUNNER S.T.G.

Year	1992
Publisher	NTVIC
Developer	Athena

ALTHOUGH ITS ART style is a little uninspired, Strike Gunner S.T.G. (which stands for, um, STrike Gunner) has a unique way of handling special weapons. Your standard weapon is always fairly unremarkable: a red laser that can be upgraded to a slightly more powerful blue laser but always has a narrow line of fire. Before each of the game's eight stages, though, you get to choose one of 15 different secondary weapons, including megabeam cannons, sonic waves and atomic missiles. Most of these weapons have their own gauge that determines how often you can use them in a stage. The twist, though, is that each weapon can only be used for one stage, meaning your favourite can't come with you for the entire journey. ◼

FACT

Strike Gunner is called Super Strike Gunner in Europe because, as you're about to find out, there aren't enough SNES games with 'Super' in the title.

STRIKER

Year	1993
Publisher	Elite / Atlus
Developer	Rage Software

LIVERPOOL-BASED RAGE SOFTWARE originally created Striker for the Commodore Amiga in 1992, before porting it to the SNES the following year. Much like Sensible Soccer, it focuses more on speed and fun than realism, with a strong focus on the ability to add swerve to your shots. There are 64 international teams to choose from, and a number of different modes to use them in ranging from the Super Cup – a knockout tournament consisting of all 64 teams – to a National League consisting of up to 16 teams. There's also an indoor football mode. The player names are real in the PAL version but the North American version, which was renamed World Soccer 94: Road to Glory, has fake names instead. ◼

FACT

Striker was rebranded in France too, where it was known as Eric Cantona Football Challenge to capitalise on the success of the Manchester United star.

STUNT RACE FX

Year	1994
Publisher	Nintendo
Developer	Nintendo EAD

STAR FOX WAS an enormous success, and the fact so much of the hype around it focused on the Super FX chip meant polygons on the SNES were suddenly a big deal. Eager to keep the momentum going, Nintendo got to work on its second Super FX game, Stunt Race FX. It's a polygonal racing game starring five cars with eyes (designed to give them personalities): the sturdy but slow 4WD, the speedy but frail F-Type, the balanced Coupe, the motorbike 2WD (who's unlockable) and the enormous truck Trailer, who only appears in a bonus mini-game. The main single-player modes are Speed Trax and Stunt Trax. The former offer three different cups, each consisting of four tracks and a bonus stage starring Trailer. The latter, meanwhile, gives players four different stunt courses to choose from and tasks them with collecting all the stars dotted around. There's also a split-screen mode called Battle Trax, where two players choose a track and race against each other. Stunt Race FX was praised for its polygonal graphics much like Star Fox was, but it was also clear that the Super FX's trademark low frame rate affected a racing game far more than it did a rail shooter. While Star Fox went on to become a much-loved Nintendo series, then, Stunt Race FX was retired after this first outing and was never seen again until 25 years later, when it was added to the Switch's library of playable SNES games in 2019. ■

> **FACT**
>
> A cross-promotion between Nintendo, Kellogg's and Mattel in the US let kids mail two proofs of purchase from Apple Jacks cereal to get a free Hot Wheels car that looked like F-Type. In reality it was a repaint of an existing Hot Wheels car called Shock Factor.

SUNSET RIDERS

Year	1993
Publisher	Konami
Developer	Konami

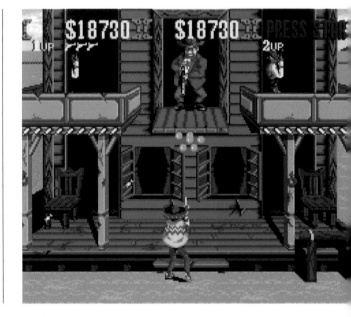

LOOK UP 'CULT game' in the dictionary and you'll find Sunset Riders (as well as numerous emails from people asking where you got your dictionary). Konami's run 'n' gun shooter was much loved in the arcade, but its home console versions were similarly adored, meaning anyone who owned it still fondly remembers it more than 25 years later. Set in the Old West, players take control of a bounty hunter as they make their way through various locales in search of eight wanted criminals, all of whom are just begging to be filled with lead and cashed in for your reward. There are four cowboys to choose from: the blue-clad revolver-shooting Billy, the shotgun-wielding and green-clothed Bob, the Mexican poncho-wearing Cormano and Steve, who wears the most garish yellow trousers you'll ever see this side of Chattanooga. After choosing your bounty hunter, you make your way through seven stages in search of the likes of the money-hungry Simon Greedwell, Mexican outlaw El Greco, the enormous Dark Horse and the knife-throwing Native American Chief Wigwam (known as Chief Scalpem in other versions of the game, but changed here and given a less stereotypical voice because Nintendo presumably felt it was a little on the nose). Sunset Riders' popularity stems from its satisfying gunplay, its brilliantly catchy music and its general sense of humour: one minute you're running along the backs of horses as they stampede through the town, the next you're gunning down a greedy banker whose solemn dying words are: 'Bury me with my money.' ■

> **FACT**
>
> The SNES version of Sunset Riders is a far more faithful port than the Mega Drive / Genesis one, which only lets you play as Billy or Cormano and only features four bosses.

SUPER 3D NOAH'S ARK

Year	1994
Publisher	Wisdom Tree
Developer	Wisdom Tree

THE NES WAS awash with games that hadn't been licensed for production by Nintendo (as you'll know if you also own the *NES Encyclopedia*, which has a full section dedicated to them). The SNES situation couldn't have been more different: only one commercially released game for the SNES in North America (during the console's active life) was unlicensed. Super 3D Noah's Ark was developed by religious studio Wisdom Tree, and was originally going to be based on the horror movie *Hellraiser*(!) before the licence expired.

In it, you play as Noah near the end of the ark's journey as he wanders its various corridors trying to calm down the restless animals, of which most are goats (so much for two of each). In order to do this, he uses a slingshot to fire fruit at them, which makes them fall asleep. If that sounds oddly harsh, that's because Super 3D Noah's Ark is actually a reskinned version of id Software's Nazi-based first-person shooter Wolfenstein 3D – made with id's full blessing, so to speak – in which the Nazi enemies are replaced with goats, sheep and ostriches and the final boss is no longer Adolf Hitler, but a large bear called Burt. One of the main reasons the SNES had so few unlicensed games is because the system had a more sophisticated copy protection chip. Wisdom Tree got around this by bundling Super 3D Noah's Ark with an adaptor that included a second slot that players had to put another, official SNES cartridge into to bypass the security check. ▪

FACT

A long-running rumour is that id Software gave Wisdom Tree the Wolfenstein 3D source code as revenge for Nintendo's heavy censorship of the SNES version of Wolfenstein. In reality, Wisdom Tree paid id for the code.

SUPER ADVENTURE ISLAND

Year	1992
Publisher	Hudson Soft
Developer	Produce!

EVEN THOUGH THERE was an Adventure Island III on the NES, Super Adventure Island is technically the third game in the series because it launched shortly after Adventure Island II. It once again stars chubby funster Master Higgins, who this time has to get through 20 stages to reach the castle of Dark Cloak, a mysterious evil entity who's turned Higgins' girlfriend Tina to stone (though she's called Jeanie Jungle in the manual for some reason). Despite releasing after the second NES game, Super Adventure Island plays more like the first with basic platforming and none of Adventure Island II's dinosaur pals to be found. One addition however is the ability to swap between your trusty stone axe and a new boomerang weapon. ▪

FACT

Super Adventure Island's soundtrack was composed by Yuzo Koshiro, who would later become known as the man responsible for the incredible music in the Streets of Rage games.

SUPER ADVENTURE ISLAND II

Year	1995
Publisher	Hudson Soft
Developer	Make Software

SUPER ADVENTURE ISLAND II was the seventh in the series (after four NES entries and a TurboGrafx-16 one), and the only one to take it beyond the standard level-based platforming routine the series was known for. Instead, it's more of an RPG-lite platformer, where Master Higgins has to travel around an island on his raft, visiting different locations and exploring them in a non-linear way. The plot's bizarre: Higgins and Tina are out at sea when a storm tears their raft apart, wiping both their memories and sending them off to different locations. A king falls in love with Tina but she's then kidnapped, so it's up to Higgins to rescue the king's future bride, even though he has the feeling he knows her from somewhere. ▪

FACT

The manual suggests that Master Higgins has never met Tina before, even though she was his love interest in most of the NES games. It also tries to draw a line under the Jeanie Jungle affair, referring to 'his disastrous relationship with Jungle Jane (sic)'.

SUPER ALFRED CHICKEN

Year | 1994
Publisher | Mindscape
Developer | Twilight Games

THIS IS THE sequel to Alfred Chicken, which was released on the NES, Game Boy and Amiga. The evil Meka Chickens have kidnapped a bunch of eggs and plan to turn them into a Meka Chicken Army. Off heads Alfred through 21 levels of platforming shenanigans as he tries to rescue his eggy chums. Like its predecessor, Super Alfred Chicken has a rather floaty feel to it, but that's what happens when you're playing as a bird. He's a rather fragile hero so even the slightest brush against an enemy will cause him to explode in a shower of feathers. What he does have, however, is the ability to dive-bomb into enemies by jumping up and slamming his beak downwards, like a sort of controllable ground pound. ■

FACT

Following the game's product manager running for election as the Alfred Chicken Party in Dorset, Alfred Chicken was cited in the UK Parliament as an example of how comedy parties mean candidates should get more signatures in order to run.

THE SUPER AQUATIC GAMES STARRING THE AQUABATS

Year | 1993
Publisher | Seika Corporation
Developer | Millennium Interactive

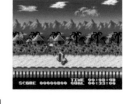

THIS MULTI-EVENT SPORTS game is a spin-off of the James Pond series, even though he isn't mentioned anywhere on the US version's packaging (the game was renamed James Pond's Crazy Sports in Europe). It consists of eight comical events, each starring a different member of the Aquabats, James Pond's athletics squad. Three of them – the 100m Splash, the Bouncy Castle and Shell Shooting – star Pond himself, while two of them – the Hop, Skip and Jump and the Leap Frog event – feature renowned sprinter F-fortesque Frog. Then there's the Tour de Grass cycling with Mark the Shark, Feeding Time with Freddie Starfish and Kipper Watching with Ceceelia the Seal. It's all deadly serious stuff, as you can imagine. ■

FACT

The training mode is called James Ponda's Workout, a reference to the hugely successful exercise video *Jane Fonda's Workout*.

SUPER BASEBALL 2020

Year | 1993
Publisher | Tradewest
Developer | Monolith Corporation

SUPER BASEBALL 2020 started life as a Neo Geo game before being ported to other systems. It's a futuristic baseball game set in the distant year 2020, where teams can consist of men, women and robots. The single stadium, the Cyber Egg, contains a number of changes that affect the game's rules: for example, you can only get a home run by hitting the ball right down the middle, otherwise it'll hit a glass roof and bounce back onto the field. Another new addition is the power-up system: as you play you earn money for strikeouts, hits and the like. This money can then be spent on powering up players to give them stronger pitches or swings. Safe to say it doesn't have the MLB licence. ■

FACT

Teams in the game include the likes of the American Dreams, Tokyo Samurais, Taiwan Megapowers and two all-female teams, the Battle Angels and Tropical Girls.

SUPER BASEBALL SIMULATOR 1.000

Year | 1991
Publisher | Culture Brain
Developer | Culture Brain

THE SECOND GAME in the Baseball Simulator series (following the original Baseball Simulator 1.000 on the NES), this follows the same general idea as its predecessor. There are 12 'normal' teams split into Atlantic and Northern leagues, as well as the six-team Ultra League where teams can trigger a series of power-ups to try and affect the outcome of the game. There are 39 Ultra moves in the game: 15 Ultra Batting techniques (like giving the ball three shadows to make it harder to catch), 20 Ultra Pitches (like the Stopper Ball, which freezes in the air right before it reaches the batter) and four Ultra Fielding moves (like the Super Catch, which can catch any ball no matter what weird power has been applied). ■

FACT

The game has a Manager mode, where you can choose to sit back and tell your pitcher and batters what plays you want them to attempt instead of trying pull them off for yourself.

SUPER BASES LOADED

Year	1991
Publisher	Jaleco
Developer	Tose

 ✔ ✗

THE BASES LOADED series was a regular fixture on the NES and it was no different after the jump to 16-bit. The first Super Bases Loaded launched at around the same time as Bases Loaded 3 hit the NES and as such it shared the 8-bit game's controversial feature that year: the search for a perfect game. Rather than having a season mode or even exhibition matches, there's one single-player mode in which you choose one of the 12 fictional teams (the Texas Tornados, Hawaii Islanders and so on) and play through a series of games where you start with 100 points and have points removed or added based on how you play. The aim is to reach a 'level 5' difficulty team and finish with a perfect score. ■

FACT

The ball physics can be a little strange: if a player bunts the ball it can sometimes pop up so slowly that the pitcher himself can run over to the home plate and catch it for an out.

SUPER BASES LOADED 2

Year	1994
Publisher	Jaleco
Developer	Tose

 ✔ ✗

THE NEXT SUPER Bases Loaded game ditched the 'perfect game' gimmick and resorted back to the usual options of a regular season, exhibition game or all-star game. There are 14 teams to choose from, plus four more teams from Urbana, Rockford, Peoria and Aurora who can be customised with new team and player names. The most interesting element of the game is its 3D infield play. Batting and pitching use the standard 'behind the batter' camera viewpoint, but when you hit the ball there's no cut to a different view: instead, the player gets a Mode 7 style 3D viewpoint as the camera follows the ball. It's only when you hit a long ball into the outfield that the camera switches to a more traditional zoomed out view. ■

FACT

Although the NES Bases Loaded games were based on the Japanese Moreo!! sports games, that isn't the case with the SNES ones. The Japanese equivalent of Super Bases Loaded 2 was fittingly called Super 3D Baseball.

SUPER BASES LOADED 3: LICENSE TO STEAL

Year	1995
Publisher	Jaleco
Developer	Tose

✔ ✗

THE SEVENTH BASES Loaded game (and the final one to be developed by studio-for-hire Tose) finally managed to get something its six predecessors didn't have: real player names. Yes, that strange title isn't just a really bad pun, it also refers to the fact that the game contains the MLBPA licence, meaning all 700 or so player names are finally real (even if the teams still don't have official logos). The game also boasts an official partnership with STATS Inc, the Chicago-based sports data and analytics company, which meant each player had their fair share of statistical information. Like the first Super Bases Loaded, the camera when pitching and batting is unusual in that it looks over the pitcher's shoulder rather than behind home plate. ■

FACT

STATS was formed in 1981 and stood for Sports Team Analysis and Tracking Systems. The company merged with Perform Content in 2019 and was renamed Stats Perform.

SUPER BATTER UP

Year	1992
Publisher	Namco
Developer	Namco

 ✔ ✗

NAMCO'S FAMISTA (FAMILY Stadium) series of baseball game has been going in Japan for over three decades, but only a handful have been localised for the west. Super Batter Up is the American version of Super Famista, the 13th(!) game in the series. Namco went the extra mile and doled out for the MLBPA licence for this one, meaning all the player names are correct as of the 1991 MLB season. While the Japanese version used 'chibi' players (with big heads), the sprites in Super Batter Up were modified to make them look a little more realistic. Which sort of goes out the window when you score a home run and are rewarded with the sight of Pac-Man flying past on a rocket. ■

FACT

The 37th Famista game was Pro Baseball: Famista Evolution on the Switch, released in 2018. It comes with a free copy of Super Famista Retro 2018, which is essentially Super Batter Up with modern (Japanese) rosters.

SUPER BATTLESHIP

Year	1993	
Publisher	Mindscape	
Developer	World Builders Synergistic	

GAMES OF CHANCE tend not to work well in a video game format, and it seems Mindscape realised this with Super Battleship. Granted, the game does have the option to play the traditional board game version of Battleship – where you try to sink your opponent's ships by guessing spaces on a grid and hoping you get a hit – but it can only be played against the CPU, which makes things even more random. Making up for it, then, is the titular Super Battleship mode, which ditches the board game format and instead offers a turn-based tactical game consisting of 16 missions that have you commanding various ships and firing at opponents while resupplying, assigning crewmen to repair damage and the like. ■

FACT

Although versions of Battleship are said to date back to 1890, the first commercial version was Salvo, which was published in 1931 in the US. The Milton Bradley version of Battleship we know today made its debut in 1967.

SUPER BATTLETANK: WAR IN THE GULF

Year	1992	
Publisher	Absolute Entertainment	
Developer	Imagineering	

EMBLAZONED WITH THE name of designer Garry Kitchen, Super Battletank puts you inside an M1A1 Abrams battle tank during Operation Desert Storm and tasks you with carrying out 10 increasingly difficult missions, all of which are basically variations on 'go and blow up some stuff'. Your targets include the likes of Soviet-made Mi-24 HIND helicopters, T-62 tanks and SCUD launchers, and missions can take place in broad daylight or under cover of night. Your tank is armed with four types of artillery: 7.62mm machine guns (which have infinite ammo but can overheat), 120mm cannons (which require you to aim your turret), a limited number of laser-guided 'fire and forget' shells, and a smoke screen which lets you escape during hairy moments. ■

FACT

Garry Kitchen was responsible for the likes of Keystone Kapers, The Simpsons: Bart vs the Space Mutants and the SNES version of Home Alone.

SUPER BATTLETANK 2

Year	1994	
Publisher	Absolute Entertainment	
Developer	Absolute Entertainment	

THE SEQUEL TO Super Battletank may have removed Garry Kitchen's name from the box but it was still more of the same, with emphasis on the 'more'. This time you're inside the improved M1A2 Abrams battle tank, with 16 more missions facing you in the Middle East (it isn't based on the Gulf War this time, just an unnamed conflict). There's a wider range of enemies facing you this time, with tanks, jeeps, infantrymen and armoured personnel carriers among your targets. On occasion you'll now get to leave the safety of inside the tank and climb top-side to take on enemy planes with the tank's mounted Phalanx machine gun: these sections are little more than elaborate shooting galleries, but fun ones nonetheless. ■

FACT

The M1A2 was an advanced version of the M1A1 which included a thermal viewer, weapon station, position navigation equipment, and an improved fire control system.

SUPER BLACK BASS

Year	1993	
Publisher	Hot-B	
Developer	Starfish	

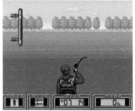

TOKYO-BASED PUBLISHER HOT-B released two fishing games on the NES: The Black Bass and The Blue Marlin. As you'd probably imagine, Super Black Bass is the sequel to the latter, and once again has you trying to be the best bass fisherman in the world. Starting off at your local amateur tournament, success there will take you onto the Amateur Bass Championship, the Pro Bass Circuit and finally the Super Bass Championship. There are eight different types of lure ranging from furry sinkers to frogs and you can select their colour too. This does have an impact: using a red lure on a foggy or cloudy day will work better because the fish will be able to notice it easier, for example. ■

FACT

The biggest largemouth bass ever caught was in 1932 when George Perry caught a fis weighing 22 pounds and 4 ounc at Lake Montgomery in Georgic That's more than two times heavier than a gallon of paint.

SUPER BOMBERMAN

Year	1993
Publisher	Hudson Soft
Developer	Produce!

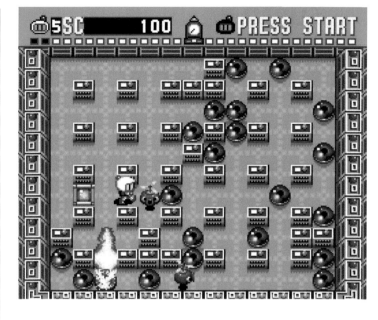

THE DEBUT OF Bomberman on the SNES was notable for a number of reasons, both trivial and important. It was the first time the series was actually called Bomberman in Europe, where it had until then been known as Dynablaster. More crucially, though, it was the first SNES game to support four players rather than the typical two. As with most main games in the series, Super Bomberman is split into two distinct modes: Normal Game and Battle Game. The former can be played alone or in co-op with a second player and has Bomberman working his way through 48 stages across six worlds, blowing up enemies in order to access the exit on each stage and occasionally taking on large boss enemies who take a number of well-placed bombs to defeat. It's the Battle Game that truly defines Bomberman, however, and the Super Bomberman battles were at the time considered to be among the best. There are 12 different battle arenas to choose from, some of which are simply themed (like the Western Zone) while others have mechanics that affect gameplay (like the Belt Zone, which is full of conveyor belts that can move bombs around the stage). Conscious that the best way to play multiplayer Bomberman is with as many players as possible, Hudson Soft released a special Party Pak version of the game which came bundled with the Super Multitap, a device allowing up to five people to play together (although only four are supported here). ■

FACT

Hudson Soft released the Super Multitap 2 later in the SNES's life, to cater for those who didn't buy Super Bomberman but still wanted to play games that supported four players. This second multitap was in the shape of Bomberman's head.

SUPER BOMBERMAN 2

Year	1994
Publisher	Hudson Soft
Developer	Produce!

THE SECOND SUPER Bomberman had nailed things the first time around so there was little reason to completely revolutionise anything this time. As such, players were treated to the four-player Battle mode again, albeit this time with 10 new stages: one covers the floor with ice, whereas another includes a trench going around the middle of the screen that ignites when it's hit with a blast. The only other major addition to Battle mode is the Gold Bomber mechanic, which colours the winner of the last round gold and lets them start off the next round with a power-up. Meanwhile, the Normal Game offers a further 40 stages divided across five worlds, with Bomberman trying to fight his way out of a prison to face the Magnet Bomber. ■

FACT

Super Bomberman 2 was so addictive that industry magazine *Edge* once wrote about development studios round the world downing tools every lunchtime to play it, coining the phrase 'Bomb o'clock'.

SUPER BOMBERMAN 3

Year	1995
Publisher	Hudson Soft
Developer	Hudson Soft

AMERICA MAY HAVE been done with Super Bomberman after two games, but Europe was given a third. The game's core remained the same: players could choose between another Normal Mode made up of six worlds, and another Battle Mode with 10 new arenas. The big addition here for SNES players though was the introduction of Louies, kangaroo-like helpers that Bomberman could ride for extra abilities. The green Louie can dash, for example, while the pink one can jump over blocks. The blue and yellow ones can kick bombs and blocks respectively, while the brown one can create a line of bombs. The multiplayer mode also introduced a bunch of different Bomberman characters from around the world, like Mexican Bomber, Bomber Cossack and Bomber Chun. ■

FACT

Super Bomberman 3 may have been the last in the series to get a western release, but that wasn't the end: Super Bomberman 4 and Super Bomberman 5 were released in Japan.

SUPER BONK

Year	1994
Publisher	Hudson Soft
Developer	AI Company

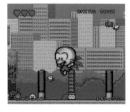

BONK (OTHERWISE KNOWN as PC Kid in Japan and BC Kid in Europe) used to be the mascot of sorts for NEC's TurboGrafx-16 console. The general consensus was that Mario was Nintendo, Sonic was Sega and Bonk was TurboGrafx. NEC's system was always a distant third, however, so when it discontinued the TurboGrafx in 1994 Bonk made the jump to the SNES. Super Bonk is the fourth game in the series, then, and once again has Bonk headbutting his way through a bunch of weird and wonderful stages, ranging from an amusement park to a large dinosaur's body. Power-ups include coloured candy that make Bonk tiny or enormous, and meat, which turns Bonk into a strange large-eyebrowed chap or a big monster depending on the type. ■

FACT

Hudson Soft was planning on resurrecting Bonk in 2011 with Bonk: Brink of Extinction on the PS3, Xbox 360 and Wii. It was about a comet colliding with the Earth, but Hudson cancelled the game after the 2011 earthquake and tsunami in Japan.

SUPER BOWLING

Year	1992
Publisher	Technos Japan
Developer	KID

THERE AREN'T MANY games that are endorsed by the Young American Bowling Alliance. In fairness, though, that would only be a useful endorsement for a bowling game. But hey, Super Bowling is a bowling game, and it's got that very endorsement, so that's nice. There are four teenage characters to choose from: two boys (all-rounder Pete 'Pins' Peterson and powerful Mars 'Muscles' Maxwell) and two girls (curve specialist Suzi 'Spinner' Spencer and accuracy champ Robin 'Red' Randall). As well as standard bowling you can also take part in Golf Bowling, where you're given nine different set-ups with certain pins laid out in a specific formation on the alley and you have to clear them in as few shots as possible. It supports up to four players. ■

FACT

One for the 'they wouldn't get away with that today' file: the description of Spinner Spencer on the back of the box says she's got 'great curves, on and off the lanes'.

SUPER BUSTER BROS

Year	1992
Publisher	Capcom
Developer	Capcom

ALSO KNOWN AS Super Pang, Super Buster Bros is the sequel to the original Pang / Buster Bros, which hit the arcades in 1989 before being ported to various home computers. The aim is exactly the same here: you have to use your harpoon gun to shoot a series of large bubbles, which have a habit of turning into two smaller bubbles when they pop. This adds an element of strategy and accuracy to the mix, as it's usually recommended to pop smaller bubbles before taking out more of the larger ones and essentially filling the screen with small ones. There are two modes: Arcade mode is your typical helping of separate levels, while Panic mode has you dealing with 99 waves of bubbles. ■

FACT

This is not to be confused with Super Pang and Super Pang II on the NES: these were unlicensed games released by Tawianese company Sachen and had nothing to do with the official series.

SUPER CAESARS PALACE

Year	1993
Publisher	Virgin Interactive
Developer	Illusion Softworks

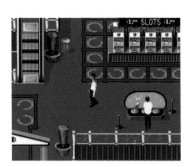

THE SEQUEL TO Virgin's Caesars Palace for the NES, Game Boy and Game Gear. Once again you play as a man arriving at Caesars Palace with just three things: a dream, a gambler's mind and $2,000 in chips. The aim is to take those chips and turn them into... well, more chips. There are eight games on offer here: Blackjack, Red Dog, Roulette, Craps, Video Power, Slots, Keno and Horse Racing. Do well enough and you'll be invited to the VIP section where the stakes are higher but so are the rewards. If that isn't enough reckless money-risking for you, you can also go to the ATM and buy some scratchcards for $100 each: this may very well be the first ever example of a video game loot box. ■

FACT

Daredevil Evel Knievel tried to jump the fountains at Caesars Palace in 1967. He fell short and crashed, suffering a crushed pelvis, crushed femur, a concussion and fractures to his hip, wrist and both ankles.

SUPER CASTLEVANIA IV

Year	1991
Publisher	Konami
Developer	Konami

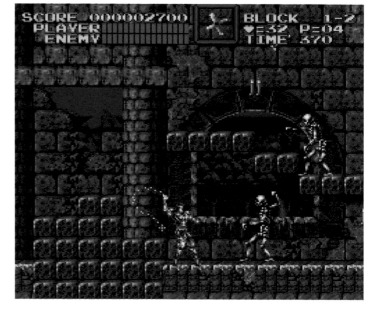

THE CASTLEVANIA SERIES had already endured its fair share of highs and lows before it made it to the SNES. The first game launched to much acclaim but was followed by the divisive Simon's Quest, a sequel that tried to mix up the formula but instead messed it up according to some. This was rectified with Castlevania III: Dracula's Curse, but the terrible arcade spin-off Haunted Castle showed that Konami was still very much hit-and-miss when it came to this franchise. Taking the various Game Boy games into account too, Super Castlevania IV was actually the eighth unique Castlevania game in just five years, but arguably the most important: could Konami whip up a memorable adventure for the series' 16-bit debut, or would it be proof that Simon Belmont's vampire-slaying days were over? Thankfully, the result turned out to be the former, and then some.

Super Castlevania IV is less a true sequel, and more a reimagining of the NES original. The plot is the same: the year is 1691 and the evil Count Dracula has risen after a 100-year slumber, so it's up to Simon Belmont, the latest in the bloodline of the vampire-killing Belmont clan, to head to Dracula's castle and see if his trusty whip can't send old Drac packing, for good this time. While it's undoubtedly a retelling of the first game's events, then – the Japanese title is simply Akumajou Dracula, which was the same as that of the original game – that doesn't mean it's

FACT

The bosses at the end of level 6 are a pair of dancing spectres. The manual refers to them as Paula Abghoul and Fred Askcare, an obvious reference to Paula Abdul and Fred Astaire.

a straight remake: it's a very different game.

As before, Simon's whip is his main form of attack. This time, however, he can whip it in eight different directions rather than simply left or right. This makes hitting higher and lower enemies far easier than it was in the NES games, and generally makes combat more satisfying. The whip can also now be used to attach to grapple points so Simon can jump over larger gaps, and sub-weapons like axes and crosses can still be used, though they're now assigned to a specific button (you used to have to hold Up on the D-pad but that's obviously now used for aiming the whip).

The Castlevania series hadn't yet reached the point in its life where it introduced the ability to explore large areas in a non-linear way: although these days it's credited for being half of the inspiration for the Metroidvania genre, it wouldn't be until 1997's Symphony of the Night that open-ended exploration would come into play. As such, Super Castlevania IV is a linear journey, but this gives Konami plenty of opportunities for set-pieces designed to make the most of the SNES hardware. This includes one of the game's most memorable sections: the rotating room (where you use the grapple points to swing in place while the stage rotates around you) which then leads to a tunnel-like room, where Mode 7 kicks in and makes the background look like you're in a huge rotating cylinder. An iconic moment in the SNES's history. ■

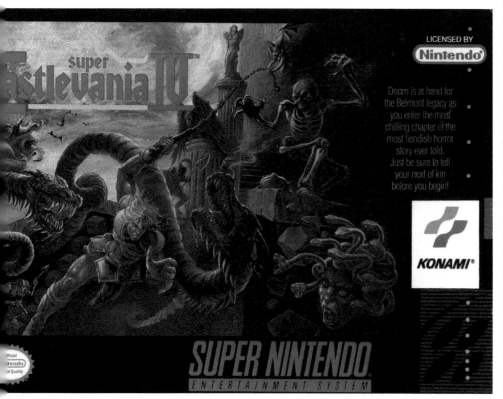

SUPER CHASE HQ

Year	1993
Publisher	Taito
Developer	Taito

THE ORIGINAL CHASE HQ was an arcade racing game with a difference: instead of simply trying to reach checkpoints before your time ran out, you were a police officer whose mission was to chase down a bunch of criminals and ram their car until it pulled over (before your time ran out, of course). Super Chase HQ follows a similar vein, but does make one notable change: instead of playing from a third-person viewpoint as in the arcade original, you play with a first-person in-car view. This makes it more like the third arcade game in the series, Super Chase: Criminal Termination, which also has a first-person view and has a few of the other features seen here, like enemies throwing and shooting things at you. ■

FACT

London-based '90s alternative dance group Saint Etienne recorded a demo song called *Chase HQ* which used samples from the game. It was eventually included in the 2009 deluxe re-release of their first album *Foxbase Alpha*.

SUPER CONFLICT

Year	1993
Publisher	Vic Tokai
Developer	Vic Tokai

SIMILAR TO ITS NES predecessor Conflict, this is a turn-based strategy game where two players go to war as the Red and Blue forces. The goal here isn't to defeat all of your opponent's troops, because war isn't like that: instead, you have to destroy your key target – a tank called the Flag Unit – before they destroy yours. There are five different skill levels to choose from, and in the fifth a second unit called the Flag Ship is added, with the game won when a team destroys either of them (meaning more tactical thinking is needed to defend both at once). Should you not have a fellow warmonger around, there's also a single-player mode where the player controls the Blue forces across 55 different scenarios. ■

FACT

Although it's never made clear who each side represents the fact the Blue forces use real life American fighters, bombers helicopters and tanks while the Red forces use Russian ones should be a heavy hint.

SUPER DANY

Year	1994
Publisher	Virgin Interactive
Developer	Cryo Interactive

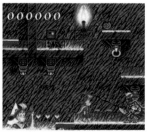

WHEN IT COMES to tie-ins, few are as niche as Super Dany. This French-only release is based on Dany, the one-time mascot for Paris-based food corporation Danone (and if you know their TV commercial jingle, you just sang it in your head without thinking). Dany and his friends are watching television together when all of a sudden they're sucked into the screen. One of their chums, Norbert, is kidnapped by the evil Doctor TV, so it's up to Dany and his other pals Mathilda and Marius to rescue him. Super Dany is a platformer where each character has their own abilities. Dany can fire a laser to defeat his enemies, while Marius can crawl into tight gaps and Mathilda can run faster than the others. ■

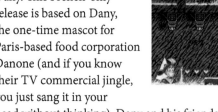

FACT

Dany is the name of a chocolate mousse product sold by Danone to this day. He and his pals used to appear in TV commercials and on the packaging in the early '90s.

SUPER DOUBLE DRAGON

Year	1992
Publisher	Tradewest
Developer	Technos Japan

THIS IS THE fourth game in the Double Dragon series (which must really annoy people who like nice numbered sequences, since this goes 1, 2, 3, Super, 5). This time the story revolves around Marian, a cop who's been investigating narcotics crime while also working as a part-time assistant at Billy and Jimmy Lee's gym. After planning to infiltrate the shady Black Shadow Warriors mob, Marian disappears, so Billy and Jimmy team up to try and find out what happened to her. The big addition to the gameplay in this fourth instalment is the new block button, which is used to nullify enemy attacks. When timed right it can also put your opponent in an armlock, acting as a counter of sorts. ■

FACT

According to lead designer Muneki Ebinuma, there were supposed to be cutscenes and a full ending sequence but they were cut due to time constraints. This means Marian never actually appears in the game.

SUPER DROPZONE

Year | 1995
Publisher | Psygnosis
Developer | Eurocom

THE ORIGINAL DROPZONE was designed by legendary British game programmer Archer Maclean and released in 1984. Maclean returned more than a decade later to create this SNES sequel, which feels more like an enhanced remake at times than a fully-fledged follow-up. As with its predecessor, Super Dropzone takes place in a series of scrolling, looping stages where the player, flying around in a jetpack, must destroy the waves of aliens descending on the surface of the moon while at the same time defending the 10 scientists running around. It's a bit like Defender in this sense, except here you have to actually collect the scientists and take them to a base. This SNES successor adds power-ups and boss battles to the mix. ■

SUPER EARTH DEFENSE FORCE

Year | 1992
Publisher | Jaleco
Developer | Jaleco

DON'T CONFUSE THIS with the other Earth Defense Force, which is a series of brilliant third-person action games where you gun down hordes of enormous bugs. This is a different Earth Defense Force, and it's a standard shoot 'em up where you pilot a ship called the XA-1. A mysterious organisation called AGYMA has started attacking small, distant planets and word through the spacevine is that they're planning to take on Earth next. As part of the (super) Earth Defense Force, you have to destroy the home bases AGYMA has already set up on Earth, in order to stop their plans. There are six stages and you have eight weapons to choose from, but you can only switch between them between stages or when you die. ■

SUPER GHOULS 'N GHOSTS

Year | 1991
Publisher | Capcom
Developer | Capcom

THE THIRD GAME in the Ghosts 'n Goblins series (after Ghosts 'n Goblins and Ghouls 'n Ghosts), Super Ghouls 'n Ghosts follows the adventures of the gallant knight Arthur as he once again tries to rescue Princess Guinevere from an evil power. This time the nasty sod in question is Emperor Sardius, who's looking for the Goddess's Bracelet weapon because it's the only thing that can beat him, and if he can get hold of it then he'll essentially be immortal. Like its predecessors, Super Ghouls 'n Ghosts is an exceptionally difficult game (not least because of the magician who occasionally appears and turns you into a duck or a baby), though this time you have the ability to double-jump, which helps matters a little. You can now upgrade your armour too: bronze armour protects you from one hit and lets you use the special 'weapons of enchantment', which are more powerful versions of the existing weapons. Gold armour, meanwhile, does the same but also gives you the ability to use magic. While these all help with the game's difficulty, it's still one hell of a challenge, especially when you consider that it shares another feature with its predecessors: you have to beat the game twice. After defeating Sardius for the first time, Princess Guinevere will tell you where she's hidden the Goddess's Bracelet. This means you have to play through the game again with the Bracelet in tow and face Sardius for a second battle, where this time you can destroy him once and for all. ■

SUPER GOAL! 2

Year	1994
Publisher	Jaleco
Developer	Tose

READY TO BE confused? The first Goal! on the SNES was simply known as Goal! in America and Super Goal! in Europe. This sequel was only released in America, so it should be called Goal! 2, but in reality it's called Super Goal! 2, even though there was never a Super Goal! in that region in the first place. Regardless, this is another Jaleco football game, offering 24 international teams (including some odd inclusions not usually associated with football's elite, such as Latvia). There are four stadiums to choose from: two sensible ones set in Milan and Tokyo, as well as two oddly named ones called Rainbow Stadium (which doesn't have a rainbow, just a wet pitch) and Snowman Stadium (which doesn't have snowmen, just snow on the grass). ∎

FACT

The Japanese version is called Takeda Nobuhiro's Super Cup Soccer, and lets you play with or against legendary Japanese striker Nobuhiro, who scored 142 goals in 357 J-League appearances.

SUPER GODZILLA

Year	1994
Publisher	Toho
Developer	Toho

THIS INTERESTING TAKE on the Godzilla franchise is part maze game, part fighting game. A series of monsters have started appearing at various Japanese locations, so the military decide to summon Godzilla to defeat them. Rather than hoping he'll get the job done on his own this time, they use a transmitter to control Godzilla, guiding him through the streets. Part of the game, then, has you exploring a map of the city – while trying not to crash through buildings and doing your best to avoid tanks firing at you – until you reach your opponent, at which point you're presented with a side-on fighting game, albeit one where you have to wait until the enemy monster's fighting spirit is low before attacking. ∎

FACT

The final boss sees Super Godzilla (he gets injected with a super serum, see) facing off against Bagan. This is interesting because Bagan was planned for several Godzilla movies but ultimately never featured in any.

SUPER HIGH IMPACT

Year	1993
Publisher	Acclaim
Developer	Iguana Entertainment

HIGH IMPACT FOOTBALL was a successful enough arcade game to warrant a sequel, and this time the sequel got a home port too. Given its coin-op roots, it should come as no surprise that Super High Impact is all about big tackles and fast-paced action rather than deep strategy. Indeed, there are only around 30 plays in the game, many of which are long bombs, so you're not going to be poring over the playbooks in this one for too long. There are 16 teams to choose from, none of which have official team or player names. In fact, the game has some odd choices for teams: there are still obvious ones like Miami and New York, but you've got the likes of Africa and 'Europa' too. ∎

FACT

One of the teams in the game is simply called LA. Two years later, both LA teams in the NFL (the Rams and the Raiders) relocated to St Louis and Oakland respectively. LA didn't have a team until 2016 when the Rams returned.

SUPER ICE HOCKEY

Year	1994
Publisher	Sunsoft
Developer	Opera House

IT'S RATHER ODD to think that a game based on a sport that's massive in North America would be denied a launch there, but that's the case with Super Ice Hockey, which was originally developed and published in Japan and then given a European launch, with not a sniff for US or Canadian players. It's a reasonably entertaining game, too: nothing that was going to make EA's NHL games quiver in their skates but fun nonetheless. Rather than focusing on teams from the NHL or any other league, Super Ice Hockey instead revolves around international teams, with 16 on offer. The main mode is Olympic mode, where teams are split into two leagues with the best qualifying for the knockout stages. ∎

FACT

The 1994 Men's Ice Hockey World Championships were won by Canada, who beat Finland in a shootout to win gold for the first time since 1961. This may seem trivial but my Canadian wife would kill me if I didn't mention it.

SUPER INTERNATIONAL CRICKET

Year	1994
Publisher	Nintendo
Developer	Beam Software

THE ORIGINAL INTERNATIONAL Cricket on the NES was one of two games released as a collaboration with Australian NES distributor Mattel and Melbourne Studio Beam Software to try to get more Australians interested in the system, with Beam and Nintendo once again teaming up with another adaptation of one of Australia's most loved sports. Super International Cricket attempted to do the same with the SNES. Players can take part in a fast match, a one-day match, a test match or a 'world series'. There are eight teams to choose from – Australia, England, India, New Zealand, Pakistan, South Africa, Sri Lanka and the West Indies – although none of them have real player names. Bad luck, then, Brian Lara fans. ◼

FACT

The longest cricket match ever took place in 1939, where South Africa and England played for 43 hours and 16 minutes.

SUPER JAMES POND

Year	1993
Publisher	American Softworks
Developer	American Softworks

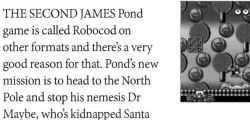

THE SECOND JAMES Pond game is called Robocod on other formats and there's a very good reason for that. Pond's new mission is to head to the North Pole and stop his nemesis Dr Maybe, who's kidnapped Santa and is holding his penguin friends hostage. There's just one problem with this mission: James is a fish. The first James Pond game took place entirely underwater, but this one is based almost exclusively on land. The solution? A fancy robotic suit which gives James special abilities. Not only does it let him breathe and run around on land, he can also pull himself into the suit and drop onto enemies from a height, or use the suit's telescopic abilities to stretch to ridiculous lengths, letting him grab high items and ledges. ◼

FACT

The reason Santa's pals are penguins is that the game had a sponsorship for Penguin chocolate biscuits. The Amiga version was more blatant, with an ad during the intro, but you can still see some Penguin wrappers in the candy stage on the SNES.

SUPER MARIO ALL-STARS

Year	1993
Publisher	Nintendo
Developer	Nintendo EAD

WHAT DO YOU do when you've already delivered one of the greatest Super Mario adventures ever created in Super Mario World but the sequel's still a number of years away and fans are eagerly anticipating more? Well, you need to give those fans at least something. That something came in the form of Super Mario All-Stars, an idea by Shigeru Miyamoto to release a compilation of Mario's NES adventures all in one cartridge. Simply bundling them all onto a cart and punting them onto shelves would have probably gotten the job done – let's face it, it's Mario – but Miyamoto and the EAD team wanted to do more to make it a worthwhile purchase for those who'd already bought the games in the past. The first and most obvious move was to use the extra power of the SNES to remaster each game. No longer restricted by palette or memory, the team was able to create versions of Super Mario

FACT

Super Mario All-Stars was perhaps a bit less exciting for Japanese gamers, because they already had access to all four games. They got the veggie version of Super Mario Bros 2 in 1992 under the new name Super Mario USA.

Bros, Super Mario Bros 2 and Super Mario Bros 3 that had a more impressive 16-bit look. Arguably the biggest selling point, however, was the addition of the Japanese version of Super Mario Bros 2, the Famicom Disk System game that Nintendo's head honchos had previously decided was too difficult for American audiences (and led to the western, veggie-throwing version of Super Mario Bros 2 instead). This version, dubbed The Lost Levels, was available to play in the west for the first time ever, offering something new even to those who'd played the other three titles to death on the NES. ◼

SUPER MARIO KART

Year	1992
Publisher	Nintendo
Developer	Nintendo

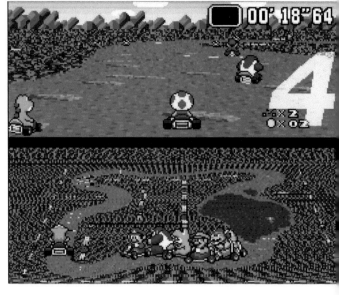

IT'S FUNNY HOW a single decision can take a game that could have been fun but ultimately forgettable, and instead make it something so iconic it created an entire genre. After finishing work on F-Zero, Nintendo's EAD team wanted to see if they could incorporate its Mode 7 racing into a split-screen view so two players could race together. They couldn't just turn the same game multiplayer, though, because as director Hideko Konno recalled in a chat with Satoru Iwata in 2008: 'With more than one player, it would have been impossible to illustrate the high speeds of F-Zero.' Looking for something with a slower pace, the team started working on a game that used go-karts instead. Since go-karts have visible drivers, they added a chap wearing overalls, and started prototyping the game. They added oil cans that could be dropped behind you, making opponents spill, they tried a basic battle mode where you had to pop your opponent's balloons and so on. About four months into development, someone jokingly decided to see what it would look like if Mario was in one of the karts. With that one decision, a genre was born.

Mario was joined by other characters from the series: Luigi, Princess Toadstool, Toad, Yoshi, Bowser, a Koopa Troopa and Donkey Kong Jr. The team started creating tracks that looked like they belonged in the Mario universe, with a heavy focus on stages from the recently completed Super Mario World:

FACT

If you win a cup with Peach she juggles her bottle of champagne in the air. If this seems odd, that's because it's a substitute animation: in the Japanese version, she takes huge drinks from the bottle and her cheeks turn red. Bowser's celebration was similarly censored.

Bowser's castle, a ghost house, Vanilla Lake, Choco(late) Island. Meanwhile, those oil cans used in the prototype were replaced with banana skins, and a bunch of other weapons were introduced. A couple of these – a feather that let you jump to reach shortcuts, a Boo that let you steal your opponent's power-up and turn invisible – were fun enough, but the rest formed a foundation that essentially laid out the blueprint for hundreds of karting games to follow. The green shell, a missile that fired straight (though there was a slight homing element to it here). The red shell, a more advanced missile that homed right in on the racer ahead of you. The mushroom, which gave you a speed boost. The lightning bolt, which affected every other racer on the track (making them smaller in this instance). The star, which sped you up and made you invincible for a while. Play any karting game and you're practically guaranteed to find weapons that may look aesthetically different to these ones, but behave in exactly the same way. With the exception of the blue shell, which would arrive in the sequel, Nintendo had nailed it the first time around.

Three decades later, there have been countless examples of games that take a licensed property, put its characters in karts and give them a bunch of wacky power-ups. It's been done with Sonic, Crash Bandicoot Star Wars, Hello Kitty, M&Ms, Nickelodeon, even Mortal Kombat. None of these would have existed had someone not suggested: 'Hey, why don't we make that guy Mario?' ∎

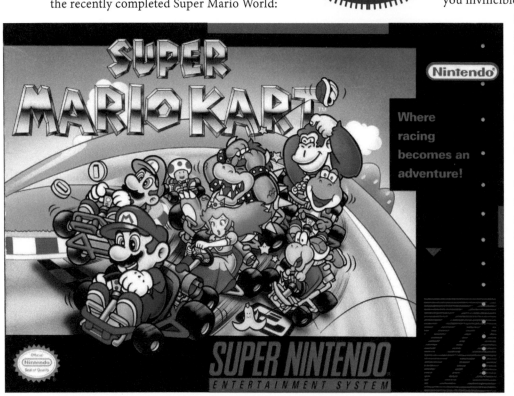

SUPER MARIO RPG: LEGEND OF THE SEVEN STARS

Year	1996	
Publisher	Nintendo	
Developer	Square	

AROUND THE BEGINNING of 1994, some executives from Square and Nintendo had a business meeting to discuss future products. Square's Final Fantasy games and other RPGs were an enormous success in Japan (second only to Enix's Dragon Quest in terms of popularity), but they'd failed to see anything but a niche following in the west: they needed a new RPG series or character that would appeal enough to make a wider audience decide to try the genre for the first time. Meanwhile, Nintendo was looking for new things to do with Mario, and Shigeru Miyamoto had expressed a desire to see him in an RPG. During the meeting the two complications clicked and the decision was made to combine each company's biggest asset – Mario and RPGs – to see what the results would be.

The answer was the inventively titled Super Mario RPG, a new adventure that lets players explore the Mushroom Kingdom and beyond from a new perspective. Literally, in this case: the game is played with an isometric viewpoint. It opens like so many other Mario games do – with Princess Toadstool being kidnapped by Bowser and Mario heading off to rescue her – but the fact that your 'final battle' against Bowser occurs five minutes in should suggest to you that maybe things are going to go differently this time. Sure enough, as the fight comes to

FACT

Super Mario RPG includes cameos from both Link and Samus, who can both be found lying in beds. Link plays the Zelda 'secret' theme when you approach him, while Samus says she's resting up for her fight with Mother Brain.

an end, a giant sword called Exor plunges into Bowser's castle, sending Mario, the Princess and Bowser flying in different directions. When Mario heads back to the castle he's informed that Exor is a member of the Smithy gang, a group of living weapons owned by an evil mechanical creature called Smithy who plans on taking over the world. So begins a quest to find Smithy and punt his metal rump.

Although it's an RPG, there's still a slight Mario-like structure here in that your journey takes you through seven separate worlds: the Mushroom Kingdom, the oddly-named 'Pond to Pipes' (which consists of many pipe-filled regions), the self-explanatory Mole Mountains, the idyllic Seaside, the edge of the map in Land's End, the cloud-based Nimbus Land and finally Smithy's factory itself. Along the way, Mario is also joined by four other party members at various points in the story: although all four become part of your group, you can only choose two of them to fight alongside Mario in battles. Mallow is a young fluffy white character who was raised by a frog and therefore thinks he's a tadpole. Geno – who's developed a cult following over the years – is a small star who possesses a doll, Child's Play style, to take part. As well as these new characters, you also find and recruit Princess Toadstool and even Bowser to your party: the phrase 'the enemy of my enemy' has never been so apt.

It's fair to say that Super Mario RPG was loved, then, at least by those who actually got it: Europe didn't, meaning the first time PAL players could legally buy it was on the Wii Virtual Console 12 years later. ∎

SUPER MARIO WORLD

Year	1991
Publisher	Nintendo
Developer	Nintendo

THERE WAS NO more obvious launch title for the SNES than a new Mario game. Nintendo was Mario, and if the console didn't launch with its most valuable asset front and centre on day one it was going to have an uphill battle on its hands (something that proved itself years down the line with the 3DS, which launched without a Mario game and severely struggled to gain momentum for the first year or so). And so, sitting happily alongside the system in Japan, North America and Europe was the fourth Super Mario Bros game, Super Mario World.

It's a fitting title. One of Super Mario World's biggest selling points is its enormous world map, which helped put across the idea that Mario was on a journey. All the previous Mario games had individual worlds, and even though Super Mario Bros 3 improved on that by adding interactive map screens, these maps were still eight separate entities that weren't linked in any way. Super Mario World changed this by presenting Dinosaur Island as a single large landmass, one that could be explored fully. It's perfectly possible – once you've unlocked all the levels, of course – to start from where the first stage is located on the map and walk all the way to Bowser's castle without stopping, taking in the entire world along the way.

It's not like this was the only addition, of course. Mario's SNES debut also saw the first appearance of one of Nintendo's most loved characters, Yoshi. Early design documents for the original Super Mario Bros show that Shigeru Miyamoto wanted to have Mario ride a dinosaur even back then, but it just wasn't possible until the SNES arrived. It was worth the wait: Mario's dinosaur chum was an instant hit with gamers and the extra gameplay mechanics he added – eating enemies, being able to dismount him in mid-air, gaining special powers depending on the colour of shells he ate – only served to add more variety to an already idea-heavy game. Consider what else featured in Super Mario World for the first time in the series: a cape power-up that let Mario fly. P-Switches that could turn certain blocks on and off. The Koopalings, Bowser's bratty children. And, most impressive of all, a host of hidden exits leading to the secret Star Road, which in turn ultimately led to a bunch of strange levels that, when cleared, completely transformed many of the game's sprites.

It could be argued that these weren't so much rewriting the book on platformers, as simply adding extra chapters. It's true that Super Mario World wasn't quite as revolutionary as Super Mario Bros or Super Mario 64 had been for the NES and Nintendo 64 respectively. And yet, sandwiched in between these two genre-defining launch offerings is a title that constantly appears in the all-time top 5 lists of gamers of a certain vintage. It may not have reinvented the wheel, but it absolutely raised the bar in every way possible: in doing so it lodged itself deep into the hearts of most who experienced it at the time, and absolutely deserves the legendary status it enjoys. ■

FACT

A SNES test cartridge used by Nintendo repair centres was discovered to contain loads of unused Super Mario World sprites from a prototype of the game. These included the Raccoon Suit from Super Mario Bros 3 and a completely different look for small Mario.

Explore nine worlds and 96 levels of non-stop action!

SUPER MARIO WORLD 2: YOSHI'S ISLAND

Year	1995
Publisher	Nintendo
Developer	Nintendo

YOSHI'S ISLAND WAS an act of rebellion. In an interview with author Stephen Kent, Shigeru Miyamoto told the story of the first time he demonstrated an early prototype of the game to Nintendo's marketing department, and had it rejected because of how it looked. Donkey Kong Country was Nintendo's golden child at this point, and Miyamoto was told that compared to its fancy pseudo-3D graphics, Yoshi's Island looked… well, like a normal Mario game. 'Everybody else was saying that they wanted better hardware and more beautiful graphics instead of this art,' Miyamoto recalled. So, rather than bow to pressure and give Yoshi's Island a pre-rendered 3D look, he doubled down and deliberately gave the game a more cartoonish, hand-drawn look, something that looked like a child (albeit a gifted one) could have created it. Characters and backgrounds were given thick outlines, and the shading was deliberately slap-dash to make it look like it had been coloured in with marker pens. He submitted the new look to Nintendo. They approved. And ultimately, when it eventually launched, so did everyone else.

Although it's technically the fifth Super Mario Bros game, Yoshi's Island is a prequel that gives a (rather odd) backstory to Mario's origin. After a Magikoopa attacks a stork while it's trying to deliver Baby Mario and Baby Luigi to their new parents, the baby brothers are separated. Baby Luigi is kidnapped by the Magikoopa, but Baby Mario falls from the sky and lands in Yoshi's Island, where he's rescued by a bunch of Yoshis. The Yoshis decide to set up a relay system, where each Yoshi carries Baby Mario through a stage before handing him off to the next one. Making things trickier is the fact that every time a Yoshi takes a hit Baby Mario floats off in a bubble, giving the player a limited period of time to catch him before he flies off and a life is lost.

Many of Yoshi's key character traits – and those of future Yoshi games – made their debut in Yoshi's Island. The mechanic of eating enemies, excreting them as eggs and then using those eggs as missiles to throw at other enemies, obstacles or collectibles began here. The concept of exploring every nook and cranny of a level to find five clouds, 20 red coins and 30 stars was first introduced here too. Perhaps more importantly though, this is where Yoshi first got his 'flutter jump', an extra little push that gives his jump a tiny bit of oomph to help him reach further and higher platforms.

Yoshi's Island was so well-loved that what was originally supposed to be the next Super Mario Bros game ended up becoming the first Yoshi's Island game. Sequels followed on the Nintendo 64 (with pre-rendered characters, no less), DS, 3DS and Wii U, and most recently on the Switch in the shape of Yoshi's Crafted World. Each of these games has carried over the egg-throwing and flutter-jumping mechanics, but more importantly they've also carried over that first SNES game's main principle: a unique, hand-made art style that puts smiles on faces. ■

FACT

Miyamoto really wasn't big on Donkey Kong Country. In another interview with Kent, he stated that: 'Donkey Kong Country proves that players will put up with mediocre gameplay as long as the art is good.'

SUPER METROID

Year	1994
Publisher	Nintendo
Developer	Nintendo

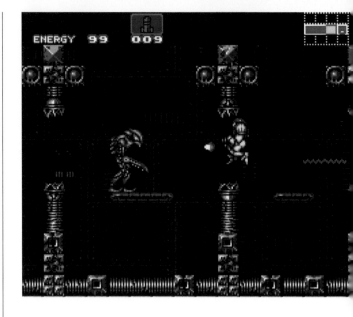

SUPER METROID MAY not have happened had Yoshio Sakamoto not visited America. Sakamoto was the co-designer of the original Metroid on the NES, but the game had only been a modest success in Japan, having sold fewer copies than his other major NES game, Kid Icarus. In the autumn of 1991, Sakamoto's boss Makoto Kano insisted that they should start working on a Metroid game for the SNES, but while Sakamoto agreed in principle, he wasn't sure it would be a success. Then, on a business trip to Nintendo of America in Seattle, Sakamoto was taken to a local mall, where he was introduced to people in every store as 'the guy who made Metroid'. Sakamoto recalled: 'Everyone knew about the game. Even a girl in a boutique who didn't look at all like a gamer reacted dramatically, explaining 'whoa!' in surprise.' Look, it was a different time: both in terms of stereotypes about female gamers and people saying 'whoa'. Convinced that Metroid absolutely did have a fanbase after all, Sakamoto returned to Japan and began working on Super Metroid with gusto. And it's a good job he did, because the result was one of the finest action games ever created.

Super Metroid follows on from the events of the Game Boy title Metroid II: Return of Samus, which ended with our hero Samus discovering a baby Metroid. After delivering the Metroid to a research station, Samus gets a distress signal saying that the station is under attack, so she heads back to find the baby being kidnapped by Ridley, the leader of the Space Pirates. Ridley escapes to Zebes, the planet from the original Metroid, so Samus chases after him and discovers that the Space Pirates have rebuilt their base there. Time to shoot loads of things until there are a lot fewer things.

FACT

Composer Kenji Yamamoto was struggling to come up with the opening theme until it suddenly hit him as he was riding his motorbike home after work. He pulled over in a parking lot, took out a tape recorder and spent 20 minutes 'belting out' the music.

As well as a few improvements to the overall gameplay – such as the ability to shoot diagonally and the introduction of many new items that would become series staples, like the Grappling Beam and Charge Beam – the biggest addition to Super Metroid was the automap. While the complex structure of the original game's non-linear world made exploring it an exercise in memorisation and patience, Super Metroid provides players with a map that fills itself in as they reach new rooms, making it much easier for them to tell at a glance where they've been and where they still have to explore.

Super Metroid's impact was more like that of Super Mario World than Super Mario Kart. On paper, it doesn't do anything truly revolutionary like create a new genre: it was the NES original that – while not the first non-linear adventure by any means – was considered the most influential game in that sub-genre, and when people use the term 'Metroidvania' the Metroid part spans all the way back to the first entry. Instead, much like Mario's SNES debut, Samus's first 16-bit adventure enhances the genre in so many ways that while it may not be the first of its era, there's a strong case for it being the best. ■

SUPER MORPH

Year | 1993
Publisher | Sony Imagesoft
Developer | Millennium Interactive

MORPH WAS AN Amiga and Atari ST game developed by Newcastle-based studio Flair Software, and this SNES port adds a few extra levels for good measure. It tells the story of Morris Rolph (Morph to his friends), a young lad who's transformed into a blob after his uncle's new invention goes wrong. Morph has to make his way through 36 stages finding the special cogs needed to repair his uncle's machine and turn him human again. The twist is that Morph can transform into four forms: a rubber ball, a cannonball, a drop of water and a cloud of gas. These let him perform various abilities such as jumping, sinking in water and passing through vents, but he's only got a limited number of transformations per stage. ■

FACT

The trick to the game is forcing transformations without using any of the limited ones you have in stock. For example, when he's a drop of water, exposing him to fire will turn Morph into a cloud without using up a transformation.

SUPER NINJA BOY

Year | 1993
Publisher | Culture Brain
Developer | Culture Brain

WHEN AN ODD man called Rub-a-Doc appeared in Chinaland's capital to sign a peace treaty, all seemed well. When Rub-a-Doc left, though, Yokan's workers started getting kidnapped, so Jack and Ryu – a pair of kung fu experts – decide to travel across Chinaland to see what's going on. Super Ninja boy is an interesting mix of role-playing games and beat 'em ups. For the most part the game looks like a standard Square or Enix RPG, where you wander around with a top-down viewpoint visiting towns, talking to people and exploring the world map. When you get into a random encounter, though, the action switches to a side-scrolling beat 'em up and you have to defeat a set number of enemies to win the fight. ■

FACT

Super Ninja Boy is actually the seventh game in the Super Chinese series of adventures. Four of its predecessors made it to the west: NES games Kung Fu Heroes and Little Ninja Brothers, and Game Boy titles Ninja Boy and Ninja Boy II.

SUPER NOVA

Year | 1993
Publisher | Taito
Developer | Taito

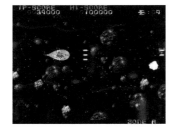

SUPER NOVA IS the western title for Darius Force, the fourth game in the Darius series of side-scrolling shoot 'em ups. Its main feature is the ability to choose between three versions of the series' Silver Hawk ship: the one from the original game (codenamed Darius Exodus War), the one from Darius II (Solar System Defend War) and a completely new version so fresh it doesn't even have a weird codename. This choice isn't arbitrary: each model has different weapons. Players can power up their shots and their bombs separately, but if they fire both at the same time their power is dropped a level. This is designed to stop players holding both buttons down continually: now they have to think which shots to fire. ■

FACT

At the time of writing, there have been seven Darius games. The last entry, Dariusburst, was released on the PSP back in 2009, so it's safe to say fans have been waiting a while for the next one.

SUPER OFF ROAD

Year | 1992
Publisher | Tradewest
Developer | Software Creations

WHILE EARLIER VERSIONS of Super Off Road were endorsed by professional off-road racer Ivan 'Ironman' Stewart, by the time the Tradewest was making 16-bit ports the licensing deal with Stewart had expired, so off went his name. The general game remains the same though: it's an off-road racer shown from a bird's-eye view, where the entire track can be seen on a single screen. Players have to complete five laps before their opponents while overcoming a variety of bumps, dips, jumps and other obstacles like hay bales. Winning earns you money that can be spent on upgrading your acceleration, top speed, steering and suspension, and any extra cash you have left over can be spent on nitro boosts to get you quickly through particularly bumpy sections. ■

FACT

The SNES version is set at the fictional 'Mickey Thompson Stadium'. Thompson was an auto racer famous for being the first American to break 400mph. In 1989 he and his wife were shot dead at their home, so his name is in Super Off Road as a tribute.

SUPER OFF-ROAD: THE BAJA

Year	1993
Publisher	Tradewest
Developer	Software Creations

THIS SEQUEL OF sorts to Super Off-Road brings back Ivan 'Ironman' Stewart for some more racing goodness inspired by the Baja 1000 race, an epic endurance contest that takes place over 1,000 miles of Mexico's California Baja peninsula. There are three different races of varying lengths to choose from here: the Mexico 250, the Ensanada 500 and the main Baja 1000 itself. Naturally, you aren't expected to do the whole race in one sitting: each consists of a number of smaller heats, and after each you can spend money to upgrade and repair your car. The top-down viewpoint of the previous Super Off-Road has been ditched (good luck fitting 1,000 miles onto one screen): instead the game is played with a third-person 'chase' camera. ■

FACT

Ivan Stewart is mainly back here in an advisory role. He appears before each race to give (fairly obvious) advice, such as: 'Start slow until you get the hang of it, then you can use your nitros to go faster.'

SUPER PINBALL: BEHIND THE MASK

Year	1994
Publisher	Nintendo
Developer	KaZe / Meldac

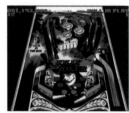

'PINBALL THE WAY it's meant to be,' promises the blurb on the back of the box for Super Pinball: Behind the Mask. Turns out the way pinball is supposedly meant to be is three fairly uninspired tables with suitably moody music playing in the background. The tables included here are all original creations: there's Jolly Joker (which apparently stars a Goth clown of sorts), Blackbeard and Ironmen (a pirate-themed table), and Wizard (look, you can probably figure it out). As well as the option to choose which table to play you can also take on Conquest mode, where you play through all three tables in a sequence: you have to hit a certain score on each table to open the 'forbidden door' taking you to the next one. ■

FACT

A sequel called Super Pinball II: The Amazing Odyssey was released in Japan and included three new tables based on sci-fi secret agents and the circus. Its tables are more varied and it's therefore more entertaining to play.

SUPER PLAY ACTION FOOTBALL

Year	1992
Publisher	Nintendo
Developer	Tose

IN 1990, NINTENDO published NES Play Action Football for, well, the NES, which lacked an NFL licence and only offered eight teams, but was entertaining enough for the time. This sequel takes things up a notch with the addition of the NFL licence, which means team names, logos and uniforms are real (there are no player names in the game, so an NFLPA licence wasn't needed). As well as this, though, there's also a college football mode with 53 (unlicensed) college teams, in case you're more into Princeton then Pittsburgh. The high school mode is a strange addition: you can enter your own high school's name and uniform and play a single game against either your rival school (which you can also name and design), or a generic one. ■

FACT

When you do the coin toss at the start of the game, 'heads' is Raccoon Mario from Super Mario Bros 3 and 'tails' is the Super Leaf power-up.

SUPER PUTTY

Year	1993
Publisher	US Gold
Developer	System 3

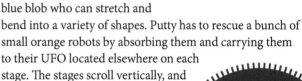

THIS QUIRKY PLATFORMER (and the predecessor to Putty Squad, seen elsewhere in this book) was developed for the Commodore Amiga and enjoyed a SNES port a year later. You're the titular Putty, a blue blob who can stretch and bend into a variety of shapes. Putty has to rescue a bunch of small orange robots by absorbing them and carrying them to their UFO located elsewhere on each stage. The stages scroll vertically, and Putty gets around by stretching, bouncing, inflating, punching and generally turning into any shape required. Putty's ability to turn into a puddle and absorb doesn't just work when picking up bots: he can also absorb some enemies and turn himself into a clone of them, acquiring their abilities. ■

FACT

In 2008 System 3 owner Mark Cale toured various UK magazines and announced in a number of interviews (including one with this book's writer) that Putty would be returning in an all-new adventure. This never happened.

SUPER PUNCH-OUT!!

Year	1994
Publisher	Nintendo
Developer	Nintendo R&D3

PUNCH-OUT!! WAS A big success on the NES – especially in its original Mike Tyson-endorsed form – with its enormous sprites and comically stereotypical boxers providing a challenge and a chuckle at the same time. Rather than following the NES game's lead when it came to the inevitable SNES follow-up, though, Nintendo instead based Super Punch-Out!! on the original arcade Punch-Out!! and its sequel, Super Punch-Out!! (confused yet?). As in the arcade titles, you no longer get to properly see your boxer Little Mac during the fight: instead, the camera is located behind him and his body is transparent, allowing you to see through him while still getting to view his punches and movement. The SNES game also brings back the power meter, which featured in the arcade originals but was ditched for the NES version. As you successfully land punches your power meter grows, while taking hits causes it to fall again. If you can manage to fill it completely, you can trigger a number of special attacks like huge uppercuts, wild hooks and rapid punches. Compared to the NES alternative – where players gained power stars for performing specific types of counter, a mechanic that was often confusing – the power meter makes it much easier to see how close you are to earning your power punches.

It wouldn't be a Punch-Out!! game without a roster of ridiculous sluggers to take on (the newly blond) Little Mac, of course, and this SNES entry doesn't disappoint. There are 16 opponents to take on

FACT

Nintendo R&D3 only made a few games, including the first four Punch-Out!! games, StarTropics and Pilotwings 64. It mainly focuses on hardware: it created the N64, GameCube, Wii and Wii U, as well as other peripherals and updates (like the New 3DS).

over the course of four different circuits, each with their own trademark attacks but, crucially, each with their own telltale weak spots too: as in previous games the player's job is to learn how to avoid each of their powerful special punches, and figure out when to attack.

Six of the 16 fighters Little Mac faces return from the two arcade entries. Speedy Cuban fighter Piston Hurricane, ram-happy Bald Bull and KO king Mr Sandman first appeared in the original 1984 arcade Punch-Out!!, while enormous Canadian lumberjack Bear Hugger, egotistical Super Macho Man and Hong Kong fighter Dragon Chan (who uses illegal kicks) made their debut in the 1985 sequel Super Punch-Out!! It's the 10 newcomers who are arguably packing the most character: these include dancing Jamaican fighter Bob Charlie, rule-breaking luchador Masked Muscle (who spits in your eyes when the ref isn't looking), Japanese kabuki Heike Kagero (who attacks you with his hair) and elderly Chinese master Hoy Quarlow, who fights with a wooden staff. Best of all, though, is Mad Clown, an Italian opera singer who had a nervous breakdown, joined the circus then decided he wanted to beat people up for a living.

Super Punch-Out!! was praised by fans of the series, but also received some criticism for being little more than the same sort of thing with better graphics. Despite the odd nod here and there over the years that followed – its blond Little Mac appeared as a hidden fighter in EA's 2005 game Fight Night Round 2 – the Punch-Out!! series wouldn't come out of retirement again until its Wii reimagining 15 years later. ■

SUPER RBI BASEBALL

Year	1995
Publisher	Time Warner Interactive
Developer	Gray Matter

THE SEVENTH GAME in the RBI baseball series offers a generous helping of options, more than in most other baseball games of its era. Although it lacks the official MLB licence it does at least have the MLBPA one, meaning all player names are accurate. While there isn't a season mode as such, the League and All Teams modes have you trying to beat every team in either your league or both the American and National Leagues one after the other. There's a home run derby mode in there, and the ability to view all of the game's stadiums (an odd choice, since it exposes how similar most of them are). Finally, there's the Game Breakers mode, where you're given 17 different scenarios and have to try to end up getting the win. ■

FACT

Forgive me American readers, but for UK readers who don't know, RBI stands for 'runs batted in', and is a stat that counts how many players have scored as a result of a batter's play (be that a home run, a good hit or being walked by the pitcher).

SUPER R-TYPE

Year	1991
Publisher	Irem
Developer	Irem

IREM'S R-TYPE SERIES enjoyed some popular home conversions: Super R-Type sadly isn't one of the better ones, thanks to a couple of issues. It's a port of sorts of R-Type II, in that levels 2, 3, 4 and 5 are taken from R-Type II whereas levels 1, 6 and 7 are new to this game. The problems, however, lie in its performance and checkpointing issues. Slowdown isn't uncommon in SNES games but Super R-Type is notorious for being one of the worst offenders, with the action slowing to a complete crawl at times when there's a lot going on. There are also no checkpoints, meaning if a player dies – which is common in a shoot 'em up – they go all the way back to the start of the level. ■

FACT

A remake of R-Type I and II called R-Type Dimensions came to the Xbox 360 in 2009, and the Switch and PS4 in 2018. It includes both 2D and 3D versions of each game, plus an infinite mode where you have endless lives.

SUPER SCOPE 6

Year	1992
Publisher	Nintendo
Developer	Nintendo

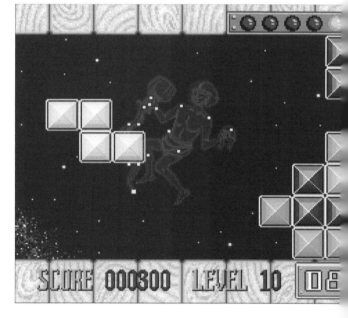

NINTENDO LAUNCHED THE Super Scope lightgun in North America in 1992 – it didn't come to Europe until nearly a year and a half later – and to get players to grips with its unique tracking and scope functions it included this cartridge containing six games (though technically it's more like three). Blastris A is a side-on take on Tetris where blocks randomly appear from the left-hand side of the screen and stack up on the right. Each time a block appears your ammo increases by two: the aim is to shoot blocks to let the rest fall into place and clear lines. Blastris B uses the more traditional vertical well of Tetris, but plays more like Sega's Columns, in that you shoot the blocks to change their colours and have to form lines of the same colour. Mole Patrol is a standard Whac-a-Mole style game where you shoot moles before time runs out. Then there's LazerBlazer, which consists of three similar shooting galleries: Intercept (where you have to shoot missiles before they reach the other end of the screen), Engage (where you shoot enemies and missiles before your fuel runs out) and Confront (where you simply shoot everything you can). The Super Scope was an impressive gun for its time, and its tracking worked relatively well as opposed to Sega's answer, the Menacer, which was plagued with issues. Sadly, a lack of 'killer' games for the peripheral meant it ultimately wasn't as successful as it could have been. ■

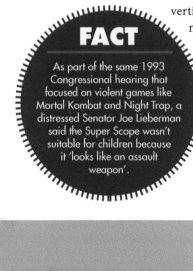

FACT

As part of the same 1993 Congressional hearing that focused on violent games like Mortal Kombat and Night Trap, a distressed Senator Joe Lieberman said the Super Scope wasn't suitable for children because it 'looks like an assault weapon'.

SUPER SLAM DUNK

Year	1993
Publisher	Virgin Interactive
Developer	Park Place Productions

IN 1993 VIRGIN Interactive decided it wanted to get in on the sports game action – because it's clear by flicking through this book that there simply weren't enough on the SNES already – and got to work on basketball and ice hockey games. The former was Super Slam Dunk, a basketball title endorsed by the legendary LA Lakers star Earvin 'Magic' Johnson, who appears before each game to give his verdict on the teams involved. It would appear that the team at Park Place was struggling to make things work graphically at the bottom of the court, because whenever the ball crosses the halfway line the court rotates 180 degrees: this means the view is always of the top half of the court and you never see the bottom. ■

FACT

The game's Playoffs mode is odd in that you have to play as a team in every game. This means you have to play four separate matches in the quarter finals, for example.

SUPER SLAP SHOT

Year	1993
Publisher	Virgin Interactive
Developer	Ringler Studios

VIRGIN'S TAKE ON ice hockey is actually a modified version of Mario Lemieux Hockey, which was released in 1991 on the Sega Mega Drive / Genesis. That version was developed by Alpine Software and designed by Ed Ringler, hence Ringler Studios. There are 16 international teams and 16 'city' teams to choose from, though there are no official licences in this game. One of its big talking points is its fighting system, which cuts to the big screen in the arena and lets you take part in an up-close fight with a variety of punches available. So proud is Super Slap Shot of its fighting that you can actually select it as an option in the main menu if you can't be bothered with all that pesky ice hockey getting in the way. ■

FACT

The game is 'endorsed' by legendary Canadian player Gordie Howe, but this just means he's on the back of the box with a fake quote saying: 'When I want a real hockey challenge, I lace up my skates and get into the fast and tough hockey action of Super Slap Shot'.

SUPER SMASH TV

Year	1992
Publisher	Acclaim
Developer	Beam Software

IN THE YEAR 1999, man's love of violence has evolved to the point that television stations think nothing of showing actual death on screen. One such example of this is Smash TV, a new game show where contestants literally fight for their lives to win prizes. If they succeed, fame and fortune is theirs. If they don't… well, at least they died doing what everyone else loved watching. Smash TV was a huge hit for Midway in the arcades thanks to its ridiculous non-stop action and its twin-stick shooting controls similar to those of Midway's iconic 1982 game Robotron 2084. Despite adding the name Super to the title, Super Smash TV isn't really much more than a port of the arcade hit, albeit a faithful one. Players have to try and make their way through three arenas, each made up of a number of separate rooms filled with enemies, in an attempt to reach the enormous bosses defending the exit doors. The key

FACT

The game's host pops up very now and then with witty catchphrases. One of these is 'I'd buy that for a dollar,' a reference to the film *RoboCop*, which offers its own satirical take on the state of television in a dystopian future.

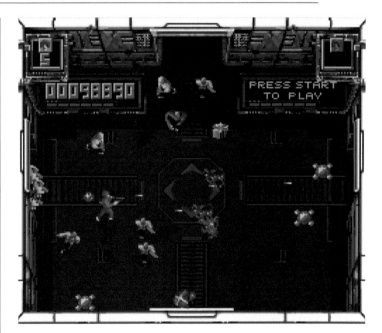

word there is 'try', because Super Smash TV is notorious for being incredibly difficult due to the constant onslaught of enemies you're up against. The SNES version at least makes this a little easier thanks to its controller: while home versions on the Mega Drive, NES, Amiga and the like had to think up creative ways to let players shoot in one direction while moving in another – a crucial skill in this game – the SNES controller's four face buttons make it a perfect match for the arcade version's twin stick controls. ■

SUPER SOCCER

Year	1992
Publisher	Nintendo
Developer	Human Entertainment

IT'S EASY THESE days to disregard Super Soccer as just another football game, but it holds a special place in the hearts of many SNES players because it was a launch title in Europe, and as such was the only football game available on the system for some time. Although it was published by Nintendo for western markets and gave the appearance of being a first-party production, Super Soccer is actually a localised version of Human Entertainment's Super Formation Soccer, itself a sequel to its PC Engine game Formation Soccer. Making use of the SNES's Mode 7 graphics, it gives the illusion of a 3D pitch, making for what was at the time one of the best looking football games around. It contains 16 international teams, all of whom have fake names, although some are suspicious: for example, Germany has two star players called Lotar and Rudi who appear to be based on Lothar Matthäus and Rudi Völler, while the best player in the game is Argentina's midfielder, simply named Diego. Beating the Tournament mode results in an interesting plot twist, in which the referee refuses to give you the trophy. 'Ha! Winning the trophy doesn't mean you are true world champions,' he tells you. 'If you want your trophy back you'll have to play against my team to determine the true world champion.' The issue of conflict of interest aside, it turns out the referee's team is the Nintendo All-Stars, seemingly made of members of Nintendo of America staff. ■

FACT

The manual has charmingly written descriptions for each of the teams. For England it says: 'This team is renowned for fair play, which is appropriate for a country of gentlemen.'

SUPER SOCCER CHAMP

Year	1992
Publisher	Taito
Developer	Taito

POPULAR ARCADE GAME Football Champ was released in 1990 and was given a slightly updated version called Euro Football Champ in 1992. This SNES release is based on that update (indeed, the SNES PAL version is called Euro Football Champ). Naturally, then, the football on offer here is very much in the arcade style, with lots of long balls, crunching tackles and over-the-top celebrations when you score a goal. The only major downside is the number of teams available, as there are only eight: Argentina, Brazil, England, Germany, Italy, Netherlands, France and USA (with Spain replacing the USA in the EU version). One unique feature is the ability to knock the ref onto the ground: while he's down you can get away with dirtier fouls. ■

FACT

Super Soccer Champ is known as Hat Trick Hero in Japan. A 1994 sequel called Hat Trick Hero 2 featured all the World Cup USA 94 teams (except for South Korea, who were replaced with Japan). It was planned for a North American release but was cancelled.

SUPER SOLITAIRE

Year	1994
Publisher	Extreme Entertainment Group
Developer	Extreme Entertainment Group

ALTHOUGH SOLITAIRE HAS obviously been popular since the 1800s, it's fair to say that the addition of a computerised version in Windows 95 led to a whole new generation of people discovering (and becoming massively addicted to) it. In a way, then, Super Solitaire was ahead of its time, offering not just the classic Klondike rules featured in the Windows version but another 11 variations: Free Cell, Golf, Cruel, Pyramid, Stonewall, Dozen't Matter, Aces Up, Florentine, Poker, Canfield and Scorpion. Each game has its own ruleset you can tinker with, and you can also change the design on the back of the cards: because who doesn't like a good game of Dozen't Matter with cards that look like fish? Complete liars, that's who. ■

FACT

The earliest mention of a game of Solitaire (or Patience if you're European) is in 1788 in the German game antholog *Das neue Königliche L'Hombre-Spiel*. You know the one.

SUPER STAR WARS

Year	1992
Publisher	JVC / LucasArts
Developer	Sculptured Software

THERE HAVE BEEN well over 100 Star Wars video games released over the years, so it takes something pretty special for one of them to be regularly namechecked any time a list of the best efforts is compiled. Do a quick search online for such lists, though, and time and time again you'll see one game constantly popping up: Super Star Wars. The first of a three-part SNES trilogy developed by Sculptured Software, Super Star Wars retold the story of the first movie, albeit with a few instances of artistic licence thrown in to make it work better as a video game.

It opens with Luke Skywalker on the vast Dune Sea desert of Tatooine. Armed with a blaster, he encounters C-3PO standing in the desert (rather than buying him from Jawas) and is informed that R2-D2 has been captured and is on a Jawa Sandcrawler, so off Luke goes to rescue it. The next step is to travel through the Land of the Sandpeople and Land of the Banthas in search for Obi-Wan Kenobi, followed by a trip to Mos Eisley and the Cantina to find Han Solo. After escaping from Mos Eisley you then head to the Death Star Hangar Bay, rescue Princess Leia and make your way to the Tractor Beam Core, after which it's into your X-Wing to take part in the Death Star Attack and the game's 15th and final stage, the Trench Battle.

Although you initially play as Luke, as the story progresses you get to play as Chewbacca and then Han: once all three have been found you can choose between them for each of the remaining stages. They each have their own strengths and weaknesses: Chewie has the most health but is the slowest character in the game, Han is the faster but his health isn't so great, and Luke is a general all-rounder but with the added ability to wield a lightsaber as a melee weapon when he earns it later in the adventure. Naturally, it wouldn't be much of a SNES adventure without the obligatory Mode 7 stages shoehorned in, and there are three to be found in Super Star Wars. Level 2 and level 6 have you piloting Luke's Landspeeder as you make your way around Tatooine: in these stages you have to destroy a certain number of Jawas before you run out of either health or fuel. Level 13, meanwhile, is the Death Star Attack stage where you fly your X-Wing over the surface of the Death Star taking out TIE Fighters and gun towers. Rounding all this off is an impressive SNES-ified rendition of John Williams' score, giving the game's audio a welcome sense of authenticity to match its impressive visuals. Super Star Wars is considered by many to be a difficult game (even though there's an Easy mode which makes it far more approachable). Despite this, the love for it and its sequels can't be denied, which is why – more than a quarter of a century later – they continue to be counted among the best interpretations of the licence. ∎

FACT

Early previews of Super Star Wars in gaming magazines showed screenshots of a trash compactor level which never ended up appearing in the game.

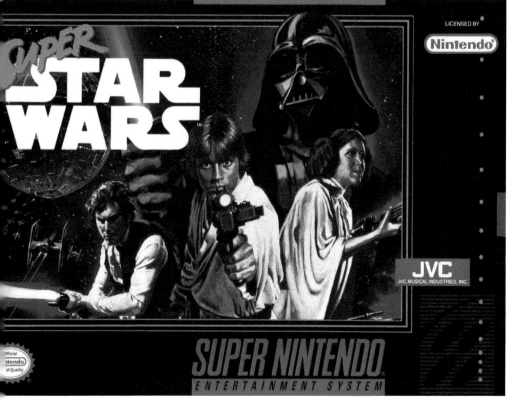

SUPER STAR WARS: THE EMPIRE STRIKES BACK

Year | 1993
Publisher | JVC / LucasArts
Developer | Sculptured Software

SINCE SUPER STAR Wars was so well-received, the obvious thing to do was to rinse and repeat with the second movie (or the fifth, depending on how seriously you take these things). Just as its predecessor followed the events of Star Wars, this retells the story of The Empire Strikes Back with a few changes here and there. Once again, you start off as Luke and eventually reunite with Han and Chewie, although this time each stage has a set character allocated to it and you don't get to choose who to play as. There's also a little more variation between the characters this time: Han now has the ability to throw thermal detonators at enemies, Chewie has a new spinning attack called the Kashyyykian Spin, and Luke can find and collect Force powers which he can store for later in the game. These include the ability to confuse enemies

FACT

As with Super Star Wars, this also had a level that was scrapped. The difference is that the cut stage here – where Luke fights bounty hunters at the Carbon Freezing Chamber – actually appears in the manual, meaning it must have been dropped at the last minute.

with mind control, deflect enemy shots, become invisible, throw your lightsaber and so on. As before, Mode 7 makes an appearance, this time in the form of three new vehicle stages. One of them has you flying your Snowspeeder through Hoth (where you have to destroy 10 probe droids and 10 speeder bikes), another lets you fly the Millennium Falcon through an asteroid field while gunning down enemy ships, and late in the game there's a stage where Luke – having finished his training with Yoda – races to Cloud City in his X-Wing, destroying 15 Cloud Cars along the way. ■

SUPER STAR WARS: RETURN OF THE JEDI

Year | 1994
Publisher | JVC / LucasArts
Developer | Sculptured Software

NES-OWNING *STAR WARS* fans were let down when they got games based on *Star Wars* and *The Empire Strikes Back* but not *Return of the Jedi*, so let's face it: it would have been downright rude if LucasArts and JVC pulled the same trick again on the SNES. Thankfully, the 16-bit trilogy was indeed completed the following year with this third and final entry, based on the muppet-heavy *Return of the Jedi*. The number of playable characters has extended to five: Luke, Han, Chewie, Leia and Wicket the Ewok. In fact, Leia technically counts as three different characters because she wears different outfits and wields different weapons depending on where you are in the story: she's got a staff when she's disguised as the bounty hunter Boushh, she uses a chain as a weapon when she's Jabba's escaped slave and when she leads the Rebels on Endor she uses a

FACT

Unlike the other two games, this was also ported to the Game Boy and Game Gear. The latter is a surprisingly good attempt considering the handheld's significant lack of power compared to the SNES.

blaster. Once again, there are a number of Mode 7 stages in here, but this time there are more: the Landspeeder and Millennium Falcon return (the latter appearing in three separate levels), but now you also get to ride a Speeder Bike on Endor. By this point the series had pretty much run its course, and while its bosses were arguably more iconic than those in its predecessors – you get to fight Jabba, the Rancor, Vader and Palpatine among others – the formula wasn't really able to go anywhere else, so in a way it was convenient that they ran out of movies. ■

SUPER STREET FIGHTER II: THE NEW CHALLENGERS

Year | 1994
Publisher | Capcom
Developer | Capcom

THE THIRD AND final version of Street Fighter II on the SNES is the most feature-heavy. Realising minor tweaks wouldn't be enough to satisfy arcade-goers who'd already spent countless hours on Street Fighter II, Street Fighter II: Champion Edition and Street Fighter II Turbo, Capcom decided to add some major new features to Super Street Fighter II to make it feel like a genuine step forward. The most obvious of these additions is the titular 'new challengers', four brand new characters for players to discover and learn how to master. Cammy is a young English special forces agent who doesn't know her past, Dee Jay is a Jamaican kickboxer with a love for music, T. Hawk is an indigenous Mexican warrior and Fei Long is basically a Bruce Lee rip-off (but that's okay). Naturally, with each of these new fighters also came new stages and new music accompanying them.

In the grander scheme of things, though, something else was added to the game that was perhaps even more important than the new characters: a combo scoring system. Combos had been present since the first version of Street Fighter II, but Super actually confirmed how many hits you'd landed and gave you a score bonus. The points were meaningless, but the fact that combos were actually counted now was a huge help for experts trying to learn new combos and looking for validation that they'd pulled them off properly. The fact that practically every fighting game these days uses a similar system speaks volumes. ■

FACT

The reason Dee Jay's trousers say 'MAXIMUM' down the side is because the letters are all symmetrical. The game flips sprites when characters face the other way, so if the letters weren't symmetrical they'd have become a mirror image when he turned.

SUPER STRIKE EAGLE

Year | 1993
Publisher | MicroProse
Developer | MicroProse

HERE'S A GAME that doesn't mind who it annoys. Your goal in Super Strike Eagle, according to the manual, is to 'bring peace to the unruly regions of the world by defeating four tyrannical regimes and bringing them back into the fold of the United Nations'. What

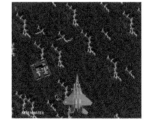

this actually means when it plays out is that you have to fly your F-15 Strike Eagle to four notorious theatres of operations – Libya, the Gulf War, North Korea and Cuba – and blow up as many MiG-29s, surface-to-air missiles and anti-aircraft artillery units as you can until that country agrees to become friends and their flag is raised at the United Nations again. If you're looking for Team America: The Video Game, this is probably as close as you'll get. ■

FACT

More than 1,500 F-15 Eagles are in service worldwide today. As well as the US Air Force and National Guard, F-15s are also used by the air forces of Israel, Japan and Saudi Arabia.

SUPER TENNIS

Year | 1991
Publisher | Nintendo
Developer | Tonkin House

THIS EARLY SNES tennis game was one of the system's five launch titles in Europe and continues to enjoy a small following of fans to this day. As well as standard singles or doubles play there's also the Circuit mode, where you choose

your player from a roster of 20 and take part in a variety of tournaments over the course of a year. Your player will get fatigued the more they play, so you have to decide whether to enter the next tournament to increase your ranking, or sit it out to recover some stamina so you'll be at your best come the next competition. The controls are simple but with four types of shot – slice, flat, top spin and lob – there's a level of depth to be discovered. ■

FACT

Tonkin House was the entertainment division of Tokyo Shoseki Media Factory, a company that specialised in all manner of media. Tokyo Shoseki still exists, but now it focuses on publishing textbooks and educational software for Japanese students.

SUPER TROLL ISLANDS

Year	1994
Publisher	American Softworks
Developer	Kemco

 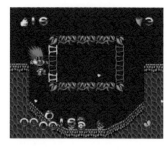

DON'T YOU JUST hate it when your land has been plunged into a murky darkness by an evil overlord? That's what's happened to the Troll Islands, so naturally the Trolls are a tad peeved. Albert, the oldest and wisest Troll, picks a crew of four young Trolls to help save the day. These Trolls – identified by their pink, red, green and blue hair – can jump high, run fast, use their strength and swim underwater respectively. Rather than a simple end-to-end platformer though, the aim is to visit each of the five islands (Forest, Beach, Castle, Outer Space and Weird) and clear their 10 stages by colouring them in. Each level starts in greyscale and by running on platforms and climbing ladders colour is added to them. ■

FACT

The game was licensed by Russ Berrie, who used to sell the original Dam Trolls until he realised their design wasn't copyrighted in the US. Berrie set up his own company and sold his own Trolls until Dam, who'd finally sorted out its US copyright, took out an injunction demanding he stop.

SUPER TURRICAN

Year	1993
Publisher	Seika Corporation
Developer	Factor 5

FOR MANY GAMERS (especially those in Europe who owned an Amiga computer), the Turrican series is synonymous with action. Super Turrican is no different: it's an action platformer that throws so many power-ups at you that your gun ends up spitting out the sort of bullets and missiles you'd be more likely to see in a shoot 'em up. As well as your gun you also have a freeze beam, which you can sweep over the screen to temporarily freeze enemies for a few seconds to make them easier to hit (just in case firing a thousand bullets at once doesn't do the trick). Its huge levels are packed with secrets and the pace is non-stop, making Super Turrican a treat for run 'n' gun fans who don't mind a little exploration. ■

FACT

Super Turrican had to be cut down, with a full level and some mechanics removed. When retro hardware company Analogue released its HD SNES alternative the Analogue Super Nt, Super Turrican: Director's Cut was built into it, making it playable for the first time.

SUPER TURRICAN 2

Year	1995
Publisher	Ocean Software
Developer	Factor 5

THE SECOND SUPER Turrican removed some of the elements that made the Turrican series so notable – specifically, the large, non-linear stages – and felt more like a standard run 'n' gun game as a result. This wasn't necessarily a bad thing, of course: all it meant was that the game had a distinctly different feel to its predecessor. This time you're also armed with a grappling hook which lets you... well, grapple onto things. There are 18 stages in total, ranging from an encounter with a flying pirate ship in the desert to a tense battle against a giant tarantula. You can now also ride vehicles at certain moments, including a dune buggy, a motorbike and a jet bike that can be operated underwater. ■

FACT

Super Turrican 2 was the last game in the Turrican series. Its creator Manfred Trenz was working on a polygonal open-world sequel called Turrican 3D in the late '90s, but it was cancelled.

SUPER VALIS IV

Year	1993
Publisher	Atlus
Developer	Telenet Japan

VALIS IV, THE final game in Telenet Japan's hack 'n' slash platformer series, was originally released on the PC Engine Super CD-ROM2 in Japan before moving to the SNES two years later. The previous game ended with its protagonist Yuko becoming a goddess, so since she's got enough on her plate this new adventure stars a new hero called Lena, a strong fighter who now has the task on her shoulders of saving Dream World from an evil king. The move from CD to cartridge meant this SNES port had to make a lot of sacrifices, including some of the levels, all the cutscenes, most of the playable characters and its magic system. As a result, most fans still believe the older PC Engine CD version to be the definitive one. ■

FACT

Telenet sold the rights to Valis to another company called Eants, who ended up releasing an erotic visual novel called Valis X, which was packed with lesbian antics and tentacle stuff. Slightly different from the original concept, then.

SUPER WIDGET

Year	1993
Publisher	Atlus
Developer	Atlus

WIDGET IS A purple 'World Watcher', whose job it is to make sure every living thing on Earth is safe. Following on from his NES adventure (cleverly called Widget), this SNES sequel has Widget exploring the Horsehead Nebula with his partner Mega-Brain in order to find and defeat a new group of alien villains who have appeared and want to destroy the Earth. As a standalone hero, Widget is a bit rubbish: not only does he look gormless, he can only take one hit before he dies. Luckily, he can find special tokens that transform his appearance and let him take extra hits. After beating each boss you're given a grade from C to S, though these grades don't unlock anything new. ■

FACT

Widget was originally a TV show designed to teach children about saving the environment. It ran for 65 episodes and became precisely nobody's favourite show of all time.

SUZUKA 8 HOURS

Year	1994
Publisher	Namco
Developer	Namco

THE SUZUKA 8 Hours race is a special annual event that's held at the Suzuka racing circuit in Japan and lasts for… well, I'll let you guess. Namco originally released an arcade game based on the event, but given that arcade machines are designed to turn over a lot of money it (perhaps understandingly) didn't let players participate in the full 8 Hours event. This SNES port doesn't either, but it does at least give you the option to take part in races that last 15 minutes, 30 minutes, 60 minutes or what it claims to be 8 hours but is instead a 90-minute race made up of eight 'virtual hours'. You can choose between a 250cc, 400cc or 750cc bike, each with their own stats for acceleration, top speed and cornering. ■

FACT

The Suzuka 8 Hours race first started in 1978. Teams owned by Honda have won it 27 times, making it by far the most successful manufacturer (the next best is Yamaha with just eight wins).

SWAT KATS: THE RADICAL SQUADRON

Year	1995
Publisher	Hudson Soft
Developer	AIM

YET ANOTHER CARTOON that tried and failed to capitalise on the success of the *Teenage Mutant Ninja Turtles*, the *SWAT Kats* are two vigilante feline fighters called Jake 'Razor' Clawson and Chance 'T-Bone' Furlong, who try to take down Megakat City's various villains while also trying to keep out of reach of the city's militarised police force. This SNES adaptation is a side-scrolling action platformer that lets you play as either Razor or T-Bone as they carry out five missions, all at the behest of Mayor Manx. This culminates in boss fights against Dr Viper, The Metallikats, Madkat, the Pastmaster and the Dark Kat. There are also some strange (and disorientating) Mode 7 shooting sections where players control the Turbokat Fighter while the screen constantly rotates. ■

FACT

The *SWAT Kats* were voiced by Barry Gorden and Charlie [A]dler, so if you've ever wondered [wh]at a team consisting of Donatello [fr]om TMNT and Buster from Tiny Toons sounds like, then I'm afraid nobody else did, which is why it only lasted 26 episodes.

SYNDICATE

Year	1995
Publisher	Ocean Software
Developer	Bullfrog Productions

SYNDICATE IS A real-time strategy game played with an isometric viewpoint. It's set in a dystopian future – the most popular type of future, it seems – where an evil corporation called EuroCorp has invented a neck implant called the CHIP which can numb a person's senses and let the corporation control them. Playing a member of a rival corporation, you have to put together a team of four cyborg agents and head to various locations around the world, taking part in a series of missions where the aim is to kill, steal, 'persuade' and infiltrate the offices of certain targets. At first your squad only owns pistols but over time you can kit them out with all sorts of serious gear like flamethrowers, sniper rifles and even an electromagnetic coilgun. ■

FACT

Syndicate was initially designed as a home computer game and enjoyed more success in that environment. It got an expansion set called American Revolt and a sequel, Syndicate Wars, which launched on PC and PlayStation in 1996.

SYVALION

Year	1993
Publisher	Toshiba EMI
Developer	Taito

AFTER YOU'VE CREATED the cute and cuddly Bubble Bobble, the next obvious step is a game featuring a giant metal dragon head that breathes fire at everything. That was the logical conclusion Fukio Mitsuji came to when he created Syvalion, which originally launched in Japanese arcades in 1988. A Darius spin-off, you play as an unnamed pilot who's stolen *Syvalion* – which is actually a giant spaceship that just happens to be shaped like a dragon's head – from an evil alien race called the Varia. Each time you play the level, the layout is completely different, with the aim being to simply reach the end before time runs out and see if you've beaten your highest score. The arcade version was played with a trackball so it loses something in the control here. ■

FACT

The Sharp X68000 computer in Japan got a port of Syvalion, which also had a hidden game called Sybubblun. This is an extremely hard sequel to Bubble Bobble where the enemies are robots.

TAZ-MANIA

Year	1993
Publisher	Sunsoft
Developer	Visual Concepts

THE TASMANIAN DEVIL is hungry. Luckily, it's Kiwi mating season (the birds, not the people), so the roads of Tasmania are lined with the little yellow birds strutting their stuff. There are 15 stages with same goal in each: Taz has to eat a certain number of Kiwis before the time runs out. This is much easier said than done, though: not only do the Kiwis have a tendency to move quickly at the drop of a hat, but Taz also has to deal with plenty of other hazards in each level, from buses and pterodactyls to the amorous She-Devil, who chases Taz looking for a smooch. You know what they say: if you can find a partner who doesn't mind the smell of Kiwi on your breath, they're a keeper. ■

FACT

Taz first appeared in the 1954 Looney Tunes cartoon *Devil May Hare*, where he tries to eat Bugs Bunny but is distracted when Bugs places a singles ad and a female Taz appears, causing the two devils to fall in love.

T2: THE ARCADE GAME

Year	1993
Publisher	LJN
Developer	Probe

THERE WERE SEVERAL different video game adaptations of *Terminator 2: Judgment Day* on a variety of formats. The SNES got its own take (which we'll get to soon), but it also received this port of Midway's popular arcade lightgun shooter, hence the 'Arcade Game' name to make it clear what you're getting. It's set over seven stages: the first four are set in 2029 and take you through a battlefield, the resistance hideout, a trip to Skynet in a pickup truck and Skynet itself. Then it's back to the 'present day' (1993) where you have to destroy as much as you can at Cyberdyne Systems, escape in a SWAT team van while trying to avoid being rammed by the T1000's helicopter and finally destroy the T1000 in a steel mill. ■

FACT

The SNES version supports the Super Scope and SNES Mouse, and has two different endings depending on whether you destroyed everything at Cyberdyne. If you didn't, you're told that Judgment Day (sic) could still happen.

TECMO SUPER BASEBALL

Year	1994
Publisher	Tecmo
Developer	Tecmo

TECMO'S ARRAY OF NES sports games sold well enough to make it worth going through the same process on the SNES. Whereas Tecmo Baseball on the NES had no licenses, however, this 16-bit take on the sport at least includes the MLBPA licence for real player names. As well as a preseason exhibition game, you can also play through an entire 1994 season. One feature here that not a lot of similar games offer is the ability to choose one of four statuses for each of the 28 teams during a season: play, coach, watch or skip. This means that in theory you could have a 28-player league, if you're happy to take part in something that could theoretically take months or years to get through. ■

FACT

One major criticism aimed at the game is that its button assignment for the plates is upside-down compared to standard convention. In most baseball video games the home plate is located at the bottom of the map, but here it's at the top.

TECMO SUPER BOWL

Year	1993
Publisher	Tecmo
Developer	Tecmo

TECMO HAD ALREADY released a game called Tecmo Super Bowl on the NES in 1991 (a sequel to Tecmo Bowl), so rather than call it Super Tecmo Super Bowl it just stuck with the same title. Containing both the NFL and NFLPA licences, it essentially improves on the NES version in every way. As well as the obvious visual improvements, there are a bunch of other random additions like user-controlled touchbacks, different weather (sun, rain and snow), the ability to block punts and the ability to change the plays in your playbook while you're in the middle of the game. The NES version was the best American football game on that system: this was a strong contender for the same crown on the SNES. ∎

FACT

Much like the NES version, there are a host of hacked updates for Tecmo Super Bowl the emulation scene, with one of the more recent examples updating the game to feature the full 2019–20 rosters.

TECMO SUPER BOWL II: SPECIAL EDITION

Year	1995
Publisher	Tecmo
Developer	Tecmo

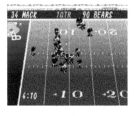

THIS IS BY far the rarest version of Tecmo Super Bowl. While the first and third SNES games were relatively plentiful in number, it's said that only 15,000 copies of Tecmo Super Bowl II were shipped to retailers, meaning most gamers skipped it and moved straight onto the Final Edition. Tecmo Super Bowl II gives its predecessor a huge graphical overhaul, changing the perspective from the straight top-down view to a more angled, realistic one. It also has the unique feature of including rosters from the 1992, 1993 and 1994 seasons, allowing you to mix and match: so if you've ever been adamant that the '92 Browns could beat the '94 Steelers, you can finally prove it to the zero people who were arguing with you. ∎

FACT

Although it's the rarest in the series, that doesn't mean copies of Tecmo Super Bowl II are going for tens of thousands online. You can find a loose cart for around $45 and a complete boxed copy (in reasonable condition) for about $110.

TECMO SUPER BOWL III: FINAL EDITION

Year	1995
Publisher	Tecmo
Developer	Tecmo

WELL, LET'S FACE it, fair play to Tecmo for making it clear when its run of NFL games was coming to an end. The Final Edition of Tecmo Super Bowl carried over all the new changes (and the improved graphical detail) from Tecmo Super Bowl 2, and added a few other little tweaks to make what it believed was the definitive, ultimate edition of the game. These included the ability to create your own players, who only have a limited number of attribute points at first but can increase their stats if they play well in Season mode. The two new expansion teams, the Jacksonville Jaguars and Carolina Panthers, were also added to the game for the first (and obviously last) time. ∎

FACT

It may have been the last 16-bit Tecmo Bowl, but Tecmo couldn't resist going back on its word a full 13 years later, when Tecmo Bowl Kickoff was released on the DS. A full HD remake called Tecmo Bowl Throwback also launched on Xbox 360 and PS3 in 2010.

TECMO SUPER NBA BASKETBALL

Year	1993
Publisher	Tecmo
Developer	Tecmo

ALL 27 TEAMS from the NBA are included in this fully licensed game, although despite being released in 1993 the teams and rosters are based on the 1991–92 season (which means no rookie Shaq, and the old Knicks logo). You can take part in a Season mode lasting 26, 42 or the full 82 game schedule, but be warned: the game also has an extensive injury system with a frankly unnecessary 14 different injuries your players can pick up, and while some of these (eye cuts, ankle sprains) can put them out for a few games, the more serious ones (broken leg, wrist fracture) can have them benched for up to 17 games, meaning you'd better hope they don't happen during a 26-game season. ∎

FACT

Tecmo Super NBA Basketball came to the Sega Genesis the following year with updated rosters, but while the SNES version included Michael Jordan and Reggie Lewis, here they were replaced with generic lads called Guard Bulls and Forward Celtics.

TEENAGE MUTANT NINJA TURTLES IV: TURTLES IN TIME

Year	1992
Publisher	Konami
Developer	Konami

IT'S RARE THAT home conversions of arcade games actually end up being better than the source material, but many believe Turtles in Time managed to do just that. With an extra stage, tighter controls, more bosses and the addition of the SNES's fancy Mode 7 effect in one particular level, it's hard to argue. The Turtles are watching the news on TV one day when Krang suddenly flies in and steals the Statue of Liberty. Deciding this isn't ideal, the three-fingered foursome head out to rescue what has to be the largest 'damsel in distress' in history, but what they don't realise is that their adventure is about to take them to places (and times) they've never been to before.

There are 10 stages to play through here, and at first things seem to play like your typical TMNT arcade beat 'em up. The first level has you crossing a bridge in New York at 3am while taking on numerous members of the Foot Clan and eventually facing off against Baxter Stockman. Then you make your way through an alley, fighting off more enemies until you encounter and defeat Metalhead (a robotic turtle designed just for this game). Following this you jump into a sewer to fight pizza monsters and the Rat King, before heading to the SNES-exclusive Technodrome level, where you go one-on-two with Tokka and Razhar from the second live-action TMNT movie. After this you have a

FACT

Ubisoft released a 3D remake called Turtles in Time Reshelled in 2009 for the Xbox 360 and PS3 digital stores. It sold well but was criticised for being far duller than the original, and was delisted just two years later due to an expired licence.

boss battle with Shredder, and then the twist: he sends you through a time warp, through which you travel to the year 2.5 billion BC (which isn't quite accurate in terms of encountering prehistoric life, but let's go with it). At this point the rest of the game becomes an attempt to make it back to the present day, with the Turtles fighting in different time periods in both the past and future. You have to make your way through a pirate stage in the year 1530, a Wild West area set in 1885, a futuristic city race on neon hoverboards in (ahem) 2020 and a base on Mars in 2100 before your final battle with Super Shredder. Quite the adventure, then.

The SNES version of Turtles in Time gives more control over your turtle's ability to perform a previously random throw move that tosses your opponent right out of the screen and into your face (pulled off here using Mode 7). Indeed, the boss battle with Shredder in the extra SNES-only Technodrome stage can only be won by throwing enemies at him in this manner. Mode 7 is also employed to dramatic effect during the Neon Night Riders stage – the one set in the distant year 2020 – where you zoom your hoverboard over F-Zero style city streets. If there was any more proof of its quality, how's this for attention to detail: the SNES version lets you choose whether to give the Turtles' skin the same bright colour as it is in the cartoon, or give each a unique, darker shade of green to give it more of a comic book look. ∎

TEENAGE MUTANT NINJA TURTLES: TOURNAMENT FIGHTERS

Year	1993
Publisher	Konami
Developer	Konami

THE NES, SNES and Mega Drive / Genesis versions of TMNT Tournament Fighters are all completely different games with entirely unique rosters, fighting mechanics and story modes. The SNES version  has the largest cast of characters, with 10 playable fighters: as well as the four Turtles and Shredder, it also includes Chrome Dome from the animated series, three characters from the Archie Comics series (Armaggon, War and Wingnut) and a brand new female ninja called Aska. There are also two bosses, Rat King and Karai – the Story mode's plot involves the latter kidnapping April and Splinter – and both can be unlocked in two-player mode using a cheat code. The gameplay and special moves are similar to Street Fighter II, though there are only four attack buttons. ■

FACT

Aska was supposed to be Mitsu from the *Teenage Mutant Ninja Turtles III* live-action movie, but after the film received a poor critical reception she was replaced with Aska.

THE TERMINATOR

Year	1993
Publisher	Mindscape
Developer	Mindscape

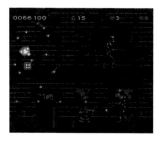

ALTHOUGH *TERMINATOR 2* was the big movie of the era, there was still a lot of love for the original movie, a love that was only renewed with the arrival of the sequel. Cue this SNES retelling of the first *Terminator*, in which you play through four extremely long stages – a battlefield in the future, the streets of present day LA, the police station and the factory – interspersed with a couple of driving stages where you have to pursue the Terminator's car for a set distance before he manages to blow your own vehicle up. Although it had a suitably Terminator-esque soundtrack, that was about the only thing going for it: the constant onslaught of enemies and the inability to fire straight up made it exceptionally difficult. ■

FACT

The soundtrack may have been a strong point but it was missing one key element: the main Terminator theme by Brad Fiedel. There must have been a reason for its removal, because there's a version of it tucked away in the cartridge's data, unused.

TERMINATOR 2: JUDGMENT DAY

Year	1993
Publisher	LJN
Developer	Bits Studios

NOT TO BE confused with T2: The Arcade Game, this is a retelling of the events of *Terminator 2* through side-scrolling action scenes (with isometric driving sections in between each stage where you travel to the next  destination). Starting at the bar where the T-800 gets his gun, you travel to John Connor's home, then the mall to find John, followed the state hospital to break out Sarah Connor, then Enrique's ranch to hide out. Then it's off to the Dyson residence to stop Sarah killing Miles Dyson, followed by a trip to Cyberdyne to blow it up, after which is the final showdown at the steel mill. A single rock track plays through the entire game until you reach the final stage, which definitely isn't annoying at all. ■

FACT

Unlike in the movie, dropping the T-1000 into a vat of molten lava still isn't enough to kill it. You have to send Arnie down with his massive Gatling gun to pump more bullets into it while it writhes around.

TERRANIGMA

Year	1996
Publisher	Nintendo
Developer	Quintet

USUALLY, DURING THE 16-bit era, RPGs were localised for North America but never released in Europe (because of the need to translate them into extra languages). Terranigma is a rare example of the opposite: an RPG originally made in Japan by Enix, translated into four languages for Europe, then never released in America. It's a fantastic game, too: it tells the story of a boy called Ark (who can be renamed) who lives in the only village in the 'under world', a subterranean version of the surface world. After accidentally opening a magical box and freezing everyone in his village, Ark is told he has to resurrect the barren surface world to save mankind. However, all is not as it seems in this extremely complex but superb plot. ■

FACT

The reason the game never made it to North America was because although Nintendo published it in Europe, Enix was due to handle publishing duties in America. By the time the game was ready, though, Enix had already closed down its US subsidiary.

TETRIS & DR MARIO

Year	1994
Publisher	Nintendo
Developer	Tose

 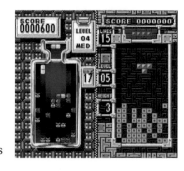

WHAT DO YOU get when you take the two most popular Game Boy puzzle games and put them on the same SNES cartridge? I mean, it's probably obvious at this point. Tetris & Dr Mario offers full versions of both much-loved games, based on the Game Boy versions rather than the NES ones (which means, yes, Tetris gets the good music). There's also a Mixed Match multiplayer mode for two players, where a time limit of 3, 5 or 7 minutes is set. Players then play their own separate game and have to clear a B-Type level of Tetris and a level of Dr Mario before moving to A-Type (endless) Tetris and trying to build the highest score with the time they have remaining. ■

FACT

The version of Dr Mario in this compilation was later made available as a standalone download on the Satellaview satellite service for the Japanese Super Famicom. Unfortunately, it was called Dr Mario BS Version.

TETRIS 2

Year	1994
Publisher	Nintendo
Developer	Bullet-Proof Software

HOW DO YOU make a sequel that lives up to one of the greatest puzzle games of all time? Well… you don't, is the answer. Tetris 2 ditches the original's rules and is a completely new puzzler: instead of clearing lines, you're using the oddly-shaped pieces to match blocks of the same colour: get three or more and they'll disappear, making the other blocks attached to them drop. Each stage has some flashing blocks: clear them all and you'll progress to the next level. As well as the standard single-player mode and two-player versus mode, there's also a Puzzle mode, where you're given a set number of blocks to clear all the flashing ones. As competent as Tetris 2 was, the general consensus was that it simply wasn't Tetris. ■

FACT

Tetris creator Alexey Pajitnov had nothing to do with Tetris 2. He was too busy working on El-Fish, a PC and Mac aquarium simulator.

TETRIS ATTACK

Year	1996
Publisher	Nintendo
Developer	Intelligent Systems

IF YOU THOUGHT Tetris 2 had little to do with the original Tetris, Tetris Attack is absolutely nothing like it: there aren't even blocks falling from the sky. That's not to say it's a bad game, however: far from it. Developed by Intelligent Systems, Tetris Attack was known in Japan as Panel de Pon and was an entirely original puzzle game starring little fairy characters. Concerned that a new IP may not set the western world alight, Nintendo did a deal with the Tetris Company founder Henk Rogers that allowed them to use the Tetris name for the western version of Panel de Pon. What's more, just to really make sure gamers in the west would pay attention to it, the fairies were ditched and replaced with characters and artwork from Yoshi's Island. The game's rules are reasonably simple: you're presented with a well that's filled with blocks with different shapes on them. The well is constantly filling up from

FACT

Henk Rogers says he regrets letting Nintendo use the Tetris name for this game, and that the decision was solely driven by cash. 'It's like naming another cartoon character Mickey Mouse just 'cause you need the money,' he said.

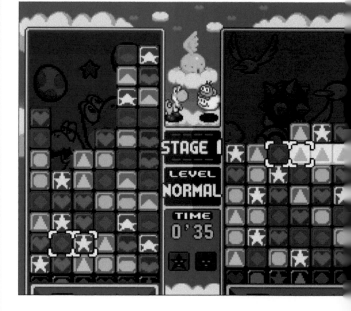

the bottom with more shapes, so you need to get rid of them by matching three of the same shape. The twist is that the only move you can make at any point is to highlight a block and move it to the left or right. There are a generous helping of modes including an Endless mode, a Timed mode (score the most points in two minutes), Stage Clear mode (where you have to clear all the blocks underneath a certain line) and a Story mode, where Yoshi takes on a variety of Yoshi's Island characters. ■

THEME PARK

Year	1996
Publisher	Electronic Arts
Developer	Bullfrog Productions

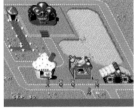

CONSIDERED TO BE the grandfather of the construction and business management simulation genre, Theme Park starts you off with an empty plot of land and asks you to create the ultimate amusement park. At first you can only build some fairly boring rides: a bouncy castle, a tree house, a cheap-looking Ghost Train. As the number of visitors increases and you start making more money, though, you can invest in research to develop new rides like rollercoasters and Ferris wheels. It's not all plain sailing, of course: rides will break down from time to time (so you'll need to hire engineers) and visitors will inevitably drop litter and vomit on the pavement, meaning a well-oiled team of janitors is essential to avoid your patrons leaving in disgust. ■

FACT

There are some sneaky tricks in here designed to wring every penny out of your customers. [Incr]ease the level of salt used at your [fr]ies stand, and visitors are more likely to want to buy a drink too (which can be watered down to save more money).

THOMAS THE TANK ENGINE & FRIENDS

Year	1996
Publisher	THQ
Developer	Software Creations

> Thomas was waiting at a junction when a bus arrived.
> "Hello," said Thomas. "Who are you?"

THERE ISN'T A child alive who doesn't like *Thomas the Tank Engine* (as long as you don't count the ones who don't), and this SNES title is aimed at those sprogs that do. It consists of a number of basic mini games, which include racing other trains, changing the signals to help Thomas get to his location and a jigsaw puzzle. There's also a number of stories for children to read, with an option to have the game read them out loud. As a result of this, there's a seriously impressive amount of recorded sound samples on here, maybe more than in any other SNES game. There are three difficulty levels: one for children aged 4 and under, one for 5–7 year olds and one for those aged 8 and over. ■

FACT

Thomas first appeared in 1946, in the second book of the Reverend W. Awdry's series of children's stories, *The Railway Series*. The first book featured Edward, Gordon and Henry, which means they actually appeared a year before Thomas did.

THUNDER SPIRITS

Year	1992
Publisher	Seika Corporation
Developer	Technosoft

THE CRITICALLY ACCLAIMED shoot 'em up Thunder Force III was modified and ported to arcades as Thunder Force AC. Technosoft wanted to port this arcade version to the SNES, but because the Thunder Force name was part-owned by Sega the title was changed to Thunder Spirits. What we have here, then, is a modified SNES port of a modified arcade port of a Mega Drive / Genesis game. Easy. Piloting the Fire LEO-03 'Styx' ship, you have to fly through eight enemy-filled stages, taking on enormous bosses and sub-bosses along the way. While the other versions let you choose the order in which to take on the first five levels, Thunder Spirits removes this option, making it a far more linear experience similar to any other shooter. ■

FACT

There are six main games in [t]he Thunder Force series (not [co]unting spin-offs and modified [por]ts like Thunder Spirits). Thunder [Fo]rce IV, known in the US as the [ba]dly-spelled Lightening Force, [i]s available on the Switch as part of the Sega Ages series.

THE TICK

Year	1994
Publisher	Fox Interactive
Developer	Software Creations

THE TICK MAY be celebrating a resurgence in popularity due to its live action Amazon Prime show, but back in the mid '90s it enjoyed its first spell of success as a comic book and animated series on Fox Kids. The SNES tie-in consists of 16 chapters split across three episodes with the extremely serious titles of Night of a Million Zillion Ninjas, Chairface Writes His Name on the Moon, and What Thrakkorzog Wants, Thrakkorzog Gets. There are two main play styles: it's a 2D side-scrolling platformer until you get into a fight, at which point the game switches to a beat 'em up where you can move in all eight directions similar to Final Fight and the like. Although light-hearted, it was criticised for being repetitive. ■

FACT

The Tick was originally created as a comedy mascot for New England Comics, a chain of comic stores in Boston. The Tick appeared on New England Comics' newsletters, and was so popular the store financed the making of a full comic book series.

TIME SLIP

Year | 1993
Publisher | Vic Tokai
Developer | Sales Curve Interactive

THE CITIZENS OF the planet Tirmat are looking for a new home, and they quite like the look of Earth. They come up with a clever plan: make use of a recently discovered time portal to travel back to five different time zones in Earth's history and conquer them before their weaponry is advanced enough to fight back. Unluckily for them, Earth scientist Dr Gilgamesh finds out about their plan and travels back in time to stop them. This Contra-like action game takes place across Medieval Britain, the Cretaceous Period, Ancient Egypt, Ancient Rome, the year 2147 and 'present day' as you gun down endless enemies. Sluggish controls, a limited number of lives and a lack of continues make this a very difficult adventure. ■

FACT

The Game Over screen is brilliant, bluntly informing you: 'Mission failure. You were never born. Earth becomes Tirmat II.'

TIME TRAX

Year | 1994
Publisher | Malibu Games
Developer | Malibu Games

 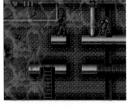

HEY! REMEMBER *TIME Trax*? The US-Australian sci-fi show that aired on the Prime Time Entertainment Network? Of course you do, it had the dad from *Pet Sematary* in it. Anyway, they made a SNES game about it which was similarly forgotten about. Playing as Captain Darien Lambert, a twenty-second century cop working for the Fugitive Retrieval Section in Enclave I-6 Middle City (formerly known as Chicago Land), you have to travel back to modern day America armed with your fancy futuristic weaponry to take down the likes of evil scientist Mordicai Sahmbi and assassin Sepp Dietrich, who've fled to the past to escape capture. This is a standard action platformer with the added ability to briefly slow down time to help you take out your more troublesome enemies. ■

FACT

The Prime Time Entertainment Network was a US channel that launched in 1993 and was dissolved four years later. *Time Trax* was the big new show that aired on opening night. It wasn't all bad news, though: PTEN also launched *Babylon 5*.

TIMECOP

Year | 1995
Publisher | JVC
Developer | Cryo Interactive

TIMECOP IS WIDELY regarded as one of the best films starring Jean Claude Van Damme, partly due to its action but also its silly time travel plot. The SNES version puts you in control of Van Damme himself (well, a digitised actor pretending to be him) as you travel through various locations in time: the Time Enforcement Commission offices in 2005, underwater at the San Andreas Fault in 1945, Wall Street in 1929, Germany in 1944 and eventually LA in the years 2144 and 2117. The main selling point of Timecop is its digitised characters, which look significantly sharper and move far smoother than those in games using a similar effect (like Mortal Kombat). However, critics complained that these smooth animations meant the game was unresponsive and sluggish. ■

FACT

The game has a ridiculous techno soundtrack, which was created by none other than David Cage, future writer of games like Heavy Rain and Beyond: Two Souls.

TIMON & PUMBAA'S JUNGLE GAMES

Year | 1997
Publisher | THQ
Developer | Tiertex Design Studios

THIS *LION KING* themed mini-game collection was originally released on PC in late 1995 – when the Windows 95 multimedia CD-ROM craze was in full swing – before coming to the SNES a couple of years later. It's a collection of four basic mini-games aimed at younger players. Burper is a shoot 'em up where Pumbaa belches gas at objects to hit them, while Hippo Hop is a Frogger clone where Timon has to cross a river to reach the grass on the other side. Jungle Pinball is a simple pinball table where the bumpers are replaced with animals, and Slingshooter is a shooting gallery where you're given 100 pellets and have to get the highest score you can. It's basic but inoffensive. ■

FACT

The PC version actually included a fifth mini-game which isn't in the SNES port. Bug Drop was a puzzle game that played similarly to Puyo Puyo.

TIN STAR

Year | 1994
Publisher | Nintendo
Developer | Software Creations

 ✔ ✘

TIN STAR IS the fruit of a collaboration between Nintendo and the Pickford brothers, the British designers behind games like Plok. It's a lightgun shooter starring a cowboy sheriff called Tin Star, whose one aim in life is to destroy all the robot bandits and bring peace to the small town of East Driftwood. It takes place over the course of Tin Star's first week on the job as sheriff, and players have to get from Monday to Sunday while collecting as much money (i.e. scoring as many points) as possible. Each day is split into a number of different missions: these range from first-person shootouts to third-person affairs, to one-on-one showdowns where players have to spot and shoot a 'draw' icon as quickly as possible. ▪

FACT

There are three endings involving the mayor's daughter. Finish with less than $750k and he refuses to marry you. Between $750k and a million, she marries your partner instead. More than a million and she reveals that she's your enemy Black Bart in disguise.

TINTIN IN TIBET

Year | 1995
Publisher | Infogrames
Developer | Infogrames

 ✘ ✔

BEFORE INFOGRAMES RELEASED The Adventures of Tintin: Prisoner of the Sun in 1996, it gave us this similarly pretty platformer based on the events of the 20th story in the *Adventures of Tintin* series. It follows Tintin as he heads to Tibet in search of his friend Chang after hearing about his plane crashing in the Himalayas. Over the course of 14 stages, Tintin makes his way to Tibet, climbs his fair share of mountains and even encounters a Yeti. While undoubtedly a beautifully designed and animated game, Tintin in Tibet is a little on the difficult side: the game does give you passwords to skip parts of the game, but you only get one after every five levels so you need to put some effort in to earn them. ▪

FACT

Tintin's creator Hergé says *Tintin in Tibet* was his most emotional story to write, because he created it while suffering from nightmares and deciding to leave his wife of 30 years for a younger woman. That poor man.

TINY TOON ADVENTURES: BUSTER BUSTS LOOSE!

Year | 1993
Publisher | Konami
Developer | Konami

 ✔ ✔

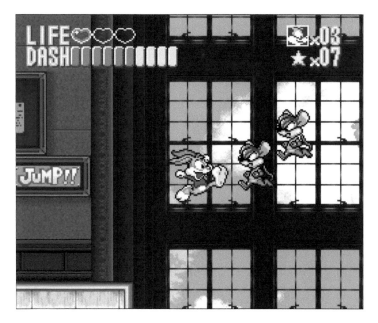

MOST GAMES ARE happy enough to have a single plot. Some, as you may have noticed while flicking through the book, barely have one. Buster Busts Loose, on the other hand, is such a greedy game that it has no fewer than six completely different plots: one for each of its levels. It's a pleasant, well-designed tie-in based on Warner Bros' Tiny Toon Adventures cartoon where the player controls Buster Bunny with just three moves: a jump, a dash and a drop kick. Despite its simplicity though, there's a lot of variety here, mainly due to those plots: the first stage is set at Acme Looniversity, where Buster realises he's late for class and has to get there pronto. Stage two takes place on the set of a Western movie, where Buster has to prove to Montana Max that he's the real star of the show. Next up

is Spook Mansion: Buster goes in to seek shelter from the rain and ends up trying to escape its ghost-riddled halls. Then it's over to an American football game, where you have to run 100 yards with Buster to win the game for the Acme Looniversity team. In stage 5, Calamity Coyote hides his treasure in the sky and forgets where he left it, so Buster heads up in a hot air balloon to get it. Finally, because there had to be a kidnapped princess in there somewhere, Buster travels to a space station to rescue Princess Babs Bunny in a *Star Wars* spoof. Phew. ▪

FACT

Despite its cult following, Tiny Toon Adventures' original run only lasted two years. Ninety-eight episodes were packed into the period between September 1990 and December 1992.

TINY TOON ADVENTURES: WACKY SPORTS CHALLENGE

Year	1994
Publisher	Konami
Developer	Konami

SPOILED RICH BOY Montana Max is holding a sports festival with a grand prize of a million dollars, so naturally the Tiny Toons are keen to get themselves some of that. Wacky Sports Challenge (or Wild & Wacky Sports, as it's known in Europe for no obvious reason) lets

you play as either Buster Bunny, Babs Bunny, Plucky Duck or Dizzy Devil as you take part in a series of mini-games with the aim being to score at least enough points in each game to qualify for the next. There are 12 events in total, ranging from the sensible (weight lifting, pole vault, swimming) to those that are a little more off-beat (bungee jumping, ice cream throwing, a birdman contest). ▪

FACT

There's a 13th event, the Marathon, which can only be played by entering Babs, Montana Max and Bookworm as a password. This brings up a level select screen which includes the otherwise unavailable Marathon.

TKO SUPER CHAMPIONSHIP BOXING

Year	1992
Publisher	SOFEL
Developer	Sting Entertainment

THIS BOXING GAME from Tokyo-based publisher SOFEL lets you create your own boxer, give him a name and chuck him into either a one-off fight or a Championship mode where he fights against a series of eight

boxers, improving his stats with each win. The eight opponents ready to face up to you range drastically in quality, from the frankly hopeless Johnnie 'The Rabbit' Murphy (who 'doesn't punch much, but moves fast', according to the game's character select screen) to the nearly invincible Thomas 'The Animal' Mitchell (of whom the game can only advise: 'Very strong! Very fast!'). The game is played from a side-on viewpoint and is zoomed out: this lets you move in all directions, making positioning more important than it is in most other boxing games. ▪

FACT

SOFEL's game publishing stint was fairly short. It was founded in 1979, and though it published a few games (like Wall Street Kid on the NES) it focused mainly on developing business software. SOFEL stands for SOFtware Engineering Laboratory.

TNN BASS TOURNAMENT OF CHAMPIONS

Year	1994
Publisher	American Softworks
Developer	Gaps

SADLY NOT A game about being the best 4-string guitar player in the world, but instead yet another bass fishing game: aliens reading this book may be starting to wonder if America has any other species of fish. It's sponsored by The Nashville Network, the TV network well known at the

time for its fishing shows (before it was renamed Spike TV in 2003). As in other similar games, the aim is to pick a lure (of which there are 24 different types), a rod and a reel, head to one of the six different available lakes, and try to catch the biggest bass you can find in what the back of the box reliably states is 'an honest to goodness bass fishin' experience right in your living room'. ▪

FACT

The Japanese version of the game is called Larry Nixon's Super Bass Fishing and is endorsed by pro fisherman Larry Nixon. When the TNN partnership bit on American Softworks' line, though, it threw Nixon back into the water.

TOM AND JERRY

Year	1993
Publisher	Hi Tech Expressions
Developer	Riedel Software Productions

EVERYONE'S FAVOURITE CAT and mouse duo (sorry, Itchy and Scratchy) make their only SNES appearance in this passable platformer. Playing as Jerry, you have to make your way through 12 areas spread across four distinct

scenarios: a movie theatre, a junk yard, a toy store and Tom's house. Jerry can arm himself with marbles, which are useful for taking out the countless other small creatures who are out to stop him for reasons that aren't entirely clear. At the end of each of the four scenarios, you face off against Tom and have to chuck marbles at him to take him out. There's also a two-player mode in which the second player takes control of Tuffy, Jerry's nephew, who otherwise plays identically. ▪

FACT

Tuffy first appeared on screen in a 1946 cartoon, where he was known as Nibbles. The name was changed to Tuffy in 1957, but in some more recent Tom and Jerry cartoons and movies he's referred to as Nibbles again.

TOMMY MOE'S WINTER EXTREME: SKIING & SNOWBOARDING

Year	1994	
Publisher	Electro Brain / Mindscape	
Developer	Loriciel	

THIS WINTER SPORTS game makes liberal use of Mode 7 to give the impression you're going downhill on a ski slope at extremely fast speeds. As the title suggests, you've got the option to ride on either skis or a snowboard, and can either take part in Competition mode – where you can choose between downhill, slalom or giant slalom events – or a Freestyle mode, which acts more like an arcade racing game with checkpoints. As well as boasting the name of US alpine skier Tommy Moe, the game is also endorsed by the Val-d'Isère ski resort: indeed, the EU PAL version of the game is instead called Val-d'Isère Championship, presumably because Tommy Moe isn't quite as well known outside of his home nation. ∎

FACT

Tommy Moe took part in 1994 Winter Olympics in [Li]llehammer and picked up [t]wo medals: a silver in the Super G event, and a gold in downhill.

TONY MEOLA'S SIDEKICKS SOCCER

Year	1993	
Publisher	Electro Brain	
Developer	Sculptured Software	

IT'S NOT OFTEN that a goalkeeper manages to get his name on a product, so fair play to the United States' goalie Tony Meola, who represented the US at the 1990 and 1994 World Cups. Sidekicks Soccer contains 32 national teams and 32 club teams, 24 of which are based in North America. If you're a European reader and are starting to think this game leans a little too heavy on the American side of things, fret not: the game was called World Soccer in Europe and contained a completely different set of club teams. In fact, not only did it have 64 club teams instead of 32, they were all based in Europe. Which is just as bad, really, when you think about it. ∎

FACT

Tony Meola played in the MLS from 1996 to 2006, where he was one of the first players to sign for the MetroStars (now known as New York Red Bulls). He also made 125 appearances for the Kansas City Wizards.

TOP GEAR

Year	1992	
Publisher	Kemco	
Developer	Gremlin Graphics	

YOU'LL FIND NO smarmy presenting styles and slightly offensive jokes in this one, because it's not that kind of Top Gear. Instead, it's a high-paced racing game designed to play like arcade racers such as Out Run. It's developed by Gremlin Graphics, who had previous experience in this sort of thing, having been responsible for the brilliant Lotus racing games on the Amiga and Mega Drive. There are four cars to choose from: the Cannibal (which has the best top speed), the Sidewinder (which has the best acceleration and grip), the Weasel (an all-rounder) and the Razor (which doesn't really have any positives and is seemingly here to provide an extra challenge). It's got 32 tracks set across eight regions: USA, Brazil, Japan, Germany, Scandinavia, France, Italy and the UK. ∎

FACT

[T]op Gear's fantastic music was [co]mposed by Barry Leitch. Leitch [a]lso composed the soundtrack [fo]r the recent retro-themed racer Horizon Chase Turbo, which includes an updated take on one of the tracks from the Top Gear soundtrack.

TOP GEAR 2

Year	1993	
Publisher	Kemco	
Developer	Gremlin Graphics	

THE SEQUEL TO Top Gear doesn't try to reinvent the wheel (ahem). Instead it simply builds on the foundations already laid by the original by improving most aspects of the game. There are now 64 tracks instead of 32, with new locations like Ireland, Canada, Greece and India added to the mix. The addition of weather now means you have to make sure your car is equipped with the right wet tyres, otherwise you'll be slipping around in the rain or snow. A new damage indicator also nestles at the side of the screen: it shows a diagram of your car which begins with an entirely green outline, but changes as you take damage. Finally, you can now spend prize money on upgrading your engine, tyres, transmission, armour and nitro system. ∎

FACT

One of the Egypt tracks is oddly named Hugh Sitton. This is the name of the Corbis photographer who took the photo of the pyramids used in the background of that track.

TOP GEAR 3000

Year	1995	
Publisher	Kemco	
Developer	Gremlin Interactive	

THE THIRD TOP Gear manages to be the least ever futuristic game set in the future. The year is 2962 and most fun has been sanitised, so 'once every millennium' (which doesn't make sense) the Top Gear 3000 race takes place. What this basically means is it's just like Top Gear 2, only the tracks are set on a bunch of different planets and you've got access to futuristic technology. The thing is, these other planets mostly look suspiciously like Earth – the sky's a funny colour but that's about it – and apparently the best technology they've come up with in nearly a thousand years is the ability to make your car jump, use a magnet to pull yourself closer to opponents and warp forward a bit. ■

FACT
According to the manual, World War XVII destroyed most of the Milky Way 'five centuries earlier'. This means we have around 440 years left to have another 15 World Wars: that's one every 30 years, so we'd better get cracking.

TOTAL CARNAGE

Year	1993	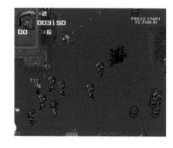
Publisher	Malibu Games	
Developer	Black Pearl Software	

THE SEQUEL TO Smash TV takes the action out of the television studio and places it on an actual battleground. It's the year 1999 and the country of Kookistan has been taken over by the evil dictator General Akhboob. Akhboob has used the radioactive goo from his bio-nuclear generators to create his own army of mutant soldiers and now he fancies taking over the world, so the Doomsday Squad – Captain Carnage and Major Mayhem – are flown in to take him out. Total Carnage plays similarly to Smash TV, right down to its twin stick control system (which again is perfectly replicated on the SNES), but this time you're taking part in actual stages with a scrolling screen rather than a set of static rooms. ■

FACT
According to the manual's 'lore', General Akhboob was driven mad when the Kookistan Burger Barn & Bait Shop he was working at closed down. This isn't a very serious game.

TOY STORY

Year	1995	
Publisher	Disney Interactive	
Developer	Traveller's Tales	

IN AN ERA where any two-bit animation studio can knock together a cheap-looking CGI film or TV show and chuck it onto YouTube or a bargain basement DVD, it may be (understandably) difficult for today's young bucks to appreciate just how revolutionary *Toy Story* was. As the first ever film that was entirely computer animated, *Toy Story* completely changed animation overnight, to the extent that some 25 years later it's now more surprising when a movie isn't made with CGI. Such a visually stunning film would require a visually stunning game to go with it, and that's what gamers got… on the Mega Drive. You see, Toy Story is a platformer whose sprites were created by having Pixar render animations of Woody and other characters, which developer Traveller's Tales would then digitise into the game. On Sega's console this was something of a revelation, but it had already been done on

the SNES with Donkey Kong Country and as such the impact was lessened a little. Regardless, the game was still a fun retelling of the events of the first movie, with players controlling Woody for the most part – though they do get to play as RC in a couple of racing scenes – as he explores various locations from the movie such as Andy's room, Pizza Planet and Sid's room. There's also a first-person stage, where Woody has to make his way through the inner workings of the claw machine while carrying one of its little green aliens. ■

FACT
The Mega Drive version has one extra stage that isn't in the SNES game. It's called Day-Toy-Na and is another racing stage, but from a third-person view rather than the top-down view of the other ones in the game.

TOYS

Year	1993
Publisher	Absolute Entertainment
Developer	Imagineering

PUTTING ROBIN WILLIAMS into a movie and simply naming it *Toys* should have been the recipe for fun, but that wasn't the case: the movie tanked and this game didn't do much better. Playing as Williams' character Leslie Zevo, you have to stop your evil uncle turning your late dad's toy factory in a weapons-building facility. You do this by exploring the three main areas of Zevo Toys – the factory, the cafe and warehouse – and using your own gadgets to take out the enemy toys in your way. Once you do, you can disable that area's camera: take out all three and you'll reach the final stage, where you pilot a toy plane through a model version of Manhattan in an attempt to crash it into your uncle's office. ■

FACT

Although *Toys* was nominated for Oscars for Art Direction and Costume Design, it was also nominated for a Razzie award for Worst Director. It didn't win any of the three so, you know, swings and roundabouts.

TRODDLERS

Year	1993
Publisher	Seika Corporation
Developer	Atod

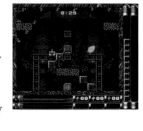

THE POPULARITY OF Lemmings led to numerous other developers trying to make lightning strike twice (particularly on the Amiga, where Lemmings began). Troddlers was one of the more obvious examples: originally released on the Amiga in 1992, it too has you trying to guide a group of tiny, mindless walking creatures to a series of exits. There are two major differences here, however: the first is that they have sticky feet, meaning they can walk up walls and ceilings. The second is that rather than controlling a cursor you're actually controlling Hokus, a sorcerer's apprentice who can run around and drop blocks directly in front of him to influence the direction the Troddlers move. There are also zombie Troddlers, who you have to deliberately kill. ■

FACT

Troddlers also boasts a 'War' mode, in which two players compete to try to protect their own Troddlers while killing those of their opponents. Sadly, Lemmings also did something similar (though most have forgotten that mode).

TROY AIKMAN NFL FOOTBALL

Year	1994
Publisher	Tradewest
Developer	Tradewest

WHEN IT COMES to getting big names for your sports game, Troy Aikman is a pretty good one. The Dallas Cowboys Quarterback had won two back-to-back Super Bowls by the time he appeared in this game (and went on to win a third in 1996) so it's safe to say his face helped shift copies. It's just as well, because while the game itself is perfectly competent there are no major selling points to make it stand out from its competitors. Despite releasing just a month before the 1994–95 season, the game focuses on the 1993–94 season instead (with the manual making it clear that the new 2-point conversion rule therefore doesn't exist yet, and that the kick-off still takes place from the 35-yard line instead of the 30). ■

FACT

The game has a fake ESRB rating on the back saying: 'Rated : All ages'. The problem is that the ESRB's 'A' rating actually means Adults Only, only given to games with strong sexual themes and graphic nudity.

TRUE GOLF: WICKED 18

Year	1993
Publisher	Bullet-Proof Software
Developer	T&E Software

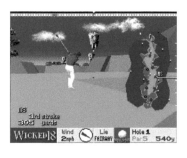

THE THIRD AND final game in the True Golf series (see over the page for the others), Wicked 18 abandons the idea of recreating classic holes and instead presents players with a completely fictional course. It isn't your standard golf course, either: this is proper fantasy stuff. The tall cliffsides and huge bunkers are tricky enough to navigate, but some holes also contain hazards like out-of-bounds areas in the middle of the course, massive stretches of water and even lava in some instances. Then there's the occasional floating island, just there for the sake of getting in the way. It's probably fair to say that if real golf was like this it would probably be a lot more dangerous, but the ratings would be huge. ■

FACT

The Japanese version of the game is called New 3D Golf Simulation: Devil's Course, which is pretty accurate to be fair.

TRUE GOLF CLASSICS: PEBBLE BEACH GOLF LINKS

Year	1992
Publisher	T&E Software
Developer	T&E Software

THE JOYS OF alphabetical order mean we're looking at this series backwards, but such is life. The second game in the True Golf Classics series offers a full recreation of the Pebble Beach Golf Links course in sunny California, believed by many to be one of the most beautiful courses in the world because of its coastline views. For the most part this plays exactly like its predecessor sitting opposite, with the same polygonal 3D course design. One change, however, is the four caddies available: whereas Waialae Country Club offered four Hawaiian chaps, here you've got four frankly ridiculous looking men called Casey, DQ, Michael and Dawg (who has an amazing moustache like Lemmy from Motörhead). ▪

FACT

The Pebble Beach course has hosted the US Open six times, the most recent being in 2019 when it was won by American golfer Gary Woodland. It's next scheduled to host it in 2027.

TRUE GOLF CLASSICS: WAIALAE COUNTRY CLUB

Year	1991
Publisher	T&E Software
Developer	T&E Software

CONTINUING OUR BACKWARDS trip through the True Golf series we finally come to the first game set in the idyllic Waialae Country Club in Honolulu, Hawaii. As with its eventual successors, True Golf Classics aims to provide players with an authentic recreation of the titular course via the use of polygonal course maps (with sprite-based scenery to ensure at least some level of detail). Before hitting each shot you have to press the B button to confirm your aim, club and stance before setting the power and accuracy. At any time you can ask your caddy for help: sometimes it's useful ('this grass is thick, so keep your head down and hit through the ball'), other times not so much ('keep your eye on the ball, that's the key'). ▪

FACT

The word wai'alae is a Hawaiian term which translates to 'spring water of the mud hen'. The location of the spring water there was closely guarded by an elderly couple in the 1830s, but it's said that King Kamehameha III (real name) drank it.

TRUE LIES

Year	1995
Publisher	LJN
Developer	Beam Software

THE BRILLIANT ARNOLD Schwarzenegger action-comedy with the terrible name got a fun tie-in game to go along with it. Naturally, you play as Arnie's character Harry Tasker as you have to snuff out the terrorist group Crimson Jihad and its leader Salim Abu Aziz's plot to detonate smuggled nuclear warheads in the US. The game is played from a top-down perspective and consists of 10 missions taking in such locations as a fortified chateau in the Swiss mountains, a Washington mall and the Forbidden City in China, before culminating in a rescue mission in which Abu Aziz takes Harry's daughter Dana prisoner in an office block. Initially armed with just a pistol, along the way you'll collect Uzis, shotguns, grenades and even landmines and flamethrowers. ▪

FACT

Arnie nearly died during the shooting of the infamous rooftop horse scene when the arm of a camera bopped the horse on the nose, causing it to start wildly flailing. He slipped off the horse and a stuntman caught him, stopping him falling 90 feet to his death.

TUFF E NUFF

Year	1993
Publisher	Jaleco
Developer	Jaleco

THIS ONE-ON-ONE FIGHTING game is set in the year 2151, where after an enormous war destroyed most of the planet all that remains is a few buildings, including the Colosseum, where warriors turn up to fight. One mysterious warlord named Jade managed to take over the Colosseum, calling himself the Fighting King, and proceeded to rule the land. You take control of one of four fighters – Japanese street fighter Syoh, his American rival Zazi, a female teenage ninja called Kotono and Dutch wrestler Vortz – and have to fight your way through the other three, then six non-playable guard fighters, until you reach the Fighting King himself. It's an entertaining enough Street Fighter clone, and thankfully there's a cheat code to unlock the other six characters. ▪

FACT

The UK and Japanese box art was actually created by UK magazine *CVG*, who commissioned the original art when it didn't have any for its preview article. Jaleco was so impressed it asked *CVG* to use the art for the box.

TURN AND BURN: NO-FLY ZONE

Year	1994	
Publisher	Absolute Entertainment	
Developer	Absolute Entertainment	

RECENT EVENTS IN the 'Mediterranean area of operations' have led to political and military instability, so the President declares the region's air space a no-fly zone. Piloting an F-14 Tomcat, you have to patrol this zone amidst rumours than an unspecified country plans to test the President's resolve by sending MiG-29 jet fighters through it. Each of the game's 16 missions starts with you taking off from an aircraft carrier, destroying a number of planes or bases, and then landing the plane on the carrier again. To help you on each mission you're armed with four different weapons: an M61A1 Vulcan cannon (which is the only weapon that can destroy bases), AIM-9 Sidewinder missiles, AIM-7 Sparrow missiles and AIM-54 Phoenix missiles. ∎

FACT

This is actually a sequel a 1992 Game Boy game called Turn and Burn: The F-14 Dogfight Simulator, which obviously was less graphically impressive.

THE TWISTED TALES OF SPIKE McFANG

Year	1994	
Publisher	Bullet-Proof Software	
Developer	Red Entertainment	

SPIKE McFANG IS a junior magician and a trainee vampire whose homeland Vladamasco – a series of islands led by three kings – falls under attack when one leader, zombie General Von Hesler decides he fancies ruling by himself. This would be bad enough were it not that one of the other kings is Spike's dad, and the third is the father of his pal Camelia. Thus begins an adventure to save both dads, give Von Hesler a kicking and restore peace. This is an action RPG where Spike can perform a spin attack with his cape and long-range attacks by throwing his hat. He can also find and equip himself with magic cards which give other perks like health recovery, elemental attacks and turning enemies into cuddly animals. ∎

FACT

The western version of the game is more difficult than the Japanese one, because enemies have higher defence stats and you don't recover all your health when you level up.

ULTIMA: RUNES OF VIRTUE II

Year	1994	
Publisher	FCI	
Developer	Origin Systems	

ALTHOUGH ULTIMA III, IV and V were released on the NES, there was always the underlying feeling that these complex computer RPGs just didn't translate well to home consoles. This was remedied with the first Runes of Virtue, a Game Boy spin-off that played more like a Zelda game. Runes of Virtue II also launched on the Game Boy first before getting a SNES port which kept the same basic structure but massively updated the graphics. You play as the Avatar – the hero who appears in all Ultima games after Ultima IV – and have been summoned by Lord British to rescue the mayors of the eight cities of Britannia, who've been kidnapped by the Black Knight. While the Game Boy version offers multiplayer co-op, the SNES game doesn't. ∎

FACT

Lord British is the ruler of Britannia throughout the Ultima series. The games' creator Richard Garriott, who grew up in America, was nicknamed British as a teenager because he greeted his friends with 'hello' instead of 'hi'.

ULTIMA VI: THE FALSE PROPHET

Year	1994	
Publisher	FCI	
Developer	Infinity Co	

Chris gets 16 points of damage!

THE SIXTH ULTIMA game is deeper than it originally appears. Playing once again as the Avatar, you find yourself returning to Britannia to help the kingdom in its war with a race of gargoyles. It isn't until much later in the game that you realise why the gargoyles are attacking (the spoiler's in the fact box), turning things on its head and revealing the game's true message of prejudice. While the NES ports of previous Ultima games made substantial concessions to work properly, the SNES version of Ultima VI is actually relatively faithful to the computer versions, other than some heavy censorship to the gargoyle designs (such as removing their horns to make them look less Satanic) and to a lot of the darker dialogue. ∎

FACT

Here's the plot twist: it turns out the gargoyles' homeland is crumbling, and their prophecy says the Avatar is the 'false prophet' who's come to kill them all. They aren't attacking, they're desperately trying to defend themselves from you.

ULTIMA VII: THE BLACK GATE

Year | 1994
Publisher | FCI
Developer | Origin Systems

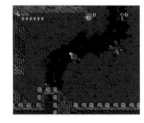

ULTIMA VI MAY have been a relatively faithful rendition of its home computer siblings, but the PC version of Ultima VII was a huge 20 megabytes in size, while the biggest ever SNES games (Japan exclusives Tales of Phantasia and Star Ocean) were only six megabytes. As such, the epic PC quest which saw the Avatar defending Britannia from a new evil called the Guardian suddenly became a lot less epic on the SNES. The story was shortened significantly, the world map was made smaller, the Avatar no longer travelled with a party and the combat was more Zelda-like than the mouse-driven PC combat. It wasn't a terrible game as such, but comparisons to the PC version were inevitable and in that sense it was eclipsed. ∎

FACT

The ninth and final Ultima game was released on PC in 1999. It didn't sell well and fans were unhappy with the way it ignored much of the story to date. One scene in which the Avatar asks 'what's a Paladin' became a well-used example of this.

ULTIMATE FIGHTER

Year | 1994
Publisher | Culture Brain
Developer | Culture Brain

THE SEQUEL TO NES fighting game Flying Warriors, Ultimate Fighter has three unique game modes as well as a two-player versus mode. The story mode revolves around Rick, a member of the Flying Warriors group, trying to defeat a demon named Dargon who wants to destroy the Flying Warriors. This mode is split into side-scrolling action sections and occasional one-on-one fighting sections. Tournament mode, meanwhile, is your typical Street fighter style affair where you pick one fighter and have to defeat the rest. Finally, the interesting Animation mode is similar to Story mode, except enemies in the side-scrolling sections are beaten with a single hit and the one-on-one fights are controlled with RPG style turn-based menus, theoretically meaning players with zero fighting game ability can still do well. ∎

FACT

Ultimate Fighter is the seventh game in the Hiryu no Ken (Fist of the Flying Dragon) series in Japan. Previous western release included Flying Dragon and Flying Warriors on the NES, and Fighting Simulator on the Game Boy.

ULTIMATE MORTAL KOMBAT 3

Year | 1996
Publisher | Williams Entertainment
Developer | Avalanche Software

WHILE MORTAL KOMBAT 3 was believed to be the best entry in the series to date – or at least the most technically impressive – there was still no denying that many fans were disappointed at some of the game's more glaring omissions. Ultimate Mortal Kombat 3 was an update designed to right some of these wrongs. Seven old characters were reinstated: Kitana, Mileena, Jade, Reptile, Ermac, the classic masked version of Sub-Zero and the most commonly requested character, Scorpion. In order to fit everything from the arcade version onto a SNES cartridge, though, other cuts were made instead. One of the existing characters, Sheeva, was removed entirely. Animality finishing moves were ditched (even though the Mercy move, which is really mainly there to trigger the Animality, stayed in). While five new stages were added, almost all of the existing ones were

FACT

Fans hoping for the truly definitive Mortal Kombat didn't have to wait long, as Mortal Kombat Trilogy launched later that year, containing all 37 characters from the first three games (although the N64 version was missing some).

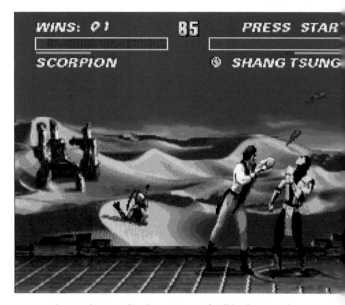

removed to make way for them. It wasn't all bad news: the SNES version let players control the boss fighters Motaro and Shao Kahn in two-player mode, and also added the arcade version's hidden CPU fighters Noob Saibot and Rain as playable characters (albeit through the use of a cheat code). It also added a new Brutality finisher, where your fighter unleashes a ridiculously fast combo of punches and kicks until your opponent explodes. Despite these positive additions, though, the underlying feeling from fans was that nearly as much was being taken away as was being given, meaning the game wasn't quite as Ultimate as the name suggested. ∎

ULTRAMAN: TOWARDS THE FUTURE

Year	1991
Publisher	Bandai
Developer	Bec

THIS TAKE ON Japan's legendary Ultra series – which began way back in 1966 – is based on the 10th series *Towards the Future*, which was an Australian-Japanese co-production. The game sees Ultraman Great fighting his way through nine of the kaiju (giant monsters) that appear in the show, from the tentacled slug Gudis to the huge ancient dragon-like beast Kilazee, who featured in the show's two-part finale. Ultraman is armed with a limited arsenal of punches and kicks, and must wear his opponent's energy down far enough that they only need a single killer blow. He then has to activate his trademark Burning Plasma arm beam move to finish them off. Later enemies will find ways to dodge the arm beam, so you have to adapt accordingly. ■

FACT

Despite being co-produced by an Australian studio and being shot entirely in Australia, *Towards the Future* never actually appeared on Australian TV (though it did make it to the US and Japan).

UNCHARTED WATERS

Year	1993
Publisher	Koei
Developer	Koei

THIS SNES VERSION of Uncharted Waters is more or less the NES game with more detailed graphics. You are a 16-year-old Portuguese lad (he's called Leon Franco on the NES but needs to be named here), and you've decided that it's time to set sail in search of fortune and fame. Accompanying you on your travels is your first mate, the sole survivor of your dad's shipwreck. As your adventure progresses, word gets back to the King of Portugal and he'll give you royal tasks to take on. These earn you noble ranking, and there are nine ranks ranging from Page all the way to Duke. The game starts in 1502, and the aim is to complete your journey within 20 years, potentially marrying the princess as a result. ■

FACT

The cover art for Uncharted Waters was created by Noriyoshi Ohrai. He was a legendary movie poster artist in Japan, famous for painting the Japanese *Star Wars* poster and numerous *Godzilla* posters.

UNCHARTED WATERS: NEW HORIZONS

Year	1994
Publisher	Koei
Developer	Koei

NEW HORIZONS OFFERS six separate six characters to choose from, each with their own standalone adventure. Joao Franco, the son of the first game's hero, wants to find Atlantis. Catalina Erantzo, a Spanish naval officer, seeks her missing brother. Otto Baynes is a British privateer on a secret mission to destroy the Spanish fleet. Dutch geographer Ernst Von Bohr wants to map the entire world. Pietro Conti is an Italian adventurer looking for treasure to pay the debt he owes his father, and Ali Vazas is a Turkish merchant in search of fortune. Each character's story occasionally crosses paths with the others', and while you still have the freedom to do what you want, following the plot is its own reward here. ■

FACT

Although New Horizons was never released in Europe, it did make it to the Wii U Virtual Console in 2013, meaning European gamers could finally (legally) play it 19 years after its original launch.

UN SQUADRON

Year	1991
Publisher	Capcom
Developer	Capcom

THE KINGDOM OF Aslan is under the control of ruthless mercenaries. The only hope of resistance is the UN Squadron, a trio of the world's finest pilots. This side-scrolling shoot 'em up gives you money after each stage which can be spent on special weapons: these can then be stored and called on when needed. Taking a hit doesn't kill you: instead, if you can avoid damage for a while you'll eventually recover. Each of the three pilots has their own special traits: Shin Kazama is a Japanese pilot who can raise his power level the quickest, Mickey Scymon was a former US Navy pilot in Vietnam and can carry the most special weapons, and Greg Gates is a Danish pilot who recovers from damage the quickest. ■

FACT

The Japanese version is called Area 88 and is based on the manga of the same name. This was one of Capcom's earliest licensed games, as the company wanted to reach larger audiences by using established characters.

UNIRACERS

Year	1994
Publisher	Nintendo
Developer	DMA Design

KNOWN AS UNIRALLY in Europe, Uniracers was the first Nintendo-only game developed by Dundee studio DMA Design, who would go on to become Rockstar North and create a small indie series by the name of Grand Theft Auto. There are significantly fewer drive-bys in this game, though, unless you're talking about the single-wheeled, gunless variety. Uniracers is a racing game where players control a unicycle on a variety of loop-filed side-scrolling courses. Your unicycle can pull off different spinning and flipping tricks: executing these is the key to success because they'll make you go faster when you land. There are also stunt tracks where performing tricks is obviously even more important, because they'll earn you the points needed to win. ■

FACT

DMA and Nintendo were sued by Pixar, who claimed Uniracers was ripping off its short movie *Red's Dream*. Despite DMA's protest that there are only so many ways you can animate a unicycle, the judge ruled in favour of Pixar and ordered no more copies to be published beyond the initial run of 300,000.

THE UNTOUCHABLES

Year	1994
Publisher	Ocean Software
Developer	Ocean Software

ALTHOUGH THE VIDEO game version of the hit 1987 movie *The Untouchables* was released on a number of different systems, the SNES port – which was the last to be released – is instead based on the 1993 TV series starring Tom Amandes as Eliot Ness and William Forsythe as Al Capone. It's the same as most other versions despite this, consisting of two different play styles. Some of your missions are side-scrolling run-and-gun affairs, while others are lightgun shooters that have you hiding behind cover and coming out occasionally to aim. Both styles feature relatively short time limits, so collecting the clock power-ups to keep the timer topped up is of the utmost importance. That and not being shot, of course. ■

FACT

The TV series lasted 42 episodes over the course of two seasons. It's (definitely) not to be confused with the classic 1959 series, which ran for four years and won Robert Stack an Emmy for Best Actor in a Dramatic Series.

URBAN STRIKE

Year	1995
Publisher	THQ
Developer	Granite Bay Software

THE THIRD GAME in EA's Strike series (after Desert Strike and Jungle Strike) took the action to the streets. Set in the year 2001, it revolves around H. R. Malone, a millionaire media mogul and cult leader who it turns out is secretly planning to make a superweapon that will destabilise the US government. Whereas the previous games mainly took place in the Gulf and a Cuba-like nation, Urban Strike focuses mostly on mainland North America, taking in San Francisco, New York and Las Vegas, as well as Hawaii and Mexico. As well as your standard helicopter, you also get to fly a larger chopper for rescue missions, as well as a ground assault vehicle. There are on-foot missions too, which see you entering buildings to carry out more intricate tasks. ■

FACT

Grantie Bay Software was the name of Desert Strike creator Mike Posehn's own development studio. It still exists to this day, but now it focuses on developing and selling timelapse software.

UTOPIA: THE CREATION OF A NATION

Year	1993
Publisher	Jaleco
Developer	Jaleco

UTOPIA IS WHAT you'd get if you crossed Populous with SimCity. The similarities to the former are obvious: this is an isometric strategy game that doesn't quite cast you as a god (as Populous does), but rather a planetary governor who arrives on one of 10 distant planets and sets about making it fit for colonisation. The similarities to SimCity come in the form of its various advisors, who pop up from time to time to tell you what you should probably focus on next. Although much of your time will be spent working on strategic planning and development, allocating tax funds and assigning personnel to exploration, construction and trade, you also need to research the development of powerful weaponry in case of alien invasion. ■

FACT

Utopia got a sequel, the Amiga-only K240. Instead of colonising a single planet it had you building multiple colonies on an asteroid belt and mining the asteroids for ore.

VEGAS STAKES

Year	1993
Publisher	Nintendo
Developer	HAL Laboratory

WHAT HAPPENS WHEN you take a usually pointless genre (the gambling game, where you win no real money) and put it in the hands of the dream team of Nintendo and HAL Laboratory? Well, the results are still

pointless, truth be told – after all, you can't polish a game of Craps – but at least there's an attempt to shoehorn a story in there. You arrive at the Golden Paradise Hotel & Casino in Las Vegas with four friends, one of whom you can choose to accompany you as you play the five games on offer: Blackjack, Slots, Roulette, Craps and Poker. You start with $1000 and as you win more money, bigger casinos are unlocked. The aim is to end up with $10 million. ∎

VENOM & SPIDER-MAN: SEPARATION ANXIETY

Year	1995
Publisher	Acclaim
Developer	Software Creations

THE SEQUEL TO Spider-Man & Venom: Maximum Carnage plays similarly to its predecessor. This time the story revolves around Venom, who was captured by the Life Foundation and had five symbiote spawn removed from him. Before the symbiotes could destroy him, Venom escaped, but now he needs to track them down to stop them creating five more creatures like Carnage, and he reluctantly needs Spider-Man's help to do it. Naturally, they're too late and they have to defeat the five symbiotes: Riot, Phage, Lasher, Agony and Scream. The big addition here is the option to play co-op as both Venom and Spider-Man. Along the way the pair can call on help from Captain America, Ghost Rider, Hawkeye and Daredevil. ∎

VIRTUAL BART

Year	1994
Publisher	Acclaim
Developer	Sculptured Software

A SEQUEL OF sorts to Bart's Nightmare, Virtual Bart is another bunch of minigames, this time without the hub world tying it all together. Instead, Bart is tied to a virtual reality exhibit at his school' science fair and must clear all

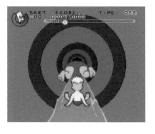

the 'virtual worlds' to get off it. There are six different mini-games: Dino Bart is a platformer with Bart as a dinosaur, Baby Bart has a young Bart escaping his bedroom and exploring Springfield's streets, and Pig Bart sees Bart as a pig who needs to escape from Krusty's Pork Factory, Meanwhile, Class Picture involves throwing tomatoes and eggs at students, Mt Splashmore has you trying to reach the bottom of a water slide and Doomsday Bart is a cross between Road Rash and Mad Max. ∎

VIRTUAL SOCCER

Year	1994
Publisher	Hudson Soft
Developer	Probe

THIS FOOTBALL GAME was originally released in Japan as J. League Super Soccer and included all 12 teams from the 1994 season of the Japanese J. League Division 1. Since Japanese football wasn't really a big deal in Europe, Hudson Soft and Probe rebranded it as Virtual Soccer and replaced the 12 J. League teams with 24 international teams instead. The main feature is the ability to choose three different camera angles: a side-on view, a vertical view (similar to Nintendo's own Super Soccer) and a more top-down, zoomed out view more reminiscent of Sensible Soccer. This feature aside, it's little more than a straightforward football game, although injuries tend to occur in it far more often than they do in real life. ∎

VORTEX

Year	1994
Publisher	Electro Brain
Developer	Argonaut Games

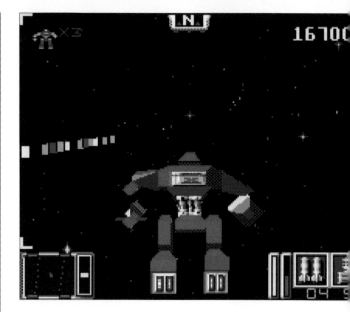

AFTER FINISHING ITS work on Star Fox with Nintendo, Argonaut was free to dabble in whatever it wanted while Nintendo got to work on its own Super FX game, Stunt Race FX. Although Argonaut could have technically made any type of game next, it did still have one thing that gave it the edge over other developers: Super FX test kits. It only made sense that the next title would be another polygonal game, then, but the team decided to keep the budget relatively low, going with smaller publisher Electro Brain. The result was Vortex, an interesting sci-fi shooter that looked more than a little like Star Fox but still had a few unique tricks up its sleeve. You play as an unnamed pilot of the Morphing Battle System (MBS), a special combat vehicle with the power to transform. Starting off in the titular Vortex, your aim is to travel to each of the five planets of

the Aki-Do system and retrieve the five pieces of core that have been captured by the enemy, so the core can be rebuilt and peace can be restored to the galaxy. Your MBS has four different forms it can transform into: Walker (a giant mech with a different selectable weapon on each arm), Land Burner (a low car that is extremely fast but hard to control), Sonic Jet (a jet aircraft that can only fire a laser but lets you reach areas you couldn't otherwise) and Hard Shell (a protective form that diverts damage to your fuel tank to protect your shield). ■

FACT

Designer Nic Cusworth says he regrets keeping the first level in the game, claiming it was too boring. 'After building the first level, I never played it again,' he told *Retro Gamer* magazine. 'I used the cheat code to skip it, a code I still remember: CTGXF.'

WAR 2410

Year	1995
Publisher	Advanced Productions
Developer	Advanced Productions

THIS IS A turn-based strategy game similar in appearance to Nintendo's Famicom Wars series. In the year 2003, scientists deciphered the code that unlocks the secrets of life, and created the perfect soldier. The

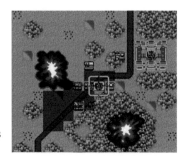

problem was, it was too perfect and the three different specimens – genetic humanoid soldiers called M.A.R.S., intelligent battle robots called Cromes and good old-fashioned Orcs – turned on their creators. It's now 2410 and the three groups of creatures are battling for control over the world, so you have to take control of the GDA – the human military – and take them out over the course of 20 missions. It's not quite clear why it took more than 400 years to do something about it, but there you go. ■

FACT

Battles are straight out of the Famicom Wars / Advance Wars playbook, with detailed animations showing the units attacking each other. These are quite lengthy but they can be turned off.

WAR 3010: THE REVOLUTION

Year	1996
Publisher	Advanced Productions
Developer	Advanced Productions

A LOT CAN happen in 600 years, and the war that previously took place on Earth has now escalated (or, rather, elevated) to outer space. The universe is now under the control of an intergalactic race called the Kyllen. A small group

of human slaves decide enough is enough and steal a few Kyllen ships, escaping with what is a frankly small battle fleet. The aim is to work your way through 16 missions, growing and upgrading your fleet as you go along until you're finally ready to take on and destroy the Kyllen once and for all. War 3010 essentially offers the same Famicom Wars style strategy gameplay, though this time with a space setting. There are also secret chess, checkers and Space Invaders mini-games that are unlocked with passwords. ■

FACT

Beat the game and the Kyllen leader warns: 'You fought bravely and your skills are impressive but your victory is not sealed. We will be back.' They weren't: Advanced Productions mysteriously disappeared with just two games under its belt.

WARIO'S WOODS

Year	1994
Publisher	Nintendo
Developer	Nintendo R&D1

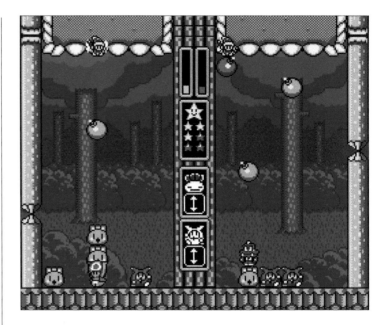

THE NES VERSION of Wario's Woods was notable for being the last ever officially licensed game on the system. The SNES version has no such historical milestone attached to it but that doesn't necessarily mean it should be dismissed, because it's a fun little puzzle game with loads of character, one with a storyline and everything. The Peaceful Woods used to live up to their name, until Wario and his crew of monsters turned up to ruin everything. Renaming the area Wario's Woods, the big man declares that peaceful creatures are no longer welcome. Toad decides to sort the situation out by entering Wario's Woods and bombing the utter hell out of the monsters that now inhabit it. Which doesn't seem very peaceful, but I suppose they aren't called the Peaceful Woods anymore. The game is played in a well similar to that in Tetris or Dr Mario, but instead of controlling falling blocks you're playing as Toad, who's located at the bottom of the screen. Toad can pick up the various monsters sitting on the ground and stack them on top of each other: in doing this he can try to arrange them into groups of matching colours. Then it's just a case of waiting for one of your sprite helpers to appear at the top of the screen and toss you a coloured bomb, which can then be lined up with enemies of the same colour to clear them. Still don't think it's like Toad to be so violent, mind you. ■

WARLOCK

Year	1995
Publisher	LJN
Developer	Realtime Associates

THIS SIDE-SCROLLING PLATFORMER is based on the second movie in the Warlock series of horror movies, *Warlock: The Armageddon*. You know the one. In the video game adaptation, you play as an unnamed druid as you try to gather six magic runestones before the titular Warlock does, so you can send him back to Hell. Your druid is armed with a small orb, which can be sent off in different directions to collect power-ups that are out of reach. These tend to give you spells, which can be cast for varying effects. One acts as a smart bomb, for example, while another protects you from some enemies. Along the way, the Warlock will keep turning up to mess things up for you: wrecking bridges, turning dogs into werewolves and the like. ■

WARPSPEED

Year	1992
Publisher	Accolade
Developer	Accolade

THERE WERE A few space dogfighting games during the 16-bit era but not a lot of them were designed specifically for consoles. WarpSpeed was, and has you piloting one of four starships – the *Stinger*, the *Striker*, the *Stalker* or the *Slasher* – as you fly through space taking out enemy ships with your machine gun and rockets. There are seven individual scenarios that you can choose at will on the main menu, as well as a short four-mission campaign. While most of the missions are pretty straightforward, it's worth bearing in mind that you only have a limited supply of fuel, so regularly landing on bases to refuel is an important habit to learn if you don't want to get caught with a chugging ship while surrounded by alien scum. ■

WATERWORLD

Year	1995
Publisher	Ocean Software
Developer	Ocean Software

WHEN YOUR FILM was the most expensive of all time and looked like it was going to be a massive financial flop, it makes sense that you probably wouldn't want to release the video game version in America. Still, the Waterworld game (developed and published by Ocean, quite fittingly) at least made it to Europe, where those who bought it discovered that it actually wasn't too bad. Playing as the nameless Mariner (portrayed by Kevin Costner in the movie), the majority of the game is presented with an isometric viewpoint as you ride around in your boat destroying the boats being sailed by the Smokers, a gang of pirates. At times you'll get to dive underwater in search of sunken treasure: these sections are viewed from side-on. ∎

FACT

The North American release of Waterworld was so close before it was pulled that *Nintendo Power* magazine actually reviewed the game, where it received 2.95 out of 5.

WAYNE GRETZKY AND THE NHLPA ALL-STARS

Year	1995
Publisher	Time Warner Interactive
Developer	Time Warner Interactive

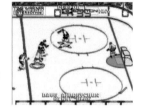

IF YOU'RE TRYING to get a famous name attached to your ice hockey game, there's simply none better than Wayne Gretzky, who was and forever will be the greatest of all time (apologies if you're reading this in 2084 and there's a hockey-playing robot breaking all records). His obligatory SNES game has the NHLPA licence – hence the superhero-like title – but doesn't have the NHL licence for teams and logos. There are also six international teams to choose from: USA, Canada, Sweden, Finland, Russia and Czechoslovakia. The latter is a bit of an odd inclusion: given that Czechoslovakia had already split into the Czech Republic and Slovakia at the start of 1993, it's safe to say someone wasn't keeping up on world affairs. ∎

FACT

At the time of writing, Wayne Gretzky holds 61 separate NHL records, including most points scored with an obscene 2,857 (second place is Jaromir Jagr, who's 'only' scored 1,921 despite playing 250 more games than Gretzky).

WAYNE'S WORLD

Year	1993
Publisher	THQ
Developer	Gray Matter

THE SATURDAY NIGHT Live sketch turned comedy movie *Wayne's World* was one of the biggest pop culture hits of the early '90s, so obviously a video game was going to follow. Rather than following the events of the movie, the plot for this one is a bit odd. Wayne and Garth are playing a game called Zantar at Noah's Arcade when they're both sucked into the machine. Garth is kidnapped by Zantar, so Wayne has to rescue him. Oddly, it turns out that this Zantar game features recreations of locations from the *Wayne's World* movie, so you'll be playing through Kramer's Music Store, Stan Mikita's Donut Shop and the Gasworks nightclub while using your guitar gun to fire deadly soundwaves at your enemies. Look, I don't know. ∎

FACT

According to the film's director, the famous car scene where Wayne, Garth and chums headbang to *Bohemian Rhapsody* was a nightmare to film because Mike Myers constantly complained that his neck was sore and that the scene wouldn't be funny.

WCW SUPERBRAWL WRESTLING

Year	1994
Publisher	FCI
Developer	Beam Software

NEW YORK BASED FCI had already published two WCW games – one for the NES, one for the Game Boy – so this SNES grappler was the last in the 'trilogy' because both companies parted ways. There are 12 WCW wrestlers to choose from: Barry Windham, Flyin' Brian Pillman, 'The Natural' Dustin Rhodes, Johnny B. Badd, Ric Flair, Rick Rude, Rick Steiner, Ricky 'The Dragon' Steamboat, Ron Simmons, Scott Steiner, Sting and Vader. Although the actual wrestling leaves something to be desired, there's a lot more personality in this game than LJN's WWF titles: the wrestlers shout at you on the character select screen and yell their catchphrases after pulling off special moves, and the commentators occasionally appear on the screen to spout one-liners. ∎

FACT

Of all twelve wrestlers in the game's roster only one of them – Dustin Rhodes – is still actively wrestling at the time of writing. Three of them are dead, of course, so it's a bit unfair to expect much from them.

WEAPONLORD

Year	1995
Publisher	Namco
Developer	Visual Concepts

AT FIRST GLANCE Weaponlord looks like an attempt to capitalise on Mortal Kombat's success by offering a similarly gory fighting game. In reality, it's an extremely deep weapons-based fighter with a host of techniques that can be learned by pros. The game was designed by James Goddard and Dave Winstead, who had previously worked with Capcom on the Street Fighter II sequels, and their expertise in the genre shines through here. Although there are only seven playable characters, each has a wealth of moves (including between 9 and 12 special moves each) as well as advanced techniques such as the ability to 'thrust block', a parry move that instantly puts players on the offensive. There were critics who suggested it was a little too complex for some, however. ■

FACT

Although it's never been confirmed or denied by Namco, Goddard and Winstead believe Weaponload inspired the studio to create the SoulCalibur series of weapons-based fighting games.

WE'RE BACK! A DINOSAUR'S STORY

Year	1993
Publisher	Hi Tech Expressions
Developer	Visual Concepts

BASED ON THE 1993 animated film of the same name by Steven Spielberg's short-lived Amblimation company, the plot for the SNES version of We're Back! doesn't follow the movie's in the slightest. Instead, you have to take friendly dinosaur Rex through five levels as he tries to rescue his human friends Louie and Cecilia from Captain Neweyes' evil twin brother, Professor Screweyes (why do they have different surnames?). Gameplay is standard for a movie tie-in platformer, although the fact you're playing as a T-Rex does make something of an impact because the massive hero sprite takes up a lot of the screen as a result. You can also call on your other dino chums Elsa, Woog, Vorb and Dweeb to pop up and lend a hand when required. ■

FACT

We're Back on Game Boy is actually a previous game called Baby T-Rex with the hero swapped out for the movie's characters. Sweden also has another version based on a cartoon character called Bamse, while Australia has one for children's TV character Agro Soar.

WHEEL OF FORTUNE: FEATURING VANNA WHITE

Year	1992
Publisher	GameTek
Developer	Imagitec Design

IF THE SNES is going to get its own version of *Jeopardy!* then the law dictates it also needs to get its own version of *Wheel of Fortune*, America's other favourite game show. It features the digitised presence and recorded speech of Vanna White, who (at the time of writing) has been playing the role of 'woman who turns the letters over' on the show for a mind-boggling 38 years. There are 4,500 puzzles to solve in the game, and while many of them are still perfectly possible to guess today (Breakfast at Tiffany's, Peanut Butter and Jelly Sandwich), some are a bit of a stretch nearly three decades later (such as Carl Yastrzemski, who retired as a baseball player in 1983). ■

FACT

Other random answers include American Dental Association, The Eruption of Krakatoa and the rather niche Don't Take Any Wooden Nickels.

WHEEL OF FORTUNE: DELUXE EDITION

Year	1994
Publisher	GameTek
Developer	Imagitec Design

FOR A GAME that's all about wordplay, it's safe to say that GameTek probably needs to read into the definition of the word 'deluxe'. This new and unimproved version of Wheel of Fortune is almost exactly the

same game as before, only with the previous 4,500 puzzles replaced with 4,000 new ones. The board looks a little different, Vanna is wearing a new outfit, the player avatars are of new people and the animation of the wheel spinning has been changed, but other than that, this is more about its new helping of puzzles than anything else. Even the back of the box can't muster up much original content, harping on once again about it 'featuring the show's popular theme music and digitised photography of the set'. ■

FACT

In case the puzzle in the screenshot is annoying you, the answer is 'Islands of the South Pacific'.

WHERE IN THE WORLD IS CARMEN SANDIEGO?

Year	1993
Publisher	Hi Tech Expressions
Developer	EA Canada

THE CARMEN SANDIEGO series is one of the rare examples of the 'edutainment' genre that actually managed to remember the 'tainment' part. Where in the World is the first instalment in the series and has you chasing after various crooks from the V.I.L.E. criminal organisation, who've been stealing famous artefacts from around the world. To find each criminal you have to follow their trail, asking at each location for clues on where they went next and then doing your own research to figure out your next destination. While you do this you also need to gather info on the suspect themselves, so you can narrow down who you need to issue an arrest warrant for. Catch enough crooks and you may be able to get Carmen herself. ◾

FACT

There have been two animated shows based on Carmen Sandiego. The first was broadcast during the mid '90s and the second was a new Netflix show that launched in 2019.

WHERE IN TIME IS CARMEN SANDIEGO?

Year	1993
Publisher	Hi Tech Expressions
Developer	EA Canada

THE ORIGINAL VERSION of Where in the World was launched in 1985, so Hi Tech Expressions was able to skip ahead a few entries for the next SNES release. Where in Time was the fifth game in the series (after Where in the World, USA, Europe and North Dakota), and this time has Carmen Sandiego and her V.I.L.E. villains travelling through time, stealing valuable items from history. As before, you have to follow the breadcrumbs by figuring out where the culprit went next, but this time rather than flying to each destination you're using your own personal chronoskimmer, a time-travel device that lets you choose both a location and an era of time, going back as far as 400 AD. ◾

FACT

As well as the animated shows, there have also been two kids' game shows based on Carmen Sandiego. *Where in the World* aired for five seasons and was then replaced with *Where in Time* for another two seasons.

WHIRLO

Year	1992
Publisher	Namco
Developer	Namco

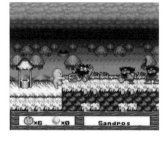

IN 1986, NAMCO released Valkyrie no Boken, a Japan-only action RPG for the Famicom about a shieldmaiden trying to save her land from darkness. One of the secondary characters in that game, Krino Xandra, was a little green lizard chap. Someone at Namco must have liked him, because he then got his own SNES platformer before being renamed Whirlo for Europe. It's a fun (but difficult) action platformer in which a strange dust has fallen over Whirlo's land, causing his family and neighbours to fall sick. Grabbing his pitchfork, Whirlo heads out to find out what's going on, and presumably decides that jabbing a lot of baddies in the process is going to help. A beautiful game but one that will test your patience. ◾

FACT

Whirlo is actually a prequel to Valkyrie no Boken, because it tells the story of how Whirlo ends up meeting Valkyrie for the first time. So don't worry about not knowing the backstory: there isn't one yet.

WHIZZ

Year	1996
Publisher	Titus Software
Developer	Flair Software

THIS ISOMETRIC PLATFORMER appeared too late in the SNES's life to make much of an impact, and its awkward marketing campaign (which asked if you ever felt 'the need for a Whizz real bad') didn't help matters much. Its small audience aside, though, this is an adequate enough platformer where you play as Whizz, a white bunny who has to make his way through 12 stages (split into four themed worlds: beach, snow, grass and board games), jumping into his hot air balloon at the end of each. One of the main criticisms levelled at Whizz is the lack of shadows, which means it can be hard to line up jumps: especially in a game with an isometric viewpoint, where shadows are often used as a reference point. ◾

FACT

Whizz was also released on the PlayStation and Saturn, where it's pretty much identical apart from a CGI intro sequence.

WILDC.A.T.S. COVERT ACTION TEAMS

Year	1995
Publisher	Playmates
Developer	Beam Software

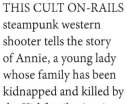

WILDC.A.T.S. WAS A comic series created by Marvel and DC writer and artist Jim Lee. The comic started in 1992 and spawned a 13-episode animated series in 1994, which was then followed by this SNES-only game. It's a beat 'em up similar to games like Final Fight, where you play as three members of the WildC.A.T.S. as they try to stop the immortal Helspont from taking over the Earth. Each of the game's stages is designed for a specific WildC.A.T. so you don't get to choose who to play as. Spartan is a cyborg who can shoot electricity, Warblade is a 'shaper' who can turn his arms into swords, and Maul is a 'titanthrope' which basically means he's the meathead. ∎

FACT

Jim Lee started at Marvel Comics in 1987 and went on to work on various projects for DC, Vertigo, Image, WildStorm, Dynamite and Dark Horse. At the time of writing, he's currently the Co-Publisher and Chief Creative Officer at DC.

WILD GUNS

Year	1995
Publisher	Natsume
Developer	Natsume

THIS CULT ON-RAILS steampunk western shooter tells the story of Annie, a young lady whose family has been kidnapped and killed by the Kid family. Annie approaches a bounty hunter called Clint and asks him to help her get revenge. Although Clint says he doesn't need Annie's help, she insists: besides, it turns out she isn't too shabby with a pistol either. Players control either Annie or Clint (or both in the two-player co-op mode) as they run left and right in the foreground. When they hold down the fire button they instead start controlling a crosshair, so they can fire at enemies. The trick, then, is to continually alternate between shooting and moving to get through the game's six stages. ∎

FACT

Natsume released an updated version called Wild Guns Reloaded for the Switch, PS4 and PC. It includes two new characters, extra stages and four-player co-op.

WILDSNAKE

Year	1994
Publisher	Spectrum Holobyte
Developer	Manley & Associates

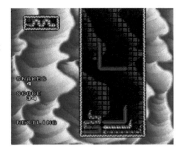

SOME PUBLISHERS SPENT a chunk of the '90s searching for the next Tetris: that next game that would transcend age, gender and gaming experience and make a small fortune in the process. WildSnake wasn't that game, but it didn't stop Spectrum Holobyte trying by putting Tetris's creator Alexey Pajitnov on the box with a 'presented by' credit (in reality he had nothing to do with the game). It's a strange cross between Tetris and the mobile game Snake, in which the usual blocks falling from the sky are replaced with snakes that you can move left and right as they fall. Make two snakes of the same colour touch and they'll disappear, but obviously that becomes harder as you end up with a big pile of serpent spaghetti. ∎

FACT

WildSnake is yet further proof that Japan is simply better at naming games. Over there, it's known as Super Snakey.

WILLIAMS ARCADE'S GREATEST HITS

Year	1996
Publisher	Williams Entertainment
Developer	Digital Eclipse Software

LIKE ITS SUCCESSOR Arcade's Greatest Hits: The Atari Collection 1 (which probably now feels like a lifetime ago if you've been reading this book in order), this is a compilation of five classic arcade games, this time all originally released by Williams. The games on offer here are Defender, Defender II, Joust, Robotron 2084 and Sinistar, and each is about as accurate as you can get on the SNES (even back in 1996 Digital Eclipse was proving itself to be the definitive studio when it came to handling compilations of retro games). Each game also has a comprehensive list of options, which essentially act like the dip switches arcade owners could mess around with on the original arcade machines to change the number of lives and such.

FACT

Williams Arcade's Greatest Hits was also released on the PlayStation and Saturn, where a sixth game, Bubbles, was added along with some video clips and concept art.

WING COMMANDER

Year	1992
Publisher	Mindscape
Developer	Origin Systems

WING COMMANDER WAS an enormous franchise throughout the '90s, and this was where it all began: or, rather, the 1990 PC version was where it all began, and this SNES port followed a couple of years later. It's a sci-fi flight sim set in the year 2654 and has you playing as a pilot on the *Tiger's Claw* strike carrier as it tries to keep the vicious Kilrathi race at bay. Depending on how well you do in your missions, you start to go down two different paths: do well and you'll get to lead an attack on the Kilrathi High Command starbase, but put in bad performances and you'll take on more defensive missions until eventually your entire strike carrier is forced to retreat. ■

FACT

Wing Commander was so successful that it ended up spawning a movie, an animated TV series, action figures and a 10-volume series of novels.

WING COMMANDER: THE SECRET MISSIONS

Year	1993
Publisher	Mindscape
Developer	Origin Systems

THE PC VERSION of Wing Commander got an add-on campaign called The Secret Missions, which added a bunch of new missions (secret ones, presumably), new ships and some new plotlines. Since the SNES had no way of applying add-on content to existing cartridges, The Secret Missions was released as a standalone sequel on Nintendo's system. In it, the *Tiger's Claw* answers a distress call but only finds wreckage and hundreds of thousands of corpses. It turns out the Kilrathi has developed a new weapon called the Graviton, which can make gravity 100 times more powerful. The Secret Missions doesn't have the original game's branching mission structure: instead, if you fail any mission you get two 'retreat' missions then it's game over. ■

FACT

Wing Commander is clearly influenced by *Star Wars*, so it's safe to say things came full circle with Wing Commander III, which featured live-action cutscenes starring Mark Hamill.

WINGS 2: ACES HIGH

Year	1992
Publisher	Namco
Developer	Namco

ORIGINALLY RELEASED AS Sky Mission in Japan, this First World War combat simulator was sold in North America as the sequel to Amiga game Wings (it actually had nothing to do with it). Europe played no part in such trickery, naming it Blazing Skies instead. You play as the leader of a squadron of British warplanes tasked with shooting down German planes and bombing German bases. There are 20 missions in total, with Mission 20 being an epic six-part affair. It's worth the effort, though, because the final part is a dogfight against the Red Baron, the notorious ace German pilot. Failing a mission results in two different outcomes: if you die you're given a funeral service, but if you survive while failing you may get a dishonourable discharge. ■

FACT

A cheat code lets you enable a radar to help you find your enemies easier, even though that type of radar didn't exist during the First World War.

WINTER GOLD

Year	1996
Publisher	Nintendo
Developer	Funcom

YOU MAY NOT expect a Europe-exclusive winter sports game to be the most graphically impressive game on the SNES, but Winter Gold is a jaw-dropping accomplishment. It's only one of three games to use the enhanced Super FX 2 chip (along with Doom and Yoshi's Island): this runs at twice the speed of the original Super FX, meaning Winter Gold's polygonal graphics aren't just more detailed than those of Star Fox and the like, the frame rate is significantly smoother too. It's just a shame that the actual game itself underwhelms slightly: with six events to choose from and fairly clunky controls, there's no denying that this is a game that should be remembered for how it looks rather than how it plays. ■

FACT

Instead of (unofficially) basing itself on a single Winter Olympics, Winter Gold lets you choose between three venues from the past and future: Albertville in France (home of the 1992 Winter Olympics), Lillehammer (1994) and Salt Lake City (2002).

WINTER OLYMPIC GAMES: LILLEHAMMER '94

Year	1994
Publisher	US Gold
Developer	Tiertex

AS THE NAME suggests, this is the official game of the 1994 Winter Olympics, which were held in Lillehammer in Norway. It consists of 10 separate events: Downhill, Super G, Giant Slalom, Slalom, Freestyle Moguls, Ski Jumping, Bobsleigh, Luge, Biathlon and Short Track Speed Skating. You can freely choose to practice any event, or take part in an Olympics mode where you take on all 10 events in a row, complete with opening and closing ceremonies. Rather than taking part as a generic character, you get to name an athlete, choose their gender and pick their nationality from a choice of 16 (sorry Kyrgyzstan, you didn't make the cut). The game was released on six formats, but the SNES version is generally considered to be the most difficult. ∎

FACT
The Winter Olympics used to be held during the same year the summer Olympics, but this was changed, beginning with the 1994 Winter Olympics. That's why there was also a Winter Olympics in 1992.

THE WIZARD OF OZ

Year	1993
Publisher	SETA
Developer	Manley & Associates

WHEN YOU'RE LOOKING for a hot new property to turn into a video game, a 1939 musical may not be your first choice. Regardless, that's what SETA chose with The Wizard of Oz, a SNES-exclusive platformer in which Dorothy tries to rescue her dog Toto from the Wicked Witch of the West (even though she didn't kidnap Toto in the film). In fact, it seems hell-bent on being nothing like the film: most stages are set in locations that were never in the movie, and the ending is completely different too: rather than Dorothy clicking together her ruby slippers and being sent home, instead the Wizard tells her that the slippers have run out of power and so he sends her home in a balloon instead. ∎

FACT
There was a 13-episode animated series of The Wizard of Oz in 1990, where the magic in Dorothy's ruby slippers was temperamental. While this may have been a more modern licence for the game, it makes no reference to the cartoon.

WIZARDRY V: HEART OF THE MAELSTROM

Year	1994
Publisher	Capcom
Developer	ASCII Entertainment

THE WIZARDRY SERIES began on home computers way back in 1981. The first two games were given NES ports, but it was decided to cut to the chase on the SNES and skip ahead to Wizardry V (even though PC gamers were onto Wizardy VII by that point). It's a pretty old-school dungeon crawler – even for then – in which you have to guide your party of adventurers through a series of tunnels called the Maelstrom in search of the Gatekeeper, who holds the ability to stop the chaotic earthquakes, floods and famine destroying your land. As is often the case with RPG ports, the SNES version of Wizardry is heavily censored, with nude sprites covered up and references to sex, alcohol and dark violence replaced. ∎

FIGHTER1 charges at Lady Stinger and hits once for 3 damage.
Lady Stinger is destroyed!

FACT
The Super Famicom version of Wizardry V was uncut and actually had the English text tucked away in its code, so in 2017 a hacked version of the game ended up online that essentially turned it into an uncensored English version.

WOLFCHILD

Year	1993
Publisher	Virgin Interactive
Developer	Core Design

TOP SCIENTIST KAL Morrow has been kidnapped by terrorist organisation Chimera, who also killed his wife and child during the skirmish. However, Kal also has a second son, Saul, who wasn't at home. Returning to find his mum and brother dead and his dad missing, Saul activates his dad's Project Wolfchild experiment, turning him into a werewolf. Off Saul heads to rescue his old man from Chimera, who probably won't end up lycan what's going to happen when he gets there (sorry). Wolfchild is an action platformer where the player starts as Saul in his human form but can then collect energy balls to eventually transform into a wolf, at which point he gains far more powerful attacks, including the ability to fire psychic energy at enemies. ∎

FACT
Wolfchild was designed by Simon Phipps, who'd also designed other action games like Switchblade and Rick Dangerous. He later moved to EA's UK team, where he helped design the first four Harry Potter games.

WOLFENSTEIN 3D

Year	1994
Publisher	Imagineer
Developer	Imagineer

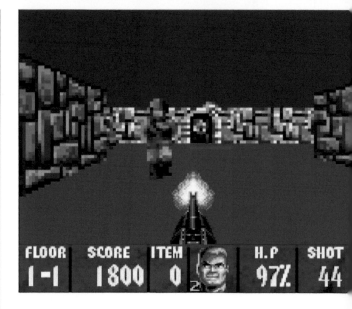

THERE'S A STRONG argument that the first-person shooter genre may never have become as popular as it is today were it not for Wolfenstein 3D. Although there were other games before it that used a first-person viewpoint, Wolfenstein 3D was the first major first-person game to show your gun at the bottom of the screen and have you gunning down enemies in what is now the standard FPS style. Its popularity saw it ported to a number of systems, but the SNES port is arguably the most interesting because of the almost comical levels of censorship that had to be carried out to get it approved by the notoriously family-friendly Nintendo.

Despite it being a game about storming a Nazi castle to kill Adolf Hitler, all reference to Nazis were removed from the SNES version. This meant no swastikas on the walls, no use of the phrase 'Nazi Germany' (it was now the 'Master State'), enemies speaking English instead of

> **FACT**
>
> When you killed Hitler in the original version of Wolfenstein 3D, he'd say 'Auf Wiedersehen' and explode in a shower of gore. In the SNES version he just falls on his bum.

German and the final boss – wee Adolf himself – having his moustache shaved off, his Nazi armband removed and his name changed to the Staatmeister. It wasn't all take, take, take, mind you: the SNES version did also add some things, like new flamethrower and rocket launcher weapons, and the extremely useful ability to bring up an automap to see which of the similar-looking rooms you hadn't visited yet. But despite these improvements, the SNES Wolfenstein will always be known more for what it took off the table than what it brought to it. ■

WOLVERINE: ADAMANTIUM RAGE

Year	1994
Publisher	LJN
Developer	Bits Studios

WHEN A MYSTERIOUS computer transmission tells Wolverine that someone has information regarding his past, he heads to Canada to see what's going on. When he reaches his destination he

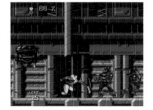

discovers that he's been tricked: he's at the Weapon X lab and it's packed with enemies. You have to fight your way through the lab and take on the Destroyer Program, before heading off on a journey that takes in the likes of Tokyo, the Hellfire Club and even a nightmare hallucination. Along the way you'll fight numerous old foes like Lady Deathstrike, Fugue, Cyber, Crystal Dragon, Geist and Tri-Fusion. Given the nature of Wolverine's powers, this is one of the first high-profile games where your health slowly begins to recover automatically after a while. ■

> **FACT**
>
> In 2016, it was discovered that the second boss fight in Adamantium Rage is the first example of a grime instrumental, some eight years before Pulse X by Youngstar, which was widely credited as the first.

WORDTRIS

Year	1992
Publisher	Spectrum Holobyte
Developer	Bullet-Proof Software

ONE OF THE earlier attempts to find a successor to Tetris, Wordtris offers more block-dropping shenanigans, except this time the blocks are single squares containing random letters. The aim is to try to form words of at least

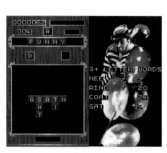

three letters either vertically or horizontally, at which point they'll disappear (as long as they're in the game's dictionary, of course: don't go expecting YOLO to work). There's also a special bonus word at the top of the screen: if you're somehow able to form that word the entire play area will wipe clean and you'll get a huge score bonus. You can also get help from the occasional special block, like a question mark block (which lets you add any letter you want) and a bomb that blows up any block. ■

> **FACT**
>
> Despite having no actual link to Tetris, Wordtris does its very best to make you think otherwise. 'It's Tetris made letter perfect,' claims the box, adding: 'It's a New Word Order in video games as those Soviet blocks fall again!'

WORLD CLASS RUGBY

Year	1993
Publisher	Imagineer
Developer	Denton Designs / Misawa

LIVERPOOL-BASED DEVELOPER DENTON Designs made World Class Rugby and its sequel World Class Rugby: Five Nations Edition for the Amiga in the early '90s, until Japanese publisher Misawa ported it over to the SNES (rugby's actually massive in Japan, you see). The SNES features 16 different international teams and the option to play either a single game, a world cup or a league for 3-8 teams. Rather than a straight port of the Amiga versions, Misawa decided to make use of the SNES's Mode 7 technique to create a 3D-style pitch, in an attempt to make the game look more realistic. While the game does look decent, it could be argued that the scales are a bit off, since the players are massive and the pitch is tiny. ■

FACT

There were actually two more rugby games released in Japan for the Super Famicom. Misawa made a sequel to World Class Rugby, and Tonkin House also developed the side-on Super Rugby.

WORLD CUP STRIKER

Year	1994
Publisher	Elite
Developer	Rage Software

WHEN YOU'VE GOT a perfectly good football game sitting there, it would be downright foolish not to capitalise on World Cup USA '94 with it. That was obviously the mindset of Elite and Rage Software, who took their existing game Striker (World Soccer '94 in North America) and upgraded it a little to World Cup Striker (which America got as Elite Soccer). At its core it's more or less the same as the previous Striker game, but while its predecessor had 64 international teams to choose from this one only has 32: that's the 24 teams who qualified for USA '94 and another eight who didn't (in other words, an excuse not to annoy Scottish and English players). On the bright side, all player names are correct. ■

FACT

You owe it to yourself to search for the title theme as the perfect example of how to use speech samples to make a brilliantly terrible song on the SNES.

WORLD CUP USA 94

Year	1994
Publisher	US Gold
Developer	Tiertex

AS THIS BOOK shows, there were numerous publishers clamouring to cash in on the 1994 World Cup in the USA, with the SNES getting far more football games than the NES did. It stands to reason, then, that there would actually be a properly official World Cup USA 94 game too, although in reality it was far from the best offering. Much like some other unofficial offerings, World Cup USA 94 included all 24 teams who'd qualified for the tournament plus another eight who hadn't qualified. Because of its official status, it also boasted an authentic World Cup mode that featured the actual groups and fixture schedule from the real-life tournament. Player names were fake, though: England's front two are Pope and Swindler, for example. ■

FACT

The Mega CD version of the game included a song by German band Scorpions called *No Pain No Gain*. The music video included footage from the game.

WORLD HEROES

Year	1993
Publisher	Sunsoft
Developer	Sunsoft

SNK'S NEO-GEO ARCADE hardware was no stranger to the one-on-one fighting genre and 1992's World Heroes was one of many examples of this. It received a SNES port a year later, and while it obviously took a hit graphically, it was still an entertaining fighter. Its plot is a little hokey: a scientist creates a time machine and decides to bring together the eight greatest fighters to see who's the best. While most of these fighters are indeed based on the actual historical figures Hattori Hanzo, Fuma Kotaro, Rasputin, Joan of Arc, Bruce Lee, Genghis Khan and Hulk Hogan – though some of them don't have those exact names – there's also Brocken, a Nazi robot who's blatantly supposed to be M. Bison from Street Fighter II. ■

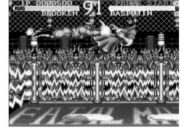

FACT

As well as standard fights, World Heroes also has a 'Fatal Match' option, where the walls of the screen are electrified. Which doesn't seem particularly fair, but there you go.

WORLD HEROES 2

Year	1994
Publisher	Takara
Developer	Saurus

WORLD HEROES' SILLY combination of electrified arenas and 'fake Hulk Hogan vs robot Nazi Bison' match-ups meant a sequel was a case of when, not if. A further six characters were added to the existing roster of eight, some of whom were once again inspired by real-life heroes: Scottish pirate Captain Kidd, Viking sailor Erik the Red, female Japanese judo legend Ryoko Tani and 1700s Muay Thai fighter Nai Khanomtom. There's also a masked witch doctor called Mudman and an enormous American football player called Johnny Maximum, who apparently only plays the sport because he loves the violence. The previous game's Fatal Match mode was tweaked a little: now players shared a single energy bar, which went back and forth as hits were landed. ■

FACT

Other characters considered but ultimately not used included Dracula, Siegfried, Ramesses III, samurai hero Yagyu Jubei and Sinbad (the sailor, not the comedian).

WORLD LEAGUE SOCCER

Year	1992
Publisher	Mindscape
Developer	Anco

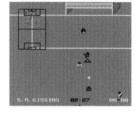

WORLD LEAGUE SOCCER is a modified SNES version of Kick Off 2, the much-loved home computer football game that gained most success on the Amiga. There are 24 international teams to choose from here (including some with questionable spelling: hello there Rumania and Columbia), and four different modes with strange names that don't always reflect what you get. Single Game is straightforward enough, and The League is a league for up to eight teams, but The Match is actually an eight-team knockout cup and World Match is a World Cup style set-up with six groups of four teams. Player names are fake, so Scotland has Row, Rhodes and Moore up front, with W. Raleigh in goal (who presumably isn't Sir Walter Raleigh). ■

FACT

There are four different pitch surfaces to choose from, including plastic. Plastic pitches were hugely controversial in English football in the '80s: QPR was the first team to install one in 1981, but were also the first team to remove one when they scrapped it in 1988.

WORLD MASTERS GOLF

Year	1995
Publisher	Virgin Interactive
Developer	Arc Developments

THIS EUROPE-EXCLUSIVE GOLF game contains four fictional courses for you to play through. Aldan Forest is a quiet, secluded course where many of the holes are surrounded by tall trees, while Cranfield Lakes has a large number of strategically placed water traps as well as uneven greens. Marston Beach is obviously packed to the brim with enormous bunkers, and 'Victoria Plains is beautifully and imaginatively contoured' (I hope they're still talking about a golf course). The game makes use of gourad shading – a technique used to add lighting to low-poly objects – to give the courses the illusion of depth, and there's a Mode 7 chase cam that follows the ball when you hit it. You can also name your golfer and choose their gender. ■

FACT

World Masters Golf was programmed by Neil Paterson, who continues to work as a programmer to this day. He was recently part of the programming team for Assassin's Creed: Syndicate.

WORMS

Year	1996
Publisher	Ocean Software
Developer	Team17

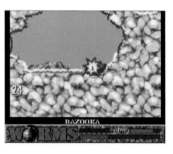

THERE WAS A period when Worms was considered the ultimate multiplayer game. It's a turn-based combat game where 2–4 players compete on a 2D battlefield with randomly generated terrain. Each player has a squad of four Worms, with a wide variety of weapons. Each weapon has its own strengths and weaknesses: Bazookas do good damage but you need to take the wind into account, while dynamite is enormously powerful and can take a big chunk out of the scenery, but you need to be able to quickly get out of the way once you've planted it. What really makes it, though, is its sense of humour: there's nothing quite like smoking an enemy out of a tunnel they've dug by sending an exploding sheep in there after them. ■

FACT

There have been more than 20 Worms games since the release of the original. The most recent was Worms WMD, which is available on the Xbox One, PS4, Switch and PC.

WWF SUPER WRESTLEMANIA

Year	1992
Publisher	LJN
Developer	Sculptured Software

THE FIRST OF three WWF (now WWE) games created by the partnership of LJN and Sculptured Software, Super WrestleMania features 10 superstars of the early '90s era, each with their own theme music: Hulk Hogan, Macho Man Randy Savage, The Million Dollar Man Ted DiBiase, Jake 'The Snake' Roberts, The Undertaker, Sid Justice, Hawk, Animal, Earthquake and Typhoon. The only modes available are one-on-one, tag team and Survivor Series matches (where two teams of four fight), and each wrestler has the same standard moveset: a punch, a kick, a dropkick, a body slam, a headbutt, a suplex and a flying elbow drop from the top turnbuckle. A rather basic first offering, then, but a foundation for the games that would follow in successive years. ∎

FACT

The Mega Drive later got its own version of the game, complete with finishing moves and an almost entirely different roster. Hogan, Savage and DiBiase were joined by The Ultimate Warrior, Papa Shango, IRS, Shawn Michaels and the British Bulldog.

WWF ROYAL RUMBLE

Year	1993
Publisher	LJN
Developer	Sculptured Software

THE SECOND ATTEMPT offered gamers a far meatier package. This time the roster consisted of 12 wrestlers: Bret Hart, The Undertaker, Shawn Michaels, Razor Ramon, Randy Savage, Crush, Lex Luger, Ric Flair, Mr Perfect, Ted DiBiase, Yokozuna and Tatanka. As well as the titular Royal Rumble mode – where up to six wrestlers fight at the same time and when one is thrown over the top rope another replaces them – there's a new Tournament mode where you choose one wrestler and beat the rest one at a time to win the WWF Championship. Players can now also knock out the referee and use illegal moves like throttling, eye raking and steel chair shots on their opponent while he's down. A big improvement. ∎

FACT

Once again, the Mega Drive version featured a different roster. Flair, Perfect, DiBiase, Yokozuna and Tatanka were ditched in favour of Hulk Hogan, IRS, Hacksaw Jim Duggan, The Model Rick Martel and Papa Shango.

WWF RAW

Year	1994
Publisher	Acclaim
Developer	Sculptured Software

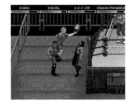

THE THIRD AND final game in LJN's WWF SNES trilogy, WWF Raw keeps all the game modes of its predecessor and adds a few more features for good measure. The shiny new 12-strong roster consists of Bret Hart, the Undertaker, Yokozuna, Bam Bam Bigelow, Razor Ramon, Lex Luger, Doink the Clown, Shawn Michaels, the 1-2-3 Kid, Diesel, Owen Hart and Luna Vachon (the first ever female wrestler in a WWF game). The new Bedlam match type is basically a tornado tag team match, with all four competitors allowed in the ring at the same time. As well as the return of finishing moves, each character now has an over-the-top Mega Move which usually throws their opponent out of the ring. Four players are also supported for the first time. ∎

FACT

There was one other WWF game created by LJN and Sculptured Software. WWF Rage in the Cage was a Mega CD exclusive with 20 characters, steel cage matches and audio samples playing before each fight.

WWF WRESTLEMANIA: THE ARCADE GAME

Year	1995
Publisher	Acclaim
Developer	Sculptured Software

THE LJN BRAND dissolved in 1995, but Acclaim (who owned it) still had the home licence for WWF games, and so published this home version of Midway's arcade WWF title. In true Midway style, this is effectively the NBA Jam or Mortal Kombat of wrestling games. The actual wrestlers were digitised into the game and pulled off ridiculous special moves: the Undertaker hits opponents with an actual tombstone, for example. The roster in other versions is small enough with only eight wrestlers, but the SNES version cuts out two more (Bam Bam Bigelow and Yokozuna), leaving players to choose between Bret Hart, the Undertaker, Shawn Michaels, Razor Ramon, Doink and Lex Luger. ∎

FACT

The brilliantly terrible promo VHS for the game has Bret Hart visiting Midway and helping the dev team fix bugs. It includes the immortal line: 'Come on guys, it was there in front of you the whole time: you're dereferencing a null pointer.'

XARDION

Year	1992
Publisher	Asmik Ace Entertainment
Developer	Asmik Ace Entertainment

THE ALPHA-1 SOLAR system is being attacked by invaders from the artificial world NGC-1611, so Alpha-1's three planets each send a hero. These are your three playable characters in this Metroidvania adventure, and you can switch between them at any time. Triton is a humanoid mech from the planet Aquata and is the only one of the three who can fire upwards. Alcedes is a beetle-like robot from the desert planet Feira, and can use its antennae to attack enemies both in front and behind. Finally, Panthera is a cat-like robot from the jungle planet Zikar who can enter small passages. Later in the game you'll also encounter the titular Xardion, a super-powerful robot who's the only one able to kill the final boss. ■

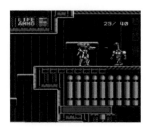

FACT

The game's manual was seemingly written by someone with a real flair for descriptions, because the introductory story refers to Alcedes as 'the telekinetic beastybot'.

X-KALIBER 2097

Year	1994
Publisher	Activision
Developer	Toshiba EMI

BY ALL ACCOUNTS, the year 2097 isn't very nice. Crime is rife and the Neo New York Special Forces are down to its last two agents, Slash (who has 'an extraordinary talismanic sword'), and Alix (who – let me just check my notes – is 'beautiful'). Alix is unsurprisingly kidnapped, so it's up to Slash to rescue her. This action platformer has a bespoke soundtrack by industrial/electronic band Psykosonik, and has you playing as Slash as he uses his X-Kaliber sword to take out numerous enemies, some extremely difficult bosses – including a chap called Tattoo who's almost identical to Street Fighter II's Blanka – and eventually the warlord ruler of Neo New York himself, Raptor. Easy! (It isn't easy: seriously, those boss fights.) ■

FACT

If you somehow don't have Psykosonik's entire discography on vinyl, you may want to track down the Japanese version. It has an entirely different soundtrack by Hitoshi Sakimoto and Hayato Matsuo, who later composed the Final Fantasy XII score.

X-MEN: MUTANT APOCALYPSE

Year	1994
Publisher	Capcom
Developer	Capcom

WHILE USING HIS snoopy, nosey Cerebro device one day, Professor X discovers that the tiny island nation of Genosha is hosting Apocalypse, who appears to imprisoning the mutants who live there. Five of the X-Men are sent to Genosha to see what's going on and try to help liberate the mutants, but it soon turns out that Apocalypse isn't the only one involved in this skulduggery. The first five stages in Mutant Apocalypse are each played with a different member of the X-Men – Beast, Cyclops, Gambit, Wolverine and Psylocke – and you can choose which order to play them. There are then another five stages that you can play as whoever you choose, followed by a final five character-specific stages again. ■

FACT

The first issue of The X-Men was published in September 1963 and introduced the original five X-Men: Angel, Beast, Cyclops, Iceman and Marvel Girl (Jean Grey).

X-ZONE

Year	1992
Publisher	Kemco
Developer	Kemco

X-ZONE IS THE only third-party SNES game that actually requires the Super Scope light gun to play (as opposed to simply offering it as an optional control method). It's set in a nondescript country called The Nation, where the huge mainframe computer that powers its defence system decides it wants to destroy the Earth. Armed with your SS6 Plasma Energy Launcher, you have to infiltrate the 'X-termination Zone' and regain control of the defence system by shooting your way through seven different levels filled with patrol tanks, drones and sentry guns. At the end of each level is an 'overseer', a large boss machine armed to the teeth with missiles and cannons. If you can't destroy them, I hope you like your Earth extra crispy. ■

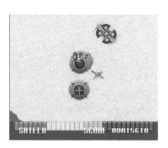

FACT

X-Zone's box makes a point of the fact that you don't actually have to hold the Super Scope up to your shoulder to play it. Instead you control an on-screen cursor with the gun's pointer, so you can aim on the TV without looking through its scope.

YOSHI'S COOKIE

Year	1993
Publisher	Bullet-Proof Software
Developer	Bullet-Proof Software

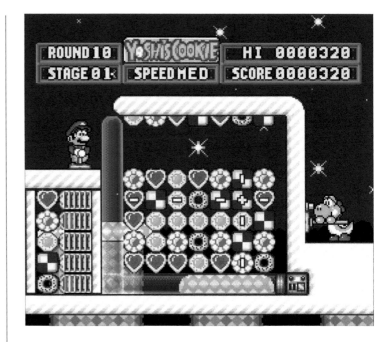

YOSHI'S COOKIE BEGAN life as a puzzle game called Hermetica, which was being developed by Bullet-Proof Software for the SNES. After Bullet-Proof showed it off at the Consumer Electronics Show in 1992, Nintendo decided it liked what it saw and negotiated the rights to publish versions for the NES and Game Boy. In order to give it a bit more character, Nintendo renamed the game Yoshi's Cookie and put Mario characters in it. Bullet-Proof, which still had the rights to make the SNES version of Hermetica, thought 'we'd like a bit of that' and so Nintendo let it Yoshi-fy the SNES game too. So what is it, then? Well, it's an odd puzzler that acts a bit like a Rubik's Cube. You're given a grid with different cookies on it and you have to rotate rows and columns to try to get a full line with the same design (which in turn makes that line disappear). If your grid overflows and becomes more than eight cookies wide, you get Game Over, but there's also a special cookie shaped like Yoshi's head that can be used as a sort of wild card to help you clear a particularly annoying section. The main single-player mode is called Action and it has you clearing increasingly larger grids over a series of stages. There's also a Versus mode and a Puzzle mode, where you're shown a specific layout of cookies and have to figure out how to clear it within a set number of moves. ■

FACT

The puzzles in the SNES-exclusive Puzzle mode were created by none other than the creator of Tetris, Alexey Pajitnov.

YOSHI'S SAFARI

Year	1993
Publisher	Nintendo
Developer	Nintendo R&D1

NINTENDO DID ITS very best to make the Super Scope a success. Not only did it get the trusted Intelligent Systems team to work on Super Scope exclusive games like Battle Clash and Metal Combat: Falcon's Revenge, it also got one of its own internal teams to make a brand new Mario spin-off that needed the peripheral to make it work. This game was Yoshi's Safari, the only lightgun game you'll see starring Mario and Yoshi. It's set in a new region called Jewelry Land, whose 12 magical gems have been stolen by the invading Bowser and his Koopalings. After the Koopas hold the king prisoner in the Dark Realm and the prince in the Light Realm, word gets to the prince's friend, Princess Peach, who asks Mario and Yoshi to head off and help. Yoshi's Safari consists of 12 stages, one for each magical gem: the first seven are set in the Light Realm, then the final five trickier levels take place in the Dark Realm. Although the game is viewed from over the back of Yoshi's head, it's actually played through a first-person perspective: you're playing as Mario, you see, sitting on Yoshi's back while armed with a Super Scope to take out approaching enemies. There's an optional two-player co-op mode, but it's fair to say it gives the second player the short end of the stick: while Player 1 operates the Super Scope, Player 2 uses a controller to make Yoshi walk (which he does automatically in single-player anyway). ■

FACT

Yoshi's Safari may not have set the world alight (or kicked off mass Super Scope sales), but it was still monumental for one reason: it was the first time Princess Toadstool was called Princess Peach in the west.

YOUNG MERLIN

Year	1994
Publisher	Virgin Interactive
Developer	Westwood Studios

WESTWOOD STUDIOS WAS known for its more serious games like Dune II and The Legend of Kyrandia, so Young Merlin was its attempt to make something that would appeal to a wider audience. It's a top-down adventure game that looks similar to Zelda: A Link to the Past, and has you playing as the great wizard Merlin, but back when he was just a young lad. When he spots a beautiful maiden drowning, Merlin tries to help but ends up getting swept by the river to an enchanted land. Discovering that the evil Shadow King plans to take over this land, Marlin decides to seek the help of the Lady of the Lake, to see if the pair can destroy the Shadow King's minions and defeat him once and for all. ∎

FACT

It's little wonder that young Merlin risks himself trying to rescue a good-looking woman: Merlin's death is different in a variety of tellings of his story, but most of them involve dying as a result of a beautiful 'femme fatale'.

YS III: WANDERERS FROM YS

Year	1992
Publisher	American Sammy
Developer	Tonkin House

THE FIRST GAME in the Ys series was released on the Sega Master System and PC in the west, but its sequel didn't get an English language release. That didn't stop Ys III making its way to North America, however. It's set three years after the events of the first two games (which took place back-to-back), and has the hero Adol and his pal Dogi heading home to discover that Dogi's hometown is in downfall thanks to failing crops and constant night-time attacks. I smell an adventure (either that or rotting corn). While many of Ys III's mechanics work the same as those in the previous Ys games, the viewpoint has been changed from a top-down view to a side-scrolling one, much like Zelda II. ∎

FACT

In case you were wondering, it's pronounced 'eez', as opposed to 'wise'. I once knew someone who pronounced it 'yiss': that person is wrong.

ZERO THE KAMIKAZE SQUIRREL

Year	1994
Publisher	Sunsoft
Developer	Iguana Entertainment

AS DISCUSSED ELSEWHERE in this book, Zero the Kamikaze Squirrel is the main henchman (well, henchsquirrel) of Edgar Ektor, the villain in the Aero the Acrobat games. At one point during Aero the Acrobat 2, Zero disappears and is nowhere to be seen, while the ending simply states that he 'quickly returned to his homeland'. That's because he had to go off on his own adventure, which this game chronicles. The reason he had to speed home was a telegram he received from his ex-girlfriend Amy, informing him that an evil lumberjack called Jacques le Sheets is destroying his homeland and cutting down all the trees so he can make counterfeit money. When Zero gets home he discovers that Amy has been kidnapped, so off he goes to both save Amy and defeat Jacques le Sheets… but is there

FACT

The Aero and Zero games were the result of father-and-son teamwork. David Siller's father Ray Siller Jr worked in the coin-op business, so David did too. When he eventually joined Sunsoft he worked with his own son, Justin Siller, to create Aero and Zero.

maybe someone else who's pulling all the strings from the shadows? Obviously there is, otherwise I wouldn't have brought it up. This is a platform game similar to the two Aero the Acrobat titles, although this time Zero is armed with his own set of abilities. He's got a double-jump that lets him reach higher areas without the use of any extra power-ups. He's got a Kamikaze Slam, a move that lets him spin in mid-air and slam down onto an enemy. And finally, he's armed with a limited number of throwing stars that he can throw at his foes (but don't worry, he can collect more along the way). ∎

ZOMBIES ATE MY NEIGHBOURS

Year	1993
Publisher	Konami
Developer	LucasArts

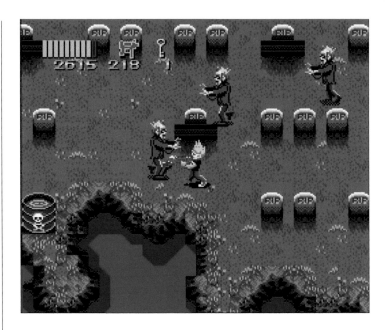

SIMPLY KNOWN AS Zombies in Europe – because rotting undead corpses are apparently fine as long as they don't nibble anyone's bum – Zombies Ate My Neighbours is LucasArts' love letter to the days of cheesy sci-fi and horror B-movies. The mysterious Dr Tongue has created a who's-who of monsters in his lab and unleashed them on the world, so it's up to two brave kids, Zeke and Julie, to head out and take them on. The aim is to rescue your various neighbours before they become victims: they're dotted around each stage and consist of the likes of cheerleaders, babies, tourists and your token 'dad operating a barbecue'. Running around the 48 maze-like stages and rounding them all up is a task in itself, and that's before you take into account the monsters. Although the title seems to suggest that zombies are the primary enemy here, in reality they're just one of a huge variety of baddies and beasts wandering around.

FACT
There's a bonus stage called Day of the Tentacle, based on the LucasArts point-and-click adventure of the same name, where all the enemies are that game's purple tentacles.

There are poisonous jelly blobs, mummies, werewolves, pod plants, evil 'Tommy' dolls (based on Chucky from *Child's Play*), chainsaw wielding maniacs (who become axe-wielding maniacs in the European version), and those are just for starters. Thankfully, you aren't entirely unarmed for this: although it may as well seem like it at first when all you have is a water pistol. Along the way you'll collect other weapons like a bazooka (which also blows holes through walls), soda can grenades, fire extinguishers and a potion that turns you into a massive purple monster. ◼

ZOOL

Year	1993
Publisher	GameTek
Developer	Gremlin Interactive

ZOOL IS A ninja from the Nth dimension whose ship encounters a powerful vortex that causes him to crash-land on a mysterious planet. The ship's computer informs Zool that his arch-enemy Krool has taken over this new planet's six different worlds, so it's up to you to do something about it. Originally released on Amiga home computers, Zool is a fast-paced action platformer where players are armed with a 'magic cannon' weapon, a spin kick and the ability to climb walls. There's a very noticeable difference between the North American and European versions of the game: the first world has a candy theme, and the European version has massive logos for Chupa Chups lollipops dotted around. These are missing in the American version. ◼

FACT
you feel the need to learn more about Zool's lore (and who doesn't), there were two oung adult novels released in 995 with the sombre, hard-hitting titles *Cool Zool* and *Zool Rules*.

ZOOP

Year	1995
Publisher	Viacom New Media
Developer	Hookstone Productions

A BASIC BUT somewhat underrated puzzle game, Zoop puts you in control of a little triangle in the middle of the screen as different coloured blobs slowly come in from the sides. You can shoot your triangle (or 'zoop' it) at these blobs, and if both are the same colour the blobs will disappear. If the triangle and the blob are a different colour, though, the colours will switch over: this lets you change the colour of your triangle so you can go and clear some other blobs elsewhere on the screen. If any blobs reach the square in the centre, the game's over. One of Zoop's selling points was its 'Opti-Challenge' backgrounds, which were designed to put you off by getting more distracting as the game progressed. ◼

FACT
Zoop had an amusing magazine ad designed to look like a public health warning showing the effects the game can have on players, including spots on their face, changing their hairstyle, dreaming of Zoop and spending their money on all nine versions.

BONUS SECTION:
THE VIRTUAL BOY ENCYCLOPEDIA

As the mid-90s approached, all eyes were on Nintendo to see what the SNES's successor was going to look like. The problem was, Nintendo wasn't anywhere near ready to release one yet: the Nintendo 64 was still at least a couple of years away, and the trusty Game Boy wouldn't get its colour upgrade until 1998. That didn't mean it didn't have another trick up its sleeve, of course, and on 13 November 1994 the *New York Times* printed a story entitled 'Nintendo counts on a new virtual game'. The next day Nintendo officially confirmed it in a press release: it was working on a new system, it would be out in 1995, and it would 'transport game players into a virtual utopia with sights and sounds unlike anything they've ever experienced'.

The Virtual Boy was a licensed version of the Private Eye, a stereoscopic prototype created by Massachusetts company Reflection Technology that showed players a 3D image while tracking their head movement. Although Sega turned it down after being given a demonstration, Nintendo's Gunpei Yokoi – the inventor of the Game & Watch and Game Boy – absolutely loved it and entered into an exclusive licensing agreement with Reflection Technology. Nintendo decided to ditch the head tracking feature, however, because it was wary of motion sickness and eye health, and Japan's new Product Liability Act of 1995 meant that anyone who suffered harm as a result of using a product would be liable to get paid damages (whereas before they had to prove that the company intended to damage them). As a result, the new system had to be mounted onto a tabletop stand, to make sure the player's head was stable and secure. It wasn't the most graceful solution, but the Virtual Boy was born nonetheless.

The Virtual Boy launched on 21 July 1995 in Japan, and came to North America a month later on 14 August (where it was bundled with Mario's Tennis). Opinion

was mixed: some thought the 3D effect was nothing short of astonishing and proposed that this could very well be the future of interactive entertainment. Others complained that the red-and-black images generated by the system could cause headaches if the system was used for too long: this was something Nintendo had anticipated and had tried to counter, by insisting an auto-pause option was added to every Virtual Boy game which would stop the action after a set period and tell the player to take a break.

The damage was already done, though, even at this early stage. Too many publications were listing the Virtual Boy's faults – it was too bulky, it hurt their eyes, it wasn't proper virtual reality – and this, combined with

the premium price of $179.99 (about $300 in today's money) meant gamers weren't exactly queuing up to buy it.

Nintendo cut its losses before the year had even ended. The Virtual Boy was discontinued in Japan on 22 December 1995, just five months after it had launched. Nintendo of America followed suit in March 1996, killing the Virtual Boy long before it even reached its first birthday. 770,000 units were sold between Japan and North America: Europeans didn't even get the chance to reject it as well.

A grand total of 22 games were released for the Virtual Boy across Japan and North America. A surprisingly large number of them were actually quite entertaining, leading many today to suggest that perhaps it was a competent little device that had been killed off before it got a chance to build any momentum. Regardless, much as I would love to write a Virtual Boy Encyclopedia, nobody in their right mind would pay full price for a book that only had 22 games in it. So here, for your reading pleasure, is that very 'book' as an extra bonus.

3D TETRIS

Year	1996
Publisher	Nintendo
Developer	T&E Soft

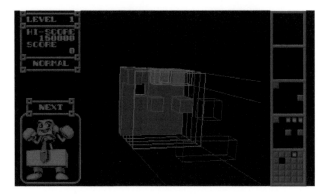

T&E SOFT WAS best known for its golfing games (see the True Golf Classics games in the SNES section and Golf below), but this was its take on Tetris. Although it looks and feels nothing like Tetris, the name is accurate: it technically is exactly what Tetris would be like if it was played in three dimensions. The aim is still to fill rows of blocks to clear them, but this time instead of playing on a grid that's 10 blocks wide you're playing on one that's five wide and five deep. Instead of just spinning blocks left and right you can now spin them back and forwards on another axis, too. Instead of just clearing single lines, then, you now have to clear entire 5x5 squares. ∎

FACT

3D Tetris was never released in Japan and didn't make it to the US until March 1996, the same month the system was officially discontinued. As such, it was the last ever Virtual Boy game released.

GALACTIC PINBALL

Year	1995
Publisher	Nintendo
Developer	Intelligent Systems

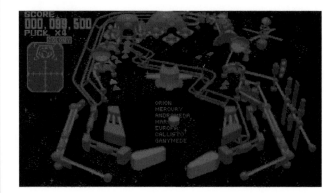

THIS IS A collection of four space-themed pinball tables called Alien, UFO, Colony and Cosmic, in which you use a puck instead of a ball for some reason (I suppose Galactic Pinpuck isn't very catchy). Each table has hidden secrets to keep things entertaining. For example, the Alien table has a trio of bumpers in the middle of the table that turn into an alien's face if you can hit a tricky-to-reach gate at the top. Each table also has star icons which can be collected: get enough of these and you'll enter a bonus table, where 12 stars swoop past like waves in an old shoot 'em up like Galaga. If you can hit all 12 stars within four waves you'll get a cool million points. ∎

FACT

The Cosmic table has a Metroid-themed bonus game where you control Samus's ship and shoot down alien ships while Metroid music plays in the background.

GOLF

Year	1995
Publisher	Nintendo
Developer	T&E Soft

YOU MAY NOT expect a golf game to be one of the better examples of what the Virtual Boy was capable of but T&E Soft's experience with the True Golf Classics series on the SNES showed it already knew how to make a decent-looking golf game. The main issue with those was that they were a little sluggish when it came to handling their polygonal environments, but the Virtual Boy's extra power makes that far less of a problem. There's a single 18-hole course here – the fictional Papillion Country Club – with a relatively straightforward helping of holes: while it has its fair share of bunkers and water hazards, none are too treacherous that they make the game remarkably difficult. The same can't be said for the shooting system, which shows an impressive 3D power arc to help you set your shot power,

but then moves a cursor extremely quickly over a ball icon and makes you try to stop it in the middle of the ball for accuracy. As such, until you get used to its timing, you can expect to be putting a lot of balls into the trees. Where the game undeniably stands out is its 3D course, though: although the Virtual Boy isn't quite powerful enough to follow behind the ball once it's hit, it does quickly cut to another angle showing you where it lands, and it does so far quicker than other previous golf games that tried the same trick in the past. ∎

FACT

T&E Soft stuck with golf games when it moved over to the Nintendo 64. It released the Japan-only Masters 98 first, then resurrected the True Golf Classics brand for a new Waialae Country Club game.

INNSMOUTH NO YAKATA

Year | 1995
Publisher | I'Max
Developer | Be Top

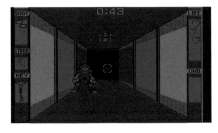

IF THERE'S ANYTHING that modern VR has taught us, it's that horror games are an easy way to get a reaction. The Virtual Boy only got one, but it was fun. Innsmouth no Yakata is a first-person survival horror game where you move through the halls of a giant building with the left D-Pad, and use the right one to move a cursor that lets you shoot any time you encounter a monster. There are 45 different possible stages but you only play through 13 in each playthrough, with the game taking you in different directions depending on how quickly you beat a stage. There are four different endings, ranging from you being hit by lightning and turning into a monster, to a joke ending where the building deflates like a balloon. ∎

FACT

The game's title is regularly referred to as Innsmouse no Yakata, which is technically an accurate translation. However, it's clearly named after the H.P. Lovecraft novel *The Shadow Over Innsmouth*.

JACK BROS

Year | 1995
Publisher | Atlus
Developer | Atlus

THIS SPIN-OFF OF the RPG series Shin Megami Tensei has you playing as its three 'Jack' brothers: Jack Frost (who uses snowballs), Jack Lantern (who uses fireballs) and Jack Skelton (who uses a knife, which is why he's known as Jack the Ripper in the Japanese version). Rather than an RPG it's s top-down action game where you have to guide your Jack of choice along a series of multi-floor stages, destroying enemies along the way and collecting keys to progress before fighting a boss at the end. Rather than taking damage when you're hit, you instead lose seconds from your timer: fail to beat the boss before the time runs out and you'll have to start the stage from the very beginning again. ∎

FACT

Jack Bros was originally going to be called Devil Busters but was renamed to include the Shin Megami Tensei characters. Despite being a spin-off it was technically the first Megami Tensei game released in the west.

MARIO CLASH

Year | 1995
Publisher | Nintendo
Developer | Nintendo R&D1

ONE OF THE games in development for the Virtual Boy was a side-scrolling platformer called VB Mario Land. The Virtual Boy didn't last long enough for this proper Mario game to get released, but Nintendo did at least take its bonus stage and turn it into a fully-fledged game. Mario Clash is a sort of 3D version of the original arcade Mario Bros, and has Mario trying to make his way up a building called the Clash House Tower. There are 99 floors in this tower, and as luck would have it every single one of them has been infested by enemies, so it's Mario's job to clear every floor as he makes his way up to the top of the tower, where there's no ending and, annoyingly, you start again from Level 1. Each stage always has a couple of Koopa Troopas wandering around (if one dies, another appears to replace it): that's because they're the most important

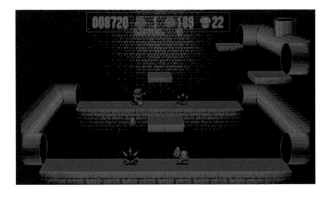

FACT

Every time you score 100,000 points, a Mario character praises you (Mario saying 'Good!', Bowser saying 'Astonishing!' and the like). Get the maximum score of 999,999 and you'll see the enemies waving a white flag with the message: 'All right, that's it: you win!'.

element of the game. The only way Mario can kill the other enemies is by stomping on a Koopa Troopa, picking up their shell and flinging it at them. The game has a background platform and a foreground one: some enemies have protection on both their front and back, which means the only way to defeat them is by travelling to the other plane and throwing a shell across the screen at them. While Mario Clash was a fun game, there's no denying it wasn't the Mario game Virtual Boy owners were waiting for and ultimately didn't get. ∎

MARIO'S TENNIS

Year	1995
Publisher	Nintendo
Developer	Nintendo R&D1

WHEN GAMES ARE bundled with consoles, it's generally best if they do a good job of demonstrating its abilities. The NES Action Set, for example, came bundled with Super Mario Bros – because, of course – and also Duck Hunt, to give the player an example of how to use that shiny new Zapper gun that was also in the box. The Wii is another shining example, with Wii Sports' games specifically designed to show the versatility of the Wii Remote and its motion controls. Given the unique selling point of the Virtual Boy, it should probably go without saying that any game bundled with it should make the most of the 3D feature and show players why the system was worth all that money they'd just paid. Mario's Tennis – which was bundled with the Virtual Boy in North America, but not in Japan – absolutely does the former, even if time obviously proved that it fell short of the latter.

Hopefully you're sitting down to withstand the shock of the revelation that Mario's Tennis is a tennis game starring Mario characters. There are seven to choose from, each with their own strengths and… you get it. Interestingly though, while most tennis games tend to grade its characters

FACT

The game's code contains the name 'Cassarin' alongside Mario, Luigi and the rest. This is one way of translating the Japanese writing of 'Catherine', which is the Japanese name for Birdo. This implies Birdo was originally planned to be in the game.

based on speed and power, Mario's Tennis takes a third stat called 'racquet contact area' into account when you're playing on the Hard difficulty level: this essentially determines how far away or close to the ball you can be while still being able to hit it. Mario is an all-rounder like he always is in things like this, and so is Luigi (although he can run a little faster, essentially making Mario pointless). Princess Toadstool and Koopa Troopa are slow, but their racquet contact area is large, meaning they can hit the ball a bit easier. Yoshi and Toad, on the other hand, are the opposite: they're fast runners but have a smaller racquet contact area. Rounding things off is Donkey Kong Jr, who's the slowest in the game and has a tiny contact area, but can also deliver extremely powerful shots.

This is all well and good, of course, but Mario's Tennis obviously wasn't bundled with the Virtual Boy so that people could study Yoshi's contact area (stop smirking). The main selling point is clearly the 3D effect, and it's one of the more impressive examples on the system. Rather than viewing the action from the usual high up, TV style vantage point you'd expect from most other Tennis games, Mario's Tennis brings the camera extremely low down behind your player, almost right to the ground. With a 2D display this makes the game almost unplayable – as anyone who wanders in the shady world of emulation will discover – but the addition of depth makes it the best possible angle, because you can easily judge how far the ball is and position yourself accordingly. It may not have been the 'killer app' the Virtual Boy needed to succeed, then, but it at least impressed early adopters looking for something to show their pals. ■

NESTER'S FUNKY BOWLING

Year	1996
Publisher	Nintendo
Developer	Saffire Corporation

NESTER WAS THE mascot of *Nintendo Power* in North America, and regularly appeared in the magazine's pages in various comics and other appearances. Nester's Funky Bowling was his real moment in the spotlight, though, as he starred in his own game for the first time. It's a bowling game in which you can play as either Nester or his twin sister Hester (who had never been seen before and was never seen again). As well as a standard 10-frame game of bowling, you can also play a Practice mode (where you can set up the pins however you like to try to master trickier shots) or a Challenge mode, where the game lays out random pin arrangements and asks you to hit them for points. ■

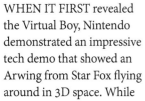

FACT

Nester was briefly name-checked in NES games StarTropics and To the Earth, but his only other visible game appearance was in NES Play Action Football, where he appears at the end of each game.

PANIC BOMBER

Year	1995
Publisher	Nintendo
Developer	Hudson Soft

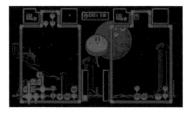

PANIC BOMBER IS a Bomberman-themed puzzle game that had already seen releases on other Japanese systems. It's sort of like Puyo Puyo, only with shapes made of three blocks instead of two. You have to try to match up three blocks of the same colour to make them disappear, which in turn makes bombs appear. These can't be cleared through normal means: instead, you have to wait for a lit bomb piece to fall from the sky. Once that lands it'll create a familiar Bomberman-style explosion, which will then trigger any other bombs it touches. If you're particularly eagle-eyed you may have noticed that the Virtual Boy only has one colour, so instead of different coloured Bomberman heads as in other versions of the game, you're matching various monsters instead. ■

FACT

An actual Bomberman game called Virtual Bomberman was in development for the Virtual Boy, with screenshots appearing in some magazines. Naturally, it was cancelled when the system was discontinued.

RED ALARM

Year	1995
Publisher	Nintendo
Developer	T&E Soft

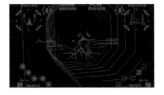

WHEN IT FIRST revealed the Virtual Boy, Nintendo demonstrated an impressive tech demo that showed an Arwing from Star Fox flying around in 3D space. While Star Fox ultimately never came to the Virtual Boy, Red Alarm at least went some way to filling the gap. Much like Star Fox, it's a polygonal on-rails shooter where you pilot a ship through a series of stages (six, in this case) while blasting away similarly polygonal enemies. The one major difference between Red Alarm and Star Fox is that polygons aren't shaded in Red Alarm, giving the game more of a wireframe effect. While that makes things massively confusing in 2D, though (as I'm sure the screenshot here shows), the added depth of 3D makes it easier to see what's going on. ■

FACT

Red Alarm offers some features that were advanced for the time, such as four different viewpoints (including a cockpit view) and the option to view a replay of your performance from different angles each time you beat a level.

SD GUNDAM DIMENSION WAR

Year	1995
Publisher	Bandai
Developer	Locomotive Corporation

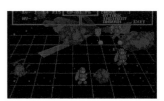

ONE OF THE last two Virtual Boy games released in Japan, SD Gundam Dimension War is a turn-based strategy game set in the Gundam universe. The player gets to put together a squad consisting of battleships and a bunch of different Gundams from all the previous Gundam series, and must take on the enemy forces, who've managed to acquire a few mobile suits of their own. While most of the game takes place on the usual sort of grid structure you'd expect from a turn-based strategy game, if two units get close enough the action will switch to a third-person view over your unit's shoulder. If your unit is a battleship the combat will play out automatically, but if it's a Gundam you'll get to control it. ■

FACT

Gundam was born in 1979 with the anime series Mobile Suit Gundam, and has since spawned countless manga, movies and further anime series, as well as over 80 video games.

SPACE INVADERS VIRTUAL COLLECTION

Year	1995
Publisher	Taito
Developer	Taito

SOMETIMES A GAME'S title says more or less all you need to know. This is indeed a collection of Space Invaders in a virtual form. Specifically, it consists of recreations of Space Invaders and Space Invaders II, both of which can be played in either 2D mode – which is basically a standard emulated version of the arcade original – or 3D mode, where everything is tilted up at an angle and it looks like the Space Invaders are floating above you.

As well as playing the standard game via either viewpoint there's also a Challenge option, which consists of Time Attack (where you have to clear a level as quickly as possible) and Score Attack: the latter adds a little twist in that some of the Invaders can shrink. ■

FACT

There's an oft-repeated myth that Space Invaders was so popular in Japan that the country saw a shortage of 100 yen coins. *The Numismatist* (a magazine about the study of coins) presented an in-depth report in 2014 that proved this was impossible.

SPACE SQUASH

Year	1995
Publisher	Coconuts Japan
Developer	Tomcat System

IF YOU'VE EVER worried that the future may not be all it's cracked up to be, Space Squash at least guarantees us that we'll still have squash. Take that however you will. Despite the name, this isn't exactly like squash, because you're still facing your opponent and you're hitting a ball back and forth at each other (instead of you both hitting the ball against a wall). Regardless, it does still have you trying to throw off your opponent's timing by hitting the ball off the side walls, ceiling and floor. Space Squash works well because it does the same trick Mario's Tennis does: puts the camera right behind your character so you can feel like the ball's coming right at you. ■

FACT

There are four power-ups you can choose from before each contest: a power boost, a speed boost and shield and a homing attack. The latter is particularly useful for boss battles where the aim is to actually hit the ball at the boss.

TELEROBOXER

Year	1995
Publisher	Nintendo
Developer	Nintendo

CONSIDERING THE WAY we look at and use virtual reality today – often as a way of seeing and exploring new environments as if we were there ourselves – it's somewhat surprising that only a couple of Virtual Boy games were actually played from a first-person perspective. Teleroboxer is probably the most effective of them, and the one that feels most like a modern day VR game. It's set in the twenty-second century and focuses on a technology called telerobotics, where people can control robots by performing the same motions remotely. A scientist called Dr Edward Maki Jr sets up a new sport called teleroboxing, where competitors can use robots to act as their avatars and take part in

FACT

Telerobotics is an actual thing and can be used to drive land rovers on the Moon in real time, handle radioactive materials or do underwater repair work that may be too dangerous for humans to carry out.

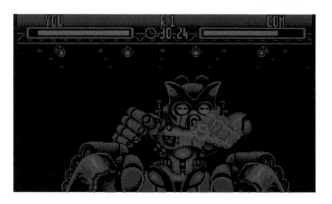

boxing on their behalf. Pacific Ring, if you will (sorry). You play as a small robot called Harry who has to defeat other robots, ranging from a sultry she-bot and a large pro wrestling bot to a robotic kangaroo with a little robot joey in its pouch (which occasionally hits you with low blows). The left and right triggers on the controller are used to throw punches, while the two D-Pads act as your left and right hands, letting you block, duck and dodge with them. Defeat all seven boxers without losing a fight and you'll face off against the 'legendary champ', who happens to be a robot cat called Milky. Which may seem silly, but to be fair, when you think about it, a robot cat would have a hell of a swipe on it. ■

V-TETRIS

Year	1995	
Publisher	Bullet-Proof Software	
Developer	Locomotive	

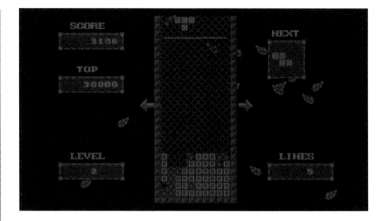

IT SAYS A lot about Tetris's importance to the Game Boy that of the Virtual Boy's meagre library of 22 titles, two of them are Tetris games. While 3D Tetris was more of an 'inspired by' situation – it didn't really play much like Tetris but the general concept of clearing rows was there – V-Tetris is instead the real deal, handled by Bullet-Proof Software (which at the time was all over Tetris). There are three main modes in V-Tetris, handily named A, B and C. The A mode is your standard endless version of Tetris, where you can happily clear lines all day until the blocks reach the top of the screen. Similarly, anyone familiar with the Game Boy or NES versions will know that the

In 2019, a Twitter user printed a fake version of the NES Tetris manual claiming the blocks had named likes Orange cky, Cleveland Z and Smashboy. Despite clearly being ridiculous, the 'fact' was used as a question in *Jeopardy!* later that year.

B mode is where you set a speed and a certain 'height' of random blocks scattered on the screen and have clear a set number of lines to win. It's the C mode that's the new one here, though, and the only one that properly makes use of the Virtual Boy's 3D. At first it looks like the standard A mode, until you realise that you can use the shoulder buttons to scroll the entire contents of the well left and right. In reality, the well has both a front and back side, and when you clear blocks on the front a random piece is dropped at the back: this means you need to keep rotating round and keeping everything in check to avoid either side scrolling to the top. ■

VERTICAL FORCE

Year	1995	
Publisher	Nintendo	
Developer	Hudson Soft	

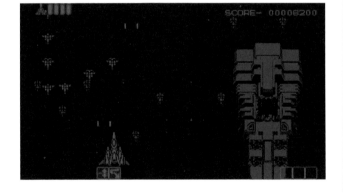

WELL, IT WOULDN'T count as a video game system if it didn't have at least one scrolling shoot 'em up. Vertical Force is set in the year 210 SE (Space Era) and tasks you with flying to a planet called Odin and destroying Mittgard, its central 'caretaker' computer, which has reprogrammed itself and now wants to extract all of Earth's minerals and kill all humans. As the number one flying ace of the United Earth Army, it's up to you to put an end to Mittgard: because as smart as its AI may be, it still somehow managed to choose that name for itself. Vertical Force's main fun gimmick is the ability to switch between a high and low altitude: each has enemies that can only be killed if you're on the same level. ■

you think Mittgard is a y name for a computer name itself, your ship s called *Ragnarok*, so don't be so quick to laugh.

VIRTUAL BOWLING

Year	1995	
Publisher	Athena	
Developer	Athena	

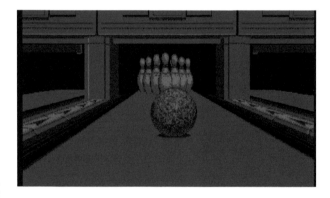

BY FAR THE rarest game on the Virtual Boy, Virtual Bowling was the other 'final game' that launched on the system along with Gundam. Since Gundam was already a known licence, that meant more copies of it were manufactured: as such, boxed copies of Virtual Bowling are rarer than getting blood from a bowling ball. What's even more depressing is that Virtual Bowling is actually a fantastic game and one of the better bowling games you'll (probably not) play, thanks not only to the detailed set-up before each throw – you change your position spin, strength and time of release – but also the brilliant way the camera follows the ball right down the lane as it crashes into the pins, followed by an impressive replay. ■

If you're curious as to just how rare Virtual Bowling is, a complete boxed copy once sold on eBay for $1300.

VIRTUAL BOY WARIO LAND

Year	1995
Publisher	Nintendo
Developer	Nintendo R&D1

THE VIRTUAL BOY may not have got the side-scrolling Super Mario Land sequel that was in development, but that doesn't mean it was completely bereft of Nintendo platformers. The Wario Land series was notable for doing things a little differently, so in a sense Virtual Boy Wario Land was maybe an even better fit for the Virtual Boy than Mario's adventure would have been. Technically, this was the second game in the Wario Land series – Nintendo cruelly pretended it didn't exist when it launched Wario Land II on the Game Boy in 1998 – and follows Wario as he finds himself on an adventure during a holiday in the Awazon rainforest (not a typo). While sunbathing, Wario spots some odd masked creatures entering a tunnel behind a waterfall: because all waterfalls in video games have something hidden behind them, after all. Deciding to follow them, Wario discovers that the tunnel leads to a huge cave containing an enormous vault of treasure. No sooner has Wario declared that the treasure now belongs to him, that a trapdoor underneath him collapses and he ends up deep underground. Wario now has to

FACT

The legendary Totaka's Song, which is hidden in numerous Nintendo games, appears at the end of Virtual Boy Wario Land if you beat the game then wait 75 seconds on the end screen.

make his way back up to the surface, smashing his way through his new enemies and collecting as much loot as he can along his journey. For the most part, Virtual Boy Wario Land plays like a typical Wario Land game: Wario is armed with a shoulder barge attack that he can use to plough through enemies, or alternatively he can jump on them to stun them, then pick them up and throw them. It wouldn't be a Mario game (or indeed a Wario one) without some power-ups, though, and there are a few here that were never seen in any other game. The Viking helmet from the original Wario Land is here, turning Wario into Bull Wario. By doing a ground pound, Bull Wario can trigger an earthquake and stun multiple enemies. As well as this, though, there's also a statue of an eagle which can turn you into Eagle Wario, who has the ability to fly thanks to his useful eagled-shaped hat. The Dragon Crystal, meanwhile, turns you into Sea Dragon Wario, who can breathe fire. Best of all, though, you can combine both the new power-ups to become King Dragon Wario, who can both fly and breathe fire.

The main gimmick here isn't the presence of new power-ups, however: these are the norm for any new platformer in the Mario universe. Virtual Boy Wario Land's most innovate gimmick is the ability to jump between two different planes at various points in the game. On occasion you'll find special arrows on the floor: if you stand on these and jump you'll leap to the back or front of the screen. Combined with the 3D effect, these moments give a fantastic feeling of depth. Even though the Virtual Boy's failure ultimately meant not enough people got to play Wario Land, this feature alone was its legacy, going on to appear in games like Donkey Kong Country Returns. ∎

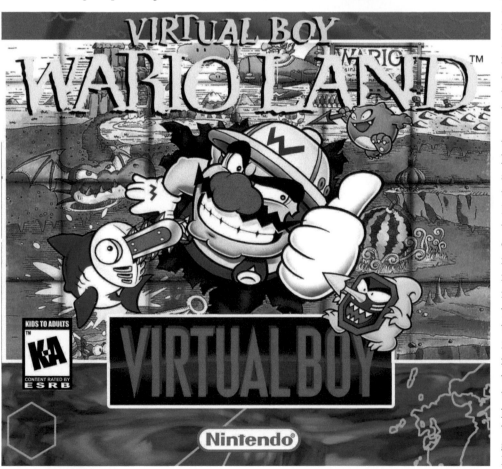

VIRTUAL FISHING

Year	1995
Publisher	Pack-In-Video
Developer	Locomotive

IT'S NEVER REALLY been clear why fishing is such a popular sport when it comes to video game adaptations, but whatever the reason, the Virtual Boy wasn't spared its own fishing title. Virtual Fishing lets you take part in fishing competitions in five different locations, as well as a practice lake where the pressure's off (well, off you that is: it's probably safe to the say the fish still aren't too relaxed). Win three tournaments and you'll unlock a sixth location, and win all six to unlock the special final seventh competition. Each time you win a tournament at a new location you'll unlock a new option there called Time Attack. Here you start with a fish already hooked, and you have to reel in five as quickly as possible. ■

FACT

Even though eight Virtual Boy games were only released in Japan, Virtual Fishing is the only one that's full of Japanese text and is therefore probably the least playable for those who can't read the language. The rest should be okay, even Gundam.

VIRTUAL LAB

Year	1995
Publisher	J-Wing
Developer	Nacoty

WIDELY BELIEVED TO be the worst game on the Virtual Boy – not to mention one of the worst games of the generation – Virtual Lab is a puzzle game that is frankly a little disturbing to play, even with its low quality sprites. It's your typical Tetris style block-dropping game, but this time the pieces are pulsating segments of some sort of wormy intestinal tract. You have to line up the pieces so that the tract connects and forms a straight line, and once you can make a fully enclosed tube the whole horrible writhing mess will disappear. Meanwhile, a little anime woman stands at the side and her boobs jiggle a bit for no real reason. You'll want to have a bath after playing this one. ■

FACT

Virtual Lab's packaging doesn't fare much better than the game itself. The back of the box refers to 'Nintenndo', while the cartridge says 'licensed by Ninntenndo'.

VIRTUAL LEAGUE BASEBALL

Year	1995
Publisher	Kemco
Developer	Kemco

AS YOU'LL HAVE already seen if you've read the SNES section of this book, you couldn't turn around in the '90s without smashing your face into another baseball video game: there were 18 on the SNES alone. Congratulations to the opportunistic Kemco, then, who managed to sneak one onto the Virtual Boy during Nintendo's brief 'you can make games now' window. There are no licences to speak of in this one: instead you can choose from 18 international teams and three all-star teams. While its pitching and batting viewpoint is similar to most other baseball games (with the exception of the 3D effect, of course), when the ball's hit in the air the game cuts to an interesting view of the entire stadium, which looks quite cool in 3D. ■

FACT

In Japan the game's called Virtual Pro Yakuu '95. Its player sprites are slightly 'cuter' with bigger heads and smaller bodies, and instead of international teams you get Nippon Professional Baseball teams.

WATERWORLD

Year	1995
Publisher	Ocean Software
Developer	Ocean Software

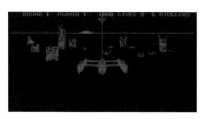

THERE WAS ONLY one licensed movie tie-in on the Virtual Boy, and in a way it's fitting that it was Waterworld. Both promised grandiose things and threatened to push their respective mediums in new directions, but ultimately both were shunned by the public (despite both actually being quite good). Not that the Waterworld game was decent, of course: it's a pretty poor sailing game where you have to destroy the enemy 'Smokers' on their jet skis in order to protect the Atollers, a group of innocent citizens who are bobbing in the water and close to drowning. The concept was sound but the execution wasn't: the controls were pretty sluggish to get to grips with and the game's performance was choppier than the seas you sailed on. ■

FACT

Waterworld got a 4K UHD Blu-ray release in 2019. You really should check it out, it's not as bad as its reputation suggests.

INDEX